Contemporary Examination of Latin America and the Caribbean:

Economy, Education, and Technology

Dale T. Mathews
University of Puerto Rico, Puerto Rico

Bryan Christiansen
Soluvex, LLC, USA

IGI Global
Publishing Tomorrow's Research Today

Vice President of Editorial — Melissa Wagner
Managing Editor of Acquisitions — Mikaela Felty
Managing Editor of Book Development — Jocelynn Hessler
Production Manager — Mike Brehm
Cover Design — Phillip Shickler

Published in the United States of America by
IGI Global Scientific Publishing
701 East Chocolate Avenue
Hershey, PA, 17033, USA
Tel: 717-533-8845
Fax: 717-533-8661
Website: https://www.igi-global.com E-mail: cust@igi-global.com

Library of Congress Cataloging-in-Publication Data

Names: Mathews, Dale T., editor. | Christiansen, Bryan, 1960- editor.
Title: Contemporary examination of Latin America and the Caribbean : economy, education, and technology / Dale Mathews, Bryan Christiansen.
Description: Hershey, PA : IGI Global Scientific Publishing, 2025. | Includes bibliographical references and index. | Summary: "The primary objective of this publication is to provide a single volume containing a variety of topics relevant particularly to the economic, educational, and technological advancements of Latin America and the Caribbean"-- Provided by publisher.
Identifiers: LCCN 2024048492 (print) | LCCN 2024048493 (ebook) | ISBN 9798369337639 (hardcover) | ISBN 9798369351079 (paperback) | ISBN 9798369337646 (ebook)
Subjects: LCSH: Caribbean Area--Economic conditions. | Latin America--Economic conditions. | Education--Caribbean Area. | Education--Latin America. | Technological innovations--Latin America. | Technological innovations--Caribbean Area.
Classification: LCC HC151 .C6675 2025 (print) | LCC HC151 (ebook) | DDC 330.9729--dc23/eng/20250114
LC record available at https://lccn.loc.gov/2024048492
LC ebook record available at https://lccn.loc.gov/2024048493

British Cataloguing in Publication Data
A Cataloguing in Publication record for this book is available from the British Library.

Table of Contents

Detailed Table of Contents

This chapter examines the phenomenon of reshoring/nearshoring. The sample studied are mature products that were initially offshored from industrialized countries to export processing zones in low wage locations. These include the production of non-knit textile articles (HTS 61), the production of knitted and crochet articles (HTS 62), shoes and related articles (HTS 64), electrical machinery and equipment related to broadcasting and television apparatus including parts and accessories (HTS 85) and medical, photographic, optical instruments and related parts and accessories (HTS 90). The data studied is restricted to U.S. imports of said products obtained since 2009, the date in which certain authors affirm that they began this strategy called reshoring and its behavior is analyzed until 2023. The methodological approach is quantitative, using for this purpose two statistical techniques: time series analysis and trend analysis with calculation of the coefficient of determination for each trend equation.

This chapter examines the impact of populism on governance, socio-economic development, and democratic consolidation in Latin America. By exploring the historical roots, socio-political mechanisms, and effects of populism, the study reveals how it can galvanize marginalized groups and disrupt existing power structures, potentially exacerbating economic inequalities and undermining democratic institutions. To address these challenges, the chapter proposes evidence-based strategies for fostering inclusive economic policies, strengthening social cohesion, and maintaining democratic integrity. Recommendations include promoting equitable growth, enhancing public trust through transparency, and supporting democratic institutions to navigate populism's complexities effectively. The analysis underscores the need for a balanced approach to achieving social justice and sustainable development amidst populist influences.

Despite fast increasing flows globally, and from emerging donors such as China, Official Development Assistance (ODA) has had limited impact on improving developmental outcomes and lived experiences in the Global South. Qualitative research can help supplement limited data availability on ODA effectiveness by offering a grounded explanation as to why donors' ODA appear to respond to that of other donors competitively and whether this can benefit recipients by increasing leverage and 'development space' or renders ODA less effective. Most research to date has concentrated on ODA competition in sub-Saharan Africa. As such, this study presents the first qualitative study on donor competition and the impacts of emerging donor ODA in Latin America. This study analyses sixteen semi-structured interviews conducted in Costa Rica and Panama to conclude that donor competition is rife, tangible, and impactful, but that Costa Rica and Panama are unable to take advantage of this competition to leverage better developmental outcomes.

This chapter examines information and analysis concerning tax evasion, bribery, and money laundering in Latin America and the Caribbean as corruption practiced by individuals, businesses, public officials, and criminal gangs. There is a wide range of conditions across the region, defined geographically as all countries or dependencies south of the United States of America (U.S.). The inquiry considers forms, causes, effects, and remedies associated with private-sector (commercial) and public-sector (political) corruption. The chapter assembles information sources and literature for comparison across countries of the region and then with other areas of the world to understand conditions in Latin America and the Caribbean. The region is a rich source of information about global networks for tax evasion, as revealed in revelations from the Panama Papers and similar sources. Several locations in the Caribbean are significant tax havens for avoidance and evasion.

The paper reports on the situation of Haitians and Haitian Creole in the Dominican Republic. It begins with a discussion of three pivotal events: the French extortion of the "Independence Debt," the period from 1822-1844 when Haiti controlled all of Hispaniola, and the 1912 purchase of 20,000 acres of Dominican land by the South Porto Rico Sugar Company. The paper then presents a discussion of the Dominican Republic's deportation of Haitians to Haiti, the poor health conditions of Haitians in the Dominican, the low status and vitality of Haitian Creole in the Dominican, and the effects of Dominican anti-Haitian policies. The paper shows that anti-Haitianism is not unique to the Dominican Republic, but has been practiced for centuries by Western countries, describes resistance within the Dominican Republic to the government's anti-Haitian policies, and ends with a discussion of what the international community should do to help Haiti.

While corporate gender diversity has substantially increased over the last decade in Latin America, there is still a large gender gap with North America and Europe. This study examines the country and firm-level drivers of this gap, providing insights into factors promoting higher gender diversity in Latin American companies. Our analysis shows that cultural dimensions greatly impact gender diversity at the board and TMT levels. Specifically, power distance and individualism positively influence gender diversity, while masculinity and uncertainty avoidance have negative effects. At the firm-level, we show that board size, board independence, ESG performance, and family ownership are important drivers of gender diversity in Latin America. We also explore the factors driving Latin American firms' commitment to SDG-5 on gender equality. Our findings highlight the necessity of understanding regional contexts to design effective policies for enhancing gender diversity in corporate leadership.

Tax evasion and bribery significantly impede the socioeconomic development of Latin America and the Caribbean. With other forms of corruption, such as extortion,

Preface

As editors of *Contemporary Examination of Latin America and the Caribbean: Economy, Education, and Technology*, we are pleased to present this comprehensive volume, which delves into the complex and vibrant dynamics of a region that holds immense cultural, economic, and technological significance in today's global landscape.

Latin America and the Caribbean represent a mosaic of indigenous cultures, European colonization, African influence, and waves of immigration that together shape the region's unique identity. This diversity creates a multifaceted social and economic environment that defies easy categorization, yet also offers immense potential for growth and development. With over 667 million people and a GDP that stands on par with other influential regions, Latin America and the Caribbean cannot be overlooked in discussions about global advancement.

This book seeks to explore a wide range of issues shaping the contemporary landscape of the region. From economic development and technology adoption to educational reforms and geopolitical challenges, we have gathered cutting-edge research and insights from scholars and practitioners who are at the forefront of their fields. The chapters in this volume span diverse areas such as macroeconomic policies, foreign direct investment, innovation, business governance, and the integration of the region into the global economy.

In addition to its economic and technological dimensions, Latin America and the Caribbean possess a rich cultural and social fabric. The region has produced some of the world's most influential thinkers, artists, and political leaders, and it faces unique challenges in areas such as public health, gender equality, and environmental sustainability. By examining these issues in depth, this volume aims to provide a holistic understanding of the region's current state and future potential.

The topics covered range from taxation and corruption to education and regional security. We also delve into specific national case studies and the transnational issues that affect the entire region, such as organized crime, Chinese investment, and the impact of U.S. interventions. By addressing these varied themes, we hope this book serves as a valuable resource for scholars, students, policymakers, and anyone with an interest in the multifaceted reality of Latin America and the Caribbean.

OVERVIEW OF CHAPTERS

In **Chapter 1**, the focus is on the phenomenon of reshoring and nearshoring, particularly in relation to mature products that were initially offshored from industrialized nations to low-wage regions. This chapter studies U.S. imports of key products from 2009 to 2023, including textiles, footwear, electrical machinery, and medical instruments. Using quantitative methods, such as time series and trend analysis, the chapter provides insights into the patterns of reshoring and the economic factors that influence it.

Chapter 2 delves into the impact of populism on governance, socio-economic development, and democratic consolidation in Latin America. By tracing the historical and socio-political mechanisms behind populism, this chapter demonstrates how populist movements both empower marginalized groups and disrupt established institutions. The chapter offers strategies to address the challenges posed by populism, advocating for inclusive economic policies, increased transparency, and strengthened democratic institutions to ensure sustainable development.

Chapter 3 shifts to the examination of Official Development Assistance (ODA) and its limited impact on developmental outcomes in the Global South, particularly Latin America. This qualitative study focuses on donor competition in Costa Rica and Panama and assesses how the influx of emerging donor ODA, such as from China, influences development. Through interviews, the chapter concludes that while donor competition is prevalent, Costa Rica and Panama struggle to leverage this competition for improved development outcomes.

In **Chapter 4**, the topic of corruption is explored, specifically tax evasion, bribery, and money laundering in Latin America and the Caribbean. This chapter investigates the regional and global networks of corruption, drawing comparisons with other parts of the world and highlighting the role of tax havens. It also examines the wide-reaching impact of these corrupt practices on economic growth and governance, referencing sources like the Panama Papers to illustrate the magnitude of the problem.

Chapter 5 examines the situation of Haitians in the Dominican Republic, beginning with a historical overview that includes events like the French extortion of the "Independence Debt" and Haiti's control of Hispaniola. The chapter then explores the Dominican Republic's policies towards Haitian migrants, including deportations, health conditions, and the status of Haitian Creole. It highlights both the deep-rooted anti-Haitian sentiment in the region and the resistance within the

Dominican Republic against these policies, proposing steps for the international community to aid Haiti.

Chapter 6 addresses corporate gender diversity in Latin America, revealing that although there has been substantial progress, the region still lags behind North America and Europe. This study identifies both cultural and firm-level drivers of gender diversity, noting that cultural factors such as power distance and individualism promote diversity, while masculinity and uncertainty avoidance hinder it. The chapter also discusses how board size, independence, and environmental, social, and governance (ESG) performance influence corporate diversity, offering recommendations for improving gender representation in leadership roles.

In **Chapter 7**, the detrimental effects of tax evasion and bribery on socioeconomic development in Latin America and the Caribbean are examined. Corruption in various forms hampers innovation, distorts markets, and erodes public trust, making reform essential. The chapter emphasizes the importance of international collaboration in combating corruption and calls for stronger legal frameworks, transparency, and judicial independence to promote equitable and sustainable growth in the region.

Finally, **Chapter 8** explores the development of intercultural competence among international business undergraduate students who participated in a virtual exchange. Through collaborative projects, students from two countries engaged with one another, fostering not only discipline-specific learning but also intercultural awareness. The chapter highlights the importance of both disciplinary and non-disciplinary interactions in fostering positive attitudes and cultural recognition, while also discussing the pedagogical and technological implications of such exchanges.

CONCLUSION

In bringing together the diverse research and perspectives presented in *Contemporary Examination of Latin America and the Caribbean: Economy, Education, and Technology*, it becomes evident that this region, with its rich historical complexity and socio-political dynamics, occupies a critical space on the global stage. From reshoring strategies and the impact of populism, to donor competition, corruption, and corporate gender diversity, the chapters in this volume illuminate the multifaceted challenges and opportunities facing Latin America and the Caribbean today.

The economic potential of the region is immense, yet it is clear that structural obstacles—such as corruption, inequitable policies, and governance issues—continue to hinder sustained development. However, as the research in this volume demonstrates, the solutions to these challenges are equally diverse. Whether through fostering stronger democratic institutions, enhancing transparency, or promoting gender diversity in corporate leadership, the region is on a path toward innovation and transformation.

Moreover, the educational and technological advancements discussed in this book highlight the importance of leveraging regional strengths to address these complex issues. As globalization continues to influence every facet of life, Latin America and the Caribbean must continue to integrate into the global economy while preserving their unique cultural and historical identity.

We hope this volume serves not only as a reference for scholars and policymakers but also as an inspiration for further research and engagement with the pressing issues of our time. Latin America and the Caribbean are poised to make significant contributions to the global landscape, and it is through a deeper understanding of the region's challenges and opportunities that we can chart a course for sustainable growth and development.

Dale Mathews
University of Puerto Rico, Puerto Rico

Bryan Christiansen
Soluvex, LLC, United States

Chapter 1
Evidence of Reshoring/ Nearshoring:
An Analysis of Imports to the United States of Selected Products

Segundo Castro-Gonzáles
University of Puerto Rico, Puerto Rico

Dale T. Mathews
https://orcid.org/0009-0009-4809-9226
University of Puerto Rico, Puerto Rico

ABSTRACT

This chapter examines the phenomenon of reshoring/nearshoring. The sample studied are mature products that were initially offshored from industrialized countries to export processing zones in low wage locations. These include the production of non-knit textile articles (HTS 61), the production of knitted and crochet articles (HTS 62), shoes and related articles (HTS 64), electrical machinery and equipment related to broadcasting and television apparatus including parts and accessories (HTS 85) and medical, photographic, optical instruments and related parts and accessories (HTS 90). The data studied is restricted to U.S. imports of said products obtained since 2009, the date in which certain authors affirm that they began this strategy called reshoring and its behavior is analyzed until 2023. The methodological approach is quantitative, using for this purpose two statistical techniques: time series analysis and trend analysis with calculation of the coefficient of determination for each trend equation.

DOI: 10.4018/979-8-3693-3763-9.ch001

INTRODUCTION

United States' President Donald Trump during his administration encouraged the return to North American territory of North American companies that had operations outside the USA, through the criterion of protectionism. For over half a century, many US firms engaged in an offshoring strategy, sending their manufacturing plants first to Mexico, the Caribbean and Central America, and then later to China, Malaysia, Vietnam and other countries with lower labor and related operating costs. Mexico and the Dominican Republic have some of the oldest programs for the attraction of US firms intending to offshore their labor-intensive segments. For example, the New York based Gulf and Western corporation established the first export processing zone for this purpose in the Dominican Republic in 1968 and for many years was closely associated with the nascent export manufacturing sector which grew under its Industrial Incentives Law # 299 (Moya Pons, 1992).

This followed Vernon's (1966) life cycle logic in the maturity stage whereby production costs are crucial for its sustainability and competitiveness, especially due to the strong imitation by rival competitive firms. It is necessary to mention that according to Kayyali, et al., (2023) the length of the stages of the life cycle of manufactures has a specific duration and their strategic needs are also different according to the type of products, external conditions and policies that occur simultaneously. For this reason, starting with the financial crisis of 2008 (Wallen & Wiberg, 2018), followed by protectionist policies implemented by former president Donald Trump (Freeman, 2019), and reinforced by successor president Joe Biden with executive order 14017, reshoring eventually became public policy in the USA. Reshoring and nearshoring constitute a relocation strategy that seeks the return of certain industrial sectors to US territory or near it (Bustamante, 2022) with the aim of achieving greater security and a recovery of the US manufacturing sector. These moves by the USA are associated with the growing view in that country of China as a geopolitical and economic threat instead of a partner (Vertinsky, et. al., 2023; Gereffi, et. al., 2021). Some North American companies thus found alternatives to minimize costs by returning their businesses to North American territory or establishing productive and export operations in some countries close to the US that have a history of special treaties or preferential trade arrangements with the latter. Prominent examples of such arrangements included the Generalized System of Preferences (1974), the Caribbean Basin Economic Recovery Act (1984), the Andean Trade Promotion and Drug Eradication Act (1991) and the Caribbean Trade Partnership Act (2000), among others (Bardos, 2017).

Hence, the primary objective of this chapter is the analytical study of whether reshoring or near-shoring may have taken place, based on US commercial data with countries close to its territory that are currently a party to bilateral or other treaties which encourage production in export processing zones. Such locations include Mexico and the Central American countries (Honduras, Nicaragua, Guatemala and El Salvador) as well as the Dominican Republic. The current special treaty known as the Central America-Dominican Republic Free Trade Agreement (CAFTA-DR), enacted in 2004, opened the way for the gradual elimination of tariffs and other barriers to international trade among member countries. Similarly, Mexico has a special treaty that updated several aspects of the North American Free Trade Agreement (NAFTA) originally enacted in 1994. In this context, it is considered that reshoring and near-shoring might play a significant role going forward as it takes advantage of incentives to relocate in or near North American territory, thereby boosting exports from both Central American countries and Mexico.

Within the stated principle objective, the focus has been restricted to the following five mature manufacturing products classified according to the accompanying Harmonized Tariff Schedule (HTS) number: a) knitted clothing and crocheted accessories HTS 61; b) Clothing and accessories not knitted or crocheted HTS 62; c) Footwear, leggings or similar items and their related parts HTS 64; d) Machinery and electrical equipment, televisions and recorders HTS 85, and e) Optical, photographic, medical, surgical products, parts and accessories HTS 90. This research work is based on empirical evidence with data obtained from the US Department of Commerce to corroborate the research hypotheses stated below. The overall reason for the choice of these particular categories of goods is their historical prominence as mature products that were offshored from industrialized countries to export processing zones in low wage locations (Cirera & Lakshman, 2017).

Based theoretically on what Kayyali, et al., (2023) state that the life cycle of products and services have different durations strategically speaking, this study purports to focus on the countries that produce the five HTS products previously described. Specifically, to investigate whether the two principal producing countries in Asia (China and Vietnam) have experienced a variation in their exports to the United States (based on US import data) and, on the other hand, whether the producing countries of Central America, the Caribbean and Mexico of said HTS items have witnessed an improvement in their exports in accordance to the overall protectionist policy embraced by Trump and crystallized by Biden.

The study begins with a detailed bibliographic review, which covers basic theories of international business, where the foundations of the life cycle theory, the concept of reshoring based on theoretical evidence and the processes of internationalization are expounded upon. This is followed by the methodology used, and subsequently the results obtained from the data and the most important conclusions that might be drawn. Finally, the practical applications and limitations of the study are noted.

REVIEW OF THE LITERATURE

It is possible to draw links between certain ownership-specific advantages of firms and the country-specific advantages likely to generate and sustain them. In this respect, a country's factor endowments and institutional or market framework have been shown to have an effect on the ownership-specific advantages of its enterprises. An example of this is the scale of the firm, with countries with large and standardized markets spawning relatively large firms. Similarly, a country with a highly skilled labor force could possess an advantage in technology and skill intensive industries, while a country with relatively large quantities of cheap labor may generate labor intensive industries.

The product Cycle and the need to re-locate

The economist Raymond Vernon developed the theory of the international product life cycle in 1966, which uses economic and location factors to provide an explanation of the evolution and movement of new products between countries, which involves an analysis beyond production in yes, involving the transfer of technology between developed and undeveloped countries (Cao & Folan, 2011). From this theory, each product has a certain life cycle that begins with its development and ends with its decline. That is, products enter the market and gradually disappear. The main stages of the model are four: introduction, growth, maturity and decline. Each stage can vary depending on the product, some can last weeks and others even decades. The useful life and how quickly the entire cycle goes through will depend on demand and how market instruments are used (Mulder, 2012).

The maturity stage is the third stage where the life cycle curve of products or industries begins to flatten, it is the longest stage and companies are most focused on maintaining their market share. Therefore, a cheap foreign labor force that offsets transportation costs, production will begin to be relevant and opt for a location in a foreign country, so the innovating country will be supplied via imports, generally by countries in development (Abasolo, 1991). In other words, when the product becomes "mature", its degree of standardization and its price elasticity of demand increase, costs become more important and its production moves to countries that export growing products (Vernon, 1966). It opens up technical possibilities to achieve economies of scale through mass production, encouraging long-term commitments to a given process and set of facility product standards (Vernon, 1966). At this stage, the different companies that manufactured products from the HTS 61, 62, 64, 85 and 90 categories in the United States moved to countries where their operational costs, especially labor and fixed costs related to macroeconomic conditions are appropriate, especially during the sixties and seventies (Garcia de Andrés, 2012). This so-called relocation signals the real beginnings of globalization.

Continuing with the life cycle theory, it is necessary to mention that in the fourth stage called: decline, the market begins to be saturated, demand and sales begin to drop, the pace varying according to each product. As competition withdraws and the market begins to decline, profits are seriously affected (Udokporo, 2021). It may thus be necessary to determine whether the product is withdrawn or the substitution for a newer product is activated (Mulder, 2012).

Theoríes of Internationalization

As described by Moran (2000), Vernon's life cycle model predicts two types of direct investment in developing countries: a) first, subsidiaries that are linked to the strategy of the parent company and advance in international markets, and b) as subsidiaries to the host market, but are not part of the parent company's global supply network. In this panorama, Moran (2000) establishes that operations in foreign investments linked to the global supply network contribute more to the host economy through the activities of the subsidiaries themselves, the backward links with local suppliers.

Given the need for mature companies to move to foreign subsidiaries, the theory of internalization and its later version, internationalization, can be considered. Internalization is mainly concerned with how to organize international business transactions, concerned with the choices and design of governance in international business (Narula & Verbeke, 2015). This is based on the assumption that the economic actors of the global system are oriented towards efficiency, and will tend to select governance approaches that best serve efficiency objectives (Narula & Verbeke, 2015). Based on Coase's theory, institutional arrangements can act as substitutes in production, improving efficiency (Narula & Verbeke, 2015).

Dunning's (1988) contribution makes a critical review of the so-called eclectic paradigm of international production, given its limited capacity to explain or predict types of international production and the individual behavior of companies. Therefore, Dunning (1988) proposes a taxonomy of three key aspects for the internationalization of companies and their decision to produce abroad, known as OLI: ownership, location and internalization.

Regarding ownership, Dunning establishes the imperfect transfer of ownership advantages that prevented companies from transferring their competitive resources or assets abroad. Regarding location (regions or countries), to have advantages, companies must have operations in place, and MNEs must take into account site-specific factors: production costs, accessibility, availability of knowledge, industrial policies, size and market power. The third component, the advantages of internalization, refers to foreign direct investment, for greater control and quality of operations (Ferreira et al., 2013). The conceptual objective of this paradigm is to explain why multinational enterprizes (MNEs) exist and why they are more successful than national ones. Dunning (1988) also establishes that there are three types of international production: search for markets (import substitution), search for resources (supply-oriented), search for efficiency (rational investment).

In his later work, Dunning (1995) considers the implications of so-called "alliance capitalism" in the theorizing of MNEs, in which companies can come together to share technology, distribution networks, technology, among others, to improve their position. competitive in the market. This implied to Dunning a reformulation of the OLI paradigm, first, in terms of expanding the analysis of the costs and benefits derived from the relationships between companies, second, the concept of location advantages needs to consider the weight of the growing need for integration of complex and changing economic activities, the conditions under which alliances occur, the role of national authorities and the spatial intersection of immobile assets in particular geographic areas (Dunning, 1995).

Thus, the theory of internationalization began to gain a relevant field both academically and industrially. Porter (1986) suggested that international competition is the most important aspect for companies, which is why trade on a global scale began to be the norm. Porter (1986) begins to focus on the industry, since it is from this basis one can measure whether a competitive advantage is successful or not, as this competition varies from industry to industry. Industries range across a broad spectrum from multi-domestic to global. Multidomestic companies are in more than one country, but they compete country by country, while global companies compete globally (Porter, 1986). Therefore, in global competitiveness, a company has to perform some functions in each country it competes, however, a global competitor must view these international activities as a general system and also maintain a country perspective. The balance between these two perspectives is the key question in global strategy (Porter, 1986).

An industry can be considered global "if there is some competitive advantage in any context, whether it be domestic or international, it is necessary to adopt a disaggregated view of the firm" (Porter, 1986, p.19). This disaggregated vision of the company is what Porter (1986) called the value chain and, on the other hand, the company's activities are called value activities. A company can have two types of competitive advantages: low cost or differentiation. A company's activities can be categorized into nine general categories: Human Resources, Technology Department, Procurement, Inbound Logistics, Operations, Marketing and Sales, Service (Porter, 1986). The activities of a company's value chain are connected through links that will consequently affect the other activities, and different amounts of links will be established in the large system of value chains, which are essential in competitive advantage (Porter, 1986).

Internationalization of the United States

By the end of the 19th century and beginning of the 20th century, the United States developed a mass production model, which broke with established production norms and marketing schemes. This was based on large assembly lines and the use of interchangeable parts, which allowed for the production in large batches of equipment, machinery, and durable consumer goods at low cost and granting affordability to people around the world (OAS, 1995). The United States also established mass production of garments, footwear and consumer electronics like radios, telephones, etc., favorably impacting the population's way of life (Grunwald & Flamm, 1985). This gave way to economies of scale where a reduced number of plants could supply mass markets.

In the 1960s, the United States economy was arguably at its apex in most productive activities; however, the increase in wages and regulations gave rise to the need for companies to contract suppliers in other parts of the world. Initially this took place in companies that manufactured final products derived from light industry (textile, footwear, plastic, etc.) (OAS, 1995). For example, the manufacture of clothing was subdivided and the labor-intensive assembly phase outsourced. Cut pieces of cloth were brought to their factories, where specific sewing, assembly, and packaging services were carried out. The complex production sharing operation complemented the purchase of raw materials, transportation, and returning of the finished products, which was done under auspices of the headquarters. With the industrial development of these countries, new companies were hired and the process was eventually completely transferred overseas (OAS, 1995). The United States was no longer about manufacturing, but about marketing agents, concentrating on service functions.

An important aspect of North American internationalization has to do with the deregulation of transportation and service markets and the privatization of public companies that began in the 1980s. At this time, salaries and the quality of labor continued to have priority in location decisions in production and service facilities, given that technology and capital were highly mobile (OAS, 1995).

In the adjacent country of Mexico, the origin of foreign direct investment was largely American, accounting for 50% of the total in the period of 1999-2018. There was a high participation of the automotive industry, placing it as the main industry integrated into the US production chain. Also, the opening of the agricultural sector with the NAFTA agreement gave the US a comparative advantage over Mexico, given that it had greater technological development and production subsidies (Correa, 2021). This opened the way for trade in agricultural products through other agreements such as CAFTA-DR (Findlay, 2019).

The Turn Towards Reshoring (reverting to nationalism)

Correa (2021) indicates that after 23 years of NAFTA, former President Donald Trump raised the need to renegotiate the treaty in 2017, given that the unemployment crisis generated in the US was attributed to bilateral trade with Mexico, as well as to rising imports from China. With his nationalist "America First" foreign policy, Donald Trump gave a twist to the international projection of the United States, advancing protectionist actions, which sparked responses in defense of free trade by China and the European Union, as well as from Latin America.

In the successor presidency of Joe Biden, antagonisms with China grew with the passage of the Uyghur Forced Labor Prevention Act (UFLPA) by the end of 2021. It stipulated that any enterprise that imports goods from the Xinjiang region must certify that those goods are not produced using "forced labor" in order to avoid penalties. According to a May 2024 textile industry report, "over the past five years, there has been a notable shift away from reliance on China due to the implementation…" of the UFLPA (Fiber2Fashion, 2024).

Therefore, new elements are added to the perspective of internationalization, with the resurgence of nationalism and geopolitical antagonisms with China, wherein the perspectives of offshoring and outsourcing activities are spurned as important elements of the discourse on manufacturing in developed economies. Emerging news in recent years shows how manufacturing companies in the Organization for Economic Co-operation and Development countries (OECD) are increasingly bringing activities back home. Prominent cases such as Apple, General Electric, NCR, and Ford Company have given visibility to the topic in public discussions (De Backer et al., 2016). According to Tate (2014), companies' consideration of changing locational or "shoring" decisions were due to the 2008 economic recession, the emphasis on sustainability and customer expectations regarding flexibility and improved economic performance.

The reshoring phenomenon in the United States has received great attention since it became a political platform during the last elections (Tate, 2014). A survey in the US Fashion Industry Association's (USFIA) 11th annual Benchmarking Study inidcated that a record 43 per cent of respondents sourced less than 10 per cent of their apparel products from China in 2023, compared to 18 per cent in 2018. Furthermore, nearly 60 per cent reportedly no longer use China as their top apparel supplier, a significant increase from pre-pandemic levels (Fibre Fashion, 2024).

The study by Fratocchi et al. (2016) conducted a literature review regarding the motivations for reshoring, highlighting that the most common explanation for why companies tend to reshoring is the rational reaction to changing conditions. Therefore, Transaction Cost Theory (TCC) and the Resource-Based View (RBV) can explain reshoring (Fratocchi et al., 2016). It is important to note that no enterprise is going to relocate a plant to the US to make low-value products, such as T-shirts. It's all focused on complicated high-value products, such as motor vehicles, chips, electrical and electronic products, heavy components and equipment, etc. Contrary to those industrial sectors, what concerns this study is the nearshoring of such low-value products south of the US border.

Bibliographic Evidence of Reshoring

There are many examples of reshoring in the public press, some such as General Electric (GE) that are putting to use their existing assets that have been idle, retrofitting buildings for current manufacturing processes (Tate, 2014). However, according to Fratocchi et al. (2016) quantitative evidence on reshoring is still very fragmented, even when there are highly visible cases of the phenomenon, making it difficult to access specific data to analyze the nature of the phenomenon. The literature has largely focused on generating conceptual approaches, trends and predictions of the future regarding reshoring (Barbieri, et al., 2018; Benstead et al., 2017; Dikler, 2021; Foerstl et al., 2016), as well as analyses on implementation regarding the decision to relocate (Boffelli, et al., 2018). Literature reviews of the reshoring phenomenon are also highlighted (Barbieri et al., 2018; Fratocchi et al., 2016; Pedroletti & Ciabuschi, 2023). The study by Barbieri et al. (2018) analyzed 57 articles on manufacturing reshoring, categorizing the main definitions for reshoring and its motivations, establishing that it can be part of the reindustrialization policies that many Western countries include in their economic agenda; and the possible relationship between reshoring and the various forms of technological innovation applied to manufacturing, popularly called "Industry 4.0".

On the other hand, Pedroletti and Ciabuschi (2023) analyzed 135 articles, and like other studies, they categorized the studies according to contingency, decisions or motivations, but additionally established the implementations and results of the relocation. They concluded that, the practice of reshoring will be shaped by the high uncertainty and rapid changes in the global economic and political scenario, which imply international relocation strategies, which companies are beginning to learn and intensify, which will have long-term effects.

Data from European companies based on the European Manufacturing Survey shows that in the period from 2010 to 2012 (data for countries available) around 4% of companies in the survey sample have moved their production activities back home. Also, in that same period of time, offshoring was found to be more important than backshoring, given that for every backshoring company, there are basically three offshoring companies (De Backer et al., 2016).

Other studies have shown evidence of reshoring activities, as is the case of Ashby, A. (2016) who presented the case study of a small medium-sized clothing company in the United Kingdom, which will bring its supply chain "home." as a way to establish sustainability through reshoring. While another study carried out in the same country indicates a relatively modest low relocation activity, due to practical restrictions such as industrial policies, which must be more "pro-manufacturing", more holistic and proactive, than until now. have shown that they can convince companies to return to their country of origin (Bailey, D., & De Propris, 2014). The study by El-Sahli, Z., & Gullstrand, J. (2023) used microdata from Sweden to identify and quantify reshoring. These authors found that reshoring is positively associated with firms' technological advances, but detected evidence supporting the notion that increased income from offshoring countries drives reshoring.

For their part, Choudhary et al. (2023) in their research, highlights the supply networks of Apple and Jaguar Land Rover, which have experienced reshoring from foreign suppliers to domestic locations, constructing the large-scale network consisting of 2,066 and 1,238 companies of these brands, finding that there is no evidence in their study that speaks to the impact of reshoring on sustainability.

The study by Zhai et al. (2016) based on 139 cases of relocation of North American companies from China. They found that quality, rather than increased labor cost, is the single primary factor driving reshoring, and cost as a group factor. In Germany, with the data available from 1,484 manufacturing companies from the European Manufacturing survey, they established the trends and changes in the companies, seeing that relocation is not only to emerging countries, but also repatriation of production to local bases and close to industrialized countries (Kinkel, 2012).

On the other hand, several of the reports from The Boston Consoulting Group (BCG) (2011, 2013, 2014) have shown data and information relevant to the relocation processes experienced in the United States. For example, according to BCG (2011) The Coleman Company moved its production from China to Wishina, Kansas due to the increase of costs in manufacturing and shipping from China. Also, Ford Motor Company brought 2,000 jobs back to the United States with a favorable agreement with United Auto Wokers, which allows new employees to be hired at $14 per hour (BCG, 2011).

According to Sirkin et al. (2014), in terms of direct costs "the US playing field is essentially level with Yangtze Rivera Delta, China's chief production zone" (p.1), because although there was a weakening of the Yen for that period, and taking into account the differences between productivity and energy costs, according to data collected by the BCG for the global manufacturing cost competitiveness index, there was a reduction from 14% in 2004 to 1% in 2016, in China's manufacturing cost advantage about the United States (Sirkin et al., 2014). Thus, when the indirect costs of shipping, inventory, among others, are included, it is now less expensive to manufacture a variety of products in the United States if that is where they will be consumed (Sirkin et al., 2014).

METHODOLOGY

This study takes as a sample the following CAFTA-DR member countries close to North American territory (El Salvador, Guatemala, Honduras and Nicaragua) along with the giant North American country of Mexico. These countries are geographically located in Central America - close to the USA - and Mexico, which has borders with the USA, so their transportation costs are economical as previously stated. In addition, due to the importance of international trade related to the amounts exported, the analysis will be considered in two groups: The first group of analysis is made up of China and Vietnam as Asian countries of reference in the analysis along with Mexico since the monetary values of the 5 HTS categories of these countries' exports to the USA are in the same range. The second group of countries are the Central American countries because the range of their exports is consistent and there is not much variability.

As a research methodology, quantitative methods will be used that include two techniques: firstly, it is established as a reference point according to the determination that 2009 marks the beginning of this phenomenon called reshoring. That year will be used for each group of countries and for each HTS category, time series analysis for which their trend equations and the type of trend will be calculated. The countries that have a substantial positive behavior will be selected in the case that they are Central American countries. This selection is determined by the nominal value of the coefficient of determination of each trend equation and that it is above + 0.45. Since the coefficient of determination, known statistically as R2, which indicates the level of proportion of the variance of the dependent variable (Y=exports) depending on the variability of the independent variables (X=years), in other words, is the level of reliability in which the values fit an estimated regression line (Castro-Gonzáles, et al., 2017). The data is analyzed from 2009 to 2023, and is expressed in dollars. Subsequently, this analysis will be reinforced by a comparative analysis of growth based on percentage growth and absolute values of growth or falls expressed in millions of dollars, according to each HTS category. All data was obtained through the official international trade website of the US government: https://hts.usitc.gov/ . After obtaining the required data for the different countries under study and for each HTS as well as a periodicity from 2009 to 2023. The results of this research are presented in the following sections.

RESULTS AND ANALYSIS OF RESULTS

As previously noted, time series analysis has been used along with trend analysis based on the coefficient of determination (R2) for each country for each HTS category. R-squared (R2) represents the proportion of the variance for the dependent variable that's explained by an independent variable. From these analyses the following results have been obtained, which are differentiated with titles to provide order to this work.

Analysis of HTS 61: Knitted or crochet clothing products and accessories among the selected countries

Graph # 1 shows the results of the time series analysis of exports to the US of knitted and crocheted clothing items and clothing accessories (HTS 61), from the countries of China, Vietnam and Mexico, which have export figures on the same scale of monetary values. During the analysis period, these three countries reached a total average of exports to the U.S. market, corresponding to 76.68% of the study sample. Hence, for the main producers of woven and crocheted clothing and textile accessories (HTS 61) from the sample, about 80% has been made by these three countries. According to the graph it is plausible that the reshoring phenomenon has affected China because there has been a negative trend since 2009 and its R2 is around 25.35% reliability.

Figure 1. Time series of HTS 61 exports to the North American market from 2005 to 2023

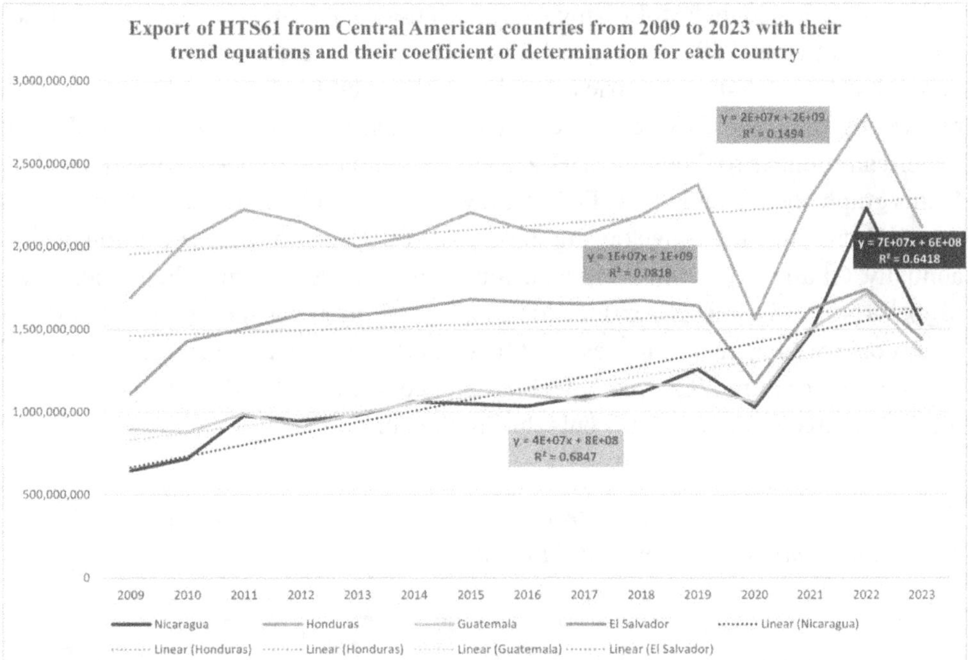

By analyzing Figure # 1 in more detail, it can be seen that China experienced significant growth in its exports from 2009 to 2015. From that year on, it is observed that there is a consistent drop until 2023 (8 years) since in absolute terms there is a decrease of $6,673 million dollars. In contrast to this result from China, Vietnam demonstrated a significant growth behavior with respect to its own exports to the United States. The latter grew by $1,563.3 million dollars between 2015 and 2023, maintaining the consistency of analysis with the same period. The coefficient of determination is 0.9031 (very significant), which suggests that US reshoring or nearshoring in this HTS category has not materialized from Vietnam.

With regard to Mexico, HTS 61 exports witnessed a sharp drop, that is, a decrease of $239.6 million dollars. Therefore, if near-shoring consists of the relocation of companies near the United States' territory, specifically in Mexico's knitted and crochet textile clothing industry, this strategy is not evident according to the US commercial data. This analysis is reinforced because the value of the coefficient of determination of Mexico's trend equation is decreasing and has a value of R2 = 0.3848. In summary, it can be asserted that reshoring or near-shoring away from China is plausible due to a very significant drop in Chinese HTS 61 exports probably due to the departure of several companies dedicated to this important industry and it means a loss of $6,673 million dollars. If such is indeed the case, it doesn't appear that Mexico or any Central American country has benefitted to any significant extent.

This is reflected in the following analysis of trends in Central American countries with regard to the HTS 61 category. Since the amounts exported are much smaller than those of the Asian countries, a separate time series analysis has been carried out among the Central American countries. Graph #2 corresponds to the Central American countries of Nicaragua, Honduras, Guatemala and El Salvador. According to this graph, the leader in this HTS 61 category among Central American countries is Honduras with an average during these years (15 years) of $2,101 million dollars annually. Of all the Central American countries, it is the one with the highest level of exports in this line of textile articles. When observing the annual exports of these countries in general, it is evident that all Central American countries suffered a significant drop in 2020, likely a consequence of the COVID-19 lockdowns and the little demand for such garments during the period.

Figure 2. Time series of exports from Central American countries of HTS 61 to the North American market from 2005 to 2023

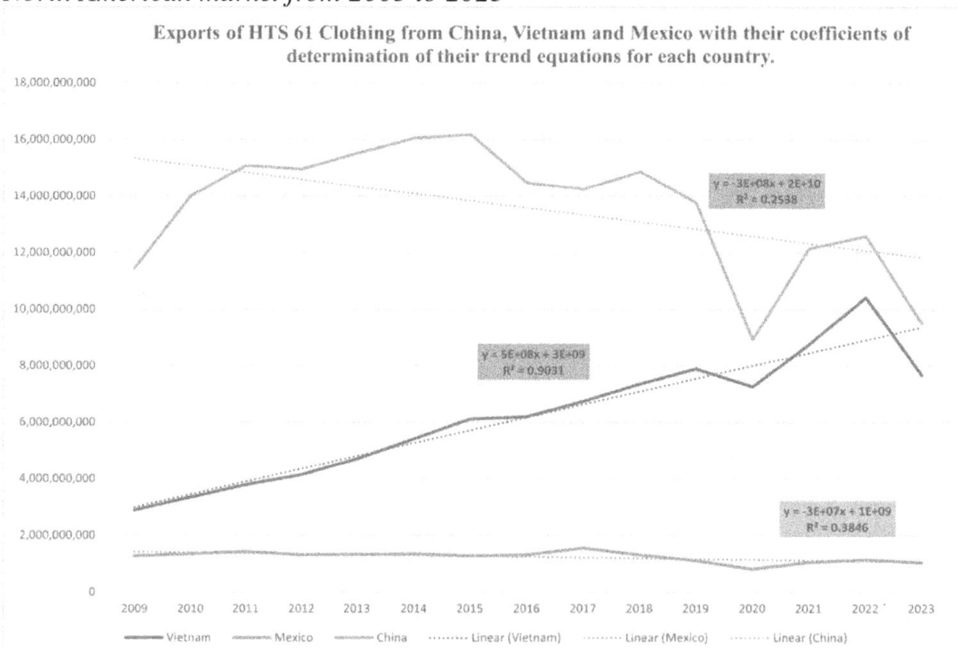

Taking into consideration that 2009 roughly marks the commencement of reshoring, it is estimated that the process was a gradual one, because it corresponds to a year after the financial crisis of 2008. Therefore, in light of Graph # 2, it is observed that the four countries have had an upward trend, undoubtedly the plausible leader of near-shoring in terms of its coefficient of determination is Guatemala with an R2 = 0.68, with a significant increase in its exports between 2009 and 2023 of $458.7 million dollars. Then comes Nicaragua, which experienced the largest, and very significant increase of $883.7 million dollars (155.22%) so it is possible to speculate that the country experienced near-shoring in this category of products, which is bolstered statistically since its R2 = 0.64.

On the other hand, it is possible that near-shoring may be occurring in Honduras given that it has a positive trend and with an R2 = 0.15. While that is not statistically very significant, when HTS 61 exports to the USA are examined it is evidenced they have increased 124% for the period 2009-2023. To conclude with the Central American countries, it can finally be seen that El Salvador has also had a percentage increase in 2023 compared to 2009 of 134%, but statistically the model is not very significant with respect to the real data because its R2 is only 0.1494, mainly due to the high variability of recent years.

Analysis of HTS 62: Clothing products and textile accessories Not knitted or crochet among the selected countries

Using the same techniques employed previously, Graph # 3 shows the results of time series analysis of the exports of products related to HTS 62, which corresponds to non-woven or crocheted clothing items and clothing accessories and involving the countries of China, Vietnam and Mexico. During the period of analysis, these three countries have registered exports to the North American market, corresponding to 93.42% of the total, while only 7.68% are accounted for by Central American countries, hence the relevance of graphs # 3 and # 4.

Once more it is observed that China appears subject to the USA's reshoring or near-shoring phenomenon. There has been a negative trend since 2009 and its R2 is around 72.38% reliability while the amount of loss since 2009 with respect to 2023 is -$5,482.8 million dollars. On the other hand, Vietnam experienced significant growth behavior with respect to its own exports. By 2023 it grew significantly with a monetary value of $4,349.5 million dollars compared to 2009. Its R2 = 0.9519 demonstrates that it has a very relevant high level of statistical significance. Hence reshoring or nearshoring by the USA from Vietnam once more seems not to have materialized.

According to Graph # 3, a sharp drop was found in Mexican exports of the order of -$310.3 million dollars. Therefore, there doesn't appear to be near-shoring in the non-knit or crocheted textile clothing industry towards Mexico. This strategy is not evident according to the US commercial values expressed in imports. The analysis is reinforced because the value of the coefficient of determination of its trend equation is declining and has a value of R2 = 0.5298.

Figure 3. Time series of HTS 62 exports to the North American market from 2005 to 2023 and their respective trend equations with their R2

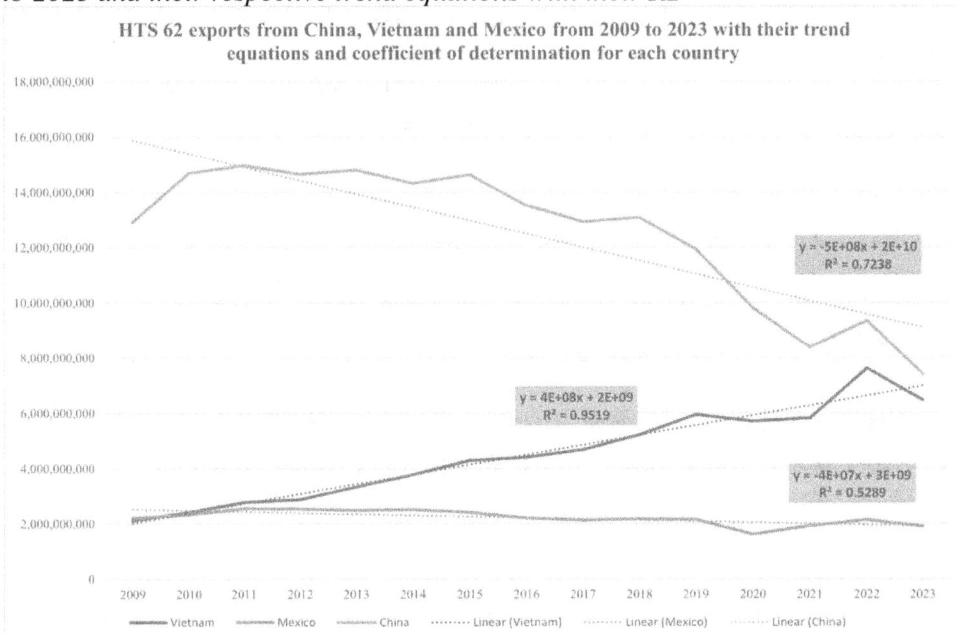

An analysis regarding the 7.68% of the total items imported to the USA under HTS 62, which corresponds to the Central American countries now follows. Since the amounts exported are much smaller than those of the Asian countries, a singular time series analysis has been carried out among the Central American countries. Graph #4 corresponds to the Central American countries of Nicaragua, Honduras, Guatemala and El Salvador. According to this graph, the leader in the HTS 62 category among the Central American countries is Honduras with an average during these years (15 years) of $467.573 million dollars annually. However, it can be seen that Nicaragua has had significant growth since 2009.

In light of Graph #4, it is evident that Nicaragua and Honduras have an upward trend, while Guatemala and El Salvador have a downward trend. The growth leader in terms of its coefficient of determination is Nicaragua with an R2 = 0.59, and a significant increase in its exports between 2009 and 2023 of $196.9 million dollars, representing a percentage increase of 80.35%. Then follows Honduras, which has had a slight increase of $1.2 million dollars (+ 0.28%) which suggests that Honduras isn't a likely candidate for US nearshoring in this product category. This is also corroborated statistically by its R2 = 0.045.

Neither is Guatemala benefitting from a possible US strategy of nearshoring, given that it has a negative trend with an R2 = 0.396 and a drop of -$58.8 million dollars (representing a 28.55% drop) for the period of 2009 to 2023. Finally, it can be seen that El Salvador isn't a plausible beneficiary of nearshoring as it experienced a percentage drop of - 42.52% for the period. Furthermore the model is statistically not very significant with respect to the data, given that its R2 is only 0.302.

Figure 4. Time series of exports from the Central American countries of HTS 62 to the North American market from 2005 to 2023.

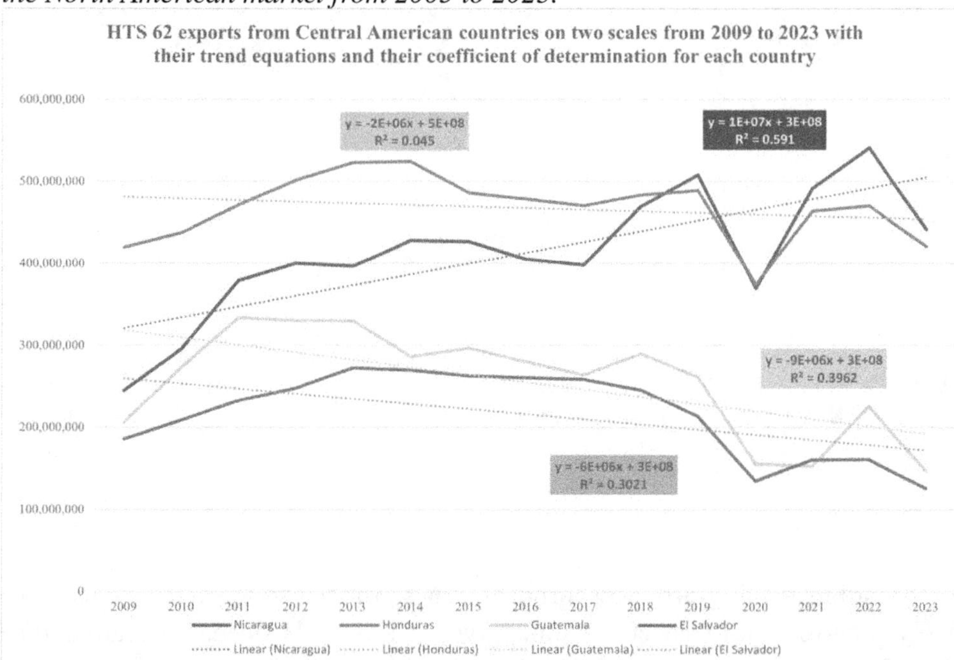

Analysis of HTS 64: Footwear, gaiters and similar articles between the selected countries.

Graph #5 illustrates the results of the time series analysis of exports of products related to HTS 64, which corresponds to footwear, leggings, and similar items originating from the countries of China, Vietnam, and Mexico. These three countries, during the analysis period, have reached a cumulative share of exports to the North American market of 99.81% of the study sample. Therefore, in this HTS 64 category, these three countries make up almost 100% of exports. Due to this circumstance, the analysis of the Central American countries was excluded since it corresponds to only 0.19% of exports in this category.

Figure 5. Time series of HTS 64 exports to the North American market from 2005 to 2023 and their respective trend equations with their R2.

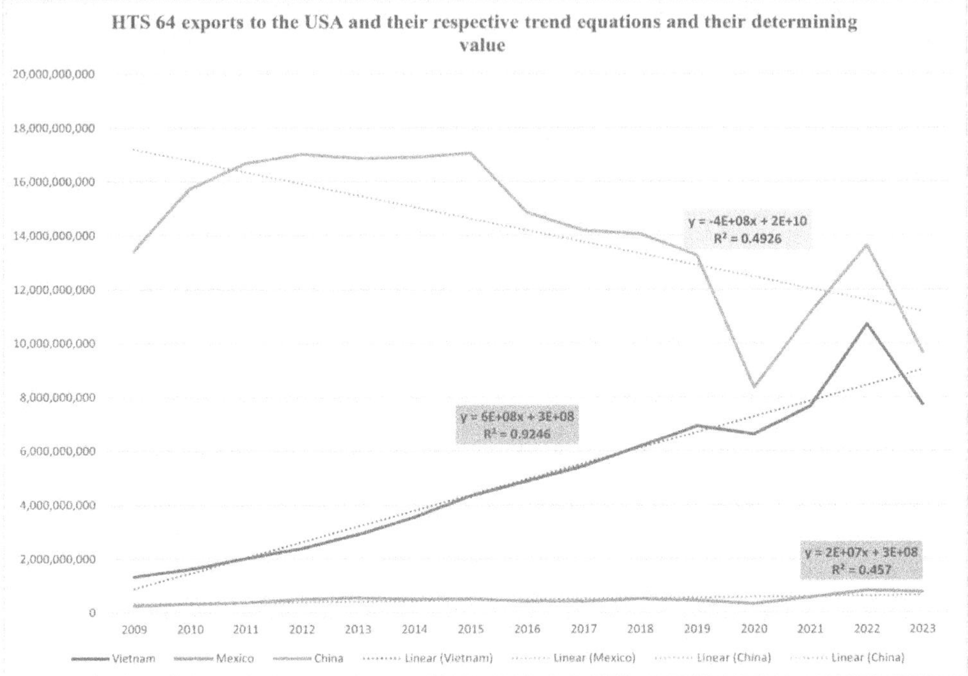

According to this graph, a reshoring or near-shoring phenomenon has once more likely occurred with respect to China, given that there has been a negative trend since 2009 and its R2 is around 72.38% reliability. The amount of loss since 2009 with respect to 2023 is -$5,482.8 million dollars. Vietnam, on the other hand has a significant growth behavior with respect to its exports to the US. It grew significantly with a monetary value of $ +6,416.1 million dollars for the period from 2009 to 2025. Its R2 = 0.9245 demostrates a high level of statistical significance, thus reinforcing the liklihood that reshoring or nearshoring in this HTS category has not ocurred. Instead, there has been a strengthening and reinforcement of offshoring of these products because both the USA and Vietnam signed expansive commercial agreements after negotiations in 2006, thereby strengthening commercial ties from 2007 when Vietnam entered the World Trade Organization. This came about above all due to its comparative advantages of having very low labor costs, infrastructure investment, increasing production capacity and economic political stability, which is reflected in its Revealed Comparative Advantage Index (RCA). The RCA basically measures the relative advantage or disadvantage of a certain country in a certain class of goods or services as evidenced by trade flows. Therefore, the RCA is based on the observed trade patterns (Balassa, 1965). In this case, according to Chi (2017), his RCA of the footwear industry for Vietnam in the given period easily explains the pattern and growth of international trade (Agbude, 2023). Vietnam's RCA between 2010 and 2013 for this footwear industry amounts to 16.43 and the share of its exports of its footwear and related products industry from Vietnam amounts to 13.61% in that same period, hence the importance of these figures exported in the HTS 64 category.

According to Graph # 5 with respect to Mexico's exports, a consistent increase in its category HTS 64 exports of the order of $ 514.9 million dollars was evidenced, with a growth in this period of 292.73%. Therefore, if near-shoring consists of the relocation of companies near US territory, specifically in the footwear and related products industry, it is likely according to the expressed commercial values of Mexico's exports. This analysis is reinforced because the coefficient of determination of its equation is on the rise and has a value of R2 = 0.457.

Analysis of HTS 85: Electrical machinery and equipment, audio players, TVs and accessories between the selected countries

Graph #6 illustrates the results of the time series of US imports of products related to HTS 85 corresponding to electrical machinery and equipment, sound players, TVs and accessories originating from China, Vietnam and Mexico. These three countries during the analysis period have reached an average total of exports to the North American market, corresponding to 99.46% of the study sample. Therefore, in this HTS 85, almost 100% has been carried out by these three exporting countries, and only 0.54% has been exported by Central American countries, hence the importance of graph # 6.

According to Graph # 6, there is no circumstantial evidence of the reshoring ornearshoring phenomenon in the Chinese case due to a growing trend since 2009, while its R2 is of the order of 0.4391% reliability. The precise amount of increase in its exports to the USA since 2009 with respect to 2023 is +$48,467.5 million dollars, or a percentage increase of 65.68%. Vietnam shows a similar behavior to that of China in that it experiences significant growth with respect to its own exports. HTS 85 exports to the US grew significantly by a value of $ 38,790.1 million dollars between 2009 and 2023. Given that the corresponding R2 = 0.7646, it can be assumed that such a high level of statistical significance makes this trend more reliable. In other words the possibility of reshoring or nearshoring for this HTS 85 category has not happened in Vietnam but to the contrary there is significant continued offshoring given its percentage increase is of the order of 6%. While in 2009 Vietnam only exported $ 639,349 million dollars, by 2023 it reached the spectacular figure of $ 14,147,210 million dollars.

Figure 6. Time series of HTS 85 exports to the North American market from 2005 to 2023 and their respective trend equations with their R2

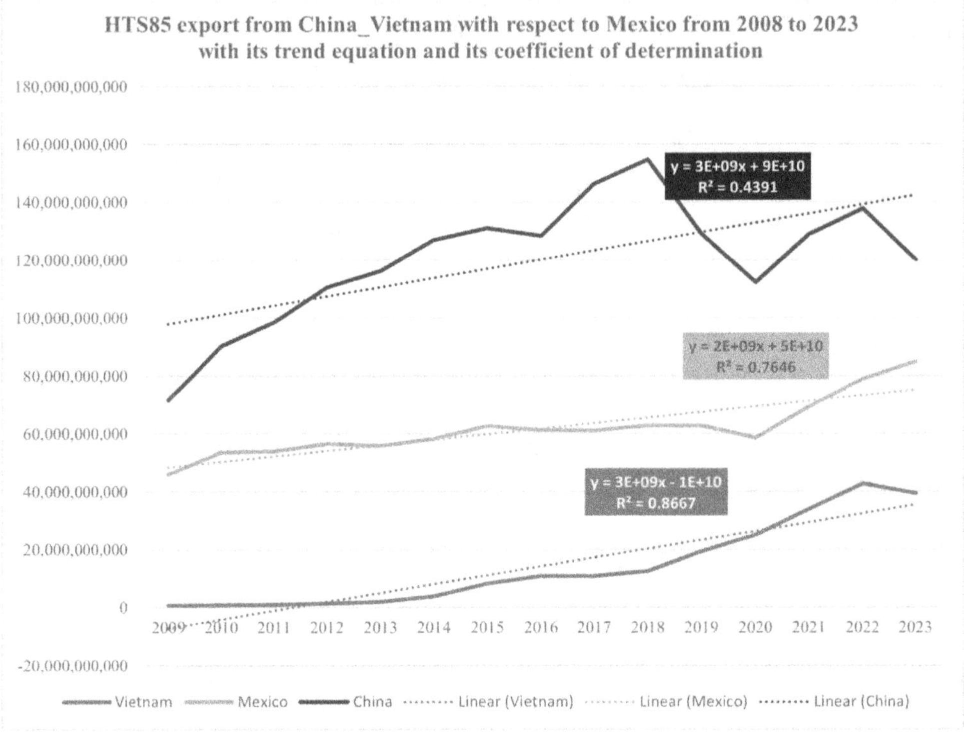

As regards Mexico's exports, it was also found that there is a strong growth in its production and export of HTS85 in the order of +$38,851 million dollars. Nearshoring towards Mexico is thus a possibility, given Mexico and the USA's proximity to one another. This analysis is reinforced by the value of the coefficient of determination which evidences a positive trend and growth equation with a value of R2 = 0.8667. The question is where is this industry drawn from?

If an analysis is carried out on the 0.47% of the total US imports of HTS 85 products that correspond to the Central American countries, a positive trend emerges from each of them, despite the fact that the amount is small. Nevertheless based on their populations, a near-shoring strategy by the USA is a possibility for these countries. Thus, based on the time series of each of the Central American countries, shown in graph # 7, the results can be analyzed as follows: According to this graph, the leader in this HTS 85 of the Central American countries is Honduras with an average increasing trend during these years (15 years) of $ 804.2 million dollars from 2009 to 2023. A nearshoring strategy is possible in Honduras since the value of its exports have increased by 323% for the period, while it exhibits an R2 of 0.5904.

Figure 7. Time series of exports from Central American HTS 85 countries to the North American market from 2005 to 2023

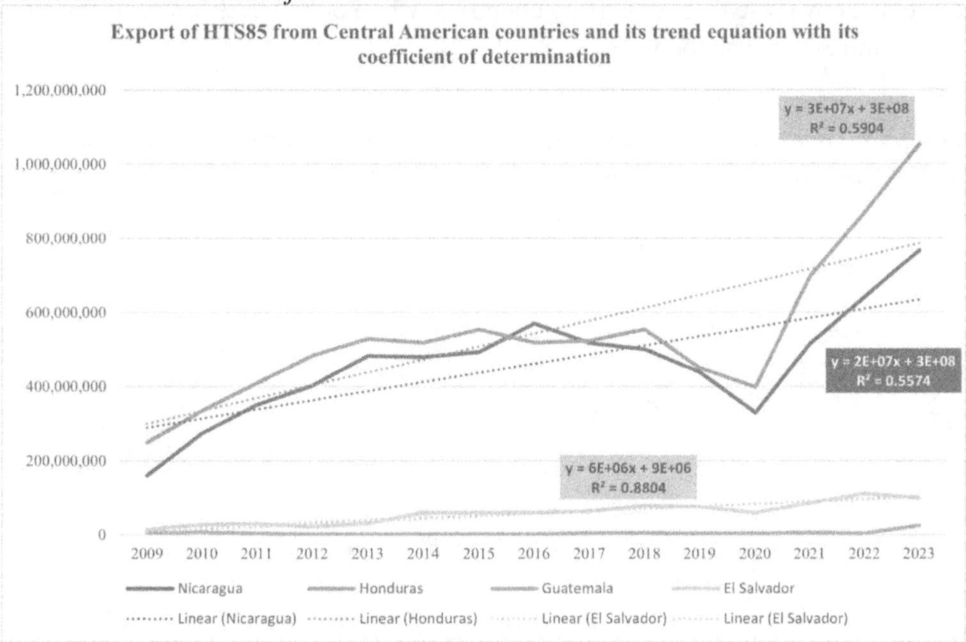

Likewise, it can be seen that Nicaragua has had significant growth from 2009 to 2023 of the order of $606.6 million dollars, reflecting an increase in its exports by 379% over the time period. These data are statistically supported because the trend equation is positive and has an R2 = 0.5574. It can therefore be assumned that in the HTS 84 category, Nicaragua may have possibly benefitted from a nearshoring strategy in economic terms.

Looking at El Salvador, there is a slight increase in its exports in this HTS 84, of the order of $86.4 million dollars with a percentage increase of the order of 67.68% in this period of time. When its trend equation is calculated, it is found to be positive and exhibits a very high coefficient of determination, that is, R2 = 0.8804. Given the small value of exports accruing to Guatemala, a detailed analysis of its commercial strategy is ommitted because on average during this period it has only exported $4.709 billion dollars.

Analysis of HTS 90: Medical, optical, photographic and cinematographic instruments between the selected countries

In Graph # 8, the results of the time series of exports of products related to HTS 90 are illustrated, which correspond to medical, optical, photographic and cinematographic instruments originating from China, Vietnam and Mexico. These three countries during the analysis period average 99.93% of the study sample of exports to the US market. Therefore, in this HTS 90 category almost 100% has been carried out by these three exporting countries, while only 0.07% has been exported by Central American countries.

Figure 8. Time series of HTS 90 exports to the North American market from 2005 to 2023 and their respective trend equations with their R2

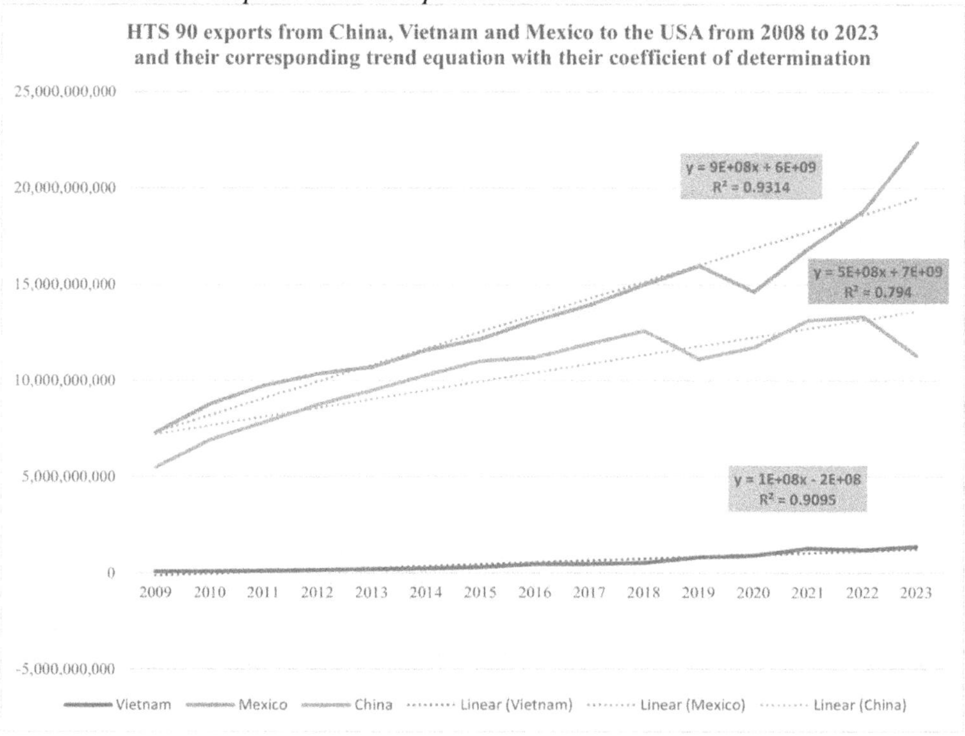

According to this graph, it is interesting to see that the leader of these three countries in this export category is Mexico, since the latter alone has 55% of the 99.93% of exports to the USA in this industry. Therefore, it can be considered that a possible US nearshoring strategy is in effect with the HTS 90 category exports from its southern neighbor. Mexico's exports to the US from 2009 to 2023, have increased a total of $15,055 million dollars for a percentage increase of 206.33%. According to its trend equation, it is observed that it is positive and has a value of R2 = 0.9314, which is extremely high and very significant, so it is possible to posit a nearshoring in the HTS 90 category beneficial to Mexico.

Interestingly, the US nearshoring phenomenon has not manifested itself with regard to China, because there is a growth trend since 2009 and the corresponding R2 is of the order of 0.7940% reliability and the precise amount of increase in its exports since 2009 with respect to 2023 is $5,806 million dollars. That is, there has been a significant growth of this HTS of the order of 105.96%.

Furthermore, Vietnam has a similar behavior to that of China, but on a smaller scale with respect to its own exports. Because in 2023 it grows with a monetary value of $1,296.7 million dollars with respect to 2009, making a percentage jump of 1,864%. Therefore, calculating its trend equation it is observed that it is positive with an R2 = 0.9095, a high level of statistical significance which makes this trend more reliable. So in other words, in this specific case, reshoring or near-shoring is not evidenced in this HTS 90 category, but on the contrary there appears to be a significant reinforcement of offshoring of this industry. The explanation in this case applies the same analysis of the HTS 64 case explained in the previous section.

CONCLUSIONS

The second and ensuing decades of the current century seem defined by multiple and persistent disruptions due to a rising wave of economic nationalism and an antagonistic rivalry between the world's two largest economies: those of the United States and China. While the first of these disruptions was arguably the 2008 financial crisis, it was the rise of the Trump administration in the US which cemented the most significant of these. His overt pursuit of protectionist measures has seemingly reversed the worldwide trend toward globalization, spearheaded by what was the most enthusiastic supporter of open markets in the post-war era. In this new context, "deglobalization" and "decoupling" have come to replace "globalization" and "liberalization". Some North American companies have found alternatives to minimize costs by returning their businesses to North American territory or locating productive and export operations in some countries close to the US that have special treaties with it such as Mexico and various Central American countries. It is the latter which has formed the basis of this chapter. Overall, this study constitutes a modest contribution to the topic of reshoring and nearshoring since the industrial sample which formed the basis of it was restricted to mature products that were initially offshored to export processing zones in low wage locations, namely garments, footwear, electronics and medical and optical devices.

This research found that in the two garment categories of HTS 61 and HTS 62, China may have experienced a loss of industrial capacity since its exports have exhibited a downward trend in both. In the case of HTS 61, this is corroborated by an overall decrease of $6,673 million dollars in the period 2009-2023 and a decrease of $5,482.8 million dollars for the period in HTS 62. Contrary to China, however, it was shown that Vietnam experienced what appears to be a reinforcement of US offshoring since its exports to the US increased by $1,563.3 million dollars with a very significant level of statistical reliability of R2=0.9031 in the case of HTS 61. In the case of HTS 62, Vietnam was found to have a positive growth performance in its exports of the order of $4,349.5 million dollars in the period 2023-2009, with its R2 = 0.9519, which might suggest a relocation of Chinese exporters to Vietnamese territory since the Vietnamese incease in value is comparable to the Chinese decrease.

What seems certain is that US garment imports were not nearshored to Mexico for the period under study. It was found that Mexican exports of HTS 61 experienced a decline of $239.6 million dollars, while a drop of $310.3 million dollars was found in its HTS 62 exports for the period. Hence Mexico has not benefitted from a US nearshoring strategy. Similarly, despite the rise in export values from some countries in Central America for both HTS 61 and 62, whatever nearshoring may have occurred seems minor at best and centered around knitted or crocheted garments (HTS 61). While the UFLPA has significantly decreased Chinese garment imports into the US, imports from the CAFTA-DR group of countries have reportedly not risen to replace them as expected (Fiber2Fashion, 2024).

The examination of the HTS 64 data that corresponds to US imports of footwear, leggings and derived articles, shows that 99.81% of imports in this category originate from China, Vietnam and Mexico, while the participation of the Central American countries is very small (0.19%). Here again, it was found that China could have suffered the effects of US reshoring or nearshoring since its exports fell considerably in the period 2009-2023 by $ -3,759.7 million dollars, although that could have been more than offset by Vietnam's increase during the period by a total of $6,416.1 million dollars (a growth by 485.12%), bolstered by an R2 of 0.9246. In this industrial sector, it was found that Mexico experienced a growth of HTS 64 goods exports to the US totalling $514.9 million dollars, (202.67%) for the period, although its R2 = 0.457.

No useful conclusions can be drawn from commercial data in the HTS 85 category, as all countries for which statistics were compiled demonstrated export value increases to the US market. As to be expected, the larger countries of China, Vietnam and Mexico eclipsed the small Central American countries on an individual basis. Neither can useful conclusions be drawn from commercial data in the HTS 90 category. Most notably, the Central American countries only account for a miniscule 0.07% of US HTS 90 imports, while the bulk is accounted for by China, Vietnam and Mexico, all of which experienced significant growth rates.

In summary, it is evident that it is still too early to draw solid conclusions that are relevant to Latin American countries concerning the acceleration of their exports of mature products, initially drawn from industrialized countries to export processing zones during the last century. Many reports from various industry media point to the process of nearshoring to the Americas as ongoing (Abdulla, H. 2024; Runde, D.F. et. al. 2024), with one declaring Honduras as the biggest winner of US apparel nearshoring in January 2024 (Husband, L. 2024).

Limitations and Future Research Avenues

Given that this book focuses on Latin America, it presents a limitation as there are other regions of the world which might benefit from nearshoring and reshoring, and not just to the United States, but to the European Union as well. Nevertheless, the most relevant limitation of this particular work is that the HTS categories studied did not consider all the producing and exporting countries to the USA of these HTS categories. Therefore it is considered as a future research endeavor to incorporate all the exporting countries of each of these 5 important HTS categories, where the role played by Latin American and Caribbean countries is also analyzed. This limitation thus becomes a future agenda to be carried out in a later opportunity.

REFERENCES

Abasolo, A. E. (1991). Un análisis empírico de los determinantes de la especialización productiva y comercial de Euskadi. *Ekonomiaz: Revista vasca de economía*, (21), 210-226.

Abdulla, H. (February 14, 2024) Data points to 2023 as turning point in US apparel nearsourcing, *JustStyle News*. https://www.just-style.com/features/data-points-to-2023-as-turning-point-in-us-apparel-nearsourcing/

Agbude, E. (2023). Changes In Export Trade Relationship Between Vietnam and the US. Norwegian University of Life Sciences. School of Economics and Business (HH). Postboks 5003 No. 1432. Norway, pp. 1-55.

Ashby, A. (2016). From global to local: Reshoring for sustainability. *Operations Management Research : Advancing Practice Through Research*, 9(3-4), 75–88. DOI: 10.1007/s12063-016-0117-9

Bailey, D., & De Propris, L. (2014). Manufacturing reshoring and its limits: The UK automotive case. *Cambridge Journal of Regions, Economy and Society*, 7(3), 379–395. DOI: 10.1093/cjres/rsu019

Balassa, B. (1965). Trade Liberalization and "Revealed" Comparative Advantage. *Manchester School*, 33(2), 99–123. DOI: 10.1111/j.1467-9957.1965.tb00050.x

Barbieri, P., Ciabuschi, F., Fratocchi, L., & Vignoli, M. (2018). What do we know about manufacturing reshoring? *Journal of Global Operations and Strategic Sourcing*, 11(1), 79–122. DOI: 10.1108/JGOSS-02-2017-0004

Bardos, P. R. (Ed.). (Nov. 2017). *A Centennial History of the USITC*. United States International Trade Commission.

Benstead, A. V., Stevenson, M., & Hendry, L. C. (2017). Why and how do firms reshore? A contingency-based conceptual framework. *Operations Management Research : Advancing Practice Through Research*, 10(3-4), 85–103. DOI: 10.1007/s12063-017-0124-5

Bhambri, S. (2015). Product Life Cycle. *International Journal of Business and Management*, II(1), 1–5.

Boffelli, A., Orzes, G., & Dotti, S. (2018). "How to reshore": Some evidence from the apparel industry. *IEEE Engineering Management Review*, 46(4), 122–127. DOI: 10.1109/EMR.2018.2886183

Borja Reyes, N. E. (2019). Las ventas desde una perspectiva del ciclo de vida del producto (Bachelor's thesis, Universidad Técnica de Ambato. Facultad de Ciencias Administrativas. Carrera Organización de Empresas).

Bustamante, V. (2022). De Vuelta a casa: La política de Reshoring del Gobierno de Estados Unidos. Universidad Pontificia de Madrid, Facultad de Ciencias Económicas y Empresariales. Junio 2022, pp. 1-57.

Canals, J. (1994). *La internacionalización de la empresa*. McGraw-Hill.

Cao, H., & Folan, P. (2011). *Product Life Cycle: the evolution of a paradigm and literature review from 1950-2009*. Department of Industrial Engineering, Tsinghua University.

Castro-Gonzáles, S., Espina, M., & Tinoco-Egas, R. (2017). Strategies and competitiveness for emerging countries: A comparative study among three South-American countries. *International Journal of Emerging Markets.*, 12(1), 125–139. DOI: 10.1108/IJoEM-12-2014-0222

Chi-Loi, C. (2017). Dinámica de las relaciones comerciales Vietnam-Estados Unidos desde una perspectiva comparada revelada. *Revista de Estudios Estrategicos.*, 4, 59–79.

Choudhary, N. A., Ramkumar, M., Schoenherr, T., Rana, N. P., & Dwivedi, Y. K. (2023). Does reshoring affect the resilience and sustainability of supply chain networks? The cases of Apple and Jaguar Land Rover. *British Journal of Management*, 34(3), 1138–1156. DOI: 10.1111/1467-8551.12614

Cirera, X., & Lakshman, R. W. D. (2017). The impact of export processing zones on employment, wages and labour conditions in developing countries: Systematic review. *Journal of Development Effectiveness*, 9(3), 344–360. DOI: 10.1080/19439342.2017.1309448 PMID: 30363912

Contractor, F. J., Kumar, V., Kundu, S. K., & Pedersen, T. (Eds.). (2011). *Global Outsourcing and Offshoring: An Integrated Approach to Theory and Corporate Strategy*. Cambridge University Press.

Correa, M. A. (2021). México y el regionalismo norteamericano. Del tlcan alt-mec. En Molano, G y Briceño, J. (Ed.) *El regionalismo en América Latina después de la Post-Hegemonía. Centro de Investigaciones sobre América Latina y el Caribe*. Universidad Autónoma de México. (pp. 15-30). México.

De Backer, K., Menon, C., Desnoyers-James, I., & Moussiegt, L. (2016). Reshoring: Myth or reality? https://www.jstor.org/stable/155557

Dikler, J. (2021). Reshoring: An overview, recent trends, and predictions for the future. *KIEP Research Paper, World Economy Brief*, 21-35.

Dunning, J. H. (1988). The Eclectic Paradigm of International Production: A Restatement and Some Possible Extensions. *Journal of International Business Studies*, 19(Spring), 1–31. DOI: 10.1057/palgrave.jibs.8490372

Dunning, J. H. (1995). Reappraising the Eclectic Paradigm in an Age of Alliance Capitalism. *Journal of International Business Studies*, 26(3), 461–491. DOI: 10.1057/palgrave.jibs.8490183

El-Sahli, Z., & Gullstrand, J. (2023). Why reshore? Evidence from Swedish firms. *Economics Letters*, 227, 111116. DOI: 10.1016/j.econlet.2023.111116

Ferreira, M., Pinto, C., Serra, F., & Santos, J. (2013). A Bibliometric Study of John Dunning's Contribution to International Business Research. *Revista Brasileira de Gestão de Negócios*, 15(46), 56–75. DOI: 10.7819/rbgn.v15i46.1163

Fiber2Fashion. (May 17, 2024) UFLPA's impact on US textile imports: A shift in global trade dynamics. https://www.fibre2fashion.com/news/printstory.aspx?news_Id=295371

Finley-Brook, M. (2018). CAFTA-DR: diverging trajectories and uneven development. In Handbook of International Trade Agreements (pp. 166-180). Routledge.

Foerstl, K., Kirchoff, J. F., & Bals, L. (2016). Reshoring and insourcing: Drivers and future research directions. *International Journal of Physical Distribution & Logistics Management*, 46(5), 492–515. DOI: 10.1108/IJPDLM-02-2015-0045

Fratocchi, L., Ancarani, A., Barbieri, P., Di Mauro, C., Nassimbeni, G., Sartor, M., Vignoli, M., & Zanoni, A. (2016). Motivations of manufacturing reshoring: An interpretative framework. *International Journal of Physical Distribution & Logistics Management*, 46(2), 98–127. DOI: 10.1108/IJPDLM-06-2014-0131

Freeman, C. P. (2019). Constructive Engagement? The US and the AIIB. *Global Policy*, 10(4), 667–676. DOI: 10.1111/1758-5899.12764

Gereffi, G., Lim, H.-C., & Lee, J. (2021). Trade policies, firm strategies, and adaptive reconfigurations of global value chains. *Journal of International Business Policy*, 4(4), 506–522. DOI: 10.1057/s42214-021-00102-z

Husband, L. (13 March, 2024) Honduras biggest winner of US apparel nearshoring drive in January 2024. *Investment Monitor*.

Kayyali, Y., Mair, S. & Seifert, R. (2023). A machine learning-based framework for forecasting sales of new products with short life cycles using deep neural networks. *International Journal of Forecasting*. Vol. 39, issue 2023, pp. 1874–1894

Kinkel, S. (2012). Trends in production relocation and backshoring activities: Changing patterns in the course of the global economic crisis. *International Journal of Operations & Production Management*, 32(6), 696–720. DOI: 10.1108/01443571211230934

Molano, G., & Briceño, J. (2021). Introducción: el regionalismo post-hegemónico. En Molano, G y Briceño, J. (Ed.) El regionalismo en América Latina después de la Post-Hegemonía. Centro de Investigaciones sobre América Latina y el Caribe. Universidad Autónoma de México. (pp. 15-30). México

Moran, T. (2000). The product cycle model of foreign direct investment and developing country welfare. *Journal of International Management*, 6, 297–311. DOI: 10.1016/S1075-4253(00)00031-4

Moya Pons, F. (1992). *Empresarios en Conflicto: Politicas de Industrializacion y Sustitucion de Importaciones en la Republica Dominicana*. Fondo para el Avance de las Ciencias Sociales.

Mulder, P. (2012). Ciclo de Vida de un Producto. Recuperado [insertar la fecha] de toolshero: https://www.toolshero.es/mercadeo/ciclo-de-vida-de-un-producto/

Narula, R., & Verbeke, A. (2015). Making internalization theory good for practice: The essence of Alan Rugman's contributions to international business. *Journal of World Business*, 50(4), 612–622. DOI: 10.1016/j.jwb.2015.08.007

Organización de los Estados Americanos (OEA). (1995). Seminario interamericano de infraestructura de transporte como factor de integración. Departamento de Desarrollo regional y medio ambiente. Secretaría ejecutiva para asuntos económicos y sociales. Washington, D.C.

Pedroletti, D., & Ciabuschi, F. (2023). Reshoring: A review and research agenda. *Journal of Business Research*, 164, 114005. DOI: 10.1016/j.jbusres.2023.114005

Runde, D. F., Bandura, R., & Hardman, A. (April 16, 2024) Expanding workforce development to enable nearshoring in the Northern Triangle. Washington DC: Center for Strategic and International Studies. https://www.csis.org/analysis/expanding-workforce-development-enable-nearshoring-northern-triangle

Sirkin, H. L., Rose, J., & Choraria, R. (2014). *Honing US manufacturing's competitive edge*. Boston Consulting Group.

Tate, W. L. (2014). Offshoring and reshoring: US insights and research challenges. *Journal of Purchasing and Supply Management*, 20(1), 66–68. DOI: 10.1016/j.pursup.2014.01.007

The Boston Consulting Group (BCG). (2011). *Made In America Again*. Why Manufacturing Will Return to the U.S.

The Boston Consulting Group (BCG). (2013). *Behind the American Export Surge: The U.S. as One of the Developed World's Lowest-Cost Manufacturers.*

The Boston Consulting Group (BCG). (2014). *The Shifting Economics of Global Manufacturing*. How Cost Competitiveness Is Changing Worldwide.

Udokporo, C. K. (2021). Understanding the Stages of the Product Life Cycle. In *Product Life Cycle-Opportunities for Digital and Sustainable Transformation.* IntechOpen. DOI: 10.5772/intechopen.99036

Verbeke, A., & Kano, L. (2016). An internalization theory perspective on the global and regional strategies of multinational enterprises. *Journal of World Business*, 51(1), 83–92. DOI: 10.1016/j.jwb.2015.08.014

Vernon, R. (1966). International investment and international trade in the product cycle. In *International economic policies and their theoretical foundations* (pp. 415–435). Academic Press.

Vertinsky, I., Kuang, Y., Zhou, D., & Cui, V. (2023). The political economy and dynamics of bifurcated world governance and the decoupling of value chains: An alternative perspective. *Journal of International Business Studies*, 54(7), 1–27. DOI: 10.1057/s41267-023-00597-z PMID: 36743261

Wallen, F., & Wiberg, M. (2018). *Growing Protectionism After the Financial Crisis: What is the evidence?* Institute of Economic Affairs.

Zhai, W., Sun, S., & Zhang, G. (2016). Reshoring of American manufacturing companies from China. *Operations Management Research : Advancing Practice Through Research*, 9(3-4), 62–74. DOI: 10.1007/s12063-016-0114-z

Chapter 2
Navigating Latin American Populism:
Economic, Educational, and Technological Implications

Surjit Singha
https://orcid.org/0000-0002-5730-8677
Kristu Jayanti College (Autonomous), India

ABSTRACT

This chapter examines the impact of populism on governance, socio-economic development, and democratic consolidation in Latin America. By exploring the historical roots, socio-political mechanisms, and effects of populism, the study reveals how it can galvanize marginalized groups and disrupt existing power structures, potentially exacerbating economic inequalities and undermining democratic institutions. To address these challenges, the chapter proposes evidence-based strategies for fostering inclusive economic policies, strengthening social cohesion, and maintaining democratic integrity. Recommendations include promoting equitable growth, enhancing public trust through transparency, and supporting democratic institutions to navigate populism's complexities effectively. The analysis underscores the need for a balanced approach to achieving social justice and sustainable development amidst populist influences.

INTRODUCTION

The political history of Latin America is characterized by its frequent oscillation between periods of stability and the disruptive force of populism. Populism, with its roots deeply embedded in the region's socio-political fabric, has manifested

DOI: 10.4018/979-8-3693-3763-9.ch002

through various leaders and movements, each leaving a distinct mark on the political landscape. From the provocative rhetoric and charismatic appeal of Juan Perón in Argentina to the more recent and influential figures such as Hugo Chávez in Venezuela and Evo Morales in Bolivia, populism has consistently influenced and reshaped the region's dynamics. These leaders have harnessed populism's power to mobilize the masses, challenge established elites, and advocate for radical change, often positioning themselves as champions of the dispossessed while igniting intense debate among policymakers, scholars, and citizens (Cachanosky & Padilla, 2020).

This chapter delves into the profound impact of populism on Latin America's socio-economic landscape, focusing on its implications across economic, educational, and technological domains. The chapter aims to unravel the historical roots of populism, tracing its evolution and examining how its various forms have emerged and transformed over time. By analyzing both historical and contemporary manifestations of populism, we seek to illuminate how these movements influence the region's progress toward inclusive growth.

Populism often challenges established institutions disrupts economic stability, and mobilizes marginalized groups, creating a complex interplay between political aspirations and practical governance. While populist movements may offer a voice to the disenfranchised and push for significant social reforms, they also pose risks by straining the mechanisms essential for sustainable development. The chapter will explore how populism impacts economic policies, educational systems, and technological advancement, highlighting its opportunities and challenges.

Readers will explore the intricate dynamics of Latin American populism, gaining insights into its far-reaching consequences and implications for the region's future. By understanding these complexities, we can better grasp the broader effects of populism on governance, socio-economic development, and the quest for equitable progress in Latin America.

BACKGROUND

The political landscape of Latin America has long been marked by its dynamism and complexity, shaped by a myriad of socio-economic factors. Over recent decades, the region has witnessed a notable surge in populist movements and leaders, who have risen to power by promising radical reforms and empowering marginalized groups. This shift towards populism has significantly impacted governance, socio-economic development, and democratic institutions, prompting extensive scholarly investigation into the phenomenon's origins, manifestations, and consequences (De La Torre, 2014).

Populism, as a concept, varies in its definitions and interpretations. Broadly, it refers to political approaches that claim to represent the interests of the common people against a perceived corrupt elite. However, definitions of populism can differ depending on the context and perspective. In Latin America, populism is often characterized by charismatic leaders who mobilize popular support through direct appeals to the masses, often bypassing traditional institutional channels. This form of populism tends to focus on significant social and economic reforms to address inequality and empower the disenfranchised.

The Latin American perspective on populism emphasizes certain unique aspects compared to other regions. For instance, Latin American populism frequently involves a strong personalist element, where leaders cultivate a direct relationship with their supporters, often positioning themselves as the sole advocates for the people's needs. This contrasts with more ideologically driven forms of populism seen elsewhere, which may focus more on specific political or economic ideologies.

Additionally, Latin American populism often emerges in response to deep-seated social and economic inequalities, reflecting the region's historical struggles with economic disparity and political instability. The dynamic interplay between populist leaders and existing political institutions in Latin America highlights the potential for transformative change and the risks of undermining democratic norms and institutional integrity.

Understanding these nuances is crucial for grasping the full impact of populism in Latin America. By exploring both the commonalities and differences in how populism is defined and experienced in the region, this chapter aims to provide a comprehensive analysis of its effects on Latin America's political and socio-economic landscape.

Examining populism in Latin America employs various theoretical frameworks from economics, sociology, and political science (Campos-Herrera & de Reguero, 2019; De La Torre, 2014; Grigera, 2017). Scholars like Kurt Weyland, Campos-Herrera G, frequently analyze populism's ideological underpinnings, discursive strategies, and mobilization tactics through the lens of political ideology. Theories of social movements, collective action, and identity politics illuminate the dynamics of populist mobilization and its resonance with diverse social groups. Furthermore, comparative politics and democratization frameworks illuminate the influence of populism on political participation, institutional stability, and democratic governance in the region.

The conceptual framework for comprehending populism in Latin America is multifaceted, encompassing ideological, socio-economic, and cultural factors. Key concepts such as charismatic leadership, mass mobilization, and appeals to the popular will fundamentally influence the analysis of populism's appeal and influence. Additionally, scholars investigate the influence of institutions, political elites, and civil society on the trajectory of populist movements and their policy agendas. Conceptual frameworks also emphasize the interplay between populism and other phenomena, including nationalism, globalization, and social inequality, thereby shedding light on the region's current intricate dynamics.

This study aims to analyze the impact of populism on specific aspects of Latin America's socio-economic landscape, focusing on its effects on governance, economic inequality, and democratic institutions. By examining selected case studies and empirical data, the study will concentrate on contemporary manifestations of populism and their historical roots. Theoretical insights from political science, sociology, and economics are integrated to explain how populism influences policy and institutional stability. This focused approach ensures a comprehensive examination of the most critical challenges and implications of populism in the region.

This investigation aims to critically examine the impact of populism on democratic consolidation and socio-economic development in Latin America. The study will focus on three main objectives: (1) analyzing the historical roots and contemporary manifestations of populism; (2) assessing its effects on democratic governance and institutional stability; and (3) evaluating the socio-economic consequences of populist policies, specifically regarding inequality and social justice. By concentrating on these areas, the study seeks to provide targeted insights into the challenges posed by populism and offer practical recommendations for fostering sustainable development in the region.

HISTORICAL ROOTS OF LATIN AMERICAN POPULISM

The evolution of populism in Latin America is deeply rooted in the region's socio-political history, with origins tracing back to the 19th century. This section focuses on the early roots of populism, particularly during the late 19th and early 20th centuries, when significant socio-economic transformations such as industrialization and urbanization were underway.

In the late 19th and early 20th centuries, populism began to take shape in response to the disparities created by rapid economic changes. Early populist movements emerged as leaders sought to address the grievances of marginalized urban and rural populations through promises of social justice and economic reform. For instance, figures like José Martí in Cuba and Manuel González Flores in Mexico began to frame populist rhetoric around national sovereignty and social equity, setting the stage for later developments in the region.

By the mid-20th century, populism became more pronounced with the rise of charismatic leaders such as Juan Perón in Argentina and Getúlio Vargas in Brazil. These leaders, who are often cited as pivotal in the development of Latin American populism, mobilized support through their promises of wealth redistribution, social justice, and state interventionism. Perón's movement, Peronism, combined elements of nationalism and corporatism, profoundly influencing Argentine politics (Teichman, 2022). Vargas's Estado Novo introduced extensive state intervention and labour rights, shaping Brazil's welfare state (Wajner, 2021).

In the contemporary context, populism manifests through leaders such as Hugo Chávez and Evo Morales, who have employed populist rhetoric to challenge traditional power structures and implement extensive social reforms. Chávez's rise in Venezuela and Morales's leadership in Bolivia are reflective of how populism has evolved to address both regional and local grievances while continuing to resonate with marginalized communities (de la Torre, 2023). This historical overview highlights how populism in Latin America has evolved from its early roots in the 19th century to its diverse contemporary forms, illustrating the ongoing impact of both early and modern populist leaders.

CONTEMPORARY MANIFESTATIONS OF POPULISM

Populism continues to significantly shape governance, society, and politics in Latin America, manifesting through various forms across the region. To provide a comprehensive understanding, it is essential to define the contemporary period as the last two decades, focusing on the early 21st century.

In Venezuela, Hugo Chávez and his successor Nicolás Maduro exemplify contemporary left-wing populism. The Bolivarian Revolution, marked by nationalization of key industries, extensive social welfare programs, and anti-imperialist rhetoric, aimed to challenge elite interests and empower marginalized populations (Dunkerley, 2013). This movement's impact on Venezuelan society and politics reflects the enduring influence of populism in the region.

Jair Bolsonaro's rise to power in Brazil signifies a notable instance of right-wing populism. Bolsonaro's campaign focused on combating corruption, addressing crime, and opposing leftist ideologies. His populist rhetoric has polarized Brazilian society and sparked debates over his authoritarian tendencies and their implications for democratic governance.

Argentina's political landscape is also shaped by populism through figures like Cristina Fernández de Kirchner. Kirchner's alignment with Peronism, which emphasizes economic redistribution and social welfare, illustrates how historical populist movements continue to influence contemporary politics despite challenges related to economic management and corruption (Feitlowitz, 2019).

In addition to these examples, populism has also emerged in other Latin American countries. In Ecuador, Abdalá Bucaram's presidency in the late 1990s highlighted the volatility and impact of populist leadership on political stability and economic policies (De La Torre, 2018; Williamson, 2000). Meanwhile, in Bolivia, Evo Morales's tenure as president represents a contemporary case of left-wing populism that emphasized indigenous rights and social reforms. Colombia has also witnessed populist rhetoric in recent years, with various leaders using populist strategies to address grievances and mobilize support (De la Torre, 2017).

Populist leaders across Latin America frequently utilize rhetoric that resonates with the public's grievances and aspirations, promising significant change and challenging established power structures. Their appeals to nationalism, anti-establishment sentiments, and promises of economic prosperity often mobilize substantial support. However, the implementation of populist policies can lead to varied outcomes. While social welfare programs and infrastructure projects may provide short-term relief, they can also exacerbate fiscal imbalances and undermine long-term economic stability (Ciccariello-Maher, 2020). Additionally, populist rhetoric can deepen political polarization and complicate consensus-building, leading to governance challenges and increased volatility in policy-making processes.

This analysis of contemporary populism highlights how populist movements have influenced Latin American politics and governance in recent decades, providing a more comprehensive view of their regional impact.

ECONOMIC IMPLICATIONS OF POPULISM

Populist economic policies in Latin America, characterized by redistributive agendas and state interventionism, significantly impact economic trajectories. For instance, Argentina's Peronist policies under Juan Perón, including expansive social welfare programs and progressive taxation, initially aimed to reduce inequality but later contributed to economic instability and inflation (Levitsky & Roberts, 2011). Similarly, Venezuela's Hugo Chávez implemented extensive social programs funded by oil revenues, which, while addressing immediate social needs, eventually led to economic distortions and a severe debt crisis (Corrales & Penfold, 2015; Watters, 2021).

Populist governments often resort to interventionist strategies like price controls and subsidies to protect domestic industries. In Brazil, President Getúlio Vargas's era saw the establishment of state-controlled industries and subsidies for key sectors, which, despite fostering initial growth, eventually led to inefficiencies and stifled competition (Campos-Herrera & de Reguero, 2019; Pinto, 2020). Similarly, Chávez's nationalization of industries in Venezuela disrupted market dynamics and impeded innovation.

Expansionary fiscal policies, such as deficit spending, are frequently employed to finance social programs and infrastructure. However, Evo Morales's expansive fiscal policies in Bolivia led to significant inflationary pressures and currency depreciation, which undermined macroeconomic stability (McCloud et al., 2023). The adverse effects of populist policies are further exemplified by Ecuador's Abdalá Bucaram, whose presidency featured erratic economic policies and fiscal mismanagement, resulting in economic instability and a decline in investor confidence (Levitsky & Roberts, 2011). While populist policies in Latin America aim to address inequality, their long-term effects often include economic instability, inflation, and reduced investor confidence.

EDUCATIONAL CHALLENGES AND OPPORTUNITIES

The economic ramifications of populist policies are not confined to fiscal and industrial spheres but also extend into social sectors, particularly education. As populist leaders seek to address inequalities and garner widespread support, education becomes pivotal for enacting change and promoting social inclusion. However, like their economic strategies, the educational policies of populist governments present a complex mix of opportunities and challenges that significantly shape the future development of Latin American societies.

Latin America's populist strategies for education reform have been lauded for their emphasis on social inclusion and criticized for their political motivations and ineffectiveness. Understanding the influence of these policies on educational access and outcomes is critical to leveraging the region's development opportunities and addressing its educational challenges.

Populist governments often prioritize policies to expand educational opportunities for marginalized communities, including indigenous communities, rural areas, and low-income families (Duncan & Ulrich-Schad, 2021; Ricee, 2022). These initiatives encompass establishing new institutions, providing scholarships and subsidies, and implementing affirmative action programs to advocate for diversity and inclusion in higher education.

Critics argue that populist regimes, such as those in Venezuela under Hugo Chávez and in Argentina during the Kirchner administration, often use education to further political agendas and promote ideological indoctrination. In Venezuela, for example, Chávez's government implemented curriculum changes that emphasized Bolivarian ideology, while in Argentina, the Kirchner governments integrated

Peronist ideals into educational materials. These actions have raised concerns about the politicization of educational institutions and the potential erosion of academic freedom and critical thinking skills.

Populist governments may prioritize expanding educational access at the expense of accountability and quality. Lack of resources, overcrowded classrooms, and a scarcity of qualified instructors can compromise the quality of education, thereby exacerbating learning outcome disparities and perpetuating cycles of poverty and inequality.

Populist education policies have led to significant growth in enrollment rates, especially at the primary and secondary levels. Government-funded scholarships and subsidies have enabled disadvantaged students to access educational opportunities that were previously out of reach, helping to reduce socio-economic disparities in educational attainment (van Slageren & Rooduijn, 2023). van Slageren and Rooduijn (2023) provide compelling evidence of a negative relationship between educational attainment and support for radical right-wing populist parties. Their analysis reveals that individuals with lower education levels are more likely to support these parties than those with higher education. The findings suggest that it is not the populist message per se that appeals to lower-educated voters but rather the nativist elements of these parties. This implies that lower-educated voters are more attracted to the nativist aspects than populism alone. The chapter underscores the importance of differentiating between nativism and populism, noting that while there is a clear educational divide, this does not necessarily extend to populism in general.

In Latin America and the Caribbean, populist education policies have indeed led to significant increases in enrollment rates at primary and secondary levels. For example, in Brazil, the Bolsa Família program, which provides financial assistance to low-income families, has contributed to higher school enrollment and reduced dropout rates among disadvantaged students. This program aligns with populist principles by directly addressing the needs of lower-income families and promoting educational access (World Bank, 2019; World Bank, 2022).

Fewer interventions address educational underachievement among boys and men, with most programs focused on high-income countries such as the United States, the United Kingdom, and various European nations. In low- and middle-income countries, limited programs exist in regions like MENA and Latin America. In the Caribbean, gender parity is typically achieved at the primary and lower secondary levels. Still, significant disparities emerge at upper secondary and tertiary levels, where boys' dropout rates are notably higher. By 2000, higher education enrollment was disproportionately female, with twice as many women as men (202.5 women per 100 men). Societal notions of masculinity contribute to boys' educational underachievement, as high returns from criminal activities and limited legitimate job opportunities make crime an attractive alternative for young men. Men adhering to traditional masculine norms often complete fewer years of education and may resort to gangs or crime to assert their manhood (World Bank, 2022).

However, challenges persist. Despite increased enrollment, the quality of education remains uneven. In rural Bolivia, for instance, schools often struggle with insufficient infrastructure and limited resources, leading to disparities in educational quality. While populist policies have improved access, these resource constraints continue to impact learning outcomes, reinforcing the gap between urban and rural education. Furthermore, political instability and economic crises have exacerbated educational inequalities in countries like Venezuela, illustrating that access alone does not ensure equitable educational quality.

In Latin America and the Caribbean, no significant difference in educational performance between girls and boys is observed due to father absence in poorer households (DeRose, Huarcaya, & Salazar-Arango, 2018). Bossavie and Kanninen (2018) note that in Latin America and the Caribbean, regional assessments such as those conducted by the Latin American Laboratory for Assessment of the Quality of Education (LLECE) reveal no significant gender performance disparities related to father absence in poorer households. Specifically, LLECE's 2013 assessments show no discernible difference in educational outcomes between boys and girls in these contexts. Despite broader trends observed in other regions, gender performance in education in Latin America and the Caribbean remains relatively balanced, with no substantial evidence suggesting that father absence uniquely affects educational achievement.

Thus, while populist education policies have expanded access, significant challenges remain in ensuring that this access translates into high-quality education for all students.

Despite improvements in accessibility, challenges persist in guaranteeing equitable access to quality education for all. Resource constraints, inadequate infrastructure, and disparities in teacher quality continue to impede educational outcomes, particularly in rural and marginalized communities. The quality of education still needs to be improved, with persistent gaps in learning outcomes between urban and rural areas and socio-economic categories. Despite strides in expanding access to education in Latin America and the Caribbean, challenges remain in ensuring equitable quality for all. For example, in rural Honduras, schools often face significant resource constraints, such as inadequate infrastructure and a lack of educational materials. According to a 2021 report by UNICEF, rural schools in Honduras frequently lack basic facilities like clean water and proper sanitation, which affects student attendance and learning. Additionally, disparities in teacher quality persist, with teachers in rural areas receiving less training and professional development than their urban counterparts. This results in a significant educational gap between students in rural areas and urban centres, with rural students lagging in key learning outcomes. This example illustrates the ongoing struggle to bridge educational disparities across different regions and socio-economic groups.

Populist educational interventions can exacerbate political polarisation and social divisions, particularly when perceived as ideologically or politically motivated. Public discourse can be further polarized, and consensus-building on education reform can be impeded by contentious debates regarding educational content and pedagogical approaches. Latin America must balance the expansion of access, the enhancement of quality, and the protection of academic freedom and institutional autonomy as it confronts the educational challenges and opportunities that populist approaches to education reform present. The region can leverage the transformative potential of education to promote social mobility, economic development, and democratic citizenship by prioritizing evidence-based policies, investing in teacher training and professional development, and fostering inclusive and participatory decision-making processes.

LEVERAGING TECHNOLOGY IN POPULIST CONTEXTS

Educational challenges in populist contexts often intersect with technology's role in addressing these issues. In regions like Latin America, populist governments may leverage technology to bridge educational gaps and enhance social inclusion. For example, technology can provide new opportunities for learning and educational access, especially when traditional educational systems face resource limitations or inequality.

Technology has become a potent instrument for social mobilization, communication, and governance in populist contexts during digital transformation. Conversely, its influence on the digital divide and technological inclusivity, as well as populist governments' utilization of technology for governance, represents both opportunities and obstacles for Latin America. Populist governments may prioritize expanding digital technology access as part of their overarching social inclusion agenda. The provision of affordable internet access, the distribution of subsidized or free devices, and the implementation of community-based digital literacy programs specifically designed to reach marginalized populations are among the initiatives to address the digital divide (Vassilakopoulou & Hustad, 2021).

Significant disparities persist along socio-economic lines despite progress in expanding access to technology. In rural areas, Indigenous communities, and low-income households, the lack of reliable internet connectivity and access to digital devices exacerbates inequalities in educational opportunities, economic participation, and civic engagement (Fang et al., 2022). Promoting digital literacy becomes crucial to address these gaps, ensuring that all citizens can fully engage in the digital economy and society. Shi et al. (2022) highlight that populist governments might allocate resources to educational initiatives to improve digital literacy. Such efforts help individuals effectively navigate online platforms, access information, and participate in digital citizenship.

Populist leaders often leverage digital and social media channels to bypass traditional media outlets and communicate directly with their supporters. These technologies facilitate the rapid dissemination of political messages, mobilize grass-roots movements, and coordinate collective action, amplifying populist discourse and political polarization (Kubin & Von Sikorski, 2021). Consequently, the role of technology in populist contexts extends beyond communication to enhance citizen engagement in governance processes. Populist administrations may use digital platforms to offer online consultations, participatory budgeting, and e-government services. These initiatives enable citizens to express opinions, report grievances, and participate in decision-making, promoting transparency, accountability, and responsiveness in governance (Afonso, 2017).

Integrating these aspects demonstrates how technology exacerbates existing disparities and serves as a tool for populist governments to influence public engagement and governance. By addressing digital access and literacy, populist administrations can potentially bridge educational and civic participation gaps while using technology to shape political discourse and governance.

In populist contexts, using technology for governance introduces critical concerns related to government control, surveillance, and privacy. Populist regimes may exploit digital tools for monitoring political opponents, suppressing dissent, and manipulating public opinion, thus potentially compromising human rights and democratic principles. For instance, research indicates that some populist governments have employed digital surveillance to track and intimidate political critics, as observed in countries like Venezuela and Nicaragua (Human Rights Watch, 2020).

In Latin America, addressing these challenges necessitates a focus on bridging the digital divide and fostering technological inclusivity while safeguarding democratic values. Evidence suggests that targeted investments in infrastructure and digital literacy can mitigate disparities in technology access. Programs that expand internet connectivity and provide digital education in underserved areas, such as Brazil's Internet for All initiative, have shown promise in reducing access gaps. Excluding Venezuela, Latin America and the Caribbean saw an average GDP growth of 1.9% in 2017, with projections of 2.6% in 2018 and 2.8% in 2019. Between 2003 and 2016, extreme poverty in the region decreased from 24.5% to 9.9%. The 2017 hurricane season prompted the World Bank to pledge $115 million for climate resilience in Dominica. Infrastructure investments included $64 million for sanitation in Brazil, $24 million for water delivery in Panama, $17 million for municipal services in the Dominican Republic, $150 million for improving over 1,500 kilometres of roads in

Argentina, and $74 million for the Paraguay Road Maintenance Project. The World Bank also issued over $1.3 billion in catastrophe bonds to insure against earthquakes in Chile, Colombia, Mexico, and Peru, marking the most significant such issuance involving multiple countries. In fiscal 2018, the Bank's commitments to the International Bank for Reconstruction and Development (IBRD) and the International Development Association (IDA) totalled over $47 billion. (World Bank, 2018).

Moreover, protecting human rights and democratic values is essential as technology becomes more integral to governance. The region must ensure that digital advancements are used to enhance rather than undermine democratic processes. For example, enhancing digital transparency and accountability through independent oversight of e-government platforms can help prevent abuses of power. By focusing on these areas, Latin America can harness technology's potential to foster socio-economic development, empower marginalized communities, and promote inclusive and accountable governance while addressing the risks posed by populist regimes.

SOCIO-ECONOMIC DEVELOPMENT AMIDST POPULIST GOVERNANCE

The intersection of technology and socio-economic development is crucial for understanding the effects of populist governance in Latin America. Leveraging technology presents significant opportunities to enhance education, healthcare, and economic participation. However, it also introduces challenges related to governance and privacy. To achieve sustainable and inclusive growth, it is essential to integrate technological advancements with effective socio-economic policies. Technological tools can drive economic diversification and entrepreneurship by offering innovative solutions and expanding access to financial services. At the same time, addressing concerns about government control and ensuring the transparent use of digital resources is critical for upholding democratic values and protecting human rights. Aligning technological initiatives with equitable economic strategies can help populist governments foster a more resilient and inclusive development framework.

Navigating socio-economic development amidst populist governance presents a complex landscape with opportunities and challenges. Governance refers to the processes by which decisions are made, implemented, and monitored, including allocating public resources and policy execution. Effective governance is vital for addressing inequality and promoting social justice, as it directly influences the implementation inclusive growth strategies and equitable resource distribution. Prioritizing investments in education, healthcare, and social services is essential for building a competent and healthy workforce that drives economic productivity and innovation. According to Cerf (2023), populist administrations can enhance economic involvement by improving access to quality education, vocational training, and healthcare services. This aligns with broader literature emphasizing that robust governance frameworks are necessary for effective policy implementation and for ensuring that economic opportunities are accessible to all segments of society, thereby fostering sustainable development and enhancing overall well-being.

Economic diversification and entrepreneurship are key to reducing dependence on volatile commodities and creating inclusive growth opportunities. Gomez et al. (2023) argue that populist regimes can bolster economic resilience and job creation by supporting small and medium-sized enterprises (SMEs), promoting innovation and technology adoption, and improving access to finance for micro-entrepreneurs. Strengthening social safety nets and targeted assistance programs is also crucial for protecting vulnerable populations from deprivation and mitigating the impact of economic shocks. During crises, populist governments may implement cash transfer programs, food assistance initiatives, and unemployment benefits to provide immediate relief and foster social cohesion (Abdullah et al., 2022).

Progressive taxation policies, which distribute the tax burden more equitably among individuals with higher incomes, can facilitate wealth redistribution and reduce income inequality. Populist governments can tax wealth, capital gains, and luxury products while offering incentives for investments in human development and social infrastructure. Addressing historical injustices and ensuring equitable access to land, natural resources, and productive assets are vital for combating inequality and advancing social justice. Populist regimes can implement land reform programs, recognize indigenous land rights, and adopt community-based resource management initiatives to tackle socio-economic disparities and empower marginalized groups (Duncan & Peter, 2016). Upholding the rule of law, strengthening democratic institutions, and combating corruption are essential for promoting social justice. Populist governments can support transparency mechanisms, anti-corruption agencies, and judicial independence to protect democratic principles and foster accountability (Schwindt-Bayer & Tavits, 2016).

In the context of populist governance, Latin America must embrace inclusive growth strategies to address socio-economic development challenges effectively. Research highlights the importance of investing in human capital, economic diversification, and social safety nets for promoting sustainable development. Prioritizing education, healthcare, and social services builds a capable workforce that drives innovation and economic productivity, as supported by Cerf (2023). Promoting economic diversification and supporting SMEs are also backed by research as effective strategies for reducing reliance on volatile commodities and fostering inclusive growth (Gomez et al., 2023). Implementing progressive taxation and addressing historical injustices are essential for reducing income inequality and advancing social justice, with academic studies confirming their effectiveness (Duncan & Peter, 2016).

This framework addresses critical issues identified in the research and offers actionable recommendations for policymakers. Integrating theoretical and empirical insights provides a comprehensive approach to navigating the complexities of populist governance, laying the foundation for a more equitable and prosperous future for all citizens. Grounding these strategies in research enhances the academic discourse on effective governance and socio-economic development in challenging political contexts.

SOLUTION AND RECOMMENDATION

To effectively address the challenges of populism in Latin America, a multifaceted approach integrating political, economic, and social strategies is essential. This approach promotes inclusive governance, sustainable development, and democratic consolidation.

1. **Strengthening Democratic Institutions:** Enhancing the resilience of democratic institutions is crucial for protecting democratic norms and principles against reactionary threats. This involves reinforcing electoral integrity, preserving judicial independence, and improving checks and balances to prevent the abuse of power. International and civil society organizations should play a pivotal role in monitoring and promoting democratic governance in the region.
2. **Implementing Inclusive Economic Policies:** To address the socio-economic grievances fuelling populist movements, it is vital to implement inclusive economic policies prioritising equitable growth, poverty reduction, and employment creation. This includes fostering entrepreneurship, promoting innovation and productive investment, and investing in education, healthcare, and social protection programs. Encouraging social dialogue and consensus-building can also help create policy agendas that balance economic efficiency with social equity.
3. **Enhancing Transparency and Combating Corruption:** Restoring public confidence in government institutions requires improved transparency and robust anti-corruption measures. Strengthening anti-corruption frameworks, promoting open government initiatives, and enhancing accountability mechanisms can build trust in public institutions and reduce the appeal of populist rhetoric.
4. **Encouraging Democratic Participation and Civic Education:** Promoting democratic participation and civic education is essential for establishing a more inclusive and resilient democracy. Governments, civil society organizations, and educational institutions should collaborate to develop civics curricula, media literacy programs, and civic engagement initiatives that empower citi-

zens to participate actively in political decision-making and hold their leaders accountable.

5. **Fostering Social Cohesion and Inclusivity:** To combat polarization and advance national unity, fostering social cohesion among diverse groups is imperative. Civil society organizations, religious institutions, and governments should work together to promote intercultural dialogue, bridge social divides, and encourage mutual understanding and respect for diversity.

By implementing these recommendations, Latin American countries can effectively confront the challenges posed by populism and advance sustainable development, inclusive governance, and democratic consolidation. Turning these recommendations into tangible actions will require collaboration among governments, civil society organizations, and international partners to foster long-term stability, prosperity, and social justice for all citizens.

FUTURE PROSPECTS AND POLICY IMPLICATIONS

Strategic foresight and evidence-based policy interventions are necessary to navigate the impact of populism on sustainable development as Latin America confronts the challenges and opportunities it presents. A multifaceted approach that promotes participatory governance, addresses structural inequalities and enhances institutional capacity is necessary to cultivate resilience and inclusivity in populist governance.

To protect democratic governance in the presence of populist tendencies, it is essential to uphold the rule of law, protect civil liberties, and ensure institutional checks and balances. Investing in independent judiciaries, electoral supervision bodies, and anti-corruption agencies can mitigate the risks of authoritarianism and safeguard democratic principles. It is imperative to pursue inclusive development strategies, prioritizing investments in social safety nets, economic diversification, and human capital to mitigate poverty, inequality, and social exclusion. Through cash transfer programs, education, and healthcare, populist governments can promote entrepreneurship, innovation, and job creation, all while offering targeted assistance to vulnerable populations.

Diversifying export markets, improving productive capacity, and advocating for sustainable resource management are necessary to enhance economic resilience and reduce vulnerabilities to external disruptions. Populist regimes can invest in infrastructure, technology, and sustainable development initiatives to reduce dependence on volatile commodities and promote long-term economic stability. To provide citizens with the necessary skills and knowledge to flourish in a rapidly changing economy, prioritize investments in education, vocational training, and lifelong learning. Foster innovation, entrepreneurship, and job creation by promoting technical training programs, STEM education, and digital literacy.

Increasing access to social safety nets, healthcare, and pension systems is imperative to guarantee universal coverage and safeguard vulnerable populations from economic disruptions and social risks. Implement progressive taxation policies to finance social programs and redistribute wealth, ensuring equitable distribution of the benefits of economic growth.

Foster dialogue, accountability, and trust between government and civil society by promoting transparent decision-making processes, citizen engagement platforms, and participatory governance mechanisms. Invest in social movements, grassroots organizations, and community-based initiatives that amplify the voices of marginalized groups and empower them in the policy-making process. Latin America must adopt a comprehensive strategy that balances economic growth, social equity, environmental sustainability, and democratic governance as it navigates the path to sustainable development in the face of populist governance. The region can address the obstacles of populism and establish a more promising future for all its citizens by promoting resilience and inclusivity through participatory decision-making and evidence-based policies.

DISCUSSION

The emergence of populism in Latin America significantly affects the region's governance, socio-economic development, and democratic consolidation. This study has illuminated the complex dynamics and far-reaching impact of populism on the region's political landscape by examining its drivers, manifestations, and consequences. This investigation's important discovery is the historical origins and development of populism in Latin America. The populist phenomenon in the region has been characterized by charismatic leaders and mass mobilization from the early 20th century to the present. From its inception in agrarian reform movements to its current manifestations marked by anti-establishment rhetoric and the promise of radical change, the research has tracked the development of populism.

The ideological underpinnings and discursive strategies of populism are also significant aspects of this study. Populist movements and leaders frequently employ nationalist, anti-elite, and anti-establishment rhetoric to garner support and challenge the status quo. Populists have gained political power and mobilized public support by appealing to the grievances and aspirations of marginalized populations.

Additionally, this investigation has explored the impact of populism on political participation, institutional stability, and democratic governance. Populist governments may restrict civil liberties, concentrate power in the hands of the executive, and undermine democratic norms and institutions in the name of defending the popular will. Nevertheless, populist movements can catalyze political change, mobilizing previously marginalized groups and challenging entrenched elites.

The study has examined the socio-economic ramifications of populist policies on social justice, inequality, and inclusive development. Populist governments may prioritize social welfare programs and redistributive policies; however, they can also exacerbate fiscal imbalances, undermine economic stability, and perpetuate clientelism. To resolve the underlying grievances that fuel populism and promote sustainable development and inclusive governance, it is essential to balance the imperatives of economic efficiency and social equity.

It underscores the multidimensional nature of populism in Latin America and its intricate relationship with governance, socio-economic development, and democratic consolidation. Policymakers, scholars, and civil society actors can develop effective strategies for addressing the challenges and fostering sustainable development, inclusive governance, and democratic resilience in the region by comprehending the drivers and consequences of populism.

CONCLUSION

Populism in Latin America is a multifaceted and intricate phenomenon with significant implications for the region's governance, socio-economic development, and democratic consolidation. This research has thoroughly examined the historical origins, ideological foundations, and socio-political dynamics of populism, as well as its manifestations, consequences, and motivations. Throughout history, Latin America has been the site of the emergence of mass movements and charismatic leaders who advocate for social justice and radical change. The region's political landscape has been shaped, and the trajectory of governance and development has been influenced by the evolution of populism in response to socio-economic transformations, political upheavals, and cultural shifts.

The influence of populism on institutional stability and democratic governance is one of the most significant discoveries of this investigation. Although populist movements have the potential to challenge entrenched elites and mobilize previously marginalized groups, they can also erode institutional checks and balances, concentrate power in the hands of the executive, and undermine democratic norms. Maintaining democratic governance and guaranteeing the rule of law requires balancing the imperatives of institutional integrity and popular sovereignty.

Additionally, this investigation has underscored the socio-economic ramifications of populism for social justice, inequality, and inclusive development. Populist governments may prioritize social welfare programs and redistributive policies;

however, they can also exacerbate fiscal imbalances, undermine economic stability, and perpetuate clientelism. To resolve the underlying grievances that fuel populism and promote sustainable development and inclusive governance, it is imperative to implement inclusive growth strategies that prioritize investments in education, healthcare, and social protection. A concerted effort is necessary to strengthen democratic institutions, promote inclusive economic policies, and cultivate social cohesion and dialogue to navigate the challenges of populism in Latin America. The region can address the root causes of populism and promote democratic resilience to create a more prosperous and equitable future for all its citizens, promote social justice, and overcome polarization. Latin America can leverage populism's transformative potential for sustainable development and positive change in the years ahead by collaborating with international partners, civil society organizations, and governments.

REFERENCES

Abdullah, A. B. M., Murad, M. W., & Ahmed, E. (2022). Social protection transfers: Types, impacts, and experiences. In *Encyclopedia of the UN sustainable development goals* (pp. 1–11). DOI: 10.1007/978-3-319-71060-0_89-1

Afonso, W. B. (2017). Citizens engaging government: Participatory budgeting in Greensboro, North Carolina. *Public Administration Quarterly*, 41(1), 7–42. DOI: 10.1177/0734914917041001 02

Bossavie, L., & Kanninen, O. (2018). *What explains the gender gap reversal in education? Theory and evidence* (Policy Research Working Paper No. 8303). World Bank. https://openknowledge.worldbank.org/handle/10986/29213

Cachanosky, N., & Padilla, A. (2020). A panel data analysis of Latin American populism. *Constitutional Political Economy*, 31(3), 329–343. DOI: 10.1007/s10602-020-09302-w

Campos-Herrera, G., & de Reguero, S. U. (2019). Populism in Latin America: Past, present, and future [Review of The Resurgence of Populism in Latin America; Political Communication and Leadership: Mimetisation, Hugo Chávez and the Construction of Power and Identity; From Fascism to Populism in History; Revolutionizing Repertoires: The Rise of Populist Mobilization in Peru, by R. R. Barr, E. Block, F. Finchelstein, & R. S. Jansen]. *Latin American Politics and Society*, 61(1), 148–159. https://www.jstor.org/stable/26779154. DOI: 10.1017/lap.2018.63

Cerf, M. E. (2023). The social-education-economy-health nexus, development and sustainability: Perspectives from low- and middle-income and African countries. *Discover Sustainability*, 4(1), 37. Advance online publication. DOI: 10.1007/s43621-023-00153-7

Ciccariello-Maher, G. (2020). Populism, universalism, and democracy in Latin America. In L. K. Jenco, M. Idris, & M. C. Thomas (Eds.), *The Oxford handbook of comparative political theory* (online edn). Oxford Academic. DOI: 10.1093/oxfordhb/9780190253752.013.16

Corrales, J., & Penfold, M. (2015). *Dragon in the Tropics: Hugo Chávez and the Political Economy of Revolution in Venezuela.* Brookings Institution Press.

De La Torre, C. (2014). Populism in Latin American politics. In *Research in political sociology* (pp. 79–100). DOI: 10.1108/S0895-993520140000022003

De la Torre, C. (2017). Populism in Latin America. In C. Rovira Kaltwasser, P. A. Taggart, P. O. Esponda, & M. M. T. (Eds.), *The Oxford handbook of populism* (pp. 115-139). Oxford University Press. DOI: 10.1093/oxfordhb/9780198803560.013.8

De La Torre, C. (2018). Populism revived: Donald Trump and the Latin American leftist populists. *The Americas*, 75(4), 733–753. DOI: 10.1017/tam.2018.39

De La Torre, C. (2023). Messianic and autocratic populism's waves in the recent history of the Americas: Continuities, twists, and rupture. In A. Akande (Ed.), *U.S. democracy in danger*. Springer Studies on Populism, Identity Politics and Social Justice. Springer, Cham. DOI: 10.1007/978-3-031-36099-2_16

DeRose, L. F., Huarcaya, G., & Salazar-Arango, Á. (2018). Father absence and the reverse gender gap in Latin America. *Journal of Family Issues*, 39(13), 3508–3534. DOI: 10.1177/0192513X18783802

Duncan, C. M., & Ulrich-Schad, J. D. (2021). Marginalization of rural communities in the U.S. *Investing in rural prosperity*. Federal Reserve Bank of St. Louis. https://www.ipp.gov/-/media/project/frbstl/stlouisfed/files/pdfs/community-development/investing-rural/chapters/chapter03.pdf

Duncan, D., & Peter, K. S. (2016). Unequal inequalities: Do progressive taxes reduce income inequality? *International Tax and Public Finance*, 23(4), 762–783. DOI: 10.1007/s10797-016-9412-5

Dunkerley, J. (2013). The Bolivian revolution at 60: Politics and historiography. *Journal of Latin American Studies*, 45(2), 325–350. DOI: 10.1017/S0022216X13000382

Fang, Y. X., Gill, S. S., Kunasekaran, P., Rosnon, M. R., Talib, A. T., & Aziz, A. A. (2022). Digital divide: An inquiry on the native communities of Sabah. *Societies (Basel, Switzerland)*, 12(6), 148. DOI: 10.3390/soc12060148

Feitlowitz, M. (2019). *A lexicon of terror: Argentina and the legacies of torture*. Oxford University Press., https://global.oup.com/academic/product/a-lexicon-of-terror-9780199744695?cc=us&lang=

Gomez, D., Aparicio, S., & Urbano, D. (2023). Entrepreneurial activity and economic growth: A literature review. In *Springer eBooks* (pp. 13–39). DOI: 10.1007/978-3-031-34386-5_2

Grigera, J. (2017). Populism in Latin America: Old and new populisms in Argentina and Brazil. *International Political Science Review / Revue Internationale de Science Politique, 38*(4), 441–455. https://www.jstor.org/stable/26940303

Human Rights Watch. (2020). *Venezuela: Government use of digital surveillance to target critics*. Human Rights Watch. https://www.hrw.org/world-report/2020/country-chapters/venezuela

Kubin, E., & Von Sikorski, C. (2021). The role of (social) media in political polarization: A systematic review. *Annals of the International Communication Association*, 45(3), 188–206. DOI: 10.1080/23808985.2021.1976070

Levitsky, S., & Roberts, K. M. (2011). *The Resurgence of the Latin American Left*. Johns Hopkins University Press. https://www.press.jhu.edu/books/title/10244/resurgence-latin-american-left

Madsen, S. R., & Wilson, I. K. (2012). Humanistic theory of learning: Maslow. In *Springer eBooks* (pp. 1471–1474). DOI: 10.1007/978-1-4419-1428-6_1022

McCloud, N., Delgado, M. S., & Jin, M. (2023). Foreign capital inflows, exchange rates, and government stability. *Empirical Economics*. Advance online publication. DOI: 10.1007/s00181-023-02490-y

Pinto, A. C. (2020). Brazil in the era of fascism: The "New State" of Getúlio Vargas. In *Springer eBooks* (pp. 235–256). DOI: 10.1007/978-3-030-46831-6_11

Ricee, S. (2022). *Marginalized communities: Addressing inequality and fostering inclusion for all.* Diversity for Social Impact. https://diversity.social/marginalized-communities/

Schwindt-Bayer, L. A., & Tavits, M. (2016). *Clarity of responsibility, accountability, and corruption*. DOI: 10.1017/CBO9781316412404

Shakeel, M. D., & Maranto, R. (2021). Introduction to the special issue: Elitism, populism, and school choice. *Journal of School Choice*, 15(1), 10–17. DOI: 10.1080/15582159.2021.1883901

Shi, G., Chan, K. K., & Lin, X. (2022). A systematic review of digital citizenship empirical studies for practitioners. *Education and Information Technologies*, 28(4), 3953–3975. DOI: 10.1007/s10639-022-11383-z

Teichman, J. (2022). Class and race in Latin America's left-populist politics. *Race & Class*, 64(2), 55–74. DOI: 10.1177/03063968221103073

van Slageren, J., & Rooduijn, M. (2023). The education divide and support for populists. In M. Gangl & others (Eds.), *The Oxford handbook of social stratification* (online edn). Oxford Academic. DOI: 10.1093/oxfordhb/9780197539484.013.48

Vassilakopoulou, P., & Hustad, E. (2021). Bridging digital divides: A literature review and research agenda for information systems research. *Information Systems Frontiers*, 25(3), 955–969. DOI: 10.1007/s10796-020-10096-3 PMID: 33424421

Wajner, D. F. (2021). Exploring the foreign policies of populist governments: (Latin) America First. *Journal of International Relations and Development*, 24(3), 651–680. DOI: 10.1057/s41268-020-00206-8

Watters, R. (2021). The economic crisis and the Chávez presidency. In *Springer eBooks* (pp. 223–251). DOI: 10.1007/978-3-030-65033-9_10

Weyland, K. (2001). Clarifying a contested concept: Populism in the study of Latin American politics. *Comparative Politics*, 34(1), 1–22. DOI: 10.2307/422412

Williamson, J. (2003). The Washington consensus and beyond. *Economic and Political Weekly*, 38(15), 1475–1481. https://www.jstor.org/stable/4413431

World Bank. (2018). *Annual Report 2018*. World Bank. https://documents1.worldbank.org/curated/en/630671538158537244/pdf/The-World-Bank-Annual-Report-2018.pdf

World Bank. (2019). *Implementation completion and results report: IBRD 7841-BR on a loan in the amount of US$200 million to the Federative Republic of Brazil for the second Bolsa Família project* (Report No. ICR00004576). Social Protection and Jobs Global Practice, Latin America and the Caribbean Region. https://documents1.worldbank.org/curated/en/578141568314136393/pdf/Brazil-Second-Bolsa-Familia-Project.pdf

World Bank. (2022). *Educational underachievement among boys and men*. World Bank. https://documents1.worldbank.org/curated/en/111041644611110155/pdf/Educational-Underachievement-Among-Boys-and-Men.pdf

ADDITIONAL READING

Cheok, A. D. (Ed.). (2021). *Analyzing Current and Future Global Trends in Populism* (pp. 1–271). IGI Global., https://www.igi-global.com/book/analyzing-current-future-global-trends/244538

Christiansen, B. (Ed.). (2019). *Global Applications of Multigenerational Management and Leadership in the Transcultural Era* (pp. 1–328). IGI Global., https://www.igi-global.com/book/global-applications-multigenerational-management-leadership/225007

Christiansen, B., & Kasarcı, F. (Eds.). (2016). *Corporate Espionage, Geopolitics, and Diplomacy Issues in International Business* (pp. 1–374). IGI Global., https://www.igi-global.com/book/corporate-espionage-geopolitics-diplomacy-issues/156639

Singha, R., & Yogesh Kanna, S. (2024). Youth, addiction, and new populism. In Chacko Chennattuserry, J., Deshpande, M., & Hong, P. (Eds.), *Encyclopedia of New Populism and Responses in the 21st Century*. Springer., DOI: 10.1007/978-981-16-9859-0_440-1

Singha, R., & Yogesh Kanna, S. (2024). Navigating peer pressure, digital age, and new populism. In Chacko Chennattuserry, J., Deshpande, M., & Hong, P. (Eds.), *Encyclopedia of New Populism and Responses in the 21st Century*. Springer., DOI: 10.1007/978-981-16-9859-0_439-1

KEY TERMS AND DEFINITIONS

Economy: The system of production, distribution, and consumption of goods and services within a region or country, influencing employment, wealth distribution, and overall prosperity.

Education: The process of acquiring knowledge, skills, and values through formal and informal means, crucial for individual development, social mobility, and economic advancement.

Inclusive growth: Economic growth that benefits all segments of society, ensuring equal opportunities, reducing poverty, and promoting social cohesion and well-being.

Latin America: Refers to the region comprising countries in Central and South America, characterized by diverse cultures, histories, and socio-economic challenges.

Populism: Political ideology emphasizing the empowerment of the "common people" against elites, often involving charismatic leaders and appeals to popular sentiment.

Socio-economic development: Improving social and economic conditions, encompassing factors such as income levels, health, education, and infrastructure.

Technology: Tools, techniques, and systems developed through scientific knowledge for practical purposes, driving innovation, productivity, and societal transformation.

Chapter 3

Has Chinese Official Development Assistance Led to More Development Space in Costa Rica and Panama?

Daniel Benson
https://orcid.org/0009-0005-0812-0191
King's College London, UK

Yundan Gong
King's College London, UK

ABSTRACT

Despite fast increasing flows globally, and from emerging donors such as China, Official Development Assistance (ODA) has had limited impact on improving developmental outcomes and lived experiences in the Global South. Qualitative research can help supplement limited data availability on ODA effectiveness by offering a grounded explanation as to why donors' ODA appear to respond to that of other donors competitively and whether this can benefit recipients by increasing leverage and 'development space' or renders ODA less effective. Most research to date has concentrated on ODA competition in sub-Saharan Africa. As such, this study presents the first qualitative study on donor competition and the impacts of emerging donor ODA in Latin America. This study analyses sixteen semi-structured interviews conducted in Costa Rica and Panama to conclude that donor competition is rife, tangible, and impactful, but that Costa Rica and Panama are unable to take advantage of this competition to leverage better developmental outcomes.

DOI: 10.4018/979-8-3693-3763-9.ch003

INTRODUCTION

Despite fast increasing flows globally, and from emerging donors such as China, overseas development assistance (ODA) has had limited impact on improving developmental outcomes and lived experiences in the Global South. While the onus for this failure has traditionally been attributed to corrupt and inept recipient governments (Alesina & Dollar, 2000), a growing body of research instead highlights a dearth of donor collaboration, donor selfishness, and mutual suspicion is likely contributing to ineffective outcomes for developing nations' development goals, inappropriately targeted support, and increased headaches for already-stretched recipient nations (Bobba & Powell, 2006; Clist, 2011; Swedlund, 2017). The contemporaneous growth in Chinese ODA offers recipient nations alternative sources of finance and bilateral understanding through non-traditional channels, threatening the long-established dominance of Western, 'traditional' donors in global ODA flows (Bräutigam, 2011; Dreher & Fuchs, 2015; Steinwand, 2015). Despite repeated and increasingly loud calls for greater donor collaboration and mutual understanding, donors' ODA allocations remain disorganized, vast, and conflicting (Fuchs et al., 2015; Nunnenkamp et al., 2013; Powell & Findley, 2012).

Previous research has argued that limited donor cooperation is rational strategy in a zero-sum game where donors seek to defend their privileged position of 'lead donor', from which they can enjoy an unbalanced flow of economic and diplomatic resources (Steinwand, 2015); the quantitative evidence for this is significant (Benson & Gong, 2022);. However, whether donors choosing to channel ODA into the same locales as other donors can causally be understood as competition is contentious and can only be answered with a more grounded, mixed methods approach. ODA competition, if it is pervasive, could reduce ODA effectiveness by duplicating already scarce development efforts on the part of donors (Olivié & Pérez, 2016); increasing recipient burden (Steinwand, 2015); and reducing donor accountability in ensuring development outcomes as they scapegoat other donors competing in the same space (Nunnenkamp et al., 2013). Alternatively, donor competition may have positive effects on recipient nations who are better able to leverage more ODA, and for projects they most strongly desire, while competing donors seek to improve the quality of their output to appeal to more discerning recipients (Kilama, 2016). From theoretical conjecture and quantitative analysis alone, it is not possible to determine whether recipient countries would more likely benefit from donor competition by leveraging competing donors to better target recipient need and increase ODA project numbers and size or lead to recipients losing out from poorly targeted aid and increasing bureaucracy.

Accordingly, qualitative research can help supplement limited data availability on ODA effectiveness by offering a grounded explanation as to why donors' ODA appear to respond to that of other donors and the impact of emerging donors on recipient nations. Moreover, it provides scope to learn whether such competitive pressures created by competing donors benefit recipients by increasing leverage and 'development space' or renders ODA less effective by leading to worse targeted aid and greater administrative burden for recipients.

Most qualitative research to date has concentrated on ODA competition and the impacts on recipient nations in sub-Saharan Africa, with little consensus on whether donor competition is beneficial for recipient nations, with outcomes appearing to differ between recipients without any clearly discernible pattern. As such, this study presents the first qualitative study on donor competition and the impacts of Chinese ODA in Latin America. This study analyses sixteen semi-structured interviews conducted in July and August 2022, in San Jose, Costa Rica and Panama City, Panama which interviewed aid practitioners, academics, and other key stakeholders concerning their interactions with and attitudes towards Chinese and traditional donor ODA, and how this has changed pre- and post-signing diplomatic relations with China [King's College London Ethical review reference number: MRSP-21/22-31851]. This chapter concludes that while there is some evidence for donor competition, Costa Rica and Panama are unable to take advantage of this competition to leverage better developmental outcomes.

The findings suggest Western donors are concerned about the rise of China in Latin America. They express this by condemning Chinese intervention in these countries, as well as sending their own diplomatic missions contemporaneously with new Chinese aid projects. Such donor competition leads to somewhat more aid and investment, but this is seldom significant to Costa Rica and Panama. Though this donor competition sounds promising for the negotiation power of Costa Rica and Panama in principle, the two nations are unable to leverage this competition to their advantage due to limited diplomatic resources and the small influence of their countries in general. Moreover, there has been a notable discord what is promised by China and its effects on the ground. Negative stereotypical views of the PRC and Chinese immigrants translate to worsening Sino-Costa Rican and Sino-Panamanian relations at the higher, diplomatic level rendering the signing of diplomatic relations much more short-term benefitting for Costa Rica and Panama than had been initially expected.

Hyperbole, emotion, and misinformation feature heavily in the discussion of the Chinese role in international development and its impact upon other donors; as such, critical, unbiased, and nuanced perspectives of ODA, its motives, and the role of China in international development are key to understanding global ODA and its efficacy. This chapter addresses this by offering a qualitative approach to better understand competition between donors and how this impacts international development efforts globally.

Thus, the findings of this chapter are instructive to policymakers seeking to understand donor interaction, and ODA effectiveness more widely. An understanding of how donors use ODA to compete across recipient countries is a critical and timely first step in pursuing greater trilateral ODA cooperation and focusing international aid efforts on recipient needs (Winters & Martinez, 2015). Should international development practitioners be aware of donor competition in ODA allocation, this can inspire greater donor coordination and ensuing aid effectiveness. Analysis of the responses of the sixteen Costa Rican and Panamanian aid practitioners, policymakers, academics and industry experts, can help comment on why Costa Rica and Panama have seemingly been unable to take advantage of competing donor interests in their countries, despite being well resourced and having some state capacity. The findings of this analysis are thus important for policymakers operating in the international development space.

LITERATURE REVIEW

The existence of multiple donors in a given locale reduces ODA effectiveness by reducing donor accountability (Knack et al., 2010) and increasing the administrative burden on the recipient nations as each donor demands face-time with the receiving agencies and reports on the progress of projects (Steinwand, 2015). In 2008, the year Costa Rica began receiving development assistance from China, the OECD recorded a further 538 development assistance projects extended to Costa Rica from 28 OECD bilateral, multilateral, and private donors operating in the country (OECD, 2019). Despite repeated calls by the OECD for donors to coordinate their efforts to reduce recipient burden and improve effectiveness, donor coordination is curiously getting worse not better (Deutscher & Fyson, 2008). As such, rationalising the inability of donors to coordinate their efforts is a critical first step into understanding why donor coordination is so elusive and why ODA is proving ineffective.

The theoretical literature concerning why donors fail to coordinate but rather compete with one another in international development finance efforts identifies donor motives for competition into two distinct categories: political motivation to retain influence over recipient nations at the expense of other donors ('a competitive motive') and bureaucratic disincentives from initiating and maintaining donor cooperation ('a path dependent motive').

Turning first to the competitive motive of donor agencies, Chandy (2011) argues that donors have not coordinated their ODA because the motive for donor competition is political not bureaucratic as OECD High Level Working Forum prescriptions often are. Instead, donors can utilise ODA allocations to support non-development objectives (Chandy, 2011). For example, Winters (2012) highlights donors unapologetically provide ODA in exchange for assurance regarding security concerns and to facilitate trade relations, both of which must come at the expense of other donors' influence and private gain from extending ODA. This reflects that donor coordination is often antithetical to individual donor interest and this is explored by Lawson (2013) and Faust et al. (2015). As such, donors rather than seeking to co-ordinate will "have a strong incentive to exercise single-agency control over projects" (Winters, 2012) so that these benefits can be rewarded to the donor associated with the project. Fuchs et al. (2015) argues similarly for the desire of donors to secure access to profitable export markets. Zeitz (2020) puts forward this donor influence game as an inhibitor for donor cooperation as donors vie for political support in international organisations. Finally, Swedlund (2013) argues that donor private benefits comprise 'voice amplification', 'a seat at the table', and 'a license to ask questions' to increase leverage over recipient policy design. Qualitative research conducted in Rwanda and Tanzania indicates that donors are often able to question policies regarding governance or fiscal management even in the cases where ODA is not being channelled into these sectors (Swedlund, 2017).

A competitive response to the ODA of other donors follows when donors fear losing access to time with recipient policymakers with whom they can discuss policies the donor has interest in influencing and as such increase their ODA to maintain this privilege, a phenomenon understood by both donor and recipient (Zeitz, 2020). The concept that donors have little incentive to cooperate as implicitly they will lose the opportunity to highlight their contribution to recipients and thus their position to influence recipient policy is echoed by Lawson (2013) and Faust et al. (2015). Finally, Fuchs et al. (2015) highlight that this visibility of ODA projects is not only critical to recipients but also the electorate in the donor nation whom donor agencies are accountable to and seek diverse, visible, and effective ODA projects to justify why their taxpayer money is not being spent domestically.

Some authors go further to suggest that the political motive for donors to maintain visibility and discourse with recipients exists beyond containing the role for other donors to do the same but that donors can convene additional privileges from being the single largest donor in each recipient country (Lebovic, 2005; Steinwand, 2015). Lebovic (2005) refers to this as a 'windfall profit' and suggests donor coordination studies inadequately control for this motive in donor allocation studies. (Steinwand, 2015) builds upon this evidencing the large existence of 'lead donorship' in practice which he conjectures is a fault of especial export promotion, diplomatic influence, and resource access that only 'lead donors' can enjoy.

Even stronger still, Winters (2012) argues that rather than evading coordination, donors may actively seek competition as ODA coordination could lead to standardisation and enforcement of aid conditionality globally which would mean donors are less able to extract the economic and political resources they seek when they extend ODA to recipients. Moreover, on a more ontological level, Faust et al. (2015) argue that if donors do not even reach consensus on how economic development is achieved and which instruments are best suited to this process then they will be unable to reach coordination in their ODA efforts in the first instance. Taken together these papers demonstrate, for reasons of political support, resource access, and commercial relations, that donors have a strong incentive to refute efforts to coordinate their ODA and seek to continue to compete with one another.

Qualitative research can help disentangle some of the causal identification issues which plagues quantitative analyses of donor allocation and supplement limited data availability by offering a grounded explanation of why donors' ODA appear to respond to that of other donors. It also allows for a more empirically sound depiction of donor competition and the impact of emerging donors on recipient nations compared to the fanaticism often exhibited by journalists and politicians (Kragelund, 2011). Moreover, it provides scope to learn whether such competitive pressures created by competing donors benefit recipients by increasing leverage and 'development space' or renders ODA less effective by leading to worse targeted aid and greater administrative burden for recipients (Walshe Roussel, 2013).

Most of the qualitative research concerning ODA competition and the impacts on recipient nations have been undertaken in sub-Saharan Africa. This is unsurprisingly given the disproportionate flows of international development financing, from both traditional and emerging donors, as well as the interest and critique of the rise of China in this region. Studies concern themselves whether China is a credible alternative to Western donors in recipient nations; the differing motives for accepting Chinese or Western ODA in recipient nations; and whether donor competition is extending or reducing development space and recipient ownership in development.

There is little consensus on whether donor competition is beneficial for recipient nations caught in its crossfire, with the outcome appearing to differ between recipients without any clearly discernible pattern. For example, Bourguignon & Platteau (2015) highlight that in Mali both donor and recipient are to blame for a lack of increased development space following increasing donor efforts from many donors. Interviewees point towards the Malian government's indecisiveness, lack of development strategy, and duplicative aid management structure as endemic to Mali's inability to leverage donors against one another in the country's interests, but also highlights donors refusal of coordination mechanisms, particularly rationalisation of communication channels, joint missions, and common pool funding, as inhibiting Mali increasing ownership of international development efforts within its borders

(Bourguignon & Platteau, 2015). On the other hand, Humphrey & Michaelowa (2019) interviewed policymakers in Ethiopia and Tanzania who believed recipient ownership had improved following Chinese ODA, by enabling their nations to enjoy more resources and provide the opportunity to be more discerning in which projects and with which conditions to accept. Yet their respondents in Malawi did not share this optimistic view, rather suggesting that they "could only passively accept what was offered" (pg. 23) and could not alter the types of projects that the World Bank offered.

Kragelund (2011, 2012, 2014, 2015) has been impactful in better understanding donor competition and the impact on recipients in Africa using qualitative methods, which the author highlights to be mostly positive regarding recipient ownership and development space. Though the role of OECD DAC donors is still critical to the development efforts of African nations, emerging donors offer these nations leverage to 'fiscally triangulate' between donors (Kragelund, 2011, 2012, 2015). At a theoretical level recipients can increase development space by trading off different donor funds in exchange for greater adherence to recipient demands, reducing dependency on any single donor which could otherwise be destabilising if funds are withdrawn, and allowing for recipients to penetrate donors and encourage them to pressure other donors into adherence to recipient demands (Kragelund, 2012). Kragelund (2015) highlights increasing ownership and development space in Zambia and Ethiopia in response to increasing donor competition in ODA as evidence for this argument. The Zambian government redrafted its development plan without directly consulting OECD donors upon receiving large flows of development finance from China and in Ethiopia, Chinese ODA was employed to develop infrastructure projects in the energy sector which OECD DAC donors had long refused based on their recommendations to prioritise other sectors (Kragelund, 2015). However, increasing development space cannot be attributed solely to the increasing numbers of ODA partners African nations can receive funding from, but also commodity price changes and debt forgiveness play a key role too (Kragelund, 2011, 2014). Considering the case study of Zambia more closely, Kragelund (2014) highlights that recipient policymakers in Zambia believe emerging donors and subsequent donor competition has facilitated an increase in Zambia's negotiation power with OECD DAC donors, "strengthen[ing] the sovereign frontier" (pg. 158). Taken together these papers suggest that developing nations in Africa can convene huge benefits from donor competition in their country.

Notwithstanding, the work of Haley Swedlund (2013, 2017) suggests through interviews with heads of development cooperation in donor agencies across fifteen African nations (Swedlund, 2013) and seventy semi-structured interviews with stakeholders in international development in Rwanda and Tanzania (Swedlund, 2017) that the role of China in bolstering development space in Africa is more limited and that the existing literature is overstated. The studies identify only a minority of interviewees believe China is reducing their bargaining power in recipient nations; a very low elasticity of probability of claiming bargaining power is reduced with respect to an increase in Chinese ODA; and very few participants give Chinese ODA much consideration when making their own ODA allocations (Swedlund, 2017). However, it would be interesting to reconsider the findings of the research today given that the relative magnitude of ODA from China relative to OECD DAC donors in these countries is much greater; already at the time of this study recipients pointed towards a preference to accept Chinese ODA over DAC ODA all else equal (Swedlund, 2017).

Qualitative research outside of Sub-Saharan Africa is scarcer, but still does not conclude whether recipients stand to benefit or lose from donor competition, nor the conditions required for a recipient to benefit from ODA competition which could provide practical guidance for recipients seeking to improve ODA effectiveness at home. As donors' roles and interest in different regions is heterogenous studies in more diverse locations are important in understanding the impacts of donor competition more generally. More pessimistic studies highlight that in Indonesia and Morocco respectively donor competition is adding to the burden of recipients and detracting from ODA effectiveness. Liao & Katada (2021) investigate Sino-Japanese development competition by considering the case study of financing the Jakarta-Bandung High Speed Rail project, which was funded by a $4bn loan from the Chinese Development Bank, seeking to understand why an apparent inflow of 'easy money' from competing Asian superpowers has not led to a beneficial outcome for Indonesians. The authors conclude that the desire of successive Indonesian presidents to accept overseas support for infrastructure development to guarantee electoral success came at the expense of adequate due diligence and long-term consideration of repayment. Indeed, the project has been plagued by budget over-runs and implementation delays (Guild, 2023). The blame lies not exclusively with Indonesia, however; competition between donors led to a deterioration in best practice, with easy credit worsening infrastructure gaps in the first instance (Liao & Katada, 2021). Moreover, Olivié & Pérez (2016) interviewed development policymakers in Morocco to better understand the practicalities of on-the-ground donor coordination. The study participants referred to the differential administrative requirements of donors and the compounding pressures these confer upon an already constrained public administration in the recipient country (Olivié & Pérez, 2016); though participants commented on state capacity in Morocco, this was less frequently cited than donors' own actions, which highlights the onus of co-operation should be with the donors. Such analysis highlights the practical hurdle many of the theoretical obstacles to donor co-ordination described in previous sections hold across the developing world.

On the other hand, in considering the interaction between emerging and traditional donors in Cambodia, Sato et al. (2011) argue that competition from emerging donors, who represent a substantial proportion of Cambodian ODA, will likely stand to benefit Cambodia by targeting sectors neglected by traditional donors and thus achieving better sectoral co-ordination; provide Cambodia more sources of international support and reduce reliance on traditional donors; and enjoy quickly delivered ODA projects. Thus, it is not puzzling that Cambodia appears to be discouraging donors from co-operating despite this focus in the international development discourse; as such, the authors caution that too much focus on donor co-ordination could come at the expense of recipient autonomy in development (Sato et al., 2011). Finally, Walshe Roussel (2013) demonstrates that Nicaragua benefitted from the rise of Venezuelan aid in the late 2000s by competing with traditional donor behaviour and incentivising a change of approach of traditional donors, in keeping with Nicaraguan interests. As emerging donors take an increasingly large role in Nicaraguan development efforts, this has "enabled the government to diversify its approach to development and gain leverage in setting its priorities" (pg. 807). Participants from European aid agencies cite changing power relations with an empowered Nicaragua who no longer depend on their aid and are less amenable to Western donor demands, but rather than reducing their ODA efforts are likely to retain funding to stay relevant to and partnered with the Nicaraguan government (Walshe Roussel, 2013). It would certainly be interesting to see whether these findings will persist in the coming years following Nicaragua signing diplomatic relations with China in December 2021 (Thaler & Mosinger, 2022), opening up to future inflows of Chinese ODA and other assistance.

Taken together these qualitative studies paint a complex, multifaceted, and diverse understanding of donor competition on the ground in developing countries, though with a heavy focus on the presence of donors in sub-Saharan Africa. This literature review has pointed to key gaps in the literature concerning donor competition in ODA, particularly with respect to the rise of China as a key development player. Qualitative, grounded research into donor competition has not considered Latin American and Asian donor competition to the same extent as that of sub-Saharan Africa despite increasing Chinese ODA to these regions and different political dynamics to that of African recipients. This chapter intends to develop this strand of literature.

CASE SELECTION

Most qualitative studies concerning the role of China in international development, donor competition, and the relationship between ODA and development space have been conducted in the context of sub-Saharan Africa, which may not be representative of donor dynamics and the role of China across the Global South. As such, we seek to select a case outside this region. We hypothesize that the role of donor competition between China and OECD donors will likely be largest in instances when there is a large, exogenous change in Chinese ODA. China rewards diplomatic partners with ODA, but consistent with its 'One-China policy' to sign diplomatic relations with China must be to rescind relations with Taiwan (Dreher & Fuchs, 2015), and so developing nations making this diplomatic 'switch' often are motivated and rewarded by large inflows of Chinese ODA in the years following signing. Thus, we investigate cases of 'diplomatic switches', outside of sub-Saharan Africa. Finally, to ensure comparison pre- and post- signing said diplomatic relations can be observed by the participants, we restrict our potential sample to countries where diplomatic relations have been signed with China between five and fifteen years before the interviews were conducted.

The subset of countries outside of sub-Saharan Africa, signing diplomatic relations with China between 2007 and 2017 is Costa Rica, Niue, and Panama. At the time of conducting the fieldwork it was not possible to travel to Niue due to COVID-19 precautions. As such, Costa Rica and Panama are quite particular cases, with respect to their diplomatic history, from which to investigate this donor competition mechanism and the findings are likely particular to this region and period.

As highlighted in the literature review, most of the qualitative research concerning ODA competition and the impacts on recipient nations have been undertaken in sub-Saharan Africa. This is unsurprisingly given the disproportionate flows of international development financing, from both traditional and emerging donors, as well as the interest and critique of the rise of China in this region. There are many reasons why donor geopolitical dynamics may differ outside of the region, but principally, the role of China is much smaller in Latin America than in Africa. Of the ODA projects committed by China between 2000 and 2020, only 11.0% were extended to recipients in Latin America, compared to 51.9% to Africa (Custer et al., 2023). Though small in project number, the growth of Chinese ODA in Latin America far outstrips that of traditional Chinese ODA strongholds, boasting a compounded annual growth rate of 7.9% between 2000 and 2020 (Custer et al., 2023).

Taken together this would suggest that the impact of donor competition could be different in Central America, the focus of this chapter, than sub-Saharan Africa. On one hand there is a more muted role of China, and as such less for Western donors to concern themselves responding to. Yet, on the other hand, it is plausible that

Western donors, principally the United States, could feel more threatened by small competitive changes in their former diplomatic strongholds. The qualitative evidence presented in this chapter can help conclude which of these outcomes is more likely.

Costa Rica and China

Costa Rica, with population 5.2 million principally exports tropical fruit, coffee, and other primary products, as well as a fast-growing sustainable tourism industry, and boasts democratic stability and environmental sustainability, but struggles with corruption, bureaucracy, and ethnic tension (World Bank, 2021). At the time of first engaging diplomatically with China in 2008, GDP per capita was $6,840 and the poverty rate 20% with respect to the $5.50 USD per day line (World Bank, 2021).

Costa Rica and Taiwan had long enjoyed decades of strong diplomatic relations, with shared commitments to human rights, liberal democracy, and environmental protection (Córdoba Ramírez, 2005). Reading Thais Cordoba's seminal book on the topic, published in 2005, the future of Taiwanese and Costa Rican relations looks bright, with increasing development commitments by Taiwan, most personified by its Bridge of Friendship committed in 2003 (Córdoba Ramírez, 2005). Not to mention the alleged large sums of money flowing from Taiwan to Costa Rican officials away from the public eye (Leffert, 2007).

Scholars have noted that the shift from focus on human rights and democracy in President Oscar Arias's first term in the late 1980s where he won the Nobel Peace Prize, made way for those of economic realism and international trade in the second between 2006 and 2010 and set the scene for the diplomatic switch (Feigenblatt, 2021). Conducted in secret, the Arias government negotiated the ODA projects that China would commit following the switch, worth approximately $400m, which were ultimately signed in June 2007 (Feigenblatt, 2021). Costa Rica was the first Latin American nation to sign diplomatic relations with China (Urcuyo, 2021). Such a shift in political focus mirrors the justification Sanchez offered the Costa Rican population, stressing the importance of the switch on economic and pragmatic rather than moral terms, at a time where the sustainability of the Costa Rican economic model looked less than certain (Feigenblatt, 2021) Taiwan immediately ended diplomatic relations with Costa Rica, reneging on $70m of ODA commitments (Leffert, 2007). In 2008 the proportion of Costa Rican imports from China was just 6% but by 2021 this had risen to 16%, with the proportion from the US constant over this period (World Bank, 2021).

Arias argued that as Taiwan lost supporters over time it had not increased its ODA allocation to each of its remaining supporters as an additional cause for the switch (Leffert, 2007). Though such ODA commitments did materialise, bureaucratic and political obstacles have plagued their progress and the scope for future Chinese involvement in Costa Rica, with the National Assembly investigating Chinese purchases of Costa Rican government bonds and pausing construction of a refinery following improper practice in feasibility studies, leading to more fraught bilateral relations (Ellis, 2014).

Panama and China

It is unsurprising that Panama's enviable geographic location and profitable canal making it the 'Hub of the Americas' was an attractive diplomatic target for China (Hafiyer Al Halim, 2021). In 2017, when Panama first engaged with China on a diplomatic level, GDP per capita exceeded $15,000 and the poverty headcount at $5.50 per day was 12.6% (World Bank, 2021). The Panamanian economy principally exports copper, bananas, and services related to trade and logistics through its canal (World Bank, 2021).

Even before signing diplomatic relations, China was the second largest user of the Panama Canal, the largest exporter to the Colón Free Trade Zone, and Panama's largest trade partner by a considerable margin (Li, 2005). After signing diplomatic relations with Costa Rica, China published several white papers detailing its intentions for foreign policy efforts in the Latin American region focussing on resource security and infrastructure construction, with the hope of securing diplomatic relations with all nations in the region (Carlos Herrera et al., 2020). Following the election of populist Varela in 2014, the Panamanian government began secretively interacting with China before signing diplomatic relations in June 2017 (Coriat, 2017). Taiwan responded disgustedly withdrawing all support and diplomatic staff immediately, with Taiwanese General Secretary Joseph Wu scolding "the purchase of diplomatic allies". Similarly, to Costa Rica, former President Varela justified the diplomatic switch according to Chinese prowess in the Global Economy and the belief that Taiwan would not be disadvantaged in its relations with Panama following the change, citing "socioeconomic reality" (Carlos Herrera et al., 2020).

ODA in Costa Rica and Panama

China does not publicly publish its ODA activities and instead most papers instead rely on the AidData Global Chinese Official Finance (AidData) dataset (Custer et al., 2023), the most accurate and granular measure for Chinese ODA flows between 2000 and 2020 (Custer et al., 2023). Similarly, the OECD Creditor

Reporting System (CRS) collates project-level ODA commitments on the part of OECD DAC Members (OECD, 2019).

Figures 1 and 2 detail ODA project flows, by sector and year, from China and OECD donors to Costa Rica and Panama respectively, noting ODA flows from the United States, Spain, and Japan, the three largest OECD donors in this region.

Figure 1a details Chinese ODA in Costa Rica between 2006 and 2016. Though there were noticeable increases in the number of ODA projects, following the introduction of Chinese ODA in Costa Rica, especially in the case of Costa Rica at a time where ODA was retreating globally, the number of projects is modest, and as can be seen, temporary. The most notable Costa Rican projects committed by China, often discussed by the interview participants are the Chinese grant for the construction of the National Football Stadium (which was committed upon the signing of diplomatic relations) and the concessional loan issued by the Chinese Exim Bank for the renovation of Route 32, a key highway in Costa Rica (Custer et al., 2023). Though both projects are categorised as physical infrastructure, the modal class of Chinese ODA projects in Costa Rica is in fact concentrated among social sectors.

Figure 1a: Chinese ODA projects committed to Costa Rica, 2006-2016

Figure 1. Chinese ODA projects committed to Costa Rica, 2006-2016

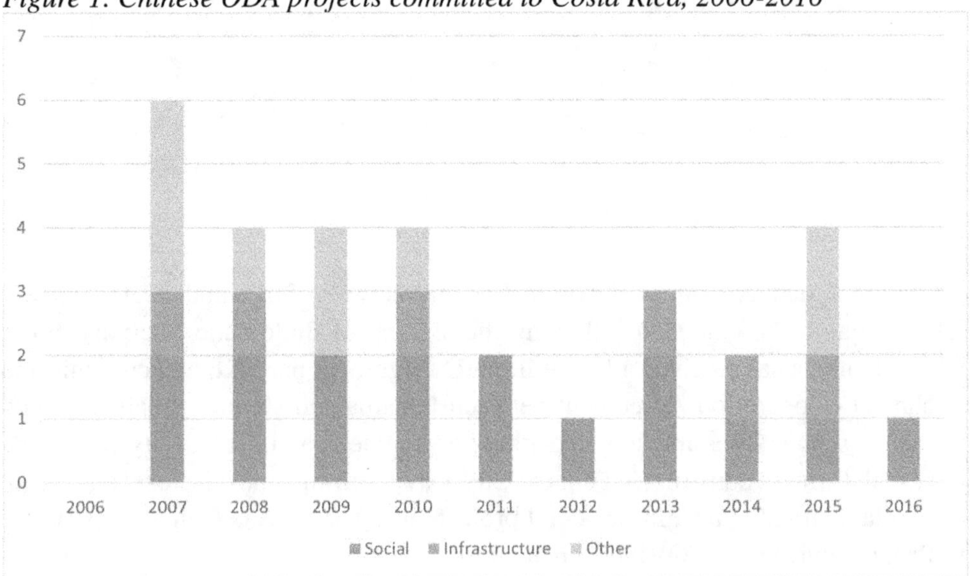

Figure 1b details OECD ODA in Cosa Rica between 2006 and 2015. OECD donor ODA to Costa Rica peaked between 2009 and 2011, in the immediate years after China signed diplomatic relations with Costa Rica, despite the negative impacts of the Global Financial Crisis on budgets for international development among

Global North donors, before tailing off in the period 2012-2016, most strongly felt in the social sectors. The largest OECD ODA projects committed to Costa Rica include the construction of the Las Pailas geothermal plant in Liberia supported by a consortium of Japanese and multilateral development agencies, and a variety of educational schemes to reduce school dropouts and youth unemployment from the United States and EU institutions.

Figure 2. OECD donor ODA projects committed to Costa Rica, 2006-2016

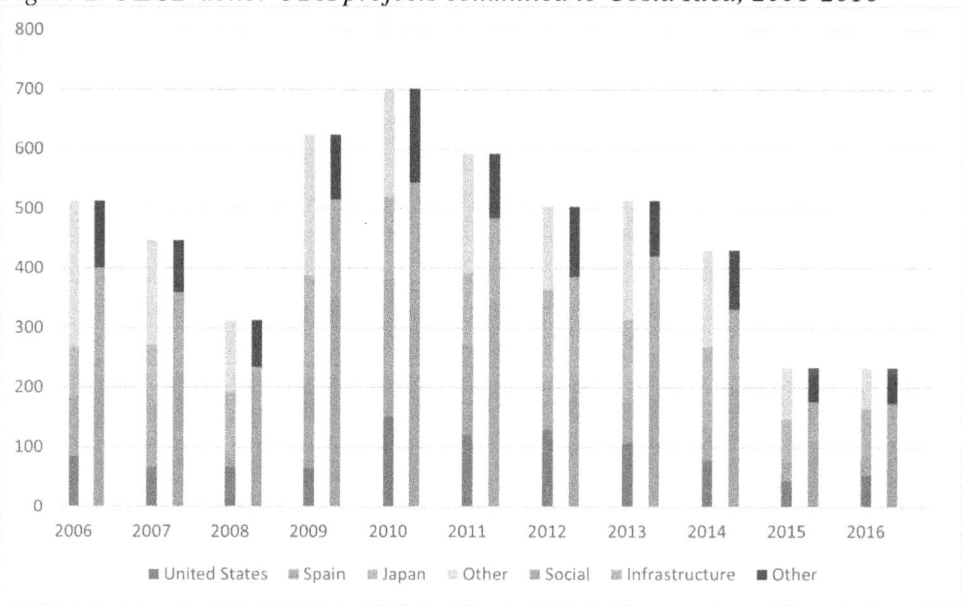

Figure 2 details Chinese ODA in Panama between 2015 and 2020. Chinese ODA began to be extended following the signing of diplomatic relations. From China, Panama has received a 100 million RMB grant as part of the "Economic and Technical Cooperation Agreement between Panama and China" which will fund academic scholarships and human capital development, and a feasibility study for a potential, Chinese constructed Panama City-David subway line (Custer et al., 2023). The notable uptake in Chinese social projects in 2020 reflects Chinese assistance to Panama during the COVID-19 pandemic.

Figure 2a: Chinese ODA projects committed to Panama, 2015-2020

Figure 3. Chinese ODA projects committed to Panama, 2015-2020

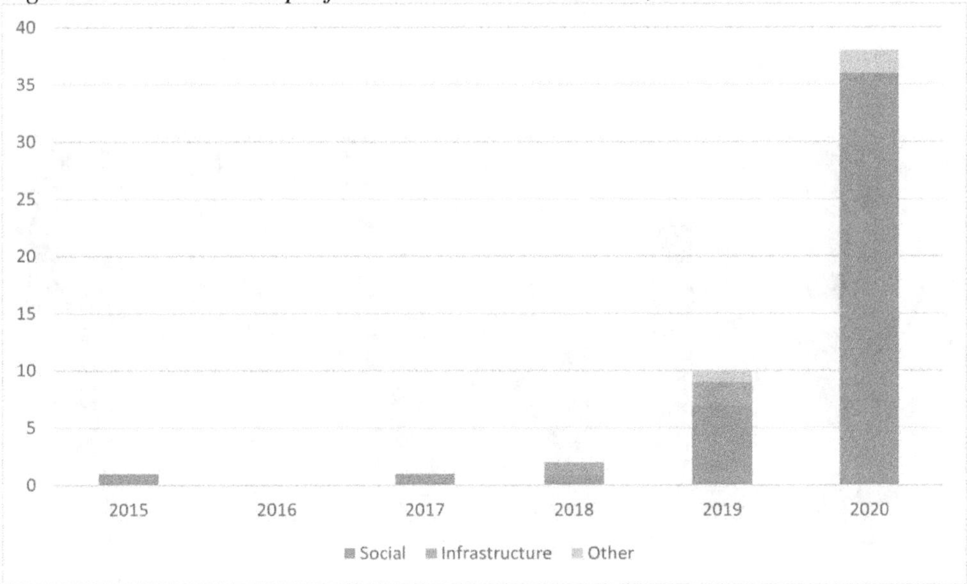

Figure 3 details OECD ODA in Panama between 2015 and 2020. There is a noticeable discontinuity from the pattern of previous years in 2018, where OECD ODA had been declining to vast increases, at a similar time to the signing of Sino-Panamanian diplomatic relations. OECD donors are principally focussed on social sector spending, but the most significant OECD donor funded projects in Panma, by size, include the development of Line 3 of the Panama City subway system by Japanese financing and the expansion of the water treatment facilities of Panama City by the European Investment Bank, both pertain to the physical infrastructure sectors.

Figure 4. OECD donor ODA projects committed to Panama, 2015-2020

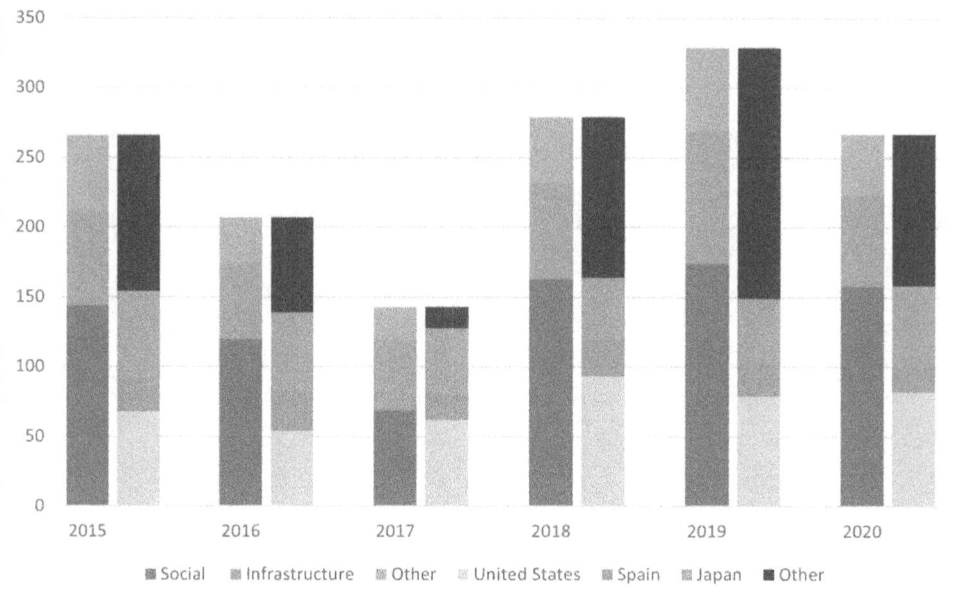

METHODOLOGY

Between July and August 2022, the primary author conducted sixteen interviews in San Jose, Costa Rica and Panama City, Panama. Though a small number, each participant had extensive experience in international development or academia that could attest to the research questions of this research, providing breadth in response. To be included in this research a participant would need to be based in Costa Rica or Panama and work in an industry related to international development or academia where they would be able to discuss the impact of Chinese aid on Western donors' behaviour in their home country pre- and post- signing diplomatic relations with China. Saturation appeared to have been reached after these sixteen interviews, evidenced by many shared experiences and repeated anecdotes. We sought a balance between participants working in academia, industry, multilateral or donor organizations, and the government, interviewing eight, three, three, and two participants respectively. The initial search for participants was by cold email, based on searching for relevant participants through LinkedIn; participants were contacted based on being expertly able to attest to the research questions from a unique perspective. This cold approach led to interviews with eight participants.

We employed a method of snowball sampling; that is, asking participants to suggest other participants to interview (Rogers et al., 2005), which was very fruitful and resulted in eight further interviews, including two who had originally not responded to cold emails. The interviews were conducted in English and thus excluded any participants who cannot speak English to a level that would be conducive to these discussions. In practice, this is not particularly restrictive as most academics and international development practitioners in this region have a very high level of English and Chinese investment activity is typically conducted in English [Interviewee 006]. There were no exclusion criteria pertaining to gender, ethnicity, or any other socioeconomic attributes.

Each interview lasted between thirty and ninety minutes and was held in a public location, as chosen by the participant. The interviews were conducted as semi-structured interviews; that is, a partially structured interview which "allows depth to be achieved by providing the opportunity on the part of the interviewer to probe and expand the interviewee's responses" (Rubin & Rubin, 2005, 88). The decision to conduct semi-structured interviews reflects the participants broad and varied experiences. Interacting with different stakeholders with different perspectives meant we hoped to learn different viewpoints from different individuals pertaining to their individual experiences and expertise. The intention is also that, not bound by a question list, the interviewee can feel comfortable to stray into a tangent that enables new understanding, or that the interviewer can follow-up on diverse points without fear of the clock, allowing for a larger and richer data collection. Kvale (1996) additionally argues that semi-structured interviews lead to less Hawthorne bias, in the sense that upon receiving a list of questions on a particular theme the participant may start to share information they think fits the interviewer's objective rather than their actual opinion. We found this to be particularly fruitful as we had few preconceived notions about our research questions in Costa Rica and Panama and were able to learn new hypotheses from our research participants and test these with other, relevant stakeholders in subsequent interviews.

To ensure ethical guidelines were in place while conducting these interviews, participants were supplied with information sheets and additionally required to give both written and oral consent. The authors had no prior relationships with any of the participants and no interviewees received any renumeration for their participation. The information sheets detailed the ability for participants to later withdraw any comments made during the interviews and the data storage plan. In accordance with UK data protection law (the UK General Data Protection Regulation (GDPR) and Data Protection Act 2018), all data was only viewed by the authors, and held anonymously, encrypted, and confidentially in the King's College London secure online storage repository. The interviews have been anonymised except for the institution to which the participant is associated with to ensure participants felt comfortable to express their own opinions rather than those expected of them. The details of the interviewees can be found in the Appendix.

As interview research relies on interpersonal relationship development and interpretation it is imperative to reflexively consider author positionality when conducting and analysing the collected data (Merriam et al., 2001; Roulston, 2010); that is, the inclusion of "an explicit and transparent exposition of an author's ethical understandin(Kendall & Thangaraj, 2013, p. 97)endall & Thangaraj, 2013, p. 97). In our case, the primary author conducted the primary data collection and analysis. The primary author is an English speaking, white-European male who has lived and been educated for most of his life in the Global North, and we are aware of the limitations this may have on understanding lived, developmental issues in the Global South (Elliott & Reid, 2019). The positionality of the primary author likely influenced the analysis of this data to some extent; namely, seeking to ignore or downplay views considered racist or ignorant towards China as stated by the research participants, and extensive research into the role of Chinese ODA in the Global South which likely paints Chinese ODA in a more positive light than that understood by the research participants. As an outsider, both linguistically and ethnically, the primary author likely had enhanced access to participants who were motivated to speak to outsiders about China; this was noted by the participants choice of location to conduct interviewees, and for one participant's desire to "face outwards" while being interviewed in a café.

During the interview, the author took extensive notes on the participants' responses, capturing their viewpoints unedited, and directly quoting any phrases or quotes that seemed particularly pertinent to their answers by hand. These were then typed out and subsequently coded. The coding process was inductive; that is, after reading the interview notes as a collective, different responses were grouped together under different themes, to structure the interview data. This process was done iteratively several times to ensure that the coding best captured the dataset.

RESULTS AND DISCUSSION

The rise in Chinese ODA extended to Latin America since 2000 has certainly not gone unnoticed by the Western donor community, with interview participants highlighting that Western donors, led by the US, have been communicating concern of Chinese development support in Costa Rica and Panama. Interview participants commented that the rise in Chinese ODA was "frightening" for Western donors who had not seen their ODA dominance contested before [Interviewee 6], leading to "paranoia" as China penetrates a sphere of influence traditionally enjoyed by Western superpowers, namely the USA [Interviewees 2 and 10]. Interviewee 4 attributed this to what they termed the US foreign "firefighter policy"; that is, the US is only waking up to reality in its influence, or lack of, amid ODA recipients in Latin America when "[it] sees a fire", i.e. the rise of Chinese ODA and other international financing. Interviewees working within the government commented that the US, among other donors, send explicit messages to receiving agencies in Costa Rica and Panama to "beware of China" [Interviewees 3, 10, and 15] citing alignment with communists [Interviewee 15], the inability to accept support from both the "sun and moon" [Interviewee 3] and African nations as case studies to exemplify these concerns [Interviewee 3], as justification not to engage with China and its ODA.

Specifically, Western donors express this concern by condemning Chinese intervention in these countries publicly, as well as sending diplomatic missions to Latin American countries after the announcement of new Chinese ODA projects [Interviewee 4]. It is notable that Mike Pompeo, US Secretary of State, visited Panama shortly after signing diplomatic relations with China and cautioned that Panama ought to "have wide eyes regarding China" (Carlos Ḥerrera et al., 2020). Interviewee 2 commented that such a response was common to even the most innocuous state visits from low-ranking Chinese state officials to Panama.

This concern has led to more aid and investment resources flowing from the US to Costa Rica and Panama. Several of the interviewees pointed to the dramatic increase in Fullbright Scholarships offered to Costa Rica after signing diplomatic relations with China and receiving ODA for the first time [Interviewees 10, 12, and 14]. Similarly, Interviewee 2 discussed "a leverage game" during the COVID-19 pandemic with the US countering a large donation of masks from China to Panama by supplying even more, "making donations for the sake of that of China". This being said, educational scholarships and masks aside, there was less reference to large ODA projects extended by OECD donors on a grander scale.

Indeed, the view that Western donors are more generous in the wake of increasing Chinese ODA was harder to substantiate among participants, with Interviewee 8 best summarising this contrasting viewpoint, suggesting that Western donors are simply not interested in 'providing the tools' for the creation of development space in Latin America. Interviewee 9 summarised this viewpoint as the feeling that this region is underrepresented in international development, commenting that "there is never a pivot to Latin America!" Interviewee 4 claimed that this could likely be a cause of the perception that Costa Rica is "a reliable ally" of the West, less susceptible to Chinese influence. This suggests that though Western donors may express concern about the rise of Chinese ODA in their sphere of influence when it comes to increasing their own ODA flows to this region that this may not be especially pertinent or tangible.

Though the donor competition ensuing following increased diplomatic and economic efforts by China in Costa Rica and Panama following signing diplomatic relations sounds promising for the negotiation power of Costa Rica and Panama in principle, through negotiating better outcomes from Western donors fearing a loss of influence in their traditional sphere of influence, the findings of the interviews unanimously and pessimistically cite that the two nations are unable to leverage this competition to their advantage. This creates a perplexing puzzle as to why Costa Rica and Panama are unable to take advantage of rising Chinese ODA in their countries. Our participants pointed to three key reasons for this: the inability of the Costa Rican and Panamanian governments to negotiate with donors; Costa Rican bureaucracy inhibiting development financing of any kind and scope for negotiation; and a discord between the promise of diplomatic relations and impacts on the ground.

The modal difficulty Panama and Costa Rica have in leveraging competing donors to their advantage is limited resources allocated to foreign diplomatic efforts. For example, Interviewee 2 points to the small size of the Panamanian foreign ministry's diplomatic teams; with only "one negotiating team" in the foreign ministry, foreign policy "can't do more than one big thing at a time". Indeed, foreign policy is argued to be too China focussed, neglecting pre-existing relationships with Western donors [Interviewees 1 and 6]. This is echoed in the Costa Rican case too [Interviewee 16]; Interviewee 4 comments that had more human resources been channelled into negotiations with China, that it would have been not only possible to access more resources from China but also to obtain more concessions from the USA in response [Interviewee 1]. Moreover, in the Costa Rican case, given the benefit of hindsight, many interviewees pointed to how this diplomatic ineptness meant that the benefits Costa Rica enjoyed from signing diplomatic relations were lost after only several years, more "symbolic than an actual, noticeable shift" [Interviewee 1]. Again, this is attributed to poor foreign policy efforts and a lack of resources dedicated to maintaining mutually beneficial relationships with China [Interviewees 4, 7, and 12], with Costa Rica unable and unaware of how to "exploit diplomatic relations" [Interviewee 4]. This leads Costa Rica and Panama to be less discerning, "take what you can get" partners [Interviewee 2] with trilateral cooperation and the fruits of these spoils low on the agenda. Interviewees 8 and 10 commented that for Costa Rica there was diplomatic ineptitude with missing ambassadors [Interviewee 10], 'piecemeal' foreign policy, with projects too short-term focussed [Interviewee 8], and the perception that diplomacy is a luxury rather than a necessity [Interviewee 10].

In the Costa Rican case, even if the government were able to simultaneously court both China and Western donors, high bureaucratic costs and inflexible legal arrangements make development finance projects and foreign direct investment in Costa Rica challenging; with one participant surmising that "the bureaucratic speed of [Costa Rica] is a big contrast with their [donor] efficiency" [Interviewee 4]. Indeed, the World Bank's Ease of Doing Business Index 2020 reveals Costa Rica has a 'Doing Business' ranking of 74, with a particularly poor ranking on establishing new business at 144 (World Bank, 2020). Interviewees typically cited environmental and labour regulation as key bureaucratic challenges frustrating, alienating, and deterring donor [Interviewees 4, 5, 9, and 15]. These regulations are often antithetical to foreign ownership of investments and development projects which limits the role of donors in Costa Rica [Interviewee 15]. Interviewee 6 spoke about how donor requests for concessions are point-blank refused, commenting that when donors ask "'Are we going to be forced to follow the specifications on quality?' We have to tell them yes you do". Interviewee 4 similarly commented that though Costa Rica is middle-income its strict specifications for overseas development assistance and foreign direct investment is very strict and mimics best practice across Europe and North America. This limits Costa Rica's ability to trade-off donors to improve developmental outcomes as there is simply too little flexibility in the role and scope of donors in Costa Rica.

This certainly contrasts with cases of increasing development space identified for many recipient nations in sub-Saharan Africa (Humphrey & Michaelowa, 2019b; Kragelund, 2015b; Swedlund, 2017) and highlights that increased legal control and regulation in Costa Rica and Panama was attributable to a lack of increased development space following the signing of diplomatic relations with China and the subsequent influx of Chinese ODA. Indeed, Interviewee 4, who had previously worked in international development projects in the Caribbean commented that Costa Rican projects were supervised constantly by government officials unlike in the Caribbean countries where they had worked, when the local government sent monthly supervisions.

Moreover, and more pessimistically still, Costa Rica and Panama have struggled to benefit from Chinese aid and investment due to the fundamental discord between the grandeur of what is promised by diplomatic relations and its effects on the ground. As such, it is rational to expect that if Western donors realise this, they will feel less need to engender a competitive response to the rise of Chinese ODA, or rather lack thereof, perhaps explaining the findings that Western donors have not increased ODA dramatically in a bid to suppress the influence of new Chinese ODA in Costa Rica and Panama. Though the justification shared by Costa Rica's Arias and Panama's Varela in signing diplomatic relations with China was the promise of widescale Chinese investment, trade and development assistance (Carlos Herrera et al., 2020; Feigenblatt, 2021), in many cases these have failed to be lived up to in Costa Rica and Panama, either on the part of China's faltering interest in the region, or resistance from recipients. Many interviewees were quick to point out that though there are many 'Chinese' projects in Panama and Costa Rica, that these projects don't include Chinese-backed capital [Interviewees 2, 3, and 4]. Interviewee 2 comments that the Bridge of the Americas and Panama City Convention Centre, often understood as Chinese ODA donations, are funded instead by loans and the Panamanian government rather than China, supported by Interviewee 3 who commented that "You don't actually see any Chinese money in Panama". Other participants commented on a melee of promised Chinese ODA and investment opportunities that have not materialised, including Air China flights [Interviewee 4] and enhanced FDI [Interviewee 12]. This led Participant 15 to exasperatedly condense the impact of Sino-Costa Rican relations to merely "A stadium and a Shakira concert!"

Many of the participants pointed towards negative stereotypical views of China and Chinese immigrants coupled with Latin America nationalism as impediments to strong Sino-Costa Rican and Sino-Panamanian relations [Interviewees 1, 2, 4, 8, 10, 15 and 16]. Many interviewees pointed to the stereotypical occupation of Chinese immigrants in both Latin American nations as convenience store owners [Interviewees 1, 2, and 15] as well as further stereotypical views which blame China for the COVID-19 pandemic [Interviewee 1], and argue Chinese imports are low quality [Interviewees 2 and 4]. Interviewee 1 comments that though Chinese commerce, investment and ODA has increased in Panama since signing diplomatic relations, this ignorance about China has unlikely changed.

Such negative stereotypical views translate to worsening Sino-Costa Rican and Sino-Panamanian relations at the higher, diplomatic level rendering the signing of diplomatic relations much more short-term benefitting for Costa Rica and Panama than had been initially expected. This finding is corroborated by Costa Rican participants, who argue that this xenophobia pervades higher level diplomacy with China [Interviewees 4 and 15], as nationalistic education and a lack of Chinese assimilation in Costa Rica continue to exist in the collective memory of Costa Ricans today. This likely inhibits trust and the potential to negotiate openly, limiting the effectiveness of Chinese ODA in these countries.

Thus, to conclude, the potential for increased development space following Costa Rica and Panama signing diplomatic relations with China is quite pessimistic. Though in a best-case scenario China would extend large volumes of ODA which make a demonstrable improvement on the development experiences of Costa Rican and Panamanian citizens following diplomatic relations being signed leading to a competitive, crowding-in response of ODA from Western donors, the analysis of the interviews has shown this does not happen. Firstly, though Western donors are critical of the increasing role of China in this region, formerly very closely tied to the USA, they do not express their criticism through increased monetary flows. Moreover, the role of China in these countries' development strategies has been less effective than promised. As such, Costa Rica and Panama will struggle to improve development space following increasing support from China.

CONCLUSION

To conclude, ODA has had limited impact on improving developmental outcomes and lived experiences in the Global South. This research contributes to the growing body of research highlighting donor competition is contributing to such ineffective outcomes. While this could be a rational strategy for donors seeking to defend their privileged position of 'lead donor', from which they can enjoy an unbalanced flow of economic and diplomatic resources (Benson & Gong, 2022; Steinwand, 2015), evidence for this can only be answered with a more grounded, mixed methods approach. Moreover, it is important to assess whether recipient countries would more likely benefit from donor competition through increased negotiation and development space or lose out from less well targeted support and increased bureaucracy. Such research is scarce, principally concentrated in sub-Saharan Africa, and though has identified donor competition, has reached little consensus on whether donor competition is beneficial for recipient nations caught in its crossfire.

As such, this study adds to the literature by presenting the first qualitative study on donor competition and the impacts of emerging donor ODA in Latin America through analysing sixteen interviews conducted in Costa Rica and Panama across aid practitioners, academics, and other key stakeholders, to conclude that though competition is apparent, Costa Rica and Panama are unable to leverage such competition to its advantage due to diplomatic ineptness and fundamental differences between their economies and that of Chinese leading to a notable discord between the grandeur of what is promised and its effects on the ground.

To extend this research, there are several potential avenues of development. Firstly, it was originally hoped that Costa Rica and Panama could form an interesting comparative case study. Most of the papers cited in the literature review investigate one recipient country only and as such comparative case studies are more limited; those that do offer comparative case studies do not dwell on the theoretical reasons why such countries benefit while others fail to take advantage of donor competition. This represents a notable gap in the literature as it could be indicative of why some recipients have been able to benefit from donor competition (e.g. Ethiopia, Tanzania, Cambodia, and Nicaragua) and why others have not (e.g. Mali, Malawi, Morocco and Indonesia) and whether this reflects failings in the donor nation or recipient, which will lead to appropriate policy recommendations. However, it quickly became apparent that the participants shared many of the same views, that many of the stakeholders interviewed had extensive experience working in relevant sectors across both countries, and that some of the multilateral donor institutions grouped Costa Rica and Panama as a collective and did not differentiate policy formation in this area. A better comparative case study would compare the findings of this chapter to stakeholders' views elsewhere in Latin America, in countries with longer established relationships with China and less strong relations with the USA, namely Chile, Brazil and Argentina.

Despite repeated and increasingly loud calls for greater donor collaboration, donor competition or lack of coordination still pervades ODA allocation today, reducing ODA effectiveness (Fuchs et al., 2015; Nunnenkamp et al., 2013; Powell & Findley, 2012). ODA competition, if pervasive, could reduce ODA effectiveness by duplicating already scarce development efforts on the part of donors (Olivié & Pérez, 2016); increasing recipient burden (Steinwand, 2015); and reducing donor accountability (Nunnenkamp et al., 2013). Hyperbole, emotion, and misinformation plague discussion of the Chinese role in international development and its impact upon other donors; as such, critical, unbiased, and nuanced perspectives of ODA, its motives, and the role of China in international development are key to understanding global ODA and its efficacy.

In understanding how donors compete with ODA across recipient countries, greater trilateral ODA cooperation can be pursued ensuring greater focus on international aid efforts upon recipient needs (Winters & Martinez, 2015). Should international development practitioners be aware of donor competition in ODA allocation, this can inspire greater donor coordination and ensuing aid effectiveness. Analysis of these responses can help comment on why Costa Rica and Panama have seemingly been unable to take advantage of competing donor interests in their countries, despite being well resourced and having some state capacity. The findings of this analysis are thus important for policymakers operating in the international development space.

From the perspective of recipients of ODA from competing donors, more human resources need to be spent on donor relationship and negotiation. Chinese attention and resource flows are noticed and a concern of more traditional regional partners such as the United States, and this can be an excellent motive for renegotiation of recipients' relations with partners from the Global North. In the absence of a grand development strategy and experienced policymakers in positions of trilateral communication, there is little hope to benefit from donor competition.

Rather than dismissing a lack of ODA effectiveness as the fault of corrupt and inept recipient governments, donor competition instead could be leading to a more inefficient and burdensome distribution of ODA resources across the developing world. Greater tripartite cooperation between traditional donors, emerging donors, and the recipients of these ODA efforts will inspire greater ODA effectiveness and lead to lasting and significant development progress. The role of Chinese ODA in disrupting the hegemony of traditional donors in international development efforts is more nuanced than the existing literature and media portray. Thus, analyses seeking to quantify and underscore donor competition in ODA allocation are a necessary first step to ensuring more reflexive donor practices going forward and improving future ODA effectiveness.

REFERENCES

Alesina, A., & Dollar, D. (2000). Who gives foreign aid to whom and why? *Journal of Economic Growth*, 5(1), 33–63. DOI: 10.1023/A:1009874203400

Benson, D., & Gong, Y. (2022). Aiding and Abetting: Is donor Official Development Assistance competition greatest in sectors key to Chinese interest? *Williamsburg, VA: AidData at William & Mary., Working Pa*(121).

Bobba, M., & Powell, A. (2006). Multilateral intermediation of foreign aid: what is the trade-off for donor countries? *Vol. Working Pa* (Issue 594). Inter-American Development Bank, Research Department, Washington, DC.

Bourguignon, F., & Platteau, J.-P. (2015). The hard challenge of aid coordination. *World Development*, 69, 86–97. DOI: 10.1016/j.worlddev.2013.12.011

Bräutigam, D. (2011). Aid 'with Chinese characteristics': Chinese foreign aid and development finance meet the OECD-DAC aid regime. *Journal of International Development*, 23(5), 752–764. DOI: 10.1002/jid.1798

Carlos Herrera, L., Montenegro, M., & Torres–Lista, V. (2020). *The'two Chinas' and Panama: an historical review of Panamanian relations with the People's Republic of China and Taiwan, 1903–2017.*

Chandy, L. (2011). It's complicated: The challenge of implementing the Paris Declaration on aid effectiveness. *Global Economy and Development at Brookings Blog, 22.*

Clist, P. (2011). 25 years of aid allocation practice: Whither selectivity? *World Development*, 39(10), 1724–1734. DOI: 10.1016/j.worlddev.2011.04.031

Córdoba Ramírez, T. M. (2005). *The significance of Costa Rica in Taiwan's diplomacy and the competition from Beijing.*

Coriat, A. (2017, August 7). Panama expects juicy investments from China. *El Siglo*, 1–1.

Custer, S., Dreher, A., Elston, T. B., Fuchs, A., Ghose, S., Lin, J., Malik, A., Parks, B. C., Russell, B., & Solomon, K. (2023). *Tracking Chinese development finance: An application of AidData's TUFF 3.0 methodology.* AidData.

Deutscher, E., & Fyson, S. (2008). Improving the effectiveness of aid. *Finance & Development*, 45(003).

Dreher, A., & Fuchs, A. (2015). Rogue aid? An empirical analysis of China's aid allocation. *The Canadian Journal of Economics. Revue Canadienne d'Economique*, 48(3), 988–1023. DOI: 10.1111/caje.12166

Elliott, S., & Reid, M. (2019). Low-income Black mothers parenting adolescents in the mass incarceration era: The long reach of criminalization. *American Sociological Review*, 84(2), 197–219. DOI: 10.1177/0003122419833386

Ellis, R. E. (2014). Costa Rica at a Crossroads in Courtship with Beijing. *China Brief*, 14, 10–13.

Faust, J., Grävingholt, J., & Ziaja, S. (2015). Foreign aid and the fragile consensus on state fragility. *Journal of International Relations and Development*, 18(4), 407–427. DOI: 10.1057/jird.2013.23

Feigenblatt, O. F. von. (2021). A case study on diplomatic competition between the People's Republic of China and the Republic of China (Taiwan): The experience of the Republic of Costa Rica from 1995 to 2010. *Dilemas Contemporáneos: Educación, Política y Valores, 9*(SPE1).

Fuchs, A., Nunnenkamp, P., & Öhler, H. (2015). Why donors of foreign aid do not coordinate: The role of competition for export markets and political support. *World Economy*, 38(2), 255–285. DOI: 10.1111/twec.12213

Guild, J. (2023, June 27). Is Indonesia's New High-Speed Rail Line Worth It? *The Diplomat*, 1–1. https://thediplomat.com/2023/06/is-indonesias-new-high-speed-rail-line-worth-it/

Hafiyer Al Halim, T. H. A. (2021). Two-Level Games Theory in Panama–Taiwan Diplomatic Relations. *Asia-Pacific Research in Social Sciences and Humanities Universitas Indonesia Conference (APRISH 2019)*, 147–153.

Humphrey, C., & Michaelowa, K. (2019a). China in Africa: Competition for traditional development finance institutions? *World Development*, 120, 15–28. DOI: 10.1016/j.worlddev.2019.03.014

Humphrey, C., & Michaelowa, K. (2019b). China in Africa: Competition for traditional development finance institutions? *World Development*, 120, 15–28. DOI: 10.1016/j.worlddev.2019.03.014

Kendall, N., & Thangaraj, M. (2013). Ethnography. In *Reviewing qualitative research in the social sciences* (pp. 82–107). Routledge.

Kilama, E. G. (2016). Evidences on donors competition in Africa: Traditional donors versus China. *Journal of International Development*, 28(4), 528–551. DOI: 10.1002/jid.3198

Knack, S., Rogers, H. F., & Eubank, N. (2010). *Aid quality and donor rankings*. The World Bank. DOI: 10.1596/1813-9450-5290

Kragelund, P. (2011). Back to BASICs? The rejuvenation of non-traditional donors' development cooperation with Africa. *Development and Change*, 42(2), 585–607. DOI: 10.1111/j.1467-7660.2011.01695.x

Kragelund, P. (2012). The Revival of Non-Traditional State Actors' Interests in Africa: Does it Matter for Policy Autonomy? *Development Policy Review*, 30(6), 703–718. DOI: 10.1111/j.1467-7679.2012.00595.x

Kragelund, P. (2014). 'Donors go home': Non-traditional state actors and the creation of development space in Zambia. *Third World Quarterly*, 35(1), 145–162. DOI: 10.1080/01436597.2014.868994

Kragelund, P. (2015a). Towards convergence and cooperation in the global development finance regime: Closing Africa's policy space? *Cambridge Review of International Affairs*, 28(2), 246–262. DOI: 10.1080/09557571.2014.974141

Kragelund, P. (2015b). Towards convergence and cooperation in the global development finance regime: Closing Africa's policy space? *Cambridge Review of International Affairs*, 28(2), 246–262. DOI: 10.1080/09557571.2014.974141

Lawson, M. L. (2013). *Foreign aid: international donor coordination of development assistance*. Congressional research service Washington, DC.

Lebovic, J. H. (2005). Donor positioning: Development assistance from the US, Japan, France, Germany, and Britain. *Political Research Quarterly*, 58(1), 119–126. DOI: 10.1177/106591290505800111

Leffert, M. (2007). *Costa Rica Boots Taiwan*. Welcomes China In Diplomatic Switch.

Li, H. (2005). Rivalry between Taiwan and the PRC in Latin America. *Journal of Chinese Political Science*, 10(2), 77–102. DOI: 10.1007/BF02877029

Liao, J. C., & Katada, S. N. (2021). Geoeconomics, easy money, and political opportunism: The perils under China and Japan's high-speed rail competition. *Contemporary Politics*, 27(1), 1–22. DOI: 10.1080/13569775.2020.1816626

Merriam, S. B., Johnson-Bailey, J., Lee, M.-Y., Kee, Y., Ntseane, G., & Muhamad, M. (2001). Power and positionality: Negotiating insider/outsider status within and across cultures. *International Journal of Lifelong Education*, 20(5), 405–416. DOI: 10.1080/02601370120490

Nunnenkamp, P., Öhler, H., & Thiele, R. (2013). Donor coordination and specialization: Did the Paris Declaration make a difference? *Review of World Economics*, 149(3), 537–563. DOI: 10.1007/s10290-013-0157-2

OECD. (2019). *Geographical Distribution of Financial Flows to Developing Countries 2019*. OECD., DOI: 10.1787/fin_flows_dev-2019-en-fr

Olivié, I., & Pérez, A. (2016). Why don't donor countries coordinate their aid? A case study of European donors in Morocco. *Progress in Development Studies*, 16(1), 52–64. DOI: 10.1177/1464993415608082

Powell, J., & Findley, M. G. (2012). *The swarm principle? A sub-national spatial analysis of donor coordination in sub-saharan Africa*. Mimeo, mimeo.

Rogers, R., Malancharuvil-Berkes, E., Mosley, M., Hui, D., & Joseph, G. O. (2005). Critical discourse analysis in education: A review of the literature. *Review of Educational Research*, 75(3), 365–416. DOI: 10.3102/00346543075003365

Roulston, K. (2010). Reflective interviewing: A guide to theory and practice. *Reflective Interviewing*, 1–216.

Rubin, H. J., & Rubin, I. S. (2005). *Continuing the design: Making the research credible*. Qualitative Interviewing.

Sato, J., Shiga, H., Kobayashi, T., & Kondoh, H. (2011). "Emerging donors" from a recipient perspective: An institutional analysis of foreign aid in Cambodia. *World Development*, 39(12), 2091–2104. DOI: 10.1016/j.worlddev.2011.04.014

Steinwand, M. C. (2015). Compete or coordinate? Aid fragmentation and lead donorship. *International Organization*, 69(2), 443–472. DOI: 10.1017/S0020818314000381

Swedlund, H. J. (2013). From donorship to ownership? Budget support and donor influence in Rwanda and Tanzania. *Public Administration and Development*, 33(5), 357–370. DOI: 10.1002/pad.1665

Swedlund, H. J. (2017). Is China eroding the bargaining power of traditional donors in Africa? *International Affairs*, 93(2), 389–408. DOI: 10.1093/ia/iiw059

Thaler, K. M., & Mosinger, E. (2022). Nicaragua: Doubling Down on Dictatorship. *Journal of Democracy*, 33(2), 133–146. DOI: 10.1353/jod.2022.0023

Urcuyo, C. (2021, June 19). Despite U.S. Pressure, China's Presence in Central America is Growing. *Latinoamérica21*, 1–1.

Walshe Roussel, L. (2013). The changing donor landscape in Nicaragua: Rising competition enhances ownership and fosters cooperation. *Journal of International Development*, 25(6), 802–818. DOI: 10.1002/jid.2932

Winters, M. S. (2012). The obstacles to foreign aid harmonization: Lessons from decentralization support in Indonesia. *Studies in Comparative International Development*, 47(3), 316–341. DOI: 10.1007/s12116-012-9114-7

Winters, M. S., & Martinez, G. (2015). The role of governance in determining foreign aid flow composition. *World Development*, 66, 516–531. DOI: 10.1016/j.worlddev.2014.09.020

World Bank. (2020). *Doing Business 2020.*

World Bank. (2021). [The World Bank.]. *World Development Indicators*, •••, 2021.

Zeitz, A. (2020). Emulation or Differentiation? China's Development Finance and Traditional Donor Aid in Developing Countries. *The Review of International Organizations*, 16(4), 933–938. DOI: 10.1007/s11558-021-09429-x

APPENDIX

Table A1: Participants Interviewed

Interviewee	Institutional Affiliation
001	International Finance Corporation
002	Panamanian Ministry of Foreign Affairs
003	Panamanian Ministry of Maritime Affairs
004	University of Costa Rica
005	Central American Institute of Business Administration
006	China Harbour Engineering Company
007	University of Costa Rica
008	University of Puget Sound
009	University of Antwerp
010	Panama Centre of Promotion of Trade & Investment Asia Pacific-Latin America
011	University of Costa Rica
012	The China Signal
013	Central American Institute of Business Administration
014	De Castro & Robles
015	University of Costa Rica
016	United Nations Development Programme Panama

Chapter 4
Tax Evasion, Bribery, and Money Laundering in Latin America and the Caribbean:
Forms, Causes, Effects, and Remedies

Duane Windsor
https://orcid.org/0000-0003-0406-1030
Rice University, USA

ABSTRACT

This chapter examines information and analysis concerning tax evasion, bribery, and money laundering in Latin America and the Caribbean as corruption practiced by individuals, businesses, public officials, and criminal gangs. There is a wide range of conditions across the region, defined geographically as all countries or dependencies south of the United States of America (U.S.). The inquiry considers forms, causes, effects, and remedies associated with private-sector (commercial) and public-sector (political) corruption. The chapter assembles information sources and literature for comparison across countries of the region and then with other areas of the world to understand conditions in Latin America and the Caribbean. The region is a rich source of information about global networks for tax evasion, as revealed in revelations from the Panama Papers and similar sources. Several locations in the Caribbean are significant tax havens for avoidance and evasion.

DOI: 10.4018/979-8-3693-3763-9.ch004

INTRODUCTION

Private sector and public sector corruption in Latin America and the Caribbean in the multiple forms of tax evasion, bribery and its twin extortion, and money laundering are significant dimensions of understanding the set of countries south of the United States of America (U.S.). Financial crimes in that set of countries are significant to the U.S. due to illegal migration from the south (Remache Lopez, 2024) and drug and human trafficking. Tax evasion is the unlawful reduction of tax liabilities, in contrast to legal tax avoidance practiced through changes in economic behavior. Bribery is the effort to influence decisions by offering something of value. Extortion is the demand for bribes. A facilitating payment is a relatively small private payment to a low-level governmental employee to expedite otherwise legally required action. Money laundering is the illegal conversion of illicit gains into clean assets, whether cash or property.

This inquiry into corruption and other financial crimes separates for comparison purposes among ten countries of Latin South America (Spanish-speaking Argentina, Bolivia, Chile, Colombia, Ecuador, Paraguay, Peru, Uruguay, and Venezuela and Portuguese-speaking Brazil), seven Spanish-speaking countries of Central America (Costa Rica, El Salvador, Guatemala, Honduras, Nicaragua, and Panama) and Mexico, and the Caribbean (with multiple languages). The guiding principle is more than just geographical. Guyana, Suriname, and French Guiana are on the continent of South America, but by language and history they are associated with the Caribbean, as is Belize in Central America. Mexico, grouped here with Central America, geographically and economically might be part of North America with Canada and the U.S., as in the trilateral North American Free Trade Agreement (NAFTA) in operation during 1994-2020. The United States-Mexico-Canada Agreement (USMCA) succeeded NAFTA in 2020.

This chapter uses the broadest definition of the Caribbean. The Caribbean Community (CARICOM), expanding from a 1973 treaty with four members, includes Guyana, Suriname, and Belize. Bermuda, together with some other British territories, is an associate member. Puerto Rico is an observer member. The Caribbean is a mix of independent countries speaking English, French, Spanish, Surinamese Dutch, or Haitian Creole (French), and British, Dutch, and French dependencies. The Commonwealth of Puerto Rico is an unincorporated island territory of the U.S. The two official languages are Spanish and English. The countries with official languages other than Spanish or Portuguese group politically with the Caribbean: French Guiana, Guyana, and Suriname on the continent of South America but officially speaking different languages (French, English, and Surinamese Dutch, respectively); and Belize (English) in Central America.

In this chapter, Belize (English-speaking) groups partly with the Caribbean and partly with Central America, depending on the purpose of the data analysis. Belize is geographically part of Central America but politically part of the Caribbean.

As a partly political conception, the Caribbean is broader than the West Indies in that the latter means strictly the islands between the Atlantic Ocean and the American continents, while the Caribbean can include Belize from Central America and French Guiana, Guyana, and Suriname from South America, and by political association Bermuda which is geographically east of North Carolina. The West Indies includes independent countries and island dependencies of France, the Netherlands, and the United Kingdom. French dependencies include Guadeloupe, Martinique, Saint Martin, and Saint Barthelemy, together with French Guiana on the continent of South America. Netherlands dependencies include Curacao, Aruba, Sint Maarten, and Caribbean Netherlands. Suriname was a Dutch territory until 1975. British dependencies include the Cayman Islands, Turks and Caicos Islands, the British Virgin Islands, Anguilla, Montserrat, and Bermuda. Guyana became a U.K. dominion in 1966 and a republic in 1970 as a member of the Commonwealth of Nations. In addition to Puerto Rico (a commonwealth), the other American dependency is the U.S. Virgin Islands (purchased from Denmark in 1917).

The region's population is about 438 million in Latin South America, 181 million in Central America and Mexico, and 46 million (roughly) in the Caribbean, including Guyana and Suriname. Brazil alone is about 49.4% of the population of Latin South America; Mexico alone is about 71.1% of the population of Central America and Mexico. In combination, Haiti, the Dominican Republic, and Cuba account for about 72.8% of the population of the Caribbean region. Table 1, in the next section, provides details and sources.

The second section provides basic information about corruption in the region (Tables 1, 2, and 3). The third section looks at some specific issues and problems of corruption. The fourth section concerns tax evasion and tax avoidance, including tax havens. The fifth section concerns money laundering in the region. The sixth section examines anti-corruption efforts. The final section discusses future directions for studying corruption and anti-corruption in Latin America and the Caribbean.

CORRUPTION IN LATIN AMERICA AND THE CARIBBEAN

Belize appears in Tables 1 and 2, grouped with Central America and Mexico for population and gross domestic product per capita (GDP p/c) reporting, but without a 2023 Transparency International Corruption Perceptions Index (CPI) score. Belize does not appear in Table 3 because the country does not have a 2023 CPI score.

Yansura, Mavrellis, Kumar, and Helms (2021) reported on financial crime conditions in Latin America and the Caribbean by country and for the whole region. The report depends on 250 expert interviews. The authors report that, generally, the region is quite violent and shows large volumes of illicit gains laundered through various channels. Quoting the report description, sources of illegal gains include "drug trafficking, mineral trafficking, corruption, and trafficking in persons and smuggling of migrants." There is prevalent "money laundering, trade-based money laundering [TBML] and terrorism financing." Corruption is the dominant source, followed by other forms of financial crime.

Corruption Perceptions Index Scores by Country within Three Groups

Tables 1, 2, and 3 use Transparency International's 2023 CPI scores to provide a general picture of corruption in three groups of the region. Overall, "Despite improvement in some countries, Sub-Saharan Africa maintains the lowest average at 33, with democracy and the rule of law under pressure.... lack of judicial independence and weak rule of law are enabling widespread impunity in the Americas" (T.I., 2024, Paragraph 1). Table 3 data indicate an estimated average for the region's 30 countries with CPI scores of about 40-41, above Sub-Saharan Africa. Nine countries are above the midpoint (50), and seven are below at or below 33 (the average for Sub-Saharan Africa).

Transparency International (T.I.) provides annual information on its Corruption Perceptions Index (CPI), launched in 1995. In 2023, the CPI scores appear for 180 countries and territories, principally Hong Kong (a dependency of China). The CPI draws on expert assessments and surveys of business people and country experts to develop estimated scores from 100 (perfectly clean) to 0 (perfectly corrupt). In 2023, the highest score was 90 (Denmark) and the lowest score was 11 (Somalia). Even if a country score involves some confidence range, the difference between the highest and lowest is marked. Although "perceptions" is the crucial term, CPI information provides a general picture of corruption conditions worldwide.

Table 1 displays CPI scores in a structure that allows comparison of countries across three groupings: Latin South America (excluding Guyana, Suriname, and French Guiana), Central America and Mexico, and the Caribbean. Regarding CPI,

Uruguay, Chile, Barbados, Bahamas, and Saint Vincent rank reasonably highly. Cosa Rica is the least corrupt country in Central America, at about the level of Dominica, Saint Lucia, and Grenada in the Caribbean, but below Uruguay and Chile. All other countries in the whole region fall below the CPI=50 midpoint score. Jamaica, Cuba, and Trinidad rank above Colombia, Guyana, and Suriname. Argentina, Brazil, Dominican Republic, Ecuador, and Peru score in the 37-33 range. Mexico and El Salvador scored 31, while Bolivia and Paraguay scored in the 29-28 range. Guatemala and Honduras drop to 23, while Nicaragua and Haiti drop to 17. Venezuela is the most corrupt country in the region at 13 (see U.S. General Accounting Office, 2023).

Table 1. 2023 CPI Comparison by Country within Latin South America, Central America and Mexico, and Caribbean

CPI	Country	GDP p/c ($ U.S.)	Population (millions) 437.9 *	CPI	Country	GDP p/c ($ U.S.)	Population (millions) 180.7 **	CPI	Country	GDP p/c ($ U.S.)	Population (millions) 46 (est.)
LATIN SOUTH AMERICA (excluding Guyana, Suriname, French Guyana)				CENTRAL AMERICA AND MEXICO (no CPI score for Belize)				CARIBBEAN (including Guyana, Suriname, dependencies) ##			
73	Uruguay	20,795	3.4	NS	Belize	6984	0.4	69	Barbados	20,239	0.3
66	Chile	15,355	19.6					64	Bahamas	31,458	0.4
								60	St. Vincent^	9125	0.1
								56	Dominica	8351	73,000
				55	Costa Rica	13,365	5.2	55	Saint Lucia	13,031	0.2
								53	Grenada	9689	0.1
								44	Jamaica	6045	2.8
								42#	Cuba	9500	11.2
								42	Trinidad	19,629	1.5
40	Colombia	6624	52.0					40	Guyana	18,199	0.8
								40	Suriname	5859	0.6
37	Argentina	13,651	45.8								
36	Brazil*	8918	216.4								
34	Ecuador	6391	18.2	35	Panama	17,358	4.5	35	Dom. Rep.^	10,111	11.3
33	Peru	7126	34.4	31	Mexico**	11,500	128.5				
29	Bolivia	3600	12.4	31	El Salvador	5127	6.4				
28	Paraguay	6153	6.9								
				23	Guatemala	5473	18.1				
				23	Honduras	3040	10.6				
13#	Venezuela	15,976	28.8	17	Nicaragua	2255	7.0	17	Haiti	1748	11.7

SOURCES: CPI: Transparency International, https://www.transparency.org/en/cpi/2023. Population: www.worldometers.info/world-population/population-by-country/ based on U.N. Department of Economic and Social Affairs, Population Division, World Population Prospects: The 2022 Revision. Latin South America and Central America and Mexico summed. Caribbean estimated. GDP p/c in current U.S. dollars: https://data.worldbank.org/indicator/NY.GDP.PCAP.CD?view=map

NOTES: All of Latin South America and Central America and Mexico is Spanish-speaking except for Brazil (Portuguese) and Belize (English). The Caribbean nations are English-speaking except for Cuba, Dominican Republic (Spanish), Dominica (French), Suriname (Surinamese Dutch), and Haiti (Haitian Creole French]). Dependencies use the home country languages (American, English, Dutch, or French).

* Brazil is about 49.4% of the total population of Latin South America.

* * Mexico is about 71.1% of the total population of Central America and Mexico.

Venezuela GPD p/c 2014 (no subsequent data); Cuba 2020 (no subsequent data).

No CPI scores in the Caribbean for Antigua and Barbuda (94,000 population, $19,920 GDP p/c); St. Kitts and Nevis (48,000 population, $20,262 GDP p/c); Commonwealth of Puerto Rico (3.3 million population, $35,209 GDP p/c). Puerto Rico has the highest GDP p/c in the grouping, followed by the Bahamas at 31,458.

^Saint Vincent and the Grenadines; Dominican Republic.

Table 1 provides each country's estimated population and estimated GDP p/c. There are three observable if weak patterns. First, the largest population countries (Argentina, Brazil, Colombia, and Mexico) are more corrupt but not the most corrupt (Bolivia, Paraguay, Venezuela, and four countries of Central America). Second, countries with higher GDP p/c (Uruguay, Chile, Costa Rica, Barbados, and Bahamas) tend to have lower corruption scores. Panama appears to be an exception in having the highest GDP p/c in Central America, associated with the Panama Canal and related trade activities, but scoring in CPI at the Dominican Republic and Ecuador level. There is more variation in the Caribbean countries. Corruption is associated with lower GDP p/c in Latin South America and Central America. Haiti has the lowest GDP p/c in the region, followed by Nicaragua. Trinidad and Guyana have lower CPI scores that do not match relatively high GDP p/c, but as with Venezuela and Suriname, the explanation may involve oil and gas extraction. Argentina's GDP p/c is the third highest in Latin America after Uruguay and Chile, but corruption is much higher in Argentina. Argentina has suffered from persistent high inflation for decades, including periods of hyperinflation (Perelman, 2024).

Inequality Measures in Relationship to Corruption

Statista Research Department (2024, March 1) points to the significant disparity in the region's income and wealth distribution. Table 2 provides information on inequality from the World Inequality Database (WID). That source provides rough estimates for the proportion of income (and some other measures) held by the top 1%, top 10%, and bottom 50% of the population by country. The higher the proportion for the top 1% or top 10% and the lower the proportion for the bottom 50%, the greater the income inequality in a country. The table provides data for Latin South America (ten countries), Central America and Mexico (seven countries plus Belize), and five selected countries of the Caribbean. The lefthand column reports data alphabetically by country. The central column sorts the data by the highest bottom 50% and then the lowest top 1% to provide a sense of inequality from the bottom up. The righthand column sorts the data by the highest top 1% and then the highest top 10% to provide a sense of inequality from the top down. Several countries receive identical proportional distributions in each category due to regional imputation rather than country-specific information.

In Latin South America, Argentina has the least inequality, appearing at the top of the central column (highest bottom 50%) and the bottom of the righthand column (lowest top 1% and 10%). In Central America, El Salvador – the smallest country – has the lowest inequality, appearing at the top and bottom of the two columns. In the Caribbean, Cuba – a communist dictatorship – has the least inequality on the same basis, followed by the Dominican Republic. In Latin South America, Uruguay and Ecuador appear to be the next best. In contrast, Chile has the worst inequality, appearing at the bottom of the central column and near the top of the righthand column. Peru has the highest 1% proportion. Central America, Mexico and Costa Rica have about the worst income distributions, but they have a high concentration in the top 10%. For comparison, New Zealand (11.6%, 34.6%, 18.6% by category) and Canada (10.6%, 35.2%, 16.9%) have much less inequality. For the U.S. the indicators are 20.9% (higher than the countries in Table 2 except for Chile 23.7% and Peru 25.2%), 48.3% (lower than most of the countries in Table 2 except for Uruguay, Ecuador, Argentina, El Salvador, the Dominican Republic, and Cuba), and 10.4% equivalent to Ecuador 10,3% (higher than most of the countries in Table 2 except for Argentina, Uruguay, Dominican Republic, and Cuba).

Table 2. Inequality Measures in Relationship to CPI: Income Shares for Top 1%, Top 10%, Bottom 50% of the Population

Country	1%	10%	50%	Country	1%	10%	50%	CPI	Country	1%	10%	50%	CPI
By Country Alphabetically				Highest Bottom 50%, Then Lowest Top 1%					Highest Top 1%, Then Highest Top 10%				
LATIN SOUTH AMERICA: ten countries excluding French Guiana, Guyana, and Suriname													
Argentina	13.4	43.9	14.7	*Argentina*	13.4	43.9	14.7	37	Peru	25.2	57.3	8.8	33
Bolivia*	18.7	52.4	9.8	*Uruguay*	17.0	47.2	14.1	73	Chile	23.7	59.0	6.8	66
Brazil	19.7	56.8	9.0	*Ecuador*	14.4	44.8	10.3	34	Brazil	19.7	56.8	9.0	36
Chile	23.7	59.0	6.8	Bolivia	18.7	52.4	9.8	29	Colombia	19.3	60.6	6.9	40
Colombia	19.3	60.6	6.9	Paraguay	18.7	52.4	9.8	28	Bolivia	18.7	52.4	9.8	29
Ecuador	14.4	44.8	10.3	Venezuela	18.7	52.4	9.8	13	Paraguay	18.7	52.4	9.8	28
Paraguay*	18.7	52.4	9.8	Brazil	19.7	56.8	9.0	36	Venezuela	18.7	52.4	9.8	13
Peru	25.2	57.3	8.8	Peru	25.2	57.3	8.8	33	*Uruguay*	17.0	47.2	14.1	73
Uruguay	17.0	47.2	14.1	Colombia	19.3	60.6	6.9	40	*Ecuador*	14.4	44.8	10.3	34
Venezuela*	18.7	52.4	9.8	Chile	23.7	59.0	6.8	66	*Argentina*	13.4	43.9	14.7	37
CENTRAL AMERICA AND MEXICO: seven countries and Belize (no CPI score)													
Belize*	18.7	52.4	9.8	*El Salvador*	12.6	42.7	10.0	31	Mexico	26.8	64.6	6.0	31
Costa Rica	20.9	57.5	4.9	Belize	18.7	52.4	9.8	NS	Costa Rica	20.9	57.5	4.9	55
El Salvador	12.6	42.7	10.0	Guatemala	18.7	52.4	9.8	23	Belize	18.7	52.4	9.8	NS
Guatemala*	18.7	52.4	9.8	Honduras	18.7	52.4	9.8	23	Guatemala	18.7	52.4	9.8	23
Honduras*	18.7	52.4	9.8	Nicaragua	18.7	52.4	9.8	17	Honduras	18.7	52.4	9.8	23
Mexico	26.8	64.6	6.0	Panama	18.7	52.4	9.8	35	Nicaragua	18.7	52.4	9.8	17
Nicaragua*	18.7	52.4	9.8	Mexico	26.8	64.6	6.0	31	Panama	18.7	52.4	9.8	35
Panama*	18.7	52.4	9.8	Costa Rica	20.9	57.5	4.9	55	*El Salvador*	12.6	42.7	10.0	31
CARIBBEAN: five selected countries													
Bahamas#	18.7	52.4	9.8	*Cuba*	14.9	45.3	13.1	42	Bahamas	18.7	52.4	9.8	64
Cuba	14.9	45.3	13.1	*Domin. Rep.*	15.3	47.8	10.9	35	Jamaica	18.7	52.4	9.8	44
Domin. Rep.	15.3	47.8	10.9	Bahamas	18.7	52.4	9.8	64	Haiti	18.7	52.4	9.8	17
Haiti#	18.7	52.4	9.8	Jamaica	18.7	52.4	9.8	44	*Domin. Rep.*	15.3	47.8	10.9	35
Jamaica#	18.7	52.4	9.8	Haiti	18.7	52.4	9.8	17	*Cuba*	14.9	45.3	13.1	42

SOURCES: World Inequality Database: https://wid.world/ based on surveys and tax data or regional imputation.

Table 1 for CPI. Higher CPI lists tied distributions.
NOTES: Domin. Rep. for the Dominican Republic.
* Same income distributions due to regional imputation.

Same income distributions due to regional imputation; imputation procedure also used for Cuba with different findings

Uruguay, the cleanest country on CPI, is next best for the highest bottom 50% but not as strong in the top 1% and top 10%. Chile performs poorly on the split between the top 1% (highest) and the bottom 50% (lowest) but better when considering the top 10%. In Central America, El Salvador has the least inequity (split between top and bottom). In contrast, Mexico and Costa Rica have the highest top 1% and lowest bottom 50% measures, reflecting considerably greater inequity. Guyana and Suriname have identical reported distributions in the Caribbean as for the Bahamas, Haiti, and Jamaica. Cuba, a communist state, has the best equality in terms of distribution, followed possibly by the Dominican Republic.

Correspondence to CPI in Latin South America weakens due to the unusual positioning of Argentina, which has the best income equality but high corruption. However, Uruguay, the cleanest country on CPI, does well regarding income equality. Interpreting correspondence is affected by the condition that corruption is commonplace throughout the entire region. Similarly, Costa Rica appears well on CPI – although considerably more corrupt than Uruguay – but has unequal income distribution, as does Mexico. The Caribbean involves a wide diversity of countries and dependencies. The Bahamas is cleaner than Costa Rica, but the income distributions for the five countries in Table 2 appear tightly grouped due to regional imputation. Cuba is the exception, with the relatively best income distribution, but it is not cleaner on CPI than Jamaica.

Regional Corruption in a Global Perspective

Table 3 places countries and dependencies of the region in a global context. There is an extensive range of perceived corruption throughout Latin America and the Caribbean. Uruguay is at the level of Belgium and Japan (CPI=73). Barbados (69) is at the level of the U.S. and U.K. (71). Chile and the Bahamas fall between Taiwan and South Korea or Israel. Saint Vincent is at the level of Latvia and Spain (60). Dominica is at the level of Italy and Slovenia (56). Costa Rica and Saint Lucia are at 55. There is then a dividing line at about the CPI=50 mark. Grenada (53) is just above this dividing line, while Jamaica (44) is between Bulgaria and Benin. Most of the other countries then receive scores of 42 or below. Cuba (42) matches Hungary. Colombia, Guyana, and Suriname match Tanzania (40). The large countries of Colombia, Argentina, and Brazil fall at or below 40 (Ukraine). El Salvador and Mexico, just below Ecuador and Peru, match Kenya and Togo at 31. Bolivia matches Pakistan at 29, just above Paraguay. Guatemala and Honduras match Iraq (23).

Table 3. 2023 CPI Rankings, Countries in Latin America and the Caribbean in **Bold Font**, *High Score Asian Countries (above 70) in Italics Font*

90-82	**Denmark, Finland, New Zealand, Norway, *Singapore*, Sweden, Switzerland**
79-75	Netherlands, Germany, Luxembourg, Ireland, Canada, Estonia, Australia, *Hong Kong*
73	Belgium, *Japan,* **Uruguay**
72-71	Iceland, Austria, France, *Seychelles,* United Kingdom (U.K.)
69	**Barbados**, United States of America (U.S.)
68-67	Bhutan, UAE, Taiwan
66	**Chile**
64	**Bahamas**, Cabo Verde
63-61	South Korea, Israel, Lithuania, Portugal
60	Latvia, **Saint Vincent and the Grenadines**, Spain
59-57	Botswana, Qatar, Czechia (Czech Republic)
56	**Dominica**, Italy, Slovenia
55	**Costa Rica, Saint Lucia**
54	Poland, Slovakia
53	Cyprus, Georgia, **Grenada**, Rwanda
52-46	Fiji, Saudi Arabia, Malta, Mauritius, Croatia, Malaysia, Greece, Namibia, Vanuatu, Armenia, Jordan, Kuwait, Montenegro, Romania
45	Bulgaria, São Tomé and Príncipe
44	**Jamaica**
43	Benin, Ghana, Oman, Senegal, Solomon Islands, Timor-Leste
42	Bahrain, China, **Cuba**, Hungary, Moldova, North Macedonia, **Trinidad and Tobago**
41	Burkina Faso, Kosovo, South Africa, Vietnam
40	**Colombia**, Cote d'Ivoire, **Guyana, Suriname**, Tanzania, Tunisia
39-38	India, Kazakhstan, Lesotho, Maldives, Morocco (38)
37	**Argentina**, Albania, Belarus, Ethiopia, Gambia, Zambia
36	Algeria, **Brazil**, Serbia, Ukraine
35	Bosnia and Herzegovina, **Dominican Republic**, Egypt, Nepal, **Panama**, Sierra Leone, Thailand
34	**Ecuador**, Indonesia, Malawi, Philippines, Sri Lanka, Turkey (Türkiye)
33-32	**Peru**, Uzbekistan, Niger (32)

continued on following page

Table 3. Continued

90-82	**Denmark, Finland, New Zealand, Norway, *Singapore,* Sweden, Switzerland**
31	**El Salvador**, Kenya, **Mexico**, Togo
30	Djibouti, Eswatini, Mauritania
29	**Bolivia**, Pakistan, Papua New Guinea
28	Gabon, Laos, Mali, **Paraguay**
27-24	Cameroon, Guinea, Kyrgyzstan, Russia, Uganda, Liberia, Madagascar, Mozambique, Nigeria, Bangladesh, Central African Republic, Iran, Lebanon, Zimbabwe
23	Azerbaijan, **Guatemala, Honduras**, Iraq
22-21	Cambodia, Congo, Guinea-Bissau, Eritrea (21)
20	Afghanistan, Burundi, Chad, Comoros, Democratic Republic of the Congo, Myanmar, Sudan, Tajikistan
18	Libya, Turkmenistan
17-16	**Haiti**, North Korea, **Nicaragua**, Yemen (16)
13, 11	South Sudan (13), Syria (13), **Venezuela (13)**, Somalia (11)

SOURCE: Transparency International, https://www.transparency.org/en/cpi/2023

Haiti (17), Nicaragua (17), and Venezuela (13) rate very low. Cuba (Castro regime), Nicaragua (Ortega regime), and Venezuela (Maduro regime), an oil-producing country, are authoritarian regimes, whether communist, leftist, or socialist. Colombia and Haiti have been in a state of internal strife for years, with gangs challenging the government in Haiti. Poverty may be a partial explanation for and a partial effect of authoritarianism.

The home countries of the dependencies all rank in the top quartile of CPI scores: the Netherlands 79, France (72), and the United Kingdom (71), a little above the U.S. (69). Whether these scores effectively translate to the dependencies is challenging to gauge. For example, Puerto Rico may or may not have greater corruption (Atiles, 2024a; Florido, Janse, & Rampton, 2022). T.I. (n.d.) reported scores of 62-63 in the period 2012-2013-2014. In July 2019, the governor resigned during widespread protests concerning in part corruption.

No country is entirely corruption-free. The highest CPI in 2023 was 90 (Denmark) of 100 possible points. The higher scores generally occur in Europe, North America, Singapore, Australia, and New Zealand (85). Scandinavia is usually clean, but the largest money laundering scandal concerning funds flowing out of Russia through Estonia into Scandinavian banks occurred in that generally clean set of countries. Uruguay (73) belongs in this set. China (42), India (39), Ukraine (36), Indonesia (34), and Russia (26) are corrupt to an increasing degree, as ordered here. Like

Latin South America, Central America, and Mexico, there is a range of corruption across Africa, the Middle East, and Southeast Asia. In general, with the exceptions of Guatemala, Honduras, Haiti, Nicaragua, and Venezuela, most countries in the region fall into a middle range below the CPI=50 midpoint but above the CPI=25 lowest quartile. Thus, countries range from reasonably clean (Uruguay and Chile), like much of the OECD, to terribly corrupt (Guatemala, Honduras, Haiti, Nicaragua, and Venezuela) in company with Equatorial Guinea, North Korea, Yemen, South Sudan, Syria, and Somalia. The last four are persistent conflict zones; North Korea is a communist dictatorship mobilized for war.

SPECIFIC CASES AND PROBLEMS OF CORRUPTION

This section examines some specific cases and problems of corruption, beginning with FDI effects of corruption and inequality, then looking at civil strife in Colombia and the drug war in Mexico, and corruption in and out of Brazil through Petrobras and Odebrecht.

FDI Effects of Corruption and Inequality

One might hypothesize that continuing economic development with foreign direct investment (FDI) should reduce corruption over time, pointing to Uruguay, Chile, Costa Rica, and the Bahamas as instances. The relationship among economic development, FDI, democracy, and corruption remains a matter of considerable empirical debate among scholars. Wu, Delios, Chen, and Wang (2024) replicate in three ways the findings of four key studies cited in the article. The authors conclude that country-level inquiry best supports theorizing about the effects of corruption on economic activity. However, corruption has different dimensions requiring further study.

A basic thesis in the empirical literature has been about the balance between the "grabbing hand" (diverting FDI to corrupt purposes) and the "helping hand" (FDI helps promote economic and democratic development). A problem is whether corruption can help facilitate business transactions in a way that serves to attract FDI. Khalid (2024) reviews the scholarship (theoretical and empirical) concerning the corruption-growth and corruption-investment arguments. An empirical analysis in a sample of 40 countries concludes that the "grabbing hand" explanation holds in the 20 least corrupt countries, and the "helping hand" explanation holds in the 20 most corrupt countries. Within the 20 most corrupt countries, the relationship for corruption-growth and corruption-investment is non-linear.

A study of corruption and income inequality in post-Soviet countries concludes that both negatively impact sustainable development. In this context, both unemployment and trade liberalization also have adverse effects. However, FDI positively supports sustainable development (Badur, Yilmaz, & Sensoy, 2024).

Chebli and Saidi (2024) assessed a global panel of 46 middle-income countries for the period 1996-2016 using a multivariate panel model with Granger causality testing to assess causal direction. The authors conclude that political instability undermines a positive relationship among FDI, gross fixed capital formation (GFCF), and GDP growth. The Granger causality test reports a bidirectional relationship given the occurrence of political instability and corruption. The authors also report a unidirectional causality from the economic measures (FDI, GDP, and GFCF) to corruption and from government effectives to FDI and GFCF.

For 1983-1999, for a panel of 21 home and 59 host countries, Egger and Winner (2006), focusing on a knowledge-capital model of multinational business activity, reported a negative relationship between corruption and FDI. The explanation was that the grabbing hand outweighed the helping hand. Corruption impeded FDI in developed but not in less developed economies. Those authors also reported a decreasing effect of corruption over time.

Two studies report interesting findings for countries in Sub-Saharan Africa. One (Gossel, 2024) uses a methodology of fixed effects and a system Generalised Method of Moments (GMM) with a panel of 38 countries (1990-2018). The author reports that FDI has no direct effect on inequality, while democracy does directly reduce disparities. Democracy operates independently of FDI or resource endowment (such as oil). FDI can reduce inequality once there is a moderate level of democracy. Thus, democracy and not FDI is the facilitator of inequality reduction. The second study (Yahyaoui, 2024) uses a panel vector autoregressive (PVAR) model and an impulse response function tool for 1996-2016. In this analysis, FDI promotes economic growth with the effect reduced by corruption. The implied policy is that reducing corruption will support the efficient application of FDI to economic growth.

Civil Strife in Colombia and Drug War in Mexico

Constitutional government in much of the region is a fragile institution, and criminal gangs and violence are endemic in much of the region (Weitzman, Caudillo, & Levy, 2024). Colombia has been through a prolonged civil war between conservatives and radicals for control of the country. Mexico is in a long-term battle with the drug cartels. In Colombia, corruption is not purely about civil strife and drug cartels (see Keefer & Roseth, 2024).

Chiquita Brands International (formerly United Fruit Co. until 1984) voluntarily disclosed in 2004 that a banana subsidiary had paid protection money during 1997-2004 amounting to more than an estimated $1.7 million to a right-wing terrorist organization Autodefensas Unidas de Colombia (AUC) (in English, United Self-Defense Groups of Colombia) (Teagarden & Schotter, 2010). Chiquita pleaded guilty in a U.S. Department of Justice investigation and paid a fine of $25 million for providing material support to a terrorist group. In 2007, various plaintiffs brought civil lawsuits for damages. Complicated legal arguments have involved the Torture Victim Protection Act (TVPA), Alien Tort Statute (ATS), Anti-Terrorism Act, and Colombia law applied in a federal court (Nanos, 2022). Earthrights (n.d.) ultimately sponsored a set of plaintiffs as "bellwether cases" in a federal district court, with trial set to begin in April 2024.

In 2006, the government of Mexico declared war on the various drug cartels in the country. Mexico is the principal throughway for moving illegal drugs into the U.S., with heroin and methamphetamine produced in Mexico, cocaine in Colombia, and fentanyl in China – all moving through Mexico. Since 2006, there have been more than 360,000 homicides in Mexico. The U.S. Drug Enforcement Agency (DEA) reports the following cartels in operation: Beltrán-Leyva Organization, Guerreros Unidos, Gulf, Jalisco New Generation, Juárez, La Familia Michoacána, Los Rojos, Los Zetas, and Sinaloa. All information in this paragraph comes from the Council on Foreign Relations (2022), which reports that "Cartels use a portion of their vast profits to pay off judges, officers, and politicians." The cartels reportedly have expanded into human trafficking across the U.S. border.

Corruption in and out of Brazil

The most prominent corruption scandals in Brazil and Latin America to date have involved Petrobras (Petróleo Brasileiro S.A.), a state-owned Brazilian petroleum multinational founded in 1953 as a legal monopoly, and Odebrecht SA (Novonor), a diversified conglomerate and the biggest construction company in Latin America stemming from a 1944 company (El-Hage, 2019; Pontes & Anselmo, 2022; Shiel & Chavkin, 2019). Braskem, the largest petrochemical firm in Latin America, is also implicated as an Odebrecht subsidiary (established in 2002). Odebrecht Agroindustrial (established in 2007) handles energy, ethanol, and sugar products. Petrobras controls some assets in Argentina, Bolivia, Ecuador, Peru, and Argentina following a 2002 acquisition of an Argentine company. Odebrecht operates throughout much of Latin America. "In 2010, the Swiss business school IMD chose Odebrecht, a

Brazilian conglomerate, as the world's best family business" (Campos, Engel, Fischer, & Galetovic, 2021, p. 171).

Operation Car Wash ("Operação Lava Jato" in Portuguese), also known as "Petrolão" ("big oil" in Portuguese) due to the connection with Petrobras, began literally with an allegation of money laundering through a car wash in March 2014 and became a widespread and politically controversial investigation (Lagunes & Svejnar, 2020; Mota Prado & De Assis Machado, 2021; Voss, Carter, & Warren, 2023) into Petrobras and Odebrecht as the tip of an iceberg of political corruption in state-owned enterprises in Brazil with various politicians including more than one former president implicated. The Brazilian judiciary has been unraveling convictions (Pooler, 2024). President Luiz I. Lula da Silva (2003-2010) was convicted of corruption and imprisoned but had his sentence overturned in 2021, allowing him to be reelected president for a third term in 2022 (Pooler, 2024). One Supreme Court justice retired and became the minister of justice in the Lula government. One estimate identified damage from corruption in Brazil at 17.8% of the value of oil refineries built, with corrupting agents receiving 13.7% of the damage (Sallaberry, Quaesner, Costa, & Flach, 2020). Some of the corruption went to various political parties. There were allegations that Odebrecht and other Brazilian construction firms operated a cartel to share government contracts (Portugal & Alves de Moraes, 2024). Odebrecht and Odebrecht family members reportedly appeared in the Paradise Papers. Both the Petrobras and Odebrecht scandals (Pohlmann, Valarini, Trombini, & Jorge, 2019; Zysman-Quirós, 2019) resulted in U.S. prosecutions (Bray & Reed, 2018; U.S. Department of Justice, 2016, 2018).

The effects spread throughout much of Latin America like tentacles. Odebrecht and Petrobras revelations included corruption in Argentina, Mexico, and specifically Pemex (Ramírez-Cendrero & Paz, 2017), Panama, and specifically the Mossack Fonseca law firm of the Panama Papers, Peru where two presidents were held for investigation together with two former presidents one of whom committed suicide, Venezuela involving campaign contributions to President Maduro; and even Singapore, where Keppel Corporation became implicated. Other countries implicated in the Odebrecht investigation included Angola, Colombia, Ecuador, Guatemala, Mozambique, the Dominican Republic, the British Virgin Islands, and the U.S. – in cases going back as far as some three decades of public contracting corruption.

In April 2024, the government of Ecuador entered the embassy of Mexico in the capital, Quito. It arrested a former vice president who had sought asylum there in December and just after Mexico granted the request. Jorge Glas had received an Ecuadorian court sentence of six years imprisonment on charges of receiving some $13.5 million in bribes in connection with the Odebrecht corruption scandal. Mexico, followed by Nicaragua, severed diplomatic relations with Ecuador. The president of Mexico demanded a public apology with reparations, filed a complaint with the International Court of Justice (ICJ), and asked the U.N. to suspend Ecuador,

TAX EVASION, TAX AVOIDANCE, AND TAX HAVENS

Tax evasion and avoidance are likely significant problems in the region, and tax havens reportedly operate in the Caribbean (Al-Asfour & McGee, 2024; McGee, 2023; Snider, 2024; Vittadini Andres, 2024). A Statista Research Department (2024, February 2) study for 2021 found the Cayman Islands to be the world's most significant tax evasion and avoidance location, with an estimated volume of greater than $US 136 billion. British Virgin Islands was second in the region at nearly $15.4 billion. The study concluded that eight Caribbean locations accounted for almost one-third of global tax evasion losses. The organization's corporate tax haven index score (up to 100 points) was high for five U.K. territories (the British Virgin Islands, Cayman Islands, Bermuda, Turks and Caicos Islands, Anguilla) and the Bahamas. FTX Trading Ltd. (FTX), the bankrupt cryptocurrency exchange and crypto hedge fund whose co-founder Sam Bankman-Fried has been convicted of fraud, was incorporated in Antigua and Barbuda with operating headquarters in the Bahamas.

In April 2024, the trial of multiple defendants commenced in Panama over charges related to the Panama Papers; the defendants included owners of the Mossack Fonseca law firm (Associated Press, 2024). The prime minister of Iceland had resigned following the 2016 leak (Associated Press, 2024). In June 2024 (Nicholls & Mendonca, 2024), the Panama judge acquitted the defendants generally on grounds that the prosecution evidence was not sufficient to establish criminality. (Defendant Mossack was acquitted; defendant Fonseca had died in May 2024.)

Hoang (2022) provides a study of the phenomenon of "spiderweb capitalism" (see review by Ortiz Casillas, 2024). Schmal, Sasse, and Watrin (2023) studied the tax haven leaks, including the Offshore Leaks, Panama Papers, Bahamas Leaks, and Paradise Papers (see also Manescu, 2022). Their study concerns changes in the disclosure behavior of American companies with subsidiaries in the tax havens concerned. (They find that tax footnotes in annual reports become less readable, suggesting attempted obfuscation, and higher tax expenses, suggesting attempts to mitigate adverse reputational effects). Schmal et al. summarize the critical leaks: the Offshore Leaks (2013), Panama Papers (2016), Bahamas Leaks (2016), and Paradise Papers (2017). All sources in this paragraph come from Schmal et al. (Other valuable sources include Berglez & Gearing, 2018; Bhuiyan, 2023; O'Donovan, Wagner, & Zeume, 2019). The Offshore Leaks – published by the International Consortium of Investigative Journalists (ICIJ) – includes the British Virgin Islands and the Cayman Islands in the Caribbean. (Other havens included the Cook Islands, Hong Kong,

Malaysia, Mauritius, Samoa, Seychelles, and Singapore – in alphabetical order per Schmal et al.) Quinn (2013), summarized by Schmal et al., reported 2.5 million files concerning over 100,000 organizations. In April 2016, someone leaked 11.5 million documents from Mossack Fonseca, a law firm in Panama, to the German newspaper *Süddeutsche Zeitung* ("South German News") in Munich, Bavaria, which in turn shared the documents with ICIJ (Stack et al., 2016; Swanson, 2017). In September 2016, the same newspaper received the Bahamas Leaks of 1.3 million files from that country's official company register and shared the documents with ICIJ concerning some 176,000 shell organizations (Garside, 2016). In late 2017, the Paradise Papers, which contained more than 13.4 million documents involving client services of the law firm Appleby in Bermuda, became public (Forsythe, 2017; Noack, 2017).

In combination, these leaks revealed considerable information about tax avoidance and possibly tax evasion occurring through tax havens and shell organizations with the assistance of law firms in certain countries. Panama, Bermuda, the British Virgin Islands, and the Cayman Islands appeared in the revelations. Scholars are conducting structural network analyses to uncover detailed information about the operation of tax havens (Fernando & Antoine, 2022; Jha & Awaate, 2024; Kejriwal & Dang, 2020).

MONEY LAUNDERING

Money laundering is the general term for moving illicit proceeds – from various criminal activities in the private and public sectors – into the legitimate economy to escape detection and punishment by the authorities.

To date, the most significant money laundering scandal occurred in Scandinavian banks, moving large amounts of funds out of Russia through Estonia in the case of Danske Bank (Denmark) (Ylönen, Raudla, & Babic, 2024).

Yansuri et al. (2021), based on 250 expert interviews, report that the channels for money laundering in the region include "financial institutions, real estate [purchasing], bulk-cash smuggling and TBML [trade-based money laundering]." Cryptocurrency is becoming a new tax haven (Noked, 2023). Noked critiques the Crypto-Asset Reporting Framework (CARF) implemented by the U.S. and 55 other legal jurisdictions. The author expects the failure of CARF to end the crypto tax haven and provides proposals for addressing shortcomings and additional measures. Cybercrime is increasing in the Caribbean (Brain & Oyadeyi, 2024).

ANTI-CORRUPTION REMEDIES

The good news in the region may be widespread resentment of corruption (World Economic Forum, 2016) and the largely symbolic value of international anti-corruption standards and the U.S. Foreign Corrupt Practices Act (Gutierrez & Peoples, 2024). Ultimately, there must be widespread revulsion against corruption and financial crimes in all their forms. T.I. (2018, 2019) paints a presently grim picture of conditions. Mexico has the highest reported rate of bribery victimization, and Peru has the highest approval of military coup to address corruption (Statista Research Department, 2024, March 1). Most people in Caribbean countries believe government officials are corrupt (World Justice Project, 2023). However, much corruption traces to and benefits the rich and powerful (Atiles, 2024b).

Effective anti-corruption reform requires several interdependent elements: political will at the top, popular demand and support, reasonably independent judiciary and media, and some form of independent anti-corruption investigation entity. Corruption spreads throughout the political system (Da Ros & Gehrke, 2024). Ultimately, radical transparency may prove necessary, particularly where there is grand and systemic corruption, as in Brazil, combined with the polarization between conservative and socialist parties (Winter, 2017). A call for reparations in the Caribbean – from European countries to former colonies – partly relies on the possible effect in reducing corruption (Mohammed, 2022).

The 250 experts interviewed by Yansura et al. (2021) rated the effectiveness of their own country's anti-financial crimes enforcement on a Likert scale of 1=weak to 5=strong. The region's average score was 2.47, less than the mid-point of 3.

Global and regional conventions exist against corrupt foreign business payments to public officials. The United Nations Convention against Corruption (UNCAC), signed in both Merida, Mexico, and New York City in December 2003, was in force in December 2005. Virtually every nation in the world is a signatory. The Inter-American Convention Against Corruption (OAS Convention), in force 1997, signed within the Organization of American States (OAS), was the first regional accord in the world. The OECD Convention on Combating Bribery of Foreign Public Officials in International Business Transactions (OECD Anti-Bribery Convention) was in force in 1999. The tenth principle of the U.N. Global Compact is an anti-corruption policy.

The Organisation for Co-operation and Economic Development (OECD, n.d.) is presently a set of 38 countries, at the core of which is the set of economically advanced democracies (North America, Europe, Japan, Australia, New Zealand, Israel, and Turkey [Türkiye]). Chile (2010), Colombia (2020), Costa Rica (2021), and Mexico (1994) are members. Since January 2022, there have been accession discussions with Argentina, Brazil, and Peru, with an accession roadmap for Argentina (March 2024). Brazil is also an OECD key partner (with China, India, Indonesia, and South Africa).

The U.S. Foreign Extortion Prevention Act (FEPA), signed into law by President Biden (December 22, 2023), asserts the authority to prosecute foreign officials (broadly defined) seeking or receiving bribes from persons or businesses of the U.S. FEPA criminalizes the demand side of foreign bribery in addition to the existing criminalization of the supply side of foreign corruption. France, Germany, and the U.K. have similar laws. FEPA penalties include fines up to $250,000 or three times the monetary equivalent of value received or up to 15 years imprisonment. FEPA may have particular significance in Latin America and the Caribbean because of the Organization of American States (OAS), drug cartels, and illegal migration.

Papada, Nord, and Lindberg (2022) argue that corruption is lower at both high levels of democracy and worst levels of dictatorship, limited democratization increases corruption falling as a country develops high-quality democracy, democratization alone is insufficient for lower corruption, and corruption can reduce support for democracy.

SOME FUTURE DIRECTIONS FOR STUDY

One direction for continuing investigation is the independence of the judiciary from both corruption and governmental pressure or interference (Voigt & Gutmann, 2015). A study (Aydin-Cakir & Ilter Akarcay, 2024) finds that verbal attacks on the judiciary in countries with reasonably independent media increase the level of corruption. Where the press is not independent, corruption is independent of verbal attacks on the judiciary. The study uses a time-series cross-section analysis for 146 countries (1975-2016). Governmental verbal attacks on the judiciary stem from an interaction between corruption and media independence. The study also examines the specific conditions in Argentina, Brazil, and Venezuela. A movement argues for an International Anti-Corruption Court to manage cases independently of national judiciaries (Lopez-Claros & Lynch, 2024; Wolf, 2014, 2018; Wolf, Goldstone, & Rotberg, 2022).

A detailed study of corruption in FIFA sports is desirable (da Costa Silva, Coimbra, & Monteiro, 2023). Sports is highly susceptible to corruption in various forms (Koenigstorfer, 2024). The soccer stadium for the 2014 World Cup (in Brazil) appeared in the Odebrecht allegations.

In a global sample of 110 countries, based on simultaneous equation modeling, the direct effect of competitiveness in reducing corruption is reinforced by the positive indirect effect operating through income inequality (Rontos, Syrmali, Salvati, & Vavouras, 2024). In countries with low human development, the direct impact of competitiveness on corruption reduction declines due to the negative indirect effect of operating through income inequality—the latter effect results from increased social turbulence due to competitiveness.

REFERENCES

Al-Asfour, F., & McGee, R. W. (2024). Tax evasion and tax compliance: What have we learned from the 100 most cited studies? In R. W. McGee & J. Shopovski (Eds.), *The ethics of tax evasion, Volume 2: New perspectives in theory and practice*. Springer (in press). Preprint available at *SSRN*: https://ssrn.com/abstract=4709193

Associated Press. (2024, April 9). "Panama Papers" trial commences. *Wall Street Journal*, CCLXXXIII(83), A6.

Atiles, J. (2024a). Anti-corruption markets: Law, public procurement, and the colonial regime of permission in Puerto Rico. *Journal of White Collar and Corporate Crime*, 5(2), 95–104. DOI: 10.1177/2631309X241234354

Atiles, J. (2024b). Crimes of the powerful in Latin America and the Caribbean: Toward a research agenda. *Sociology Compass*, 18(2), e13172. DOI: 10.1111/soc4.13172

Aydin-Cakir, A., & Ilter Akarcay, E. (2024, March 13). When do the governments attack the judiciary? The explanatory power of corruption. Available at *SSRN*: https://ssrn.com/abstract=4757545 DOI: 10.2139/ssrn.4757545

Badur, M. M., Yılmaz, E., & Sensoy, F. (2024). Do corruption and inequality shape sustainable development? Evidence from the post-Soviet countries. *International Journal of Social Economics*, 51(1), 115–132. DOI: 10.1108/IJSE-01-2023-0065

Berglez, P., & Gearing, A. (2018). The Panama and Paradise Papers. The rise of a global fourth estate. *International Journal of Communication*, 12, 4573–4592. https://ijoc.org/index.php/ijoc/article/view/9141/2501

Bhuiyan, S. (2023). The Pandora Papers opens up Pandora's Box: Integrity in crisis. *Public Integrity*, 25(2), 245–256. DOI: 10.1080/10999922.2022.2035945

Brain, S., & Oyadeyi, O. (2024). Funding crime online: Cybercrime and its links to organised crime in the Caribbean. *The Commonwealth Cybercrime Journal, 1*(1), 84–110. https://thecommonwealth.org/publications/commonwealth-cybercrime-journal-volume-1/funding-crime-online-cybercrime-and-its-links-organised-crime-caribbean#:~:text=Organised%20crime

Bray, C., & Reed, S. (2018, January 3). Petrobras of Brazil to Pay $2.95 Billion Over Corruption Scandal. *New York Times*.https://www.nytimes.com/2018/01/03/business/dealbook/brazil-petrobras-corruption-scandal.html

Campos, N., Engel, E., Fischer, R. D., & Galetovic, A. (2021). The ways of corruption in infrastructure: Lessons from the Odebrecht case. *The Journal of Economic Perspectives*, 35(2), 171–190. https://pubs.aeaweb.org/doi/pdfplus/10.1257/jep.35.2.171. DOI: 10.1257/jep.35.2.171

Chebli, M., & Saidi, K. (2024). Economic growth in middle-income countries: The role of political stability and foreign direct investment. *Journal of Quantitative Economics*, 22(3), 641–665. DOI: 10.1007/s40953-024-00394-x

Council on Foreign Relations. (2022, September 7). Mexico's Long War: Drugs, crime, and the cartels: Violence continues to rage more than a decade after the Mexican government launched a war against drug cartels. https://www.cfr.org/backgrounder/mexicos-long-war-drugs-crime-and-cartels

da Costa Silva, P. H., Coimbra, L. W. P., & Monteiro, V. S. (2023). FIFA World Cup and corruption: an analysis by the Synthetic Control Method applied to the host countries from 2006 to 2014. *Espacio abierto: cuaderno venezolano de sociología, 32*(3), 51–75. Available at Dialnet-FIFAWorldCupAndCorruptionAnAnalysisBy-TheSyntheticC-9076835.pdf

Da Ros, L., & Gehrke, M. (2024). Convicting politicians for corruption: The politics of criminal accountability. *Government and Opposition*, 59(3), 951–975. Advance online publication. DOI: 10.1017/gov.2023.48

Earthrights. (n.d.). Doe v. Chiquita Brands International: Banana Giant Chiquita Paid Terrorist Group for Security. https://earthrights.org/case/doe-v-chiquita-brands-international/

Egger, P., & Winner, H. (2006). How corruption influences foreign direct investment: A panel data study. *Economic Development and Cultural Change*, 54(2), 459–486. DOI: 10.1086/497010

El-Hage, J. (2019, November 4). Shaking the Latin American equilibrium: The Petrobras & Odebrecht corruption scandals. *Fordham Journal of Corporate & Financial Law* [Blog]. https://news.law.fordham.edu/jcfl/2019/11/04/shaking-the-latin-american-equilibrium-the-petrobras-odebrecht-corruption-scandals/

Fernando, G. A., & Antoine, M. (2022). The network structure of global tax evasion evidence from the Panama Papers. *Journal of Economic Behavior & Organization*, 197, 660–684. DOI: 10.1016/j.jebo.2022.03.024

Florido, A., Janse, A. M., & Rampton, R. (2022, May 12). In Puerto Rico, the arrests of elected officials worsen trust in government. https://www.npr.org/2022/05/12/1098585366/in-puerto-rico-the-arrests-of-elected-officials-worsen-trust-in-government

Forsythe, M. (2017, November 5). Paradise Papers shine light on where the elite keep their money. *The New York Times*. https://www.nytimes.com/2017/11/05/world/paradise-papers.html

Garside, J. (2016, September 21). Bahamas files leaks expose politicians' offshore links. *The Guardian*.https://www.theguardian.com/business/2016/sep/21/leaked-bahamas-files-expose-politicians-offshore-links

Gossel, S. (2024). FDI and inequality in Sub-Saharan Africa: Does democracy matter? *International Journal of Emerging Markets*, 19(1), 33–55. DOI: 10.1108/IJOEM-03-2021-0321

Gutierrez, B. N., & Peoples, C. D. (2024). The Foreign Corrupt Practices Act (FCPA) as a symbolic policy in the broader "Anti-Corruption Movement": A case study of Latin American prosecutions. *Journal of White Collar and Corporate Crime*, 5(2), 85–94. DOI: 10.1177/2631309X241234358

Hoang, K. K. (2022). *Spiderweb capitalism: How global elites exploit frontier markets*. Princeton University Press.

Jha, S., & Awaate, S. (2024). Offshore FDI, tax havens, and productivity: A network analysis. *Global Strategy Journal*, 14(2), 350–382. DOI: 10.1002/gsj.1466

Keefer, P., & Roseth, B. (2024). Transparency and grand corruption: Lessons from the Colombia school meals program. *Journal of Comparative Economics*, 52(2), 445–462. DOI: 10.1016/j.jce.2024.02.003

Kejriwal, M., & Dang, A. (2020). Structural studies of the global networks exposed in the Panama papers. *Applied Network Science*, 5(1), 63. Advance online publication. DOI: 10.1007/s41109-020-00313-y

Khalid, A. M. (2024). Does corruption hinder foreign direct investment and growth in Asia and beyond? The grabbing versus the helping hand revisited. In Teramura, N., Nottage, L., & Jetin, B. (Eds.), *Corruption and illegality in Asian investment arbitration* (pp. 39–67). DOI: 10.1007/978-981-99-9303-1_2

Koenigstorfer, J. (2024). Corruption in connection to major sport events. In Solberg, H. A., Storm, R. K., & Swart, K. (Eds.), *Research handbook on major sporting events* (pp. 591–606). Edward Elgar Publishing. DOI: 10.4337/9781800885653.00057

Lagunes, P. F., & Svejnar, E. (Eds.). (2020). *Corruption and the Lava Jato scandal in Latin America*. Routledge., DOI: 10.4324/9781003024286

Lopez-Claros, A., & Lynch, I. J. (2024). Combatting corruption to advance good governance: Exploring options for an International Anti-Corruption Court. In Falk, R., & Lopez-Claros, A. (Eds.), *Global governance and international cooperation* (pp. 428–443). Routledge India. DOI: 10.4324/9781032699028-29

Manescu, D. M. (2022). Pandora Papers and the latest European efforts to combat money laundering, tax evasion and tax avoidance. *Technium Social Sciences Journal*, 27, 384–390. DOI: 10.47577/tssj.v27i1.5668

McGee, R. W. (2023, November 14). Studies in tax evasion: A bibliography. Available at *SSRN*: https://ssrn.com/abstract=4632770

Mohammed, K. (2022). Reparations to the Caribbean could break the cycle of corruption – and China's grip. *The Guardian*.https://www.theguardian.com/global-development/2022/jan/25/reparations-caribbean-cycle-of-corruption-china

Mota Prado, M., & De Assis Machado, M. R. (2021). Using criminal law to fight corruption: The potential, risks, and limitations of Operation Car Wash (Lava Jato). *The American Journal of Comparative Law*, 69(4), 834–879. DOI: 10.1093/ajcl/avac008

Nanos, E. (2022, September 7). Federal appeals court [11th Circuit] resurrects major lawsuit against Chiquita for funding Colombian terrorist organization. https://lawandcrime.com/federal-court/federal-appeals-court-resurrects-major-lawsuit-against-chiquita-banana-for-funding-colombian-terrorist-organization/

Nicholls, C., & Mendonca, D. (2024, June 29). Panama court acquits 28 implicated in Panama Papers and Operation Car Wash scandals. https://www.cnn.com/2024/06/29/americas/operation-car-wash-panama-papers-acquittals-intl/index.html

Noack, R. (2017, November 6). Leaked documents reveal financial habits of Queen Elizabeth and Trump officials. *The Washington Post*.https://www.washingtonpost.com/news/worldviews/wp/2017/11/06/paradise-papers-reveal-how-the-wealthy-and-even-the-politicians-are-still-hiding-their-wealth-from-the-taxman/

Noked, N. (2023, July 1). Ending the crypto tax haven. *Harvard Business Law Review, 15* (in press). Available at *SSRN*: https://ssrn.com/abstract=4618310 DOI: 10.2139/ssrn.4618310

O'Donovan, J., Wagner, H. F., & Zeume, S. (2019). The value of offshore secrets: Evidence from the Panama Papers. *Review of Financial Studies*, 32(11), 4117–4155. DOI: 10.1093/rfs/hhz017

Organisation for Economic Co-operation and Development. (n.d.). Retrieved May 23, 2024, from https://www.oecd.org/about/members-and-partners/

Ortiz Casillas, S. (2024). Book review: Kimberley Kay Hoang, Spiderweb Capitalism: How Global Elites Exploit Frontier Markets. *Administrative Science Quarterly*, 69(1), NP18–NP20. DOI: 10.1177/00018392231213822

Papada, E., Nord, M., & Lindberg, S. I. (2022, December). Can democracy limit corruption? V-Dem Institute, V-Dem Policy Brief No. 36. Available at *SSRN*: https://ssrn.com/abstract=4787135

Perelman, M. (2024). Living with inflation in Argentina. *Current History (New York, N.Y.)*, 123(850), 50–55. DOI: 10.1525/curh.2024.123.850.50

Pohlmann, M., Valarini, E., Trombini, M., & Jorge, M. (2019). Systemic corruption in Brazil: An autopsy of the Odebrecht case. *Journal of Self-regulation and Regulation*, 5, 55–78. https://journals.ub.uni-heidelberg.de/index.php/josar/article/download/69286/62621

Pontes, J., & Anselmo, M. (2022). *Operation Car Wash: Brazil's institutionalized crime and the inside story of the biggest corruption scandal in history*. Bloomsbury Publishing. DOI: 10.5040/9781350265646

Pooler, M. (2024, May 22). Brazil's supreme court overturns 'Car Wash' corruption convictions [of José Dirceu, Marcelo Odebrecht]: Reversal of high-profile rulings comes as country backtracks on graft probe. *Financial Times*. https://www.ft.com/content/c0d84b0f-1f0b-40d0-8ebe-8bf6c60b4fbe

Portugal, M. A., & Alves de Moraes, E. (2024). Operation Car Wash: Uncovering corruption pathways in the Brazilian construction industry through bid law blind spots. *Public Integrity*, 1–19. Advance online publication. DOI: 10.1080/10999922.2024.2316492

Quinn, B. (2013, June 15). Offshore Leaks app puts secret users of tax havens in the public eye. *The Guardian*.https://www.theguardian.com/technology/2013/jun/15/database-app-icij-tax-havens

Ramírez-Cendrero, J. M., & Paz, M. J. (2017). Oil fiscal regimes and national oil companies: A comparison between Pemex and Petrobras. *Energy Policy*, 101, 473–483. DOI: 10.1016/j.enpol.2016.11.009

Remache Lopez, A. A. (2024). *Political corruption: An explanation for Latin American migration*. [Master's thesis, Harvard University Division of Continuing Education]. https://nrs.harvard.edu/URN-3:HUL.INSTREPOS:37378447

Rontos, K., Syrmali, M. E., Salvati, L., & Vavouras, I. (2024). Competitiveness, corruption, and income inequalities: Approaching the 'Janus' face of development with simultaneous equation modelling. *Quality & Quantity*, 58(1), 343–364. DOI: 10.1007/s11135-023-01644-5

Sallaberry, J. D., Quaesner, L. S., Costa, M. C., & Flach, L. (2020). Measurement of damage from corruption in Brazil. *Journal of Financial Crime*, 27(4), 1239–1239. DOI: 10.1108/JFC-04-2020-0057

Schmal, F., Sasse, K. S., & Watrin, C. (2023). Trouble in paradise? Disclosure after tax haven leaks. *Journal of Accounting, Auditing & Finance*, 38(3), 706–727. DOI: 10.1177/0148558X20986348

Shiel, F., & Chavkin, S. (2019, June 25). Bribery Division: What is Odebrecht? Who is involved? International Consortium of Investigative Journalists (ICIJ). https://www.icij.org/investigations/bribery-division/bribery-division-what-is-odebrecht-who-is-involved/

Snider, L. (2024). Globalized tax evasion and corruption: Two steps forward, one step back. *Journal of White Collar and Corporate Crime*, 5(2), 113–121. DOI: 10.1177/2631309X241236202

Springer, Singapore. https://link.springer.com/chapter/10.1007/978-981-99-9303-1_2

Stack, L., Erlanger, S., Rousseau, B., Forsythe, M., MacFarquhar, N., & Castle, S. (2016, April 4). What are the Panama Papers? *The New York Times.*https://www.nytimes.com/2016/04/05/world/panama-papers-explainer.html

Statista Research Department. (2024, February 2). Largest enablers of tax avoidance and tax evasion in Latin America and the Caribbean in 2021 (in million U.S. dollars). https://www.statista.com/statistics/1224443/tax-evasion-avoidance-latin-america-caribbean-country/

Statista Research Department. (2024, March 1). Corruption in Latin America – statistics & facts. https://www.statista.com/topics/6468/corruption-in-latin-america/#topicOverview

Swanson, A. (2017, June 1). The ultra-rich are hiding way more money overseas than anyone realized. *The Washington Post.*https://www.washingtonpost.com/news/wonk/wp/2017/06/01/researchers-are-figuring-out-just-how-much-wealth-the-super-rich-are-hiding-overseas/

Teagarden, M. B., & Schotter, A. (2010, November 11). *Blood Bananas: Chiquita in Colombia*. Harvard Business School Publishing. TB0245-PDF-ENG

Transparency International. (2019). Global Corruption Barometer: Latin America & the Caribbean 2019: Citizens' views and experiences of corruption. https://www.transparency.org/en/gcb/latin-america/latin-america-and-the-caribbean-x-edition-2019

Transparency International. (2024, January 30). CPI 2023 for the Americas: Lack of independent judiciary hinders the fight against corruption. Luciana Torchiaro, Regional Advisor for the Americas. https://www.transparency.org/en/news/cpi-2023-americas-lack-independent-judiciary-hinders-fight-against-corruption

Transparency International (T.I.). (2018, February 21). Perceptions remain unchanged despite progress in the Americas: Regional analysis by Alejandro Urizar and Luciana Torchiaro. https://www.transparency.org/en/news/perceptions-remain-unchanged-despite-progress-in-the-americas

Transparency International (T.I.). (n.d.). Our Work in Puerto Rico. Retrieved May 23, 2024, from https://www.transparency.org/en/countries/puerto-rico

U.S. Department of Justice, Press Release 16-1515. (2016, December 21). Odebrecht and Braskem plead guilty and agree to pay at least $3.5 billion in global penalties to resolve largest foreign bribery case in history. https://www.justice.gov/opa/pr/odebrecht-and-braskem-plead-guilty-and-agree-pay-least-35-billion-global-penalties-resolve

U.S. Department of Justice, Press Release 18-1258. (2018, September 27). Petróleo Brasileiro S.A. – Petrobras agrees to pay more than $850 million for FCPA violations. https://www.justice.gov/opa/pr/petr-leo-brasileiro-sa-petrobras-agrees-pay-more-850-million-fcpa-violations

U.S. Governmental Accountability Office (GAO). (2023, July 10). Venezuela: Illicit financial flows and U.S. efforts to disrupt them. GAO-23-105668. https://www.gao.gov/products/gao-23-105668

Vittadini Andres, S. N. (2024). Moral and cultural perspectives of tax evasion in Latin America. In R. W. McGee & J. Shopovski (Eds.). *The ethics of tax evasion, Volume 2: New perspectives in theory and practice.* Springer (in press). Preprint available at *SSRN*: https://ssrn.com/abstract=4686864

Voigt, S., & Gutmann, J. (2015). On the wrong side of the law – Causes and consequences of a corrupt judiciary. *International Review of Law and Economics*, 43, 156–166. DOI: 10.1016/j.irle.2014.04.005

Voss, B. L., Carter, D. B., & Warren, R. (2023). A car wash: Post-truth politics, Petrobras and ethics of the real. *Accounting, Auditing & Accountability Journal*, 36(2), 437–463. DOI: 10.1108/AAAJ-03-2020-4460

Weitzman, A., Caudillo, M., & Levy, E. J. (2024). Hybrid interpersonal violence in Latin America: Patterns and causes. *Annual Review of Criminology*, 7(1), 163–186. DOI: 10.1146/annurev-criminol-022422-014603 PMID: 38304058

Winter, B. (2017). Brazil's never-ending corruption crisis: Why radical transparency is the only fix. *Foreign Affairs*, 96(3), 87–94. https://www.jstor.org/stable/44823734

Wolf, M. L. (2014, July 23). The case for an International Anti-Corruption Court. Brookings Institution. https://www.brookings.edu/articles/the-case-for-an-international-anti-corruption-court/

Wolf, M. L. (2018). The world needs an International Anti-Corruption Court. *Daedalus*, 147(3), 144–156. https://www.jstor.org/stable/48563086. DOI: 10.1162/daed_a_00507

Wolf, M. L., Goldstone, R. J., & Rotberg, R. I. (2022, August 24). The progressing proposal for an International Anti-Corruption Court. American Academy of Arts and Sciences. https://www.amacad.org/publication/proposal-international-anti-corruption-court

World Economic Forum. (2016, June 15). Corruption in Latin America is skyrocketing. Here's why that's good news. https://www.weforum.org/agenda/2016/06/corruption-in-latin-america/

World Justice Project. (2023). *Corruption in the Caribbean: Insights from the General Public 2022*. Washington, DC. https://worldjusticeproject.org/sites/default/files/documents/Corruption-in-the-Caribbean-report-v4.pdf

Wu, T., Delios, A., Chen, Z., & Wang, X. (2023). Rethinking corruption in international business: An empirical review. *Journal of World Business*, 58(2), 101410. DOI: 10.1016/j.jwb.2022.101410

Yahyaoui, I. (2024). How corruption mitigates the effect of FDI on economic growth? *Journal of the Knowledge Economy*, 15(1), 1344–1362. DOI: 10.1007/s13132-023-01098-y

Yansura, J., Mavrellis, C., Kumar, L., & Helms, C. (2021, October 15). Financial crime in Latin America and the Caribbean: Understanding country challenges and designing effective technical responses. Global Financial Integrity. https://gfintegrity.org/report/financial-crime-in-latin-america-and-the-caribbean/

Ylönen, M., Raudla, R., & Babic, M. (2024). From tax havens to cryptocurrencies: Secrecy-seeking capital in the global economy. *Review of International Political Economy*, 31(2), 563–588. DOI: 10.1080/09692290.2023.2232392

Zysman-Quirós, D. (2019). White-collar crime in South and Central America: Corporate-state crime, governance, and the high impact of the Odebrecht corruption case. In Rorie, M. L. (Ed.), *The handbook of white-collar crime* (pp. 363–380). John Wiley., DOI: 10.1002/9781118775004.ch23

ADDITIONAL READING

Brown, C. M. (2023). *Failed democracies in Latin America and the Caribbean: Democratic purgatory and the viability of consolidated democratic regimes*. Palgrave Macmillan Cham., DOI: 10.1007/978-3-031-38481-3

De Coteau, D. (2024). *Black fins white sharks: Unmasking the genealogy of Caribbean political corruption: Decolonising Caribbean corruption studies*. Palgrave Macmillan. DOI: 10.1007/978-3-031-47479-8

Griffith, I. L. (2024). *Challenged sovereignty: The impact of drugs, crime, terrorism, and cyber threats in the Caribbean*. University of Illinois Press. DOI: 10.5622/illinois/9780252045660.001.0001

Husted, B. W. (1994). Honor among thieves: A transaction-cost interpretation of corruption in third world countries. *Business Ethics Quarterly*, 4(1), 17–27. DOI: 10.2307/3857556

Kemsley, D., Kemsley, S. A., & Morgan, F. T. (2024). Tax evasion on lawful income: Is it a form of money laundering? *Journal of Financial Crime*, 31(1), 33–43. DOI: 10.1108/JFC-11-2022-0268

Latinobarómetro [Latin Barometer]. (2023). https://www.latinobarometro.org/lat.jsp

McGee, R. W., & Benk, S. (Eds.). (2023). *The ethics of bribery: Theoretical and empirical studies*. Springer. DOI: 10.1007/978-3-031-17707-1

Sonneland, H. K. (2022, January 11). Chart: Evaluating Latin American Democracies in 2022. https://www.as-coa.org/articles/chart-evaluating-latin-american-democracies-2022

U.S. Congressional Research Service. (2019, May 21). Combating corruption in Latin America: Congressional considerations. https://crsreports.congress.gov/product/pdf/R/R45733

U.S. Congressional Research Service. (2022, February 1). Anti-corruption efforts in Latin America and the Caribbean. https://crsreports.congress.gov/product/pdf/IF/IF12031

U.S. Congressional Research Service. (2023, September 27, updated). Democracy in Latin America and the Caribbean: A compilation of selected indices. https://crsreports.congress.gov/product/pdf/R/R46016

KEY TERMS AND DEFINITIONS

Anti-Corruption Reform: Desirable efforts by private, governmental, and international entities to reduce corruption in particular countries.

Bribery: Whether in a commercial or governmental setting, an illegal offer or transfer of something of value to another actor in exchange for something of value, such as a contract or license. A bribe may result from an act of extortion by the recipient rather than from a demand by the payor.

Corruption: Based on the definitional conception of Transparency International, illegitimate abuse of a position of trust or power, especially public office, for private gain obtained typically through bribery by or extortion of others. Corruption may be grand (occurring at higher levels of government or business management), petty (occurring in daily life including private transactions and at lower levels of government of business), or systemic (broad abuse of power by governmental and political elites and typically occurring together with authoritarianism). A "culture of corruption" is a condition of corruption sufficiently pervasive that most of the population have grown to tolerate because they are unable to change the condition.

Facilitating Payment: A relatively small private payment to a low-level government official to expedite an otherwise legal action typically reflecting extortion. Such payment is legal under the U.S. Foreign Corrupt Practices Act but illegal under the U.K. Bribery Act. Payment may be unlawful under the domestic laws of a host country. In December 2009, the OECD called for prohibiting such "grease payments."

Money Laundering: The general conception is concealing the source of money or other forms of value, typically coming from illicit activities such as corruption, criminal trafficking, embezzlement, gambling, and tax evasion.

Tax Avoidance: Tax avoidance is any legal action, independent of any ethical considerations, by which a taxpayer reduces tax liability with transparency. Tax avoidance by businesses and wealthy individuals, especially elected officials, raises issues of tax fairness.

Tax Evasion: Any illegal action to reduce tax liability, typically involving concealment of the action from tax authorities. Tax evasion may occur in various ways, including at lower income levels use of cash transactions only to avoid reporting liability.

Chapter 5
The Situation of Haitians and Haitian Creole in the Dominican Republic

Clifton Deed Armstrong
https://orcid.org/0000-0002-6023-6766
University of Puerto Rico, Puerto Rico

ABSTRACT

The paper reports on the situation of Haitians and Haitian Creole in the Dominican Republic. It begins with a discussion of three pivotal events: the French extortion of the "Independence Debt," the period from 1822-1844 when Haiti controlled all of Hispaniola, and the 1912 purchase of 20,000 acres of Dominican land by the South Porto Rico Sugar Company. The paper then presents a discussion of the Dominican Republic's deportation of Haitians to Haiti, the poor health conditions of Haitians in the Dominican, the low status and vitality of Haitian Creole in the Dominican, and the effects of Dominican anti-Haitian policies. The paper shows that anti-Haitianism is not unique to the Dominican Republic, but has been practiced for centuries by Western countries, describes resistance within the Dominican Republic to the government's anti-Haitian policies, and ends with a discussion of what the international community should do to help Haiti.

THE SITUATION OF HAITIANS AND HAITIAN CREOLE IN THE DOMINICAN REPUBLIC

Since the late 1800's, Haitians have been migrating to the Dominican Republic (henceforth, the DR) to work and to escape the difficult situation that has been Haiti almost since it became independent in 1804. In 2018 (the last year for which such

DOI: 10.4018/979-8-3693-3763-9.ch005

figures are available), the DR government released the results of its immigration survey. The publication indicates that 849,979 (8.3% of the total DR population) people living in the country are immigrants[1] or are descendants of immigrants (Oficina Nacional de Estadística, 2018, p. 25), and that 88.5% of the immigrants are of Haitian origin (p. 29). Haiti's security situation has deteriorated since 2018 and, though no official numbers are available, it appears safe to assume that the number of Haitian immigrants in the DR has greatly increased.

The situation of Haitians in the DR is difficult; those without documentation are subject to deportation to Haiti and sometimes people with documentation get deported. Haitians tend to be paid less than Dominicans for similar work and Haitians with advanced degrees from universities in the DR are not allowed to practice in their chosen field. Disease rates and malnutrition are higher among Haitians than within Dominican society at large. Further, there is widespread clamor for all Haitians in the DR to be sent to Haiti. Under such conditions, it is hardly surprising that Haitian is not being acquired by children of Haitian immigrants.

The rest of the paper first presents a discussion of three pivotal events that have led to the current situation. The paper then turns to the situation of Haitians in the DR, giving further details, referencing sources that verify the claims made above regarding the difficult lives of Haitians in the DR. A discussion of the language issues then ensues, briefly discussing the origin of Haitian Creole, but focusing on its status in the DR.

The paper ends by reporting on resistance by Haitians and Dominicans of Haitian descent to the discrimination they experience in the DR, and then briefly discusses attempts by the International community to help Haiti. A value of the paper is that by describing the difficult lives of Haitians in the DR, it shows the need to find ways to help Haiti become a successful state. Haitians could then stay safely in Haiti and would leave by choice, not out of desperation.

Historical Background: Three Pivotal Events

Here the paper presents discussion of the "Independence Debt" that France demanded Haiti pay, Haiti's control over all of Hispaniola from 1822 to 1844, and the 1912 purchase by the South Porto Rico Sugar Company of 20,000 acres of Dominican land near La Romana. The three events are pivotal in that the changes they entailed greatly contributed to the development of the current situation in Haiti and the DR.

The "Independence Debt"

The nation of Haiti came into being on 1 January 1804. So far it is the first and only case in which slaves revolted, defeated by war their former enslavers, and set up their own country. As reported by Phillips (2008, pp. 4-5) and Henochsberg (2016, pp. 12-13), representatives of the French government came to Port-au-Prince in 1825 and, accompanied by the French navy, demanded payment of 150 million francs in return for diplomatic recognition. The money was supposedly for reparations to the former French slave owners who, because of the rebellion, had lost much of what they owned, and for businesses that lost money invested in Haiti. Haitian refusal would mean a French blockade of Port-au-Prince. The Haitians agreed to the terms. Haiti paid off the "debt" to the French by 1883, but interest payments on the loans the government took to make the payments were not retired until 1947, with payments for the final 25 years being made to the bank known today as Citibank (Phillips, 2008, p. 6).

The Haitian government needed almost all its revenue to pay the debt. In 1915, for example, payments servicing the debt took up 80 percent of the government's income (Phillips, 2008, p. 7). Throughout the 122-year repayment period, the country had little money for education, infrastructure, or healthcare. The French extortion led to the poverty, illiteracy, and low life-expectancy that has been the rule in Haiti for generations. The United Nations Human Development Index indicates that as of 2022, Haiti was the lowest ranking country in the Caribbean and Latin America, with a life expectancy of 63.7 years, a mean of 5.6 years of schooling and annual per-person income of $2,802, just over half the per-person income of Honduras, the next higher country on the Caribbean/Latin America list. The DR ranks much higher on the list, with an annual per-person income of $18,653, more than six times greater than the per-person income of Haiti (United Nations, 2022).

The 1822-1844 Unification of Hispaniola

The second pivotal event is the 22-year unification of Hispaniola under Haitian rule from 1822-1844. It is pivotal because much of the long-standing discord between the two countries can be seen as stemming from the unification period.

On 9 February 1822, Jean-Pierre Boyer, President of Haiti, arrived in the Dominican capital city of Santo Domingo to announce the annexation of the country by Haiti and declared freedom for all slaves being held in the DR (Vega, 1994, p. 170). There was little or no resistance to the unification, and most Dominicans, at least initially, appear to have supported it (Walker, 2019). Their support apparently related to Boyer's promises to end slavery and redistribute the land (Vega, 1994, pp. 177-187). At that time, the Catholic Church and less than 5% of the population controlled approximately 90% of Dominican land (Venator-Santiago, 2011, p. 761).

In May 1822, three months after unification, in Galindo, a Santo Domingo community near what is today known as the Zona Colonial, three Dominican jail escapees murdered a man and his three daughters. The accused were arrested, tried, and sentenced (Lovaton, 1953, p. 335; García-Peña, 2016, p. 25; and Venator-Santiago, 2011, p. 762). As time went on and Dominicans began to see the unification period in a negative light, the national memory of the murders changed. According to the revised version, brutal black Haitians were the perpetrators, not Dominican common criminals (Venator-Santiago, 2011, pp. 762-764 and Garcia-Peña, 2016, p. 25). The murders became symbolic of the negative perception of the 22 years of Haitian domination. An entry on the site "Historia Dominicana en Gráficas," describes the members of the murdered family and then turns to the crime (throughout the paper, quotations originally in Spanish appear in English as translated by the present writer):

This family was the protagonist of one of the darkest episodes of Haitian domination, … the murder of "The Virgins of Galindo:" Haitian soldiers, commanded by officers Condé and Lenoir, brutally murdered on 29 May 1822, Andrés Andújar and his three daughters. This episode, narrated by several Dominican writers (Félix María Del Monte Fernández de Castro in "Las Vírgenes de Galindo" (1885), César Nicolás Pénson in his work "Cosas Añejas" (1891), and more recently, Joaquín Antonio Balaguer (1970) in his work "Centinela de la Frontera") served to increase the repudiation the Dominican people feel towards Haiti. The "Virgins of Galindo" in the 19th century had a similar impact to that created by the murder of the Mirabal sisters during the Trujillo dictatorship (Guerra-Sánchez, 2016).

The post is remarkable for the acceptance as settled facts that, first, the murders were committed by Haitians and, second, that Dominicans reject all things Haitian. The full title of the 1885 work the post refers to, "The Virgins of Galindo or the Haitian Invasion of the Spanish part of the Island of Santo Domingo" (Del Monte, 1885), equates the two events, showing how the murders and the period of unification have been seen as equally important and interchangeable. The "Mirabel sisters" mentioned by Guerra-Sánchez were three women who, with their husbands, actively resisted the Trujillo dictatorship. While returning home after visiting their imprisoned husbands, the sisters were assassinated by Trujillo's men on 25 November 1960. In their honor, the International Day of Elimination of Violence Against Women is observed every November 25th (United Nations, n.d.).

The 1970 publication by Balaguer, president of the DR from 1960-1962, 1966-1978, and from 1986-1996, was followed in 1983 by his "La Isla al Revés: Haití y el Destino Dominicano" (The Upside-Down Island: Haiti and Dominican Destiny). The 1983 publication does not discuss Galindo; instead the book is full of racist commentary about Haitians and how Haitians have supposedly repeatedly invaded the county, as follows:

The Hispanic language and tradition were ... the only walls that served as a defense against the terrifying wave of color and the disintegrative forces that since 1795 have been invading Dominican territory in an uninterrupted and systematic manner. Without the glue of language and the cohesive power of customs, Santo Domingo would have already disappeared under the push of what Menéndez y Pelayo has called "the savage Gallo-Ethiopian domination" (Balaguer, 1983, p. 63).

Regarding the "Galindo Virgins," in 2020, a review of Pénson's account appeared in Diario Libre, a Dominican newspaper. Journalist, Emila Pereyra, writing in the paper's literature section, uncritically accepts Pénson's work as historical and comments (Pereyra, 2020, para 5), "El autor manifiesta su desprecio por los haitianos, a los que llama 'mañeses' y les critica sus 'bailes salvajes', sus 'ranchos nauseabundos' y su 'castiza brujería' " (The author expresses his contempt for Haitians, whom he calls "mañeses,"[2] and criticizes their "wild dances," their "nauseating smells," and their "pure witchcraft"). Pereyra writes, with expressions similar to those of Guerra-Sánchez (2016), that the murders "increased the rejection of the invaders, as several Haitians were involved in the events" (Pereyra, 2020, para 2). Pereyra does not specifically endorse Pénson's negative appraisal of Haitians, but her uncritical repetition of his offensive expressions appears to signal at least tacit support for such racist attitudes.

A striking aspect of the Dominican attitude towards the unification period is that, as Venator-Santiago (2005) points out, those twenty-two years were

"The most progressive period of Dominican history in more than 400 years. More importantly, while Dominican national identity narratives continue to be constituted in repudiation of the Haitian unification period, ... the Dominican Republic continues to use legal narratives and institutions that were introduced by the Haitians" (p. 63).

The discussion of the unification period ends with comment on a street sign seen on streets in the DR in the early months of 2024.

The top of the sign reads, "180 AÑOS DE DOMINICANIDAD de pura cepa" (180 years of pure-bred Dominicanness) (Highway Motion, 2024, 7:32). And then written in red, appears "¡Pa'que le sepa!" (So that you know!). The man depicted in the sign is Juan Pablo Duarte, a leader of the movement against Haitian domination.

The reference to one hundred and eighty years refers to the time between 2024 and the 1844 end of the unification period and indicates that 1844 is the recognized independence date for the DR. The rebellion against the Haitians started on 27 February 1844, and a main artery in Santo Domingo is in fact named "February 27th Avenue."

Other independence dates are available, as the DR became independent from Spain in 1821 and again in 1865 (Dominican Republic, 1989, p. 758). The choice of 1844 appears to relate to the fact that independence can have a political dimension and a social/identity dimension. The independence from Spain had a political dimension, but little in the way of a social/identity dimension, since Dominicans, as well as other Latin American countries, see Spain as "La Madre Patria." As the preceding discussion makes clear, the social/identity aspect of independence from Haiti is at least as important as the political dimension. Thus, 1844 is the logical choice for the beginning of Dominican independence; it marks the political reality of the break with Haiti, and represents a disavowal of Haiti and things Haitian. It is striking that expressions referring to concepts such as "freedom" and "liberty" do not occur on the sign. The emphasis is on Dominican ethnicity.

Finally, the "So that you know!" language comes across as aggressive. Given the current situation with hundreds of thousands of Haitians in the DR and more coming every day, "So that you know!" appears to be telling Haitians who see the sign, "You are not part of us and you never will be."

The notion expressed on the sign that Dominican independence was and continues to be an expression of ethnic identity, implies, especially at a time when Haitians are believed to be entering the country in increased numbers, that their increased presence in the DR threatens national sovereignty, and supposedly justifies efforts to deport them. Such attitudes are an apparent result of Dominican attitudes towards the unification period (1822-1844). Guerra-Sánchez's post, quoted previously, is seemingly correct when he notes that the murders increased "the repudiation the Dominican people feel towards Haiti."

The South Porto Rico Sugar Company's Purchase of 20,000 Acres

The third pivotal event is the 1912 purchase by the South Porto Rico Sugar Company of 20,000 acres of land near La Romana (Central Romana, n.d.). Within the DR, it was one of the first large purchases of land by a foreign company and the ensuing growth of the sugar cane industry changed the country forever. While much of the land in the DR was owned by less than 5% of the people, before the advent of widespread sugarcane farming, most of the population famed land their families had lived on for generations (Calder, 1984, p. xxviii). The growth of the sugar industry led to the displacement of many people from their land and way of life. The United States governed the DR from 1916 through 1922 by means of an American military government. During that time, an armed rebellion sprang up. An American soldier noted, "The principal thing the provincial peasants have been taught about the foreigner is that he is trying to deprive the peasant of his land and

… to impose new and undesirable forms of living" (Calder, 1984, pp. 119-120). In 1922, as military rule was ending, American officials came to understand that a principal reason for the uprising was the displacement of the peasants. The outgoing military government tried to get the sugar companies to provide land for the workers so they could sustain themselves when not working in the sugar harvest. An official wrote, "any lack of employment will have the most disastrous results in the increase of [armed insurrection]" (Calder, 1984, p. 120).

As the sugar industry grew, Haitians began migrating to the DR in large numbers. Because conditions in Haiti were so difficult due to the "Independence Debt," Haitians had few opportunities to prosper in Haiti. Since they were and are willing to work for lower pay than Dominicans (Guilamo, 2018, p. 502), they have become an important part of the Dominican work force.

The sugar companies provided places for the workers to stay, constructing neighborhoods known as bateyes, which consisted of small, poorly built homes with no electricity, no running water, and no sewage systems. People living in the bateyes had no access to education for their children, and no access to healthcare.

In 1926, an American official described conditions in the bateyes. He wrote that conditions were "primitive in the extreme … most of these laborers exist solely on a diet of yams, bananas, and other fruits," and went on to note that people wore clothes until they were useless and that children went naked for years (Calder, 1984, p. 95).

The present writer traveled to rural areas of the DR in 2014 and noted the following: *"The next day, we went to two bateyes. A church in the first of these neighborhoods was made rather poorly of wood. As it filled up with children, I saw one boy who had a three-inch bump where his belly button was supposed to be. I assume it was some kind of parasite.*

The houses in this neighborhood were made of narrow planks of wood on the outside, supported, on the inside, by poles cut from trees and looked pretty rickety. The roofs consist of cheap zinc panels. Though the houses cost little to build, they are not big. I got inside one of them and saw that it was big enough for only the beds of the people who lived there. The kitchen consisted of a pot being cooked over a hibachi-like thing on the floor.

On the way to the house of a pastor of a church, we passed a barely-moving waterway that apparently serves as water source and sewer for the neighborhood. We saw pigs walking around loose, including one that probably weighed over 250 pounds."

The account of the present writer's visit to the two bateyes indicates little difference between the conditions of the 1920's and modern times.

The South Porto Rico Sugar Company is now known as Central Romana Corporation. On their website, the following appears for 1982:

Central Romana has the largest sugarcane harvest by one sugar mill, worldwide, exceeding 480,000 tons, which consolidates it as one of the largest and most productive mills in the world. The level of prosperity achieved during these years allows the company to develop numerous social and economic programs with vast repercussions for the whole country (Central Romana, n.d.).

Given the "vast repercussions," one wonders why contemporary conditions are so poor. The Central Romana website (https://centralromana.com.do/memorias/?lang=en). features photos and videos replete with gleaming machinery, private jets, polo players, golf courses and shining hospitals with no mention or evidence of conditions in the bateyes. In contrast to the picture presented by Central Romana, Filiau (2023, p. 11) indicates that in La Romana, 130,000 people live in 160 bateyes, and shows, as will be seen in the section on the health of Haitians in the DR, that conditions in the bateyes are poor.

In summing up the discussion of the three pivotal events, the "Independence Debt" extortion, the attitudes that formed as a result of interpretations of the unification period, and the advent and growth of the sugar industry, led to the current situation in which Haitians in the DR find themselves.

The Current Situation of Haitian and Haitians

The study now turns to discuss aspects of Haitian life in the DR. Specifically, the deportations of thousands of presumed Haitians to Haiti, the health of Haitians in the DR, the status and vitality of Haitian Creole in the DR, and the so-called Dominican "anti-Haitianism" that is a fact of life for Haitians in the DR. The paper concludes with accounts of how Haitians within the DR are peacefully and creatively resisting the difficulties they confront.

Deportations

In recent years, the DR government has deported many thousands of people to Haiti. The supposed targets of the deportations are Haitians and people of Haitian descent. Actually, anyone who looks Haitian or speaks Spanish with a Haitian accent or has a Haitian-sounding name or has dark skin can get deported (Childers, 2023, p. 110). The DR government indicates it deported 174,677 Haitians in 2023, 122,838 in 2022, and 44,082 in 2021, referring to the deported people as foreigners (Oficina Nacional de Estadísticas, 2024). The historical background to the deportations is described in the discussion of the three pivotal events. The supposed legal basis for the deportations comes from various laws and legal proceedings, the most important of which is the 2013 decision commonly referred to as "La Sentencia," that took citizenship away from nearly all Dominicans of Haitian descent born after 1929

(Silverio, 2013). Hundreds of thousands of people lost their citizenship and became stateless. Since they were stateless, they became illegal aliens and were and are subject to deportation. The government operates specially constructed busses with "Control Migratorio" painted on the side, that collect captured presumed Haitians and transport them to Haiti (see Associated Press (2024) for a picture of such a bus).

As will be seen as the discussion continues, fear of being deported can affect much of a person's life.

The Health of Haitians in the Dominican Republic

Health services in the DR tend to be in urban areas, and since most bateyes are in rural or semi-rural areas, bateyes residents often have problems accessing health care (Simmons, 2010, p. 13). With their low salaries, they frequently cannot afford to pay for transportation and thus are not able to get to a hospital. Even if they can pay for transportation, those without documentation are hesitant to leave the batey for fear of being "stopped by local authorities and imprisoned or deported" (Simmons, 2010, p. 13).

Given the distance from health care facilities and the issues that can arise when one leaves a batey (a fear even more well-founded after the 2013 "Sentencia"), a greater incidence of disease among batey residents compared to the overall Dominican population would be expected and is what medical researchers have found.

Filiau (2023, p. 4), for example, indicates that in 2020, the HIV prevalence rate in the Dominican population was 0.9%, and that the HIV rate for batey inhabitants was 3.0 – 9.0%. She attributes the disparity to "limited access to health services, endemic poverty, barriers to citizenship status, and discrimination" (p. 5), exactly the issues seen in the discussion so far. She notes that the prevalence of HIV in Haiti is 1.9% (p. 4), much lower than the 3.0% - 9.0% prevalence in the bateyes, which suggests, as "endemic poverty" is characteristic of Haiti as well as the bateyes, that it is the "barriers to citizenship status and discrimination" occurring within the DR that most contribute to the higher HIV prevalence rates in the bateyes.

Jaskolka-Brown (2022) cites many studies of the health of Haitians in the bateyes and paints a grim picture, especially regarding children. In one town, 99.2% of children aged 2-15 had at least one gastrointestinal parasite (p. 3). She indicates that less than 50% of rural populations in the DR (not just Haitians and not just in bateyes) have access to safe drinking water and only 16% "dispose of sewage in a sanitary manner" and that 95% of the deaths of children aged 0 – 4 relate to lack of clean water (p. 3). She also reports that many people in bateyes do not know what causes malaria and cannot name a symptom of the disease (p. 4). Given our previous discussion, it is unsurprising that of the DR residents surveyed, only Haitians indicated that "cost, a lack of respect, and a lack of legal documents were preventing them from seeking care" (Jaskolka-Brown, 2022, p. 4).

Jaskolka-Brown (2022) reports that after the government conducted a survey of health conditions in the bateyes, it instituted programs to counteract the spread of lymphatic filariasis, a mosquito-borne parasite. The program reduced the spread of the disease, but Jaskolka-Brown reports that more was done among poor non-Haitian Dominicans than in the bateyes (p. 5).

Madrid (2014) studied malnutrition rates for children five years old or younger living the DR. His focus was on the stunting rates of children of Haitian descent growing up in bateyes compared to non-Haitians growing up elsewhere in the DR. As might be expected, he found that batey children were more frequently malnourished, 15.9% in bateyes vs. 10.8% of children in the DR population, and as a result, batey children were shorter than similar-aged non-batey children. Similar to the health research cited above, Madrid notes that the children of the bateyes are stateless and are denied access to education, healthcare and civil rights. He concludes, "all of these factors combined indicate that the Haitian community [in the DR] is subjected to a constant state of poor well-being and quality of life" (Madrid, 2014, p. 15).

The studies by Simmons, Filiau, Jaskolka-Brown, and Madrid indicate that batey residents experience poorer health than non-batey residents. The studies connect the poorer health with the social and economic problems named in the present study as being common among Haitians in the DR.

Haitian Creole in the Dominican Republic

Given the difficulties Haitians have in the DR, one would expect that Haitian Creole, the language Haitians bring with them when they migrate to the Dominican, would not be passed on to the migrant's children as a first language. Instead, the children would learn Spanish, the majority language in the DR.

Jansen (2013) indicates that such changes are occurring in the bateyes; the children of Haitian descent born in the bateyes are acquiring Spanish as their first language. She relates that her consultants, all women of Haitian descent, born in bateyes, spoke to children and to each other in Spanish. They spoke Haitian when they spoke to older people who did not know Spanish and in situations in which they wanted to conceal what they were saying from Dominicans (p. 84). Her consultants frequently asked those around them for help in coming up with a Haitian word and would say they did not know Haitian well.

Jansen relates (2013, p. 97) that Dominicans tend to see the bateyes as islands where Haitians speak only Haitian. The present writer encountered such attitudes on a humanitarian trip to the DR in 2014. The group he was with was informed that if they were going to a batey, they would need a translator. The group hired a middle-aged Haitian man to translate. He translated almost nothing the group said into Haitian, but spoke Spanish with most people, reserving Haitian for older adults, exactly the scenario Jansen describes. A Haitian church in the batey, furthermore, conducts its services in Spanish.

Smith (2020) reports the following based on her conversations with batey residents:

To be of Haitian descent was something shameful and even though speaking Creole could be a useful skill on the job, many preferred to pretend that they did not know the language so they would not be categorized as "Haitian." Many feared if others, especially co-workers or employers, knew that they were of Haitian descent, they would lose their jobs or would face discrimination and harassment at work. Instead, they hide their identity to protect their job security (p. 104).

Smith's remarks indicate that Haitian Creole and being Haitian is highly stigmatized in the DR. She notes that "lighter skinned" Haitians are able to "pass" as Dominicans (p. 104), and avoid some discrimination.

On a trip with another group to a batey in June of 2023, the present writer's group needed no translator and spoke Spanish with everyone, including young adults recently arrived from Haiti, who asked a group member for help with Spanish vocabulary.

In April 2024, the writer visited a Haitian church in the DR, but not in a batey, attended by adult migrants from Haiti and their children. On that day, there were four Sunday school classes. Three of the four were for different-aged adults and were conducted in Haitian. The fourth class was for the children of the adults. As Haitian children in the DR are not acquiring Haitian, the children's class was conducted in Spanish.

As seen in the following quotation (Morgan, 1987), the shift from Haitian to Spanish has been occurring for some time: "Continued immigration helps maintain use of Haitian Creole, but … the educational system, the immigrant's desires of economic improvement, and social pressures to conform to the language and culture of the Dominican Republic strongly encourage use of Spanish" (p. 133).

The government's 2018 study referred to earlier, reported that 89.3% of the descendants of immigrants speak Spanish "well or very well" (Oficina Nacional de Estadística, 2018, p. 36).

The government publication, Jansen (2013), Smith (2020), Morgan (1987), and the experience of the present writer, indicate that among Haitians in the DR, a shift to Spanish from Haitian is underway. In the literature on language shift, such changes are commonly reported. Grenoble (2021) identifies factors commonly in play when language shift occurs:

A nexus of factors—historical, political, social, and economic— often provides the impetus for a community to cease speaking their ancestral language, and to replace it with the language of the majority, and usually politically dominant, group.

Language shift is thus a social issue, and often coupled with other indicators of social distress (para 4).

The discussion so far has identified historical, political, social, and economic factors affecting the Haitian population in the DR and thus the shift from Haitian Creole to Spanish represents something normal and expected. Further, Joo et al. (2024) cite numerous studies on language shift, showing that the children of immigrants commonly learn the new majority language, not their heritage language. From all of the preceding, one can conclude that the shift from Haitian to Spanish underway among Haitians in the DR would probably be occurring whether or not Haitian and its speakers were stigmatized.

Anti-Haitianism: Just a Dominican Phenomenon?

In work on Haitians in the DR, one frequently encounters the term "antihaitianismo" or its English equivalent, "anti-Haitianism." In Jaskolka-Brown (2020), the term occurs twelve times. The term occurs numerous times in Jansen (2013), Martínez (2007), and is in the title of Simmons (2010). Sagas (2000) defines anti-Haitianism as "the manifestation of the long-term evolution of racial prejudices, the selective interpretation of historical facts and the creations of a nationalist Dominican 'false consciousness'" (p. 21). Whenever the term is mentioned, it is seen as a contributing factor to the difficult lives Haitians live in the DR.

That anti-Haitianism appears to be taken a given among Dominicans, can be seen in Guerra-Sánchez's remarks cited earlier, especially his statement that the murders "*increase* the repudiation" [emphasis added].

The writer has seen how anti-Haitianism affects people: he knows a Haitian living in the DR who was trained as a doctor at Dominican universities, who, because he is Haitian, was not allowed to practice medicine in the DR. After years of grinding poverty, he is now a medical doctor in Ecuador. Another man with an engineering degree from a Dominican university, is not allowed to get his license and work as an engineer. Instead, he sells sausages in the street.

Nationalist groups within the DR advocate for the removal of Haitians from the country. They support the deportations and want them expanded. A YouTube video posted 21 February 2024, calls for all Haitians to leave the DR within seven days. The video is strongly militaristic, showing tanks and soldiers and features aggressive speech. One woman says on the video that they are giving Haitians in the DR seven days to leave and, she finishes, "we are not playing" (@el_meneoTV, 2024). Three minutes into the video, the narrator strongly criticizes a candidate for public office for using Haitian Creole in her publicity. The narrator says, with obvious frustration "there are many Haitians who are able to vote" (As of 4 June 2024, the video had been cut from 18 minutes to 3 minutes and 8 seconds. At forty seconds, the narrator refers to the woman's speech (now cut), repeating her "we are not playing" remarks). Comments on the video number in the hundreds, all supporting the nationalist views the video expresses.

Estrella (2024) reports on the activities of various nationalist groups in the DR. She indicates that one group, the Antigua Orden Dominicana (henceforth, AOD), routinely disrupts marches and vigils organized by feminist and anti-racist groups and has as its goal the expulsion of all Haitians from the DR. The AOD Facebook page reveals that they have more than 77,000 followers (Antigua Orden Dominicana, n.d.).

Although nationalist groups appear to be relatively few in number, they enjoy widespread support. The fact that there has been little protest within the DR to the deportations nor to the wall the government is building on the border (Associated Press, 2024 May 21, para 7), indicates that anti-Haitian sentiment has significant support within the DR. Shortly after the 2013 "Sentencia," for example, a Gallup poll showed that 83% of Dominicans believed that the government should, by whatever means possible, prevent the entry of Haitians to the country. The same poll also indicated that 48.5% of Dominicans believed Haitians with irregular status should be expelled from the country (Carrón, 2013, p. 29).

As reported by Jansen (2013, p. 97) and in the present writer's experience when told he would need a translator if he went to a batey, Dominicans commonly see the language issue as a point of separation between Dominicans and Haitians. Of course, when different languages are involved, a language difference will always exist. In the case of the contact between Haitian and Spanish in the DR, however, an important difference between the languages is that Spanish is spoken natively in many countries and has greater apparent international prestige than Haitian, which, though spoken by millions of Haitians, is not as widely spoken internationally as Spanish and thus to many Dominicans, is less prestigious than Spanish.

Balaguer's remarks, quoted earlier, about the Spanish language and traditions being a protective wall against Haitian domination appear to reflect a common Dominican attitude towards Haitian Creole. Such attitudes might not be so pronounced if Haitians spoke a major European language instead of the African and French-based creole they do speak.

The origins of Caribbean creoles such as Haitian are debated by linguists, but there is general agreement that the languages came into existence as a byproduct of slavery and the slave trade, and have a lexicon derived mainly from a European language and a grammar at least partly based on one or more African languages.

In the case of Haitian Creole, the vocabulary mainly comes from French (Aboh & deGraff, 2017, p. 24) and much of the grammar has been attributed to the African language Gbe (Lefebvre, 2008, pp. 197-198 and Aboh & deGraff, 2017, p. 59).

Though the African dimension of Haitian Creole is not widely known, it is obvious to people that Haitian is not French, but a creole language, originally spoken by slaves from Africa. That factor, along with the general perception that Haitians look to Africa for their roots, seen in the practice of voodoo (though voodoo, like Haitian Creole, contains African and European elements) and in the intentional identification of themselves as black (Garcia-Peña, 2016, p. 32), correlates with the ostracism Haiti has experienced from the rest of the world. An example can be seen by comparing international responses to the U.S. takeovers of Haiti (1915-1934) and the DR (1916-1924). Calder (1984, pp. 199-204) details opposition throughout Latin America to the U.S. presence in the DR. International opposition to the American presence on Hispaniola primarily had to do with U.S. presence on the Dominican side of the island; there was little Latin American opposition to the simultaneous U.S. presence in Haiti. Latin American opposition to the situation in the DR and its non-involvement in the situation in Haiti correlate with the shared heritage of Latin America and the DR on the one hand and the lack of shared heritage between Haiti and Latin America on the other. The nearly non-existent international response to the current situation in Haiti provides additional evidence of Haiti's ostracism.

Scholarly work mentioning Dominican anti-Haitianism, typically criticizes the DR for its racism. Soiney (2003), for example, refers to Pénson's account of the *Virgins of Galindo* and comments that it is "required reading for every public-school student in the Dominican Republic — demonstrating that notions of Dominican 'purity' are extant in the country, kept alive by the linguistic violence present in the nation's education system" (p. 140).

On the international level, the United Nations has issued statements criticizing the government's actions towards Haitians. Remarks by Volker Türk, UN High Commissioner for Human Rights, regarding deportations of Haitians provide a typical example:

> *A week ago, I called for deportations to Haiti to stop, given the human rights and humanitarian crises the country is facing. I am troubled to see that forced returns of Haitians to Haiti from the Dominican Republic are continuing.*
>
> *Unremitting armed violence and systematic human rights violations in Haiti do not currently allow for the safe, dignified and sustainable return of Haitians to the country. I reiterate my call to all countries in the region, including the Dominican Republic, to halt the deportation of Haitians.*
>
> *I also call on the Dominican Republic authorities to step up efforts to prevent xenophobia, discrimination and related forms of intolerance based on national, racial or ethnic origin, or immigration status (Türk, 2022).*

Haiti's problems are largely the result of actions by the international community. First there was slavery and the slave trade, instituted and managed by European powers. Then, following independence in 1804, there was international ostracism of

Haiti. Then came the "Independence Debt" extortion by France, that challenged the Monroe Doctrine but was never opposed by the United States. Later, while the U.S. governed Haiti from 1915-1934, American banks took over the Haitian loans. Then, when Haitian President Jean-Bertrand Aristide announced that Haiti was preparing to sue France to get back the extorted money, France and the U.S. supported a coup (Phillips, 2008, p. 7 and Valdman, 2015, p. 7) and he was thrown out of office. Finally, after centuries of abuse, the United Nations, of which the United States and France are veto-wielding members, criticizes the DR for being anti-Haitian.

Perhaps Haitians leave Haiti for the DR because they prefer DR anti-Haitianism to the international anti-Haitianism all Haitians experience in Haiti.

Resistance to Anti-Haitianism

In the face of deportations and racist government policies, people in the DR are resisting. Here, the paper presents ways people are responding and making a difference. One group, "Muñecas Negras RD" (Black Dolls Dominican Republic) consists mainly of women and girls of Haitian descent. They make dolls with skin color like that of their makers. The dolls provide a source of income for the batey residents that make them. The organization (website: https://www.conectora.org/2020/11/munecas-negras-rd-emprendimiento-social.html) also teaches literacy and creative writing and participates in protests and other activities focused on changing the government narrative that, as seen in the work of Balaguer and many of the Dominican sources cited throughout the paper, that being black is a negative.

Another group, "Reconoci.do" (website: https://www.reconoci.do/), focuses on protests and getting the government to change its policies. Casey (2023) reports that the group is "petitioning the Dominican government to change its history curriculum" (para 17), so that Black Dominicans and Haiti are not presented as enemies. They report (Civicus.org, 2020) that nationalist groups such as the Antigua Orden Dominicana, threaten them via Facebook, and that when the AOD disrupts their public events, police arrest Reconoci.do members, not AOD people.

One place where Haitian and being Haitian is not stigmatized is a Haitian church in a city of the DR. The present writer was there for a day in 2023, and it was obvious that Haitian identity is important to the people at the church. The services are conducted in Haitian and French. He listened to the church's choir rehearsing a French song that they sang in parts under the leadership of a conductor and has video taken in March 2024 of church members celebrating the dedication of their new church building by parading down the streets of the city, singing in Haitian, accompanied by drums and brass instruments.

Despite deportations, deportation threats, discrimination, and abuse, the groups described above are not going to keep quiet.

Anti-Haitianism in the DR is deep-seated. But as long as there is resistance, there is hope.

Addressing the Situation of Haiti

Whatever the DR accomplishes in reducing anti-Haitianism, such efforts will have little or no effect on conditions within Haiti, conditions which drive Haitians to leave Haiti for the DR and many other countries. Much work has been published on the problems of Haiti and what to do about them. Here, the present paper briefly presents assessments of the current situation and proposals for addressing Haiti's problems. The works listed in "For Further Reading" present information on conditions in Haiti and international responses to those conditions.

For many years, countries have sent armed forces to Haiti to rein in the lawless groups in Haiti and establish peace. The efforts have not had success because, instead of establishing ties with civil society groups within Haiti, they inevitably prop up whatever typically corrupt government is in power, thereby alienating the people most in need of help (Murray & Bernotavicius, 2024, pp. 102-106 and Ward & Brown, 2024, pp. 1-2).

In opposition to the top-down, security-oriented approaches so often employed, organizations such as Christian Aid (Kurien et al., 2024) and researchers such as Boese (2022) advocate for holistic methods that involve the international community but also give agency to affected groups within Haiti. Such efforts appear to have a greater likelihood of success as they do not only work with the government, but allow otherwise disenfranchised people to have a say and a role in how aid is distributed, thereby spreading the benefits of international assistance more widely throughout Haitian society.

CONCLUSION

The paper began by discussing three pivotal events: first, the "Independence Debt," second, the unification period and the attitudes and beliefs Dominicans have about it, and finally, the purchase of land by Central Romana. The paper relates the three events to the difficult lives of Haitians in the DR. The study discussed Dominican and international anti-Haitianism and described resistance within the DR to such attitudes. Finally, the paper discussed international attempts to improve the situation in Haiti. The difficult living conditions of Haitians in the DR underscore the need for the international community to create conditions for Haiti to become a successful country. Massive emigrations do not occur from successful states. If

Haiti were not a failing state, few Haitians would be leaving their homeland and the situations described in the present paper would not be occurring.

REFERENCES

Aboh, E., & deGraff, M. (2017). A null theory of creole formation based on universal grammar. In Roberts, I. (Ed.), *The Oxford handbook of universal grammar* (pp. 401–467)., DOI: 10.1093/oxfordhb/9780199573776.013.18

Antigua Orden Dominicana. (n.d.). Home [Facebook page]. Antigua Orden Dominicana. Retrieved June 10, 2024 from https://www.facebook.com/Antiguaordendominicana1844

Associated Press. (2024, May 21). ¿Que sigue en las restricciones migratorias a los Haitianos en República Dominicana? *Voz de America.*https://www.vozdeamerica.com/a/que-sigue-en-las-restricciones-migratorias-a-los-haitianos-en-republica-dominicana/7620661.html#comments

Balaguer, J. (1970). *Centinela de la frontera.* (n.p.).

Balaguer, J. (1983). *La isla al revés: Haití y el destino dominicano*. Librería Dominicana.

Boese, H. K. (2022). Nou bouke – we are tired: Human security as a tool for foreign aid in Haiti. [Bachelor's thesis, University of Arizona, Tucson, USA]. http://hdl.handle.net/10150/665729

Calder, B. (1984). *The impact of intervention.* University of Texas Press.

Carrón, H. (2013). Borrando la huella africana: La sentencia 168-13 del Tribunal Constitucional Dominicano y la identidad nacional. *Afro-Hispanic Review, 32*(2), 27-40. https://www.jstor.org/stable/24585141

Casey, M. (2023) Black activists take on Dominican government and society in quest for justice and recognition. *Cronkite Borderlands Project.* https://cronkitenews.azpbs.org/2023/09/15/black-activists-dominican-government-justice-and-recognition/

Central Romana. (n.d.). *History*. Retrieved June 5, 2024 from https://centralromana.com.do/memorias/?lang=en

Childers, T. B. (2023). The role of anti-Haitian racism in Dominican mass deportation policy. *Georgetown Journal of International Affairs*, 24(1), 107–113. DOI: 10.1353/gia.2023.a897708

Civicus.org. (2020, August 13). *Dominican Republic: We are part of a global anti-racist movement*. Retrieved June 6, 2024, from https://www.civicus.org/index.php/media-resources/news/interviews/4562-dominican-republic-we-are-part-of-a-global-anti-racist-movement

Del Monte, F. M. (1885). *Las vírgenes de Galindo.* https://curiosity.lib.harvard.edu/latin-american-pamphlet-digital-collection/catalog/43-990061373890203941

Dominican Republic. (1989). In P. W. Goetz (ed.). *The New Encyclopaedia Britannica* (29, pp. 753-758). Chicago. @el_meneoTV (2024, February 21). *Dijeron la orden! Los Haitianos tienen 7 dias para abandonar todos La República Dominicana* [Video]. YouTube. Retrieved June 5, 2024, from https://www.youtube.com/watch?v=q84GXB7xBws&t=219s

Estrella, A. (2024). Dominican Republic's neofascist paramilitaries double down on right-wing repression: New expressions of ultranationalist violence censoring Black women and migrants harken back to the Trujillo dictatorship. Anyone deemed a threat to Dominican values is a potential target. *NACLA Report on the Americas*, 56(1), 42–49. https://www.tandfonline.com/doi/full/10.1080/10714839.2024.2323399?casa_token=S1wJuIhdWEAAAAA:xlu5XU0aMmQf1P_Y59GOadrBVCBEpDIcrDsvzcCp8MAc6q90lIi3OjGkXqWkuEX5YbWYfzBbZ9qOSg. DOI: 10.1080/10714839.2024.2323399

Filiau, A. (2023). *Hope for the future: Key informants' perspectives on HIV prevention in Dominican Republic batey communities* [Doctoral dissertation, UMass Chan Medical School]. https://repository.escholarship.umassmed.edu/handle/20.500.14038/52149

García-Peña, L. G. (2016). *The borders of dominicanidad: Race, nation, and archives of contradiction*. Duke University Press.

Grenoble, L. (2021). Language shift. In Aronoff, M. (Ed.), *Oxford Encyclopedia of Linguistics*., DOI: 10.1093/acrefore/9780199384655.013.347

Guerra-Sánchez, A. J. I. (2016). El crimen de las vírgenes de Galindo. *Historia dominicana en graficas*. Retrieved June 6, 2024, from https://historiadominicanaengraficas.blogspot.com/2016/06/el-crimen-de-las-virgenes-de-galindo.html?view=flipcard

Guilamo, D. (2018). Dominican attitudes toward Haitian immigrants following the 2010 earthquake and before the 2013 sentencing. *The Journal of Pan African Studies*, 12(4), 488–509. https://www.jpanafrican.org/docs/vol12no4/12.4-14-Guilamo.pdf

Haitian unification period (1822-1844): Towards a Dominican perspective. *Cleveland State Law Review, 52*(1), 63-78. https://engagedscholarship.csuohio.edu/clevstlrev/vol52/iss1/5/

Henochsberg, S. (2016). Public debt and slavery: The case of Haiti (1760-1915). [Master's thesis, Paris School of economics.] http://piketty.pse.ens.fr/files/Henochsberg2016.pdf

Highway Motion. (2024, April 6). *Avenida Independencia* [Video]. YouTube. Accessed June 6, 2024 at https://www.youtube.com/watch?v=nylP7oGktlQ&t=587s

Jansen, S. (2013). Language maintenance and language loss in marginalized communities: The case of the bateyes in the Dominican Republic. *International Journal of the Sociology of Language*, 2013(221), 77–100. https://www.degruyter.com/document/doi/10.1515/ijsl-2013-0024/html. DOI: 10.1515/ijsl-2013-0024

Jaskolka-Brown, A. (2022). Haitians In the Dominican Republic: Marginalization and its relationship with public health. *The Macksey Journal, 3*(1).

Joo, S. J., Chik, A., & Djonov, E. (2024). From my parents' language to my language: Understanding language ideologies of young Australian Korean heritage language learners at the primary and secondary school level. *Journal of Multilingual and Multicultural Development*, 45(2), 147–160. DOI: 10.1080/01434632.2020.1871359

Kurien, A., Fevrin, W. L., & Di Vicenz, S. (2024). Haiti: It's time to strengthen homegrown solutions. *Christian Aid.* https://coilink.org/20.500.12592/ht76pq6

Lefebvre, C. (2008). On the principled nature of the respective contributions of substrate and superstrate to a creole's lexicon. In Michaelis, S. (Ed.), *Roots of creole structure: Weighing the contribution of substrates and superstrates* (pp. 197–224). John Benjamins. DOI: 10.1075/cll.33.11lef

Lovaton, R. L. (1953). *Boletin del archivo de la nación.* Editora Montalvo.

Madrid, F. (2014). A comparative analysis of the health status of children under 5 years of age in the Dominican Republic and Dominican bateyes. [Master's thesis, Georgia State University]

Martínez, S. (2007). *Decency and excess: Global aspirations and material deprivation on a Caribbean sugar plantation.* Routledge.

Morgan, N. T. (1987). *Language maintenance and shift among Haitians in the Dominican Republic* (Order No. 8808137) [Doctoral dissertation, University of New Mexico]. ProQuest Dissertations and Theses Global.

Murray, I., & Bernotavicius, C. (2024). *Stabilizing Haiti: A Guide for Policymakers.* Texas National Security Review.

Oficina Nacional de Estadística. (2018). *ENI-2017: Segunda encuesta nacional de Inmigrantes.* https://www.one.gob.do/publicaciones/2018/segunda-encuesta-nacional-de-inmigrantes-en-la-republica-dominicana-eni-2017-informe-general/

Oficina Nacional de Estadística. (2024). *Extranjeros deportados por año, según nacionalidad, 2021-2023.* https://one.gob.do/datos-y-estadisticas/temas/estadisticas-demograficas/migracion/

Pénson, C. N. (1891). *Cosas añejas.* https://archive.org/details/cosas-anejas

Pereyra, E. (2020, April 16). Las vírgenes de Galindo: Estremecedor relato de César Nicolás Penson. *Diario Libre.* Retrieved June 6, 2024, from https://www.diariolibre.com/revista/cultura/las-virgenes-de-galindo-estremecedor-relato-de-cesar-nicolas-penson-KO18168345

Phillips, A. (2008). Haiti, France and the independence debt of 1825. *Canada Haiti Action Network, 24.* https://canada-haiti.ca/sites/default/files/Haiti,%20France%20and%20the%20Independence%20Debt%20of%2018250.pdf

Sagás, E. (2000). *Race and politics in the Dominican Republic.* University Press of Florida.

Silverio, R. (2013, October 13). Protests hit Dominican Republic's expulsion of Haitians. *Workers World.* Retrieved June 3, 2024, from https://www.workers.org/2013/10/11266/

Simmons, D. (2010). Structural violence as social practice: Haitian agricultural workers, anti-Haitianism, and health in the Dominican Republic. *Human Organization*, 69(1), 10–18. DOI: 10.17730/humo.69.1.8271r0j17372k765

Smith, E. (2020). *Livelihoods in the balance: Haitians, Haitian-Dominicans and precarious work in the Dominican Republic.* [Master's Thesis, Pennsylvania State University]. https://etda.libraries.psu.edu/catalog/18182ees238

Soiney, M. (2023). The weaponization of language against ethnic Haitians in the Dominican Republic. *Tensões Mundiais, 19*(39), 157-181. https://revistas.uece.br/index.php/tensoesmundiais/article/view/10135/9071

Türk, V. (2022). *Comment by UN High Commissioner for Human Rights Volker Türk on deportation of Haitians from Dominican Republic.* https://www.ohchr.org/en/press-releases/2022/11/comment-un-high-commissioner-human-rights-volker-turk-deportation-haitians

United Nations. (2022). *Human development index.* https://hdr.undp.org/data-center/human- development-index#/indicies/HDI

United Nations. (n.d.). *International day for the elimination of violence against women 25 November*. https://www.un.org/en/observances/ending-violence-against-women-day/background

Valdman, H. (2015). *Haitian Creole: Structure, Variation, Status, Origin*. Equinox.

Vega, W. B. (1994). *Los documentos básicos de la historia dominicana*. (n.p.).

Venator-Santiago, C. R. (2005). Race, nation-building and legal transculturation during the

Venator-Santiago, C. R. (2011). When literature becomes law: Clarifying Cesar Nicolas Penson's rendition of the case about the prisoners of Galindo. *Rev. Juridica U. Inter. PR, 46*, 759-766. https://heinonline.org/HOL/Page?handle=hein.journals/vjuriprc46&id=825&collection=journals&index=

Walker, A. (2019). All spirits are roused: The 1822 antislavery revolution in Haitian Santo Domingo. *Slavery & Abolition, 40*(3), 583-605. https://ww w.tandfonline.com/doi/abs/10.1080/0144039X.2019.1565438

Ward, H., & Brown, S. (2024). Beyond intervention: Sustainable solutions for Haiti's security needs. *GNSI Decision Brief*. https://digitalcommons.usf.edu/gnsi_decision_briefs/13/

Belony, M. S. (2024). Humanitarian response by NGOs to the 2010 Haiti earthquake: Expectations vs. realities. *McGill Journal of Global Health*, 13(1), 16–27. DOI: 10.26443/mjgh.v13i1.1357

Jean-Baptiste, S. (2024). *Ou pa moun bò isit: Haitian imaginaries of Non-Governmental Organizations* (Doctoral dissertation, Loyola University Chicago). https://www.proquest.com/docview/3069873586?pq-origsite=gscholar&fromopenview=true&sourcetype=Dissertations%20&%20Theses

Paul, B., & Storchevoi, D. (2024). *No. 2* (Vol. 51). Does colonial institutional legacy fully explain why nations fail? Theoretical and empirical confrontations using the case of Haiti. *Forum for Development Studies*. Routledge., DOI: 10.1080/08039410.2023.2255217

Pinheiro, J. S., & Pinheiro, D. S. (2018). Social power and stabilization strategies: A case study of Brazilian troops deployment in Haiti. *ERUDITIO*, 71. https://eruditio.worldacademy.org/files/vol2issue5/reprints/Social-Power-and-Stabilization-Strategies-JSPinheiro-DSPinheiro-Eruditio-V2-I5-Reprint.pdf

Shakibaei, H., Moosavi, S. A., Aghsami, A., & Rabbani, M. (2024). Designing a sustainable-resilient humanitarian supply chain for post-disaster relief process: An earthquake case study in Haiti. *Journal of Humanitarian Logistics and Supply Chain Management*. https://www.emerald.com/insight/content/doi/10.1108/JHLSCM-08-2023-0071/full/html

Steckley, M., Civil, M., Osna, W., Steckley, J., & Sider, S. (2024). A community-engaged tool for evaluating food sovereignty in Haiti and beyond. *Agroecology and Sustainable Food Systems*, 48(10), 1–27. DOI: 10.1080/21683565.2024.2388694

Viau, B. K. (2024). *The nexus between official development aid and economic development in Haiti* [Master's thesis, Virginia State University].

Wood, R. E. (2024). *From Marshall Plan to debt crisis: Foreign aid and development choices in the world economy* (Vol. 15). University of California Press. DOI: 10.2307/jj.15552458

KEY TERMS AND DEFINITIONS

Anti-Haitianism: negative attitudes towards and treatment of Haitians. A point the paper makes is that anti-Haitianism is not only a Dominican phenomenon, but has long been characteristic of the international community.

Batey: any one of the approximately 400 impoverished neighborhoods originally provided by sugarcane companies to house Haitian workers during the sugarcane harvest season, but now inhabited year-round.

Deportations: officially, the practice of the Dominican government to expel to Haiti Haitians and people of Haitian descent who do not have proper documentation. In practice, however, anyone with dark skin can be deported even if they have documentation.

Documented/Undocumented Status in the Dominican Republic: Haitians entering the DR with a valid visa are considered legal aliens. Haitians entering without such a visa enter illegally. Visas must be kept current by traveling once a month to an entry point and paying $50.00 U.S. at an immigration office. Haitians who have a visa but do not keep it current are considered documented but illegal.

Haitian Creole: the language spoken natively by the people of Haiti. Creolists debate the existence of linguistic features distinguishing creole languages from other languages, but there is general agreement that creole languages form as a result of language contact. Most, if not all Caribbean creoles (for example, Jamaican Creole, Haitian Creole, and Papiamentu), originated as byproducts of slavery and the Atlantic slave trade. Each Caribbean creole typically has a vocabulary taken mainly from one European language and a grammar based, at least in part, on one or more West-African languages.

Independence Debt: money (150 million francs) France, in 1825, demanded Haiti pay to compensate for French losses due to the Haitian rebellion. Haiti needed 122 years to pay off the "debt," and the financial burden of making the payments has seemingly permanently crippled the Haitian government.

Language Shift: occurs when speakers of a language stop speaking it in favor of a competing language.

Language Stigmatization: occurs when a language is seen as having low prestige. When a stigmatized language is in competition with another language, speakers of the stigmatized language will tend to use it less and less, leading to language shift. Haitian Creole is stigmatized in Haiti (creoles are frequently stigmatized in their place of origin) and in the Dominican Republic. In Haiti, no shift is underway as Haitian is not in competition with any other language. In the Dominican Republic, Haitian is stigmatized and in competition with Spanish, with the apparently inevitable result that speakers of Haitian in the DR are shifting to Spanish.

ENDNOTES

1 All people in the DR are, ultimately, immigrants or descendants of immigrants; the group being referred to are people descended from recent immigrants from another country.

2 *Mañeses,* used by some Spanish speakers as a disrespectful way to refer to Haitians, has no specific meaning.

Chapter 6
What Drives Corporate Gender Diversity in Latin America?

Kurt Desender
https://orcid.org/0000-0002-6528-8004
Universidad Carlos III de Madrid, Spain

Mónica LópezPuertas Lamy
Universidad Carlos III de Madrid, Spain

ABSTRACT

While corporate gender diversity has substantially increased over the last decade in Latin America, there is still a large gender gap with North America and Europe. This study examines the country and firm-level drivers of this gap, providing insights into factors promoting higher gender diversity in Latin American companies. Our analysis shows that cultural dimensions greatly impact gender diversity at the board and TMT levels. Specifically, power distance and individualism positively influence gender diversity, while masculinity and uncertainty avoidance have negative effects. At the firm-level, we show that board size, board independence, ESG performance, and family ownership are important drivers of gender diversity in Latin America. We also explore the factors driving Latin American firms' commitment to SDG-5 on gender equality. Our findings highlight the necessity of understanding regional contexts to design effective policies for enhancing gender diversity in corporate leadership.

DOI: 10.4018/979-8-3693-3763-9.ch006

INTRODUCTION

Gender diversity in corporate leadership has gained significant attention in recent years. Regulators, politicians, and investors are increasingly urging companies to address the lack of gender diversity at the board and executive levels (Zattoni, Leventis, Van Ees & De Masi., 2022). The literature on board diversity underscores numerous advantages associated with increased gender diversity, including the stimulation of creative thinking and the incorporation of novel perspectives (Adams & Ferreira, 2009; Benton, 2021; Post & Byron, 2014; Desender & LópezPuertas-Lamy, 2024). A 2022 survey of US corporate directors revealed that gender diversity ranked highest in terms of introducing new ways of thinking to the boardroom (PwC Report, 2022). The tension between the suggested benefits and the relatively slow increase in gender diversity at the board and top management team (TMT) level, combined with important differences across countries, raises the question about what drives gender diversity, both at the country and firm-level.

Zattoni et al. (2022) analyze 184 empirical studies on board diversity published in high ranked journals and highlight that only a limited number of papers address the drivers of diversity (13 percent). Yao (2022) develops an integrative review of the drivers of gender diversity at the board and TMT levels and shows that most studies focus on a single country (83 percent), most frequently the US, the UK, and Australia. While the insights gained from the drivers in those settings are relevant, the findings may not readily apply to the case of Latin America characterized by high levels of uncertainty avoidance, low levels of trust in public institutions, traditional gender roles and concentrated ownership structures (Fainshmidt, Judge, Aguilera & Smith, 2018). The lack of comparative evidence is noteworthy considering the well-established institutional theory that emphasizes the influence of broader social structures and various types of institutions on organizations' decision-making, including the promotion of gender diversity (Campbell, 2007). In this regard, Husted and de Sousa-Filho (2019) highlight that Latin America presents a unique configuration of institutional attributes which may lead to results that differ from the mainstream literature.

Latin America lags significantly behind North America and Europe in terms of corporate gender diversity. A recent study by Deloitte (2023) highlights that the average board gender diversity is 15.1 percent in 2023, compared to 7.9 percent in 2018, which is well below the average of other regions, as the average in North America is 28.5 percent and 33.8 percent in Europe. The objective of this study is twofold. First, we aim to add evidence to country-level factors that help to explain the gap in gender diversity between Latin America and other regions. Specifically, we examine the role of cultural dimensions, while controlling for other known institutional and firm-level characteristics. Second, we aim to provide novel insights into the firm-level drivers of gender diversity that apply to Latin American listed firms, to better understand the drivers of companies in Latin America towards higher levels of gender diversity.

Most early studies that focus on gender diversity in Latin America have focused on outcomes such as firm performance, risk, or CSR, providing mixed evidence (e.g., Marquez-Cardenas, Gonzalez-Ruiz & Duque-Grisales, 2022; Moreno-Gómez, Lafuente, & Vaillant, 2018; Mastella, Vancin, Perlin & Kirch, 2021). To better understand the consequences of gender diversity, it is important to understand what shapes gender diversity. To date, to our knowledge, there are no studies that examine corporate governance drivers of gender diversity focused on Latin America, considering both the board and TMT levels.

Focusing on 393 listed firms headquartered in Latin America and 10,856 from other regions over the period 2006-2023, our study aims to contribute to the expanding research on gender diversity in corporate leadership. We find that cultural dimensions have a significant impact on gender diversity both at the board and TMT levels, even after controlling for other known factors. Specifically, we find that power distance and individualism are positively related to gender diversity at both the board and TMT levels. In contrast, masculinity and uncertainty avoidance is negatively related. These findings allow for a better understanding of the reasons behind regional differences in gender diversity. In addition, we focus on firm-level determinants to better understand what drives Latin American companies to increase gender diversity. Our results uncover that board size, board independence, ESG performance and family ownership are important drivers of gender diversity at the board and TMT levels. We also uncover that firm size does not influence board gender diversity, but that it is negatively related to TMT diversity. Our findings also show that board gender diversity and state ownership are relevant drivers of TMT gender diversity. Next, we examine the corporate governance factors that influence the likelihood that Latin American companies commit to the Sustainable Development Goal 5 (SDG 5) on gender equality. We find that ESG performance is one of the main drivers, while other board dimensions show no significant relationship. Finally, we compare the relevance of several corporate governance drivers between Latin America and a global sample and uncover important differences.

Our study makes several notable contributions. Firstly, it addresses the call for more research in understanding the wide range of factors influencing gender diversity variation at both the board and TMT levels, as well as the impact of informal institutions on gender diversity variation. While the literature on the drivers of gender diversity has seen significant development in the past decade, only a limited number of studies explore institutional drivers and regional differences in the firm-levels drivers. Therefore, there is still much to explore regarding how cross-national institutional factors contribute to the variation in gender diversity at the board and

TMT levels. Additionally, our study focuses on an important underexplored region. Our results highlight the significant impact of cultural dimensions on gender diversity in corporate leadership and help to better understand why gender diversity is generally lower in Latin America, compared to other parts of the world. While high Power Distance and Uncertainty Avoidance create rigid structures resistant to change, low Individualism and high Masculinity reinforce traditional gender roles and may restrict women's access to board and TMT positions.

Secondly, we contribute to a better understanding of the corporate governance drivers of gender diversity in Latin America, and how they compare to a global sample. Our findings reveal importance differences. For example, while firm size is a key driver of board gender diversity for a global sample, in Latin America this dimension is not significant for Latin America. Another important difference is the role played by family ownership. While this is not significantly related to board gender diversity and negatively related to TMT gender diversity for a global sample, family ownership is positively related to both board and TMT gender diversity in Latin America. Overall, our findings underscore the importance of understanding local contexts when designing and implementing policies aimed at enhancing gender diversity.

THEORETICAL BACKGROUND AND HYPOTHESES DEVELOPMENT

Institutional Drivers of Gender Diversity

Institutions are widely understood as the "humanly devised constraints that structure human interaction" (North, 1990). They comprise formal rules, informal constraints, and the enforcement characteristics of both. Institutional theory suggests that institutional forces within a given context shape societal expectations about what is appropriate and legitimate, thereby constraining or guiding choices and actions (Scott, 2001). Companies are therefore social entities embedded in an institutional order set (Desender & Epure, 2021). They tend to shape their organizational structures to fit the established social order and gain legitimacy. Indeed, authors such as Aguilera and Jackson (2003) or Lubatkin, Lane, Collin and Very (2007) indicate how differences in the institutional environment are the basis for divergences in corporate governance structures.

Most early studies that focus on drivers of gender diversity examine a single institutional setting and focus on firm and industry characteristics to explain the variance in board gender diversity (e.g., Brammer, Millington & Pavelin, 2007; Hillman, Shropshire & Cannella, 2007; Guldiken et al., 2019; Knippen, Shen & Zhu, 2019).

The review by Zattoni et al. (2023) reveals that only a few multi-country studies (e.g., Chizema et al., 2015; Grosvold & Brammer, 2011) have examined the legal, cultural and social institutions are key drivers of board gender diversity (Zattoni et al., 2023), mostly focused on highly developed economies. For instance, Terjesen and Singh (2008) argue that a country's social, political, and economic frameworks significantly influence the representation of women on corporate boards. Their research reveals that nations with greater female representation on boards also tend to have more women in senior management roles and fairer gender pay ratios. Grosvold and Brammer (2011) find that national institutional systems explain a large portion of the differences in women's board representation. They emphasize that cultural and legal orientations within these systems play a crucial role in shaping board diversity. Similarly, Carrasco et al. (2015) explore how cultural characteristics impact women's directorships in 32 countries, including two Latin American countries, for the year 2010. They find that that nations with lower board gender diversity often tolerate higher power inequalities and uphold traditional gender roles. Chizema et al. (2015) examine the influence of religiosity on board gender diversity, and find that traditional gender stereotypes associated with religiosity are negatively correlated with diversity. Grosvold et al. (2016) identify several institutional factors that positively correlate with female board representation, including divorce rates, female labor force participation, female managerial participation, government investment in daycare facilities, and legal protections for mothers returning to work post-childbirth.

While extensive research has explored the relationship between institutional factors and board gender diversity, most of the prior research do not account for a comprehensive sample of emerging economies or considers the recent surge in gender diversity. Finally, few studies examine whether drivers of board diversity play a similar role for diversity at the TMT level (Yao, 2023).

Informal Institutions and Gender Diversity

According to institutional theory, firm decision makers are influenced by "common understandings of what is appropriate and, fundamentally, meaningful behavior" in the environment in which they are embedded (Zucker, 1983: 105). North (1990) describes these common understandings as informal institutions. If institutions are seen as "the rules of the game," then informal institutions are the unwritten, unspoken rules—collective beliefs, values, and social norms—that constrain the behavior of individuals and organizations (Desender, Castro & Escamilla de León, 2011). These informal institutions are often collectively referred to as "culture." At the core of culture are value emphases, which are the implicitly or explicitly shared abstract ideas about what is good, right, and desirable within a society (Williams, 1970). Culture provides motivation and justification for types of behavior that are consistent with beliefs, assumptions, values, and practices prevailing within a given country (Deephouse, Newburry, & Solemani, 2016; Guiso, Sapienza & Zingales, 2006; Licht, Goldschmidt, & Schwartz, 2007).

Hofstede (1980, 2001) provided a foundational framework for understanding cultural values, centered on four cultural dimensions that remain central to cultural research: Individualism, Power Distance, Uncertainty Avoidance, and Masculinity. Latin American countries generally exhibit high Power Distance, low Individualism (indicating collectivism), varying levels of Masculinity, and very high Uncertainty Avoidance. These cultural characteristics taken together highlight the regional tendencies in Latin America towards hierarchical structures, collective social frameworks, and a strong preference for stability and order.

Gender schema theory posits that individuals in society develop culture-specific cognitive structures, or schemas, that dictate role expectations for females and males (Bem, 1981). These gender schemas foster stereotyped attitudes and can result in discriminatory behaviors (Lemons & Parzinger, 2007). The decisions individuals make about themselves and others are influenced by how these schemas shape the processing of information (Bem, 1981; Starr & Zurbriggen, 2017), including beliefs about appropriate roles for men and women in society (Lemons & Parzinger, 2007). Through gender-schematic processing, individuals feel pressured to conform to societal norms regarding gender-appropriate behaviors (Bem, 1981). Building on the cultural dimensions defined by Hofstede (1980; 2001) and prior work by Carrasco et al. (2015), we next develop how Power Distance, Individualism, Uncertainty Avoidance, and Masculinity is related to gender diversity.

Power Distance

Power distance refers to the extent to which less powerful members of a society accept and expect that power is distributed unequally (Hofstede, 2001). In cultures with high power distance, hierarchical structures are deeply entrenched, and authority is rarely questioned (Lewellyn, & Bao, 2017). The relationship between power distance and gender diversity could be positive or negative. On the one hand, societies that score high on power distance may struggle with gender diversity as traditional power structures often favor male leadership and maintain the status quo, limiting opportunities for women to ascend to board and TMT positions (Sealy, Vinnicombe & Doldor, 2009). Conversely, in cultures with low power distance, there is a greater emphasis on egalitarianism and meritocracy. Organizations in these cultures are more likely to challenge traditional gender roles and promote women based on their qualifications and competencies, thereby enhancing gender diversity at the top levels.

Empirically, Carrasco et al. (2015) find support for a negative link between power distance and board gender diversity.

On the other hand, decisions and initiatives often come from the top of the hierarchy in high power distance cultures. When top leaders are committed to gender diversity, they can effectively implement policies and quotas that promote the inclusion of women at board and TMT levels. This may be especially relevant in settings where companies are controlled by its founders, and the involvement of family members in key executive positions is very common, like in Latin America (Bertrand & Schoar, 2006). The hierarchical nature ensures compliance with these directives throughout the organization, even when there may be resistance towards gender diversity. As arguments are presented at both sides, we hypothesize

H1a: Board and TMT gender diversity is lower/higher in cultures with high power distance.

Individualism

Individualism measures the degree of interdependence a society maintains among its members. In highly individualistic cultures, personal achievements and individual rights are paramount (Desender et al., 2011). This cultural focus encourages organizations to adopt fair evaluation and promotion practices, ensuring that women have equal opportunities to ascend to leadership roles based on their performance and capabilities, rather than being held back by gender biases. Individualistic societies are also more likely to support work-life balance initiatives and flexible working arrangements, which can facilitate the participation of women in the workforce and their progression to senior positions. Policies such as remote work, parental leave, and childcare support can significantly enhance women's ability to pursue and sustain leadership roles.

On the other hand, in cultures with high institutional collectivism, people rely on membership in groups for identity and status (Hofstede, 2001). For instance, in highly collectivist cultures like China, acting outside of well-accepted group norms and belief systems is seen as 'losing face' or 'shameful' (Lewellyn, & Bao, 2017). As a result, collectivist cultures, which emphasize group harmony and collective decision-making, may prioritize traditional gender roles and familial responsibilities, potentially hindering women's advancement to top leadership roles. Empirically, Carrasco et al. (2015) find no significant link between individualism and board gender diversity. Taking the arguments together, we hypothesize that:

H1b: Board and TMT gender diversity is higher in individualistic cultures.

Masculinity

The masculinity dimension captures the extent to which a society values traditionally masculine traits such as competitiveness, assertiveness, and material success, as opposed to feminine traits like care, cooperation, and quality of life (Hofstede, 2001). In highly masculine cultures, business environments are often competitive and dominated by male norms, which can create barriers for women aspiring to reach board and TMT levels (Eagly & Carli, 2007). Such environments may be less open to women and may devalue leadership styles typically associated with women, such as collaboration and empathy. This can deter women from aspiring to or being selected for top management roles. Furthermore, the traits traditionally valued in leaders—such as toughness, decisiveness, and competitiveness—are often associated with male leaders, in masculine cultures. This bias can lead to the systematic exclusion of women from leadership roles, as they may not fit the stereotypical image of a leader in these cultures (Carrasco et al., 2015). In contrast, cultures with lower masculinity (more femininity) emphasize collaboration, care, and gender equality, fostering an environment where women can thrive and attain leadership positions. These societies are more likely to implement gender-inclusive policies and support initiatives aimed at reducing gender disparities in the workplace. Empirically, Konrad et al. (2000), and Oakley (2000) lend support to the idea that the attribution of stereotyped values to women can negatively bias their appointment to corporate boards. Carrasco et al. (2015) find a negative link between masculinity and board gender diversity. Taking these arguments together, we hypothesize:

H1c: Board and TMT gender diversity is lower in masculine cultures.

Uncertainty Avoidance

Uncertainty avoidance indicates the degree to which members of a society feel uncomfortable with uncertainty and ambiguity (Hofstede, 2001). High uncertainty avoidance cultures prefer structured environments with clear rules and stability. These cultures might resist changes to traditional gender roles and be slower to adopt gender diversity initiatives, fearing that such changes could disrupt established norms and create uncertainty. In addition, women are often expected to conform to conventional roles in high uncertainty avoidance societies, which limits their opportunities to ascend to leadership positions. The societal pressure to maintain these roles can discourage women from pursuing high-level careers and can prevent organizations from recognizing and promoting female talent. In contrast, cultures with low uncertainty avoidance are more open to innovation and change, which can include embracing gender diversity as a means to enhance organizational adaptability and performance. These cultures are more likely to experiment with and adopt policies that support the inclusion of women in leadership roles, viewing diversity as a strategic advantage in navigating a complex and dynamic business environment. Empirically, Carrasco et al. (2015) find no significant relationship between uncertainty avoidance and board gender diversity. Taking the arguments together, we hypothesize that:

H1d: Board and TMT gender diversity is lower in societies with high uncertainty avoidance

Corporate Governance Drivers of Gender Diversity in Latin America

Most early studies that focus on gender diversity in Latin America have focused on outcomes such as firm performance, risk, or CSR, providing mixed evidence. Marquez-Cardenas, Gonzalez-Ruiz and Duque-Grisales (2022) show that board gender diversity in Latin America does not lead to any change in firm performance. In contrast, Moreno-Gómez, Lafuente, and Vaillant (2018) find a positive link for a sample of Colombian firms and, Mastella, Vancin, Perlin, and Kirch (2021) find that women on the board has a positive effect on accounting and market performance measures for a sample of Brasilian firms. De Abreu, Soares, Daniel-Vasconcelos and Crisóstomo (2023) find no significant link between board diversity and CSR activities for a sample of firms from Brazil, Mexico, and Chile. To gain a better understanding of the consequences of gender diversity, it is important to understand what drives gender diversity, at the board and TMT levels, in the first place. We focus on several relevant corporate governance dimension, including board size, board independence, family and state ownership and ESG performance.

Board Size and Gender Diversity

Board size has been identified as a significant factor influencing gender diversity on corporate boards. Larger boards tend to encompass a broader talent network, increasing the likelihood of including female directors. This relationship is supported by evidence from North America (Burke, 1999; Hillman et al., 2007), Malaysia (Abdullah, 2014), and China (Farag & Mallin, 2016). These findings suggest that as the size of the board increases, the opportunities and scope for appointing female directors expand due to the need to fill more positions and the access to a wider pool of candidates. However, this relationship is not universal, as Kang et al., (2007) find no significant correlation between board size and the proportion of female directors for a sample of Australian firms. This suggests that the impact of board size on gender diversity may be contingent upon regional or contextual factors. Taking the arguments together, we hypothesize that:

Hypothesis 2a: There is a positive relationship between board size and gender diversity on corporate boards.

Board Independence and Gender Diversity

Board independence, defined by the presence of independent directors versus insiders, is likely to shape gender diversity. In the United States, boards with more insiders tend to have fewer female directors (Carter et al., 2003). This could be due to insiders less inclined to disrupt existing power dynamics by introducing diverse members. Independent directors, who are not part of the company's management, may be more open to advocating for gender diversity as part of good governance practices and as the broader push for inclusion and diversity. Taking the arguments together, we hypothesize that:

Hypothesis 2b: There is a positive relationship between board independence and gender diversity on corporate boards.

Family and State Ownership and Gender Diversity

Ownership structure plays a crucial role in determining board composition and, consequently, gender diversity. In family-owned businesses, there is often a higher proportion of female directors, particularly those with familial ties, as observed in French and Indian firms (Nekhili & Gatfaoui, 2013; Saeed et al., 2019). This might be due to the willingness of family-owned businesses to integrate female family members into leadership roles. In addition to a positive role played by family ownership, we expect a positive relationship between state ownership and gender diversity. Companies with state participation are likely to be sensitive towards gender diversity, as they are often subject to greater public scrutiny. As such, they may face more reputational risks associated with unethical or discriminatory practices. Empirically, the evidence is mixed however. In Indian firms, state ownership does not significantly affect board gender diversity (Saeed et al., 2019), whereas in Chinese listed companies, state ownership is associated with lower gender diversity (Farag & Mallin, 2016). These mixed findings indicate that the relationship between state ownership and gender diversity may be influenced by country-specific governance practices and cultural norms. Taking the arguments together, we hypothesize that:

Hypothesis 2c: Family and State ownership is positively associated with gender diversity on corporate boards.

ESG and Gender Diversity

Environmental, Social, and Governance (ESG) factors have increasingly been linked to corporate decision-making and stakeholder value. Companies with strong ESG practices may show greater commitment to ethical values and moral standards (LópezPuertas, Desender & Epure, 2017). In addition, Desender et al., (2020) highlight that consistency across different ESG dimensions is critical to obtain the potential benefits associated with ESG. As a result, firms that prioritize ESG principles may view gender diversity not only as a moral imperative but also as a strategic asset that enhances reputation, drives innovation, and improves decision-making processes. Taking the arguments together, we hypothesize that:

Hypothesis 2d: There is a positive relationship between a firm's commitment to ESG practices and gender diversity on corporate boards.

METHODOLOGY

Sample

The sample for this study is obtained from combining several datasets. We start from all firms within the Refinitiv ESG database, which provides data on ESG and corporate governance dimensions across the world. We combine this data with financial and ownership data from Refinitiv Eikon, and country level data from the worldbank database. We winsorize our firm-level financial variables at the one percent top and bottom levels to avoid outlier-related problems. Our final sample consists of 11,249 firms, of which 393 have their headquarter in Latin America, and contains a total of 78,232 firm-year observations.

Model and Variables: Country-Level Analysis

Our empirical analysis is organized around two key questions. The first analysis focuses on uncovering the relationship between cultural values and gender diversity; while the second analysis focuses on company-level drivers of gender diversity. To estimate the relevance of culture on gender diversity, we estimate the following models:

Board Gender Diversity% = f(Power distance, Individualism, Masculinity, Uncertainty Avoidance, country-level controls, firm-level controls, year, industry) (1)

TMT Gender Diversity% = f(Power distance, Individualism, Masculinity, Uncertainty Avoidance, country-level controls, firm-level controls, year, industry) (2)

Dependent Variables

Board Gender Diversity (%) is measured as the percentage of female directors on a company's board, while *TMT Gender Diversity (%)* represents the percentage of women in top management teams. Both measures are obtained from the Refinitiv ESG database.

Independent Variables: Country Level

Power Distance measures the extent to which less powerful members of a society accept and expect power to be distributed unequally. Higher power distance scores are associated with hierarchical organizational structures that may impede gender diversity. *Individualism* reflects the degree of interdependence a society maintains among its members. Higher scores indicate individualistic societies that emphasize personal achievements. *Masculinity* measures the preference in society for achievement, heroism, assertiveness, and material rewards for success. Higher scores denote more competitive, masculine-oriented cultures. *Uncertainty Avoidance* indicates the extent to which members of a society feel uncomfortable with uncertainty and ambiguity. Higher scores reflect societies that prefer structured conditions. The data for the cultural dimensions is obtained from https://geerthofstede.com/.

Country-Level Control Variables

Ln(GDP per capita) is the natural logarithm of the Gross Domestic Product per capita, representing economic development. Economic development correlates with better educational opportunities, higher living standards, and progressive values, and is therefore likely to foster more inclusive workplace cultures. *Rule of Law* is an index variable that measures the extent to which agents have confidence in and abide by the rules of society. Confidence in and adherence to legal systems, reflects a country's commitment to enforcing anti-discrimination laws and gender equality policies, promoting a fair environment for gender diversity. *Control of Corruption* is an index variable that measures the extent to which public power is exercised for private gain; lower corruption levels are linked to transparent and merit-based business practices, enhancing gender diversity. The country-level variables are obtained from the WorlBank Database.

Firm-Level Control Variables

Ln(total assets) is the natural logarithm of a company's total assets, representing firm size. Larger firms are likely to have resources and structures that support gender diversity, but may also be under greater scrutiny. *Leverage* is the ratio of a company's total debt to its total equity. Market to Book Ratio is the ratio of the market value of a company's equity to its book value. Firms with higher growth opportunities and valuations may be more likely to promote gender diversity. The data for the firm-level financial controls is obtained from Refinitiv Eikon. *Family Ownership* measures the ownership stake held by individuals and families. The data is obtained from Refinitiv Eikon. Finally, we include year, industry fixed effects.

Model and Variables: Firm-Level Analysis

To estimate the relevance of firm-level corporate governance on gender diversity, we estimate the following 3 models:

Board Gender Diversity% = f(Board Size, Board Independence, CEO-Chair Duality, Family Ownership, State Ownership, ESG performance, firm-level controls, year, industry, country) (3)

TMT Gender Diversity% = f(Board Gender Diversity%, Board Size, Board Independence, CEO-Chair Duality, Family Ownership, State Ownership, ESG performance, firm-level controls, year, industry, country) (4)

SDG5 – Gender diversity (0/1) = f(Board Gender Diversity%, TMT Gender Diversity%, Board Size, Board Independence, CEO-Chair Duality, Family Ownership, State Ownership, ESG performance, firm-level controls, year, industry, country) (5)

Dependent Variables

Board Gender Diversity (%) is the percentage of female directors on a company's board. *TMT Gender Diversity (%)* is the percentage of women in top management teams. *SDG 5 Gender Equality (0/1)* is a binary variable indicating a firm's commitment to Sustainable Development Goal 5 (SDG 5) on gender equality. The three gender diversity dimensions are obtained from Refinitiv ESG.

Independent Variables

CEO-Chairman Duality is a binary variable indicating whether the CEO also serves as the chairman of the board. *Board Independence* is measured as the proportion of independent directors on the board. *Board Size* is measured as the total number of directors on the board. ESG Performance is a measure of a firm's performance in environmental, social, and governance (ESG) aspects. *Family Ownership* measures the ownership stake held by individuals and families. *Government Ownership* captures the ownership stake held by regional and national governments. In addition, we include year, industry and country fixed effects. Data on board composition and ESG is obtained from Refinitiv ESG, while ownership data is obtained from Refinitiv Eikon.

RESULTS

Descriptive Statistics

Table 1 presents descriptive statistics for firm-level variables in a global sample compared to a subset from Latin America. The global sample consists of 78,232 observations with a mean board gender diversity of 17.1 percent, while the Latin American subset has 2,803 observations with a lower mean of 9.7 percent. Similarly, TMT gender diversity is higher globally at 13.7 percent compared to 9.1 percent in Latin America. The commitment to SDG 5 on gender equality shows a mean of 27.0 percent globally and 44.7 percent in Latin America, indicating much stronger commitment.

Table 1. Descriptive statistics of the firm-level variables

	Global Sample			**Latin America**		
	Obs	**Mean**	**Std. Dev.**	**Obs**	**Mean**	**Std. Dev.**
Board Gender Diversity%	78,232	0.171	0.139	2,803	0.097	0.105
TMT Gender Diversity%	75,501	0.137	0.147	2,797	0.091	0.110
SDG 5 Gender equality	38,356	0.270	0.444	1,442	0.447	0.497
Ln(total assets)	78,232	22.149	1.956	2,803	22.280	1.619
Leverage	78,232	0.559	0.232	2,803	0.591	0.207
Market to Book Ratio	78,232	3.051	4.210	2,803	1.877	2.488
CEO-chairman duality	78,232	0.364	0.481	2,803	0.278	0.448
Board Independence	74,535	0.583	0.259	2,785	0.371	0.225
Board Size	78,202	9.773	3.515	2,802	10.451	3.995
ESG Performance	78,232	43.536	20.707	2,803	47.066	22.017
Family Ownership	70,634	0.086	0.168	2,570	0.051	0.142
Government Ownership	70,634	0.014	0.082	2,570	0.017	0.099
Power Distance	78,232	49.936	17.634	2,803	67.901	9.043

continued on following page

Table 1. Continued

	Global Sample			Latin America		
	Obs	**Mean**	**Std. Dev.**	**Obs**	**Mean**	**Std. Dev.**
Individualism	78,232	64.807	27.785	2,803	31.721	9.569
Masculinity	78,232	59.253	17.361	2,803	51.416	12.989
Uncertainty Avoidance	78,232	53.654	20.784	2,803	80.937	4.368
Ln(GDP per capita)	75,560	10.435	0.851	2,803	9.163	0.270
Control Of Corruption	78,232	1.161	0.788	2,803	-0.137	0.632
Rule of Law	78,232	1.226	0.714	2,803	-0.106	0.584

The Latin American subset shows a significantly higher mean power distance (67.901) compared to the global sample (49.936), suggesting that Latin American cultures are more accepting of hierarchical structures and inequalities in power distribution. Individualism is markedly different, with the global sample having a high mean score (64.807) compared to the Latin American subset (31.721). Finally, we observe a large difference in uncertainty avoidance, which is substantially higher in Latin America (80.937) compared to the global sample (53.654). Considering relevant control variables, control of corruption and rule of law are notably weaker in Latin America, compared to a global sample.

Table 2. Descriptives statistics of the main variables of interest by country over the period

	N Obs	Board Gender Diversity%	TMT Gender Diversity%	SDG 5 Gender equality	Power Distance	Indivi-dualism	Mascu-linity	Uncertainty Avoidance	Ln(GDP per capita)	Control Of Corruption	Rule of Law
Argentina	316	8.5%	6.7%	36.7%	49	46	56	86	9.29	-0.18	-0.41
Brazil	1,088	10.1%	8.1%	53.8%	69	38	49	76	9.13	-0.26	-0.15
Chile	417	8.4%	7.7%	40.3%	63	23	28	86	9.55	1.25	1.21
Colombia	190	15.8%	20.7%	46.6%	67	13	64	80	8.77	-0.30	-0.37
Mexico	593	8.5%	6.9%	43.2%	81	30	69	82	9.13	-0.70	-0.59
Peru	199	9.5%	15.9%	33.3%	64	16	42	87	8.78	-0.48	-0.46
Australia	3,581	18.9%	17.7%	21.0%	38	90	61	51	10.89	1.85	1.74
Austria	300	22.4%	5.3%	53.5%	11	55	79	70	10.80	1.55	1.85
Belgium	478	25.7%	13.6%	36.5%	65	75	54	94	10.71	1.48	1.39
Canada	3,858	18.6%	14.9%	23.3%	39	80	52	48	10.72	1.85	1.76
China	5,888	12.8%	14.5%	20.7%	80	20	66	30	9.11	-0.22	-0.21
Denmark	563	23.2%	11.2%	46.3%	18	74	16	23	10.97	2.30	1.91
Finland	586	28.3%	20.3%	31.3%	33	63	26	59	10.76	2.24	2.03

continued on following page

Table 2. Continued

	N Obs	Board Gender Diversity%	TMT Gender Diversity%	SDG 5 Gender equality	Power Distance	Indivi-dualism	Mascu-linity	Uncertainty Avoidance	Ln(GDP per capita)	Control Of Corruption	Rule of Law
France	1,759	31.9%	15.0%	52.1%	68	71	43	86	10.59	1.33	1.42
Germany	1,973	21.2%	7.2%	32.0%	35	67	66	65	10.70	1.85	1.64
Greece	320	11.2%	17.2%	42.5%	60	35	57	112	9.97	0.03	0.43
Hong Kong	1,795	11.1%	17.0%	24.3%	68	25	57	29	10.59	1.72	1.64
India	2,012	14.1%	7.1%	29.1%	77	48	56	40	7.47	-0.31	-0.02
Indonesia	568	9.2%	15.2%	47.1%	78	14	46	48	8.19	-0.47	-0.41
Ireland	552	19.1%	13.3%	28.2%	28	70	68	35	11.05	1.60	1.60
Israel	286	20.0%	19.2%	21.8%	13	54	47	81	10.55	0.80	1.01
Italy	931	28.4%	9.1%	52.3%	50	76	70	75	10.42	0.31	0.35
Japan	6,725	4.7%	1.5%	43.4%	54	46	95	92	10.60	1.48	1.43
Korea	1,597	3.8%	2.5%	34.8%	60	18	39	85	10.26	0.58	1.09
Luxembourg	167	19.2%	12.0%	44.5%	40	60	50	70	11.63	2.07	1.79
Malaysia	1,162	19.2%	28.1%	40.3%	104	26	50	36	9.24	0.22	0.59
Morocco	73	18.5%	16.1%	35.6%	70	46	53	68	8.01	-0.35	-0.09
Netherlands	679	22.3%	12.4%	31.9%	38	80	14	53	10.82	1.99	1.81
New Zealand	464	26.6%	22.1%	21.4%	22	79	58	49	10.63	2.23	1.92
Norway	575	40.7%	21.4%	45.5%	31	69	8	50	11.24	2.11	1.98
Pakistan	22	10.8%	2.0%	50.0%	55	14	50	70	7.08	-0.84	-0.69
Philippines	332	12.1%	33.4%	51.7%	94	32	64	44	7.99	-0.53	-0.47
Poland	378	18.0%	15.6%	29.1%	68	60	64	93	9.55	0.65	0.61
Portugal	71	28.2%	19.8%	68.3%	63	27	31	104	10.03	0.80	1.16
Russia	388	6.9%	15.2%	30.5%	93	39	36	95	9.35	-0.96	-0.78
Singapore	846	12.1%	26.0%	26.2%	74	20	48	8	10.87	2.16	1.77
Spain	758	19.3%	13.5%	56.4%	57	51	42	86	10.26	0.87	1.04
Sweden	1,776	31.2%	21.8%	45.4%	31	71	5	29	10.87	2.15	1.86
Switzerland	1,531	14.9%	7.0%	24.1%	34	68	70	58	11.30	2.06	1.87
Taiwan	1,842	10.1%	12.8%	43.4%	58	17	45	69	-	0.90	1.12
Thailand	830	17.8%	30.8%	39.0%	64	20	34	64	-	-0.41	0.03
Turkey	596	14.6%	13.2%	65.3%	66	37	45	85	9.19	-0.20	-0.20
United Kingdom	4,963	20.9%	15.3%	29.2%	35	89	66	35	10.65	1.77	1.66
United States	24,146	19.2%	15.1%	12.2%	40	91	62	46	10.96	1.29	1.53
Vietnam	58	19.3%	27.3%	32.8%	70	20	40	30	7.93	-0.40	-0.10

We next consider the differences at country level in Table 2, which reveals notable differences. Argentina has relatively low board gender diversity at 8.5 percent and TMT gender diversity at 6.7 percent. Brazil shows slightly higher figures, with board gender diversity at 10.1 percent and TMT gender diversity at 8.1 percent.

Chile exhibits similar board gender diversity to Argentina at 8.4 percent but a slightly higher TMT gender diversity at 7.7 percent. Colombia stands out with the highest gender diversity in both dimensions among the Latin American countries listed, with board gender diversity at 15.8 percent and TMT gender diversity at 20.7 percent. Mexico has board gender diversity at 8.5 percent and TMT gender diversity at 6.9 percent, showing similar figures to Argentina and Chile. Peru presents a higher TMT gender diversity at 15.9 percent, but its board gender diversity is 9.5 percent which is moderate compared to other Latin American countries. In terms of commitment to SDG 5 (gender equality), Brazil leads with 53.8 percent of its firms showing this commitment, followed by Mexico at 43.2 percent, and Colombia at 46.6 percent. Peru and Argentina have the lowest commitment among these countries, with 33.3 percent and 36.7 percent respectively.

Table 3. A comparison of Gender Diversity and Commitment to SDG 5 for 2013, 2018 and 2023

country	Obs	SDG 5 gender equality	Board Gender Diversity	TMT Gender Diversity	Obs	Board Gender Diversity	TMT Gender Diversity	Obs	Board Gender Diversity	TMT Gender Diversity
Year	2023	2023	2023	2023	2018	2018	2018	2013	2013	2013
Argentina	54	51.9%	10.3%	8.7%	57	6.0%	5.0%	-	-	-
Brazil	112	75.0%	15.4%	10.6%	136	9.3%	7.6%	137	6.7%	7.5%
Chile	34	76.5%	16.9%	14.6%	46	7.5%	7.2%	46	5.0%	3.0%
Colombia	14	78.6%	21.9%	19.0%	25	16.5%	20.9%	25	12.8%	18.9%
Mexico	86	55.8%	12.0%	11.4%	101	6.7%	5.2%	101	7.3%	6.7%
Peru	15	66.7%	19.8%	25.5%	35	5.8%	15.1%	35	7.4%	7.1%
Australia	384	36.9%	28.5%	22.6%	392	18.9%	18.9%	394	11.2%	13.8%
Austria	36	75.0%	31.0%	8.3%	36	21.6%	3.3%	36	14.1%	4.7%
Belgium	47	48.9%	36.9%	18.4%	51	30.3%	16.6%	51	14.8%	11.1%
Canada	366	38.1%	29.6%	18.8%	432	20.4%	14.6%	436	10.5%	14.1%
China	1245	32.8%	15.3%	16.6%	1305	11.3%	12.9%	1305	7.5%	11.3%
Denmark	63	65.1%	33.0%	16.4%	65	25.8%	10.7%	65	18.8%	8.5%
Finland	74	41.9%	31.7%	24.4%	77	35.8%	20.3%	77	26.2%	15.6%
France	174	66.7%	44.9%	22.4%	189	43.7%	14.2%	189	23.5%	12.9%
Germany	245	45.7%	27.5%	11.4%	274	25.8%	6.8%	276	16.4%	5.0%
Greece	24	70.8%	20.9%	16.0%	30	10.5%	18.1%	30	10.7%	18.4%
Hong Kong	162	41.6%	15.7%	21.5%	172	10.8%	18.2%	172	8.9%	15.5%
India	703	28.0%	18.2%	9.4%	717	13.4%	6.1%	717	6.2%	4.1%
Indonesia	80	56.3%	14.3%	19.7%	87	7.9%	14.7%	87	5.0%	10.7%
Ireland	44	59.1%	33.2%	19.2%	49	19.9%	12.9%	49	12.4%	10.7%

continued on following page

Table 3. Continued

country	Obs	SDG 5 gender equality	Board Gender Diversity	TMT Gender Diversity	Obs	Board Gender Diversity	TMT Gender Diversity	Obs	Board Gender Diversity	TMT Gender Diversity
Israel	35	22.9%	24.8%	18.7%	40	20.0%	16.1%	40	15.9%	19.6%
Italy	125	68.8%	38.9%	11.4%	132	34.4%	7.8%	132	14.6%	5.7%
Japan	478	70.9%	12.1%	3.4%	499	5.5%	1.7%	499	2.9%	0.8%
Korea	149	59.5%	12.3%	5.1%	172	2.7%	2.2%	172	0.8%	0.5%
Luxembourg	36	52.8%	24.1%	12.1%	37	15.5%	14.2%	37	16.8%	11.8%
Malaysia	344	44.3%	23.4%	31.2%	349	19.7%	25.2%	349	8.9%	25.7%
Morocco	46	34.8%	19.1%	16.0%	46	0.0%	0.0%	46	8.3%	25.1%
Netherlands	65	44.6%	36.9%	18.1%	69	25.8%	12.0%	69	13.7%	9.6%
New Zealand	61	33.3%	33.9%	26.4%	61	24.8%	18.7%	61	16.9%	18.0%
Norway	79	67.1%	44.2%	25.1%	82	40.3%	20.5%	82	42.7%	16.7%
Pakistan	11	54.5%	10.9%	1.7%	11	7.1%	2.5%	-	-	-
Philippines	38	65.8%	19.4%	34.8%	39	10.0%	32.7%	39	7.1%	32.6%
Poland	31	54.8%	25.0%	14.9%	39	17.2%	15.5%	39	9.8%	14.7%
Portugal	14	78.6%	35.0%	21.8%	15	17.0%	15.6%	15	5.6%	9.9%
Singapore	95	38.9%	20.1%	31.9%	101	11.1%	22.3%	101	7.6%	22.8%
South Africa	114	54.4%	32.3%	25.6%	117	23.5%	21.7%	117	19.4%	18.0%
Spain	67	76.1%	33.5%	20.1%	74	21.2%	14.6%	74	14.0%	12.7%
Sweden	300	56.3%	33.9%	25.3%	315	35.0%	20.1%	315	27.8%	20.4%
Switzerland	183	37.0%	21.6%	10.2%	195	18.2%	6.6%	195	8.8%	5.3%
Taiwan	178	60.7%	13.6%	18.4%	183	10.8%	13.9%	183	7.1%	8.5%
Thailand	163	53.4%	21.3%	34.1%	179	14.1%	28.1%	179	12.6%	27.0%
Turkey	107	78.5%	20.0%	15.9%	116	10.4%	11.9%	116	9.4%	10.7%
United Kingdom	576	42.3%	32.5%	21.6%	602	22.6%	15.5%	603	13.5%	12.5%
United States	3063	17.4%	27.1%	18.8%	3358	15.4%	13.9%	3362	14.8%	13.0%
Vietnam	18	38.9%	20.7%	24.4%	27	0.0%	0.0%	-	-	-

Note: We limit the table to countries that have at least ten listed company with their headquarter in the focal country in 2022.

Over the last decade, gender diversity has gained much attention and firms have started to make important changes. In Table 3, we compare the level of gender diversity in 2023, country by country to the situation 5 years ago and 10 ago. Analyzing the changes in gender diversity in Latin America from 2013 to 2023 reveals significant progress.

In Argentina, between 2018 and 2023, board gender diversity increased from 6.0 percent to 10.3 percent, and TMT gender diversity rose from 5.0 percent to 8.7 percent. Brazil exhibited substantial improvements over the decade: board gender diversity increased from 6.7 percent in 2013 to 15.4 percent in 2023, and TMT gender diversity increased from 7.5 percent to 10.6 percent. Chile showed notable progress as well, with board gender diversity increasing from 5.0 percent in 2013 to 16.9 percent in 2023, and TMT gender diversity increasing from 3.0 percent to 14.6 percent. Colombia also saw significant improvements, with board gender diversity rising from 12.8 percent in 2013 to 21.9 percent in 2023, and TMT gender diversity increasing from 18.9 percent to 19.0 percent. Mexico's board gender diversity saw an increase from 7.3 percent in 2013 to 12.0 percent in 2023, while TMT gender diversity rose from 6.7 percent to 11.4 percent. Peru showed the most dramatic improvement in TMT gender diversity, rising from 7.1 percent in 2013 to 25.5 percent in 2023, and board gender diversity increased from 7.4 percent to 19.8 percent.

Regression Results

Table 4 presents the results of regression analyses exploring the relationship between cultural dimensions and gender diversity on corporate boards and TMT, as well as the commitment to SDG 5 on gender equality. The analyses use Ordinary Least Squares (OLS) for board and TMT gender diversity and Logit regression for SDG 5 commitment, controlling for various factors. The analysis reveals significant relationships between Hofstede's cultural dimensions and gender diversity in corporate leadership, as well as the commitment to SDG 5 on gender equality.

The first model explores the relationship between various cultural and control variables and board gender diversity using an Ordinary Least Squares regression. The results reveal that Power Distance and Individualism positively influence the percentage of female directors on corporate boards. Conversely, Masculinity and Uncertainty Avoidance negatively impact board gender diversity, indicating that traditional masculine values and a preference for stability can hinder the inclusion of women on boards. Among the control variables, firm size shows a strong positive effect, indicating that larger firms are more likely to have diverse boards. The market-to-book ratio also positively impacts board diversity, suggesting that firms with higher growth potential tend to include more women on their boards.

The second model examines the factors influencing TMT gender diversity. Similar to board gender diversity, Power Distance and Individualism are positively associated with TMT gender diversity. This indicates that even in cultures that accept hierarchical structures and emphasize individual merit, there is an effort to promote gender diversity within TMT. On the other hand, higher scores in Masculinity and Uncertainty Avoidance negatively correlate with TMT gender diversity, suggesting that competitive, achievement-oriented cultures and those that avoid uncertainty are less likely to include women in top management. Control variables such as firm size also show a significant positive impact on TMT gender diversity. Additionally, the rule of law negatively affects TMT diversity, whereas control of corruption positively impacts TMT gender diversity. Interestingly, the market-to-book ratio does not show a significant impact on TMT diversity in this model.

Table 4. Regression analysis on the relationship between cultural dimensions and gender diversity

Dependent variable	**Board Gender Diversity%**	**TMT Gender Diversity%**
Estimation Method	OLS	OLS
	1	2
Power Distance	0.001***	0.002***
	(0.000)	(0.000)
Individualism	0.001***	0.001***
	(0.000)	(0.000)
Masculinity	-0.001***	-0.001***
	(0.000)	(0.000)
Uncertainty Avoidance	-0.001***	-0.001***
	(0.000)	(0.000)
Ln(total assets)	0.017***	0.002***
	(0.000)	(0.000)
Leverage	0.000	0.003
	(0.003)	(0.003)
Market to Book Ratio	0.001***	0.001***
	(0.000)	(0.000)
Fam Ownership	0.085***	-0.013
	(0.012)	(0.014)
Ln(GDP per capita)	-0.003**	0.015***
	(0.001)	(0.002)
Rule of Law	-0.054***	-0.031***
	(0.003)	(0.004)
Control Of Corruption	0.054***	0.023***
	(0.002)	(0.003)
Constant	-0.384***	-0.362***
	(0.107)	(0.126)

continued on following page

Table 4. Continued

Dependent variable	Board Gender Diversity%	TMT Gender Diversity%
Year- Effects	Y	Y
Industry- Effects	Y	Y
R-squared	0.35	0.165
N	67595	64951

* p<0.10, ** p<0.05, *** p<0.01. Standard errors are reported in parentheses.

We next focus on firm-level determinants to better understand what drives Latin American companies to increase gender diversity. Table 5 presents a comparative analysis of the key drivers of gender diversity in corporate leadership between a global sample and Latin American countries, using three models to evaluate board gender diversity, TMT gender diversity, and commitment to SDG 5 gender equality. The analysis highlights how these determinants differ across the two contexts.

Focusing on the drivers of board gender diversity, board independence is a significant driver of gender diversity in both samples, highlighting the importance of independent boards in promoting gender diversity. Similarly, larger boards are associated with greater gender diversity in both contexts, suggesting that increasing board size can be an effective strategy for enhancing gender diversity. Interestingly, family ownership positively impacts board gender diversity in Latin America, contrasting with a non-significant relationship globally. This suggests that family-owned firms in Latin America are more likely to include women on their boards, possibly due to family ties and succession planning. Government ownership does not significantly affect board gender diversity in either context.

In term of the control variable, it is worth noting that larger firms tend to have more women on their boards, as indicated by the significant positive relationship between the natural logarithm of total assets and board gender diversity, in the global sample. This finding, however, does not hold in Latin America, where firm size does not significantly influence board gender diversity. The market-to-book ratio positively influences board gender diversity in both the global and Latin American samples, with the relationship being more pronounced in Latin America.

Moving to the drivers of TMT gender diversity, the analysis reveals that larger firms tend to have less gender diversity in their top management teams in both the global and Latin American samples. This negative relationship is stronger in Latin America. Board independence shows a significant positive effect on TMT gender diversity in Latin America, whereas the relationship is not significant globally. Family ownership, however, presents a stark contrast between the two contexts. While it has a significant negative impact globally, it shows a strong positive relationship with TMT gender diversity in Latin America. This highlights cultural differences, suggesting that family-owned firms in Latin America are more likely to promote women to top management positions.

The commitment to SDG 5 gender equality shows different determinants in the global and Latin American contexts. Globally, larger firms are more likely to commit to SDG 5. In contrast, this relationship is not significant in Latin America. Board independence has a significant negative impact on SDG 5 commitment globally, whereas it does not significantly affect SDG 5 commitment in Latin America. In contrast, family ownership does not significantly affect SDG 5 commitment globally but shows a strong positive relationship in Latin America. This suggests that family-owned firms in Latin America are more likely to commit to gender equality initiatives, potentially due to internal family values and succession planning practices that emphasize inclusivity. Finally, government ownership shows a significant negative impact on SDG 5 commitment in Latin America, whereas the relationship is not significant globally.

Table 5. Regression analysis on the relationship between firm-level corporate governance and gender diversity

Sample	Global	Global	Global	Latin America	Latin America	Latin
Dependent variable	Board Gender Diversity%	TMT Gender Diversity%	SDG 5 Gender equality	Board Gender Diversity%	TMT Gender Diversity%	SDG 5 Gender equality
Estimation Method	OLS	OLS	Logit	OLS	OLS	Logit
	1	2	3	4	5	6
Ln(total assets)	0.006***	-0.006***	0.163***	0.000	-0.011***	-0.086
	(0.000)	(0.000)	(0.021)	(0.002)	(0.002)	(0.071)
Leverage	0.001	0.001	0.027	-0.016	0.017	0.011
	(0.003)	(0.003)	(0.138)	(0.011)	(0.011)	(0.436)
Market to Book Ratio	0.001***	0.000	0.005	0.003***	-0.001	-0.012
	(0.000)	(0.000)	(0.006)	(0.001)	(0.001)	(0.035)
CEO-chairman duality	0.001	0.000	0.181***	-0.005	0.006	0.106
	(0.001)	(0.001)	(0.055)	(0.004)	(0.005)	(0.189)
Board Independence	0.055***	-0.005	-0.485***	0.032***	0.021**	0.183
	(0.003)	(0.003)	(0.144)	(0.010)	(0.010)	(0.391)
Board Size	0.002***	0.001**	0.019**	0.001**	0.002**	0.018
	(0.000)	(0.000)	(0.008)	(0.001)	(0.001)	(0.029)
ESG Performance	0.001***	0.001***	0.050***	0.001***	0.001**	0.071***
	(0.000)	(0.000)	(0.002)	(0.000)	(0.000)	(0.006)
Family Ownership	-0.001	-0.006*	-0.010	0.045***	0.050***	-0.843

continued on following page

Table 5. Continued

Sample	Global	Global	Global	Latin America	Latin America	Latin
	(0.003)	(0.004)	(0.159)	(0.014)	(0.015)	(0.565)
Government Ownership	0.005	-0.008	-0.355	-0.023	0.061***	-1.727*
	(0.005)	(0.006)	(0.275)	(0.020)	(0.021)	(0.928)
Board Gender Diversity%		0.289***	0.222		0.132***	-0.420
		(0.005)	(0.233)		(0.021)	(0.738)
TMT Gender Diversity%			0.046			0.006
			(0.180)			(0.659)
Constant	-0.128**	0.066	16899	-0.037	0.229**	-0.192
	(0.060)	(0.069)	16899	(0.107)	(0.113)	(1.878)
Year- Effects	Y	Y	Y	Y	Y	Y
Industry- Effects	Y	Y	Y	Y	Y	Y
Country- Effects	Y	Y	Y	Y	Y	Y
(Pseudo) R-squared	0.409	0.281	0.294	0.217	0.229	0.294
N	65068	64194	26899	2618	2618	1177

* p<0.10, ** p<0.05, *** p<0.01. Standard errors are reported in parentheses.

Overall, the analysis highlights significant differences in the determinants of gender diversity and commitment to gender equality between the global and Latin American contexts, and underscore the importance of considering regional cultural and institutional factors when designing policies and strategies to promote gender diversity in corporate leadership.

DISCUSSION AND CONCLUSION

Gender diversity in corporate leadership has gained significant attention in recent years. While the literature on board diversity underscores numerous advantages associated with increased gender diversity, the increase in gender diversity at the board and TMT levels has been relatively slow. Latin America lag significantly behind North America and Europe in terms of corporate gender diversity. In this study, we aim to better understand the role of cultural dimensions to explain the gender diversity differences between Latin American countries and other regions, and to provide novel insights into the firm-level drivers of gender diversity that apply to Latin American listed firms.

Focusing on a large sample of listed firms in Latin America and other regions over the period 2006-2023, we find that cultural dimensions have a significant impact on gender diversity both at the board and TMT levels, even after controlling for other known factors. Specifically, we find that power distance and individualism is positively related to gender diversity at both the board and TMT levels. In contrast, masculinity and uncertainty avoidance is negatively related. Our results highlight the significant impact of cultural dimensions on gender diversity in corporate leadership and help to better understand why gender diversity is generally lower in Latin America, compared to other parts of the world. While high Power Distance and Uncertainty Avoidance create rigid structures resistant to change, low Individualism and high Masculinity reinforce traditional gender roles and may restrict women's access to board and TMT positions.

In addition, we focus on firm-level determinants to better understand what drives Latin American companies to increase gender diversity. We find that board size, board independence, ESG performance and family ownership are important drivers of gender diversity, at the board and TMT levels. We also uncover that while firm size does not influence board gender diversity, it is negatively related to TMT diversity. Our findings also show that board gender diversity and state ownership are relevant drivers of TMT gender diversity. Our findings contribute to a better understanding of the corporate governance drivers of gender diversity in Latin America, and how they compare to a global sample. For example, we reveal that family ownership is not significantly related to board gender diversity and is negatively related to TMT gender diversity for a global sample. In contrast, family ownership is positively related to both board and TMT gender diversity in Latin America. Finally, we examine the corporate governance factors that influence the likelihood that Latin American companies commit to the SDG5 objective on gender equality. We find that ESG performance is one of the main drivers, while other board dimensions show no significant relationship.

Our study opens several promising avenues for future research. Firstly, while we highlight the significant role of cultural dimensions and corporate governance factors in influencing gender diversity, there is a need for more granular research exploring how these factors interact with other regional specificities, such as political stability, economic development, and regulatory environments. Comparative studies across different Latin American countries could provide deeper insights into the contextual nuances that drive or hinder gender diversity. Secondly, further research could explore the long-term impacts of increased gender diversity on corporate performance, risk management, and decision-making processes in Latin

REFERENCES

Abdullah, S. N. (2014). The causes of gender diversity in Malaysian large firms. *The Journal of Management and Governance*, 18(4), 1137–1159. DOI: 10.1007/s10997-013-9279-0

Abdullah, S. N., Ismail, K. N. I. K., & Nachum, L. (2016). Does having women on boards create value? The impact of societal perceptions and corporate governance in emerging markets: Women on Boards. *Strategic Management Journal*, 37(3), 466–476. DOI: 10.1002/smj.2352

Adams, R. B., & Ferreira, D. (2009). Women in the boardroom and their impact on governance and performance. *Journal of Financial Economics*, 94(2), 291–309. DOI: 10.1016/j.jfineco.2008.10.007

Aguilera, R. V., & Jackson, G. (2003). The cross-national diversity of corporate governance: Dimensions and determinants. *Academy of Management Review*, 28(3), 447–465. DOI: 10.2307/30040732

Bem, S. L. (1981). Gender schema theory: A cognitive account of sex typing. *Psychological Review*, 88(4), 354–364. DOI: 10.1037/0033-295X.88.4.354

Benton, R. A. (2021). Women in the inner circle: Gender and director networks after the fracturing of the corporate elite. *Organization Science*, 32(6), 1492–1522. DOI: 10.1287/orsc.2021.1433

Bertrand, M., & Schoar, A. (2006). The role of family in family firms. *The Journal of Economic Perspectives*, 20(2), 73–96. DOI: 10.1257/jep.20.2.73

Brammer, S., Millington, A., & Pavelin, S. (2007). Gender and ethnic diversity among UK corporate boards. *Corporate Governance*, 15(2), 393–403. DOI: 10.1111/j.1467-8683.2007.00569.x

Burke, R. (1999). Women on Canadian corporate boards of directors: Getting the numbers right! *Corporate Governance*, 7(4), 374–378. DOI: 10.1111/1467-8683.00167

Campbell, J. L. (2007). Why would corporations behave in socially responsible ways? An institutional theory of corporate social responsibility. *Academy of Management Review*, 32(3), 946–967. DOI: 10.5465/amr.2007.25275684

Carrasco, A., Francoeur, C., Labelle, R., Laffarga, J., & Ruiz-Barbadillo, E. (2015). Appointing women to boards: Is there a cultural bias? *Journal of Business Ethics*, 129(2), 429–444. DOI: 10.1007/s10551-014-2166-z

Carter, D. A., Simkins, B. J., & Simpson, W. G. (2003). Corporate governance, board diversity, and firm value. *Financial Review*, 38(1), 33–53. DOI: 10.1111/1540-6288.00034

Chen, G., Crossland, C., & Huang, S. (2016). Female board representation and corporate acquisition intensity. *Strategic Management Journal*, 37(2), 303–313. DOI: 10.1002/smj.2323

Chizema, A., Kamuriwo, D. S., & Shinozawa, Y. (2015). Women on corporate boards around the world: Triggers and barriers. *The Leadership Quarterly*, 26(6), 1051–1065. DOI: 10.1016/j.leaqua.2015.07.005

Cumming, D., Leung, T. Y., & Rui, O. (2015). Gender diversity and securities fraud. *Academy of Management Journal*, 58(5), 1571–1593. DOI: 10.5465/amj.2013.0750

de Abreu, M. C. S., Soares, R. A., Daniel-Vasconcelos, V., & Crisóstomo, V. L. (2023). Does board diversity encourage an environmental policy focused on resource use, emission reduction and innovation? The case of companies in Latin America. *Corporate Social Responsibility and Environmental Management*, 30(3), 1161–1176. DOI: 10.1002/csr.2411

Deephouse, D. L., Newburry, W., & Soleimani, A. (2016). The effects of institutional development and national culture on cross-national differences in corporate reputation. *Journal of World Business*, 51(3), 463–473. DOI: 10.1016/j.jwb.2015.12.005

Deloitte. (2024). *Women in the boardroom: a global perspective*. Deloitte Global Boardroom Program, Eight Edition.

Desender, K., & Epure, M. (2021). The pressure behind corporate social performance: Ownership and institutional configurations. *Global Strategy Journal*, 11(2), 210–244. DOI: 10.1002/gsj.1390

Desender, K. A., Castro, C. E., & Escamilla de León, S. A. (2011). Earnings management and cultural values: Earnings management and cultural values. *American Journal of Economics and Sociology*, 70(3), 639–670. DOI: 10.1111/j.1536-7150.2011.00786.x

Desender, K. A., LópezPuertas-Lamy, M., Pattitoni, P., & Petracci, B. (2020). Corporate social responsibility and cost of financing—The importance of the international corporate governance system. *Corporate Governance*, 28(3), 207–234. DOI: 10.1111/corg.12312

Eagly, A. H., & Carli, L. L. (2007). *Through the labyrinth: The truth about how women become leaders*. Harvard Business School Press.

Fainshmidt, S., Judge, W. Q., Aguilera, R. V., & Smith, A. (2018). Varieties of institutional systems: A contextual taxonomy of understudied countries. *Journal of World Business*, 53(3), 307–322. DOI: 10.1016/j.jwb.2016.05.003

Farag, H., & Mallin, C. (2016). The impact of the dual board structure and board diversity: Evidence from Chinese initial public offerings (IPOs). *Journal of Business Ethics*, 139(2), 333–349. DOI: 10.1007/s10551-015-2649-6

Grosvold, J., & Brammer, S. (2011). National institutional systems as antecedents of female board representation: An empirical study. *Corporate Governance*, 19(2), 116–135. DOI: 10.1111/j.1467-8683.2010.00830.x

Grosvold, J., Rayton, B., & Brammer, S. (2016). Women on corporate boards: A comparative institutional analysis. *Business & Society*, 55(8), 1157–1196. DOI: 10.1177/0007650315613980

Guiso, L., Sapienza, P., & Zingales, L. (2006). Does culture affect economic outcomes? Social Science Research Network. CEPR Discussion Paper No. 5505.

Guldiken, O., Mallon, M. R., Fainshmidt, S., Judge, W. Q., & Clark, C. E. (2019). Beyond tokenism: How strategic leaders influence more meaningful gender diversity on boards of directors. *Strategic Management Journal*, 40(12), 2024–2046. DOI: 10.1002/smj.3049

Hillman, A. J., Shropshire, C., & Cannella, A. A.Jr. (2007). Organizational predictors of women on corporate boards. *Academy of Management Journal*, 50(4), 941–952. DOI: 10.5465/amj.2007.26279222

Hofstede, G. (1980). *Culture's consequences: international differences in work related values*. Sage.

Hofstede, G. (2001). *Culture's Consequences: Comparing Values, Behaviors, Institutions, and Organizations Across Nations* (2nd ed.). Sage.

Husted, B. W., & de Sousa-Filho, J. M. (2019). Board structure and environmental, social, and governance disclosure in Latin America. *Journal of Business Research*, 102, 220–227. DOI: 10.1016/j.jbusres.2018.01.017

Kang, H., Cheng, M., & Gray, S. J. (2007). Corporate governance and board composition: Diversity and independence of Australian boards. *Corporate Governance*, 15(2), 194–207. DOI: 10.1111/j.1467-8683.2007.00554.x

Knippen, J. M., Shen, W., & Zhu, Q. (2019). Limited progress? The effect of external pressure for board gender diversity on the increase of female directors. *Strategic Management Journal*, 40(7), 1123–1150. DOI: 10.1002/smj.3014

Konrad, A. M., Kramer, V., & Erkut, S. (2008). Critical mass: The impact of three or more women on corporate boards. *Organizational Dynamics*, 37(2), 145–164. DOI: 10.1016/j.orgdyn.2008.02.005

Lemons, M. A., & Parzinger, M. (2007). Gender schemas: A cognitive explanation of discrimination of women in technology. *Journal of Business and Psychology*, 22(1), 91–98. DOI: 10.1007/s10869-007-9050-0

Lewellyn, K. B., & Bao, S. (2017). The role of national culture and corruption on managing earnings around the world. *Journal of World Business*, 52(6), 798–808. DOI: 10.1016/j.jwb.2017.07.002

Lewellyn, K. B., & Muller-Kahle, M. I. (2020). The corporate board glass ceiling: The role of empowerment and culture in shaping board gender diversity. *Journal of Business Ethics*, 165(2), 329–346. DOI: 10.1007/s10551-019-04116-9

Licht, A., Goldschmidt, C., & Schwartz, S. H. (2005). Culture, law, and corporate governance. *International Review of Law and Economics*, 25(2), 229–255. DOI: 10.1016/j.irle.2005.06.005

Lubatkin, M. H., Lane, P. J., Collin, S. O., & Very, P. (2007). An embeddedness framing of governance and opportunism: Towards a cross-nationally accommodating theory of agency. *Journal of Organizational Behavior*, 28(1), 43–58. DOI: 10.1002/job.402

Marquez-Cardenas, V., Gonzalez-Ruiz, J. D., & Duque-Grisales, E. (2022). Board gender diversity and firm performance: Evidence from Latin America. *Journal of Sustainable Finance & Investment*, 12(3), 785–808. DOI: 10.1080/20430795.2021.2017256

Mastella, M., Vancin, D., Perlin, M., & Kirch, G. (2021). Board gender diversity: Performance and risk of Brazilian firms. *Gender in Management*, 36(4), 498–518. DOI: 10.1108/GM-06-2019-0088

Moreno-Gómez, J., Lafuente, E., & Vaillant, Y. (2018). Gender diversity in the board, women's leadership and business performance. *Gender in Management*, 33(2), 104–122. DOI: 10.1108/GM-05-2017-0058

Nekhili, M., & Gatfaoui, H. (2013). Are demographic attributes and firm characteristics drivers of gender diversity? Investigating women's positions on French boards of directors. *Journal of Business Ethics*, 118(2), 227–249. DOI: 10.1007/s10551-012-1576-z

North, D. C. (1990). *Institutions, Institutional Change, and Economic Performance*. Harvard University Press. DOI: 10.1017/CBO9780511808678

Oakley, J. G. (2000). Gender-based barriers to senior management positions: Understanding the scarcity of female CEOs. *Journal of Business Ethics*, 27(4), 321–334. DOI: 10.1023/A:1006226129868

Post, C., & Byron, K. (2015). Women on boards and firm financial performance: A meta-analysis. *Academy of Management Journal*, 58(5), 1546–1571. DOI: 10.5465/amj.2013.0319

PwC Report (2022). ESG-Focused Institutional Investment Seen Soaring 84% to US$33.9 Trillion in 2026, Making up 21.5% of Assets under Management.

Saeed, A., Sameer, M., Raziq, M. M., Salman, A., & Hammoudeh, S. (2019). Board gender diversity and organizational determinants: Empirical evidence from a major developing country. *Emerging Markets Finance & Trade*, 55(8), 1803–1820. DOI: 10.1080/1540496X.2018.1496421

Scott, W. R. (2001). *Institutions and organizations*. Thousands Oaks: Sage.

Sealy, R., Vinnicombe, S., & Doldor, E. (2009). *Female FTSE index and report 2009*. Cranfield University.

Starr, C., & Zurbriggen, E. L. (2017). Sandra Bem's gender schema theory after 34 years: A review of its reach and impact. *Sex Roles*, 76(9-10), 566–578. DOI: 10.1007/s11199-016-0591-4

Terjesen, S., Sealy, R., & Singh, V. (2009). Women directors on corporate boards: A review and research agenda. *Corporate Governance*, 17(3), 320–337. DOI: 10.1111/j.1467-8683.2009.00742.x

Williams, R. M. (1970). *American society: A sociological interpretation*. Knopf.

Yao, T. (2023). Antecedents of top management team and board gender diversity: A review and an agenda for research. *Corporate Governance*, 31(1), 227–248. DOI: 10.1111/corg.12495

Zattoni, A., Leventis, S., Van Ees, H., & De Masi, S. (2023). Board diversity's antecedents and consequences: A review and research agenda. *The Leadership Quarterly*, 34(1), 101659. DOI: 10.1016/j.leaqua.2022.101659

Zucker, L. (1983). Organizations as institutions. In Bacharach, S. (Ed.), *Research in the sociology of organizations* (Vol. 2, pp. 1–47). JAI Press.

Chapter 7
Uncovering the Nexus of Tax Evasion and Bribery in Latin America and the Caribbean

Surjit Singha
https://orcid.org/0000-0002-5730-8677
Kristu Jayanti College (Autonomous), India

ABSTRACT

Tax evasion and bribery significantly impede the socioeconomic development of Latin America and the Caribbean. With other forms of corruption, such as extortion, they stifle innovation, distort markets, compromise education, and undermine public trust. Robust legal frameworks, transparency, judicial independence, and robust anti-corruption measures must address these issues. International cooperation through exchanging information, treaties, and technical assistance is essential. The socio-educational and technological repercussions of corruption in various forms underscore the necessity for reform. Ultimately, the region can establish a more egalitarian society with broader access to resources and opportunities by promoting equitable, competitive, and sustainable growth through international collaboration and transparency.

INTRODUCTION

Endemic tax evasion and bribery issues substantially impact Latin America and the Caribbean's economy, education, and technology sectors. These challenges persist, exacerbating inequality, undermining governance, and impeding sustain-

DOI: 10.4018/979-8-3693-3763-9.ch007

able development despite the concerted efforts of governments and international organizations to address them.

The chapter examines the complex dynamics of tax evasion and bribery, revealing their interconnectedness and ubiquitous impact on the socioeconomic fabric of the region. This chapter aims to propose actionable solutions and foster a more profound comprehension of these issues by analyzing the fundamental causes, prevalent practices, and systemic implications.

In Latin America and the Caribbean, the situation has been characterized by the proliferation of corruption due to the legacy of colonialism, political instability, and economic disparities. Bribery and tax evasion are not isolated incidents but are interwoven into the fabric of daily living and institutional operation. Elites frequently evade justice, and ordinary citizens are left to bear the burden of these corrupt practices, perpetuated by a culture of impunity, weak enforcement of laws, and a lack of transparency.

Due to tax evasion, governments are deprived of the revenue necessary to finance public services, including infrastructure, healthcare, and education. This deficit results in public services that are inadequately funded and inefficient, which, in turn, exacerbates social inequality and impedes human development. The burden is shifted to those who cannot afford it when individuals and corporations fail to pay their reasonable share of taxes, further entrenching poverty and restricting economic opportunities.

Conversely, bribery results in an uneven playing field and distorts market mechanisms. It erodes trust in public institutions, undermines the rule of law, and discourages foreign investment. Bribery frequently coincides with tax evasion, as businesses and individuals may pay officials to mitigate their tax obligations or avoid scrutiny altogether. This vicious cycle is complex to break due to the symbiotic relationship between tax evasion and bribery.

The implications for technology and education are staggering. In the education sector, bribery can misallocate resources, leading to substandard educational materials, poorly trained instructors, and inadequate facilities. It diminishes the competitiveness of the region's personnel in the global economy, restricts the innovation potential, and impairs the quality of education. Corruption can impede the development of a robust digital infrastructure and stifle entrepreneurship in the technology sector, further isolating the region from economic growth and technological advancements (Kumar, 2023).

A multifaceted approach is necessary to address tax evasion and extortion. Stabilizing institutional frameworks, cultivating a culture of integrity, and improving transparency and accountability are essential measures. These issues can also be significantly mitigated through international cooperation and implementing global standards for financial transparency and anti-corruption measures. Furthermore, from the grassroots level, meaningful change can be affected by empowering citizens to hold their governments accountable and engage civil society (McGee, 2023). Bribery can be commercial, involving businesses and their stakeholders, or governmental, involving public officials.

Examining the historical and socio-political context facilitating tax evasion and bribery proliferation in Latin America and the Caribbean. It examines empirical data and case studies to demonstrate the extent and influence of these concerns. Lastly, it provides strategic interventions and policy recommendations to reduce tax evasion and extortion, promoting a more prosperous, transparent, and equitable region.

This chapter offers valuable insights to policymakers, scholars, and practitioners pursuing sustainable development in Latin America and the Caribbean by revealing the connection between tax evasion and bribery. Developing effective strategies to combat these forms of corruption and promote a more just and inclusive society is contingent upon understanding the complex interplay between them.

BACKGROUND

The socioeconomic development of Latin America and the Caribbean is substantially impeded by endemic issues such as tax evasion and bribery. These corrupt practices are deeply entrenched in historical, cultural, and institutional origins, perpetuating inefficiency and inequality cycles. Tax evasion and extortion persist despite numerous initiatives designed to address these challenges. These practices undermine public trust, distort market dynamics, compromise educational infrastructure, and stifle technological innovation. Their persistence underscores the necessity of a comprehensive and multifaceted strategy to address these issues effectively.

This chapter examines the complex dynamics of tax evasion and bribery in Latin America and the Caribbean, focusing on their interconnectedness and ubiquitous impact on the region's socioeconomic fabric. This chapter aims to promote a more profound comprehension of these issues and to suggest actionable solutions by investigating the underlying causes, prevalent practices, and systemic implications of these corrupt activities.

This chapter thoroughly examines the multifaceted consequences of tax evasion and extortion in Latin America and the Caribbean. It incorporates a variety of dimensions, such as economic, socio-educational, and technological aspects. Initially, it examines the complex relationship between tax evasion and extortion, contextualizing them within the region's history and investigating their intersections with corruption and the informal economy. In the subsequent section, the chapter assesses the economic consequences of these corrupt practices, including their impact on market dynamics, revenue generation, foreign direct investment, and overall economic development. In addition, it examines the socio-educational repercussions of tax evasion and extortion, with a particular emphasis on the exacerbation of social inequality, compromised educational infrastructure, and erosion of public trust.

Furthermore, it examines the technological obstacles resulting from these corrupt activities, such as cybersecurity risks, technological adoption impediments, and entrepreneurship barriers. Additionally, the chapter investigates regulatory responses to combat tax evasion and extortion, focusing on legislative reforms, transparency measures, and the significance of judicial independence. Finally, it emphasizes the importance of international cooperation in resolving these issues, emphasizing the participation of international organizations, cross-border collaboration initiatives, and capacity-building programs designed to improve the region's anti-corruption efforts.

The objectives of this study are to conduct a thorough investigation of the widespread issues of tax evasion and extortion in Latin America and the Caribbean. Initially, it endeavours to investigate the historical, cultural, and institutional factors that underlie these corrupt practices, thereby elucidating their persistence in the region. Consequently, it evaluates the economic consequences of tax evasion and bribery by examining their effects on the investment climate, market competitiveness, and revenue generation. The study also intends to examine the socio-educational consequences of these corrupt activities, particularly emphasizing their impact on social equality, educational quality, and public trust. Furthermore, it intends to examine the technological obstacles that tax evasion and extortion present, such as cybersecurity risks and innovation barriers.

Additionally, the research aims to suggest comprehensive regulatory reforms that will effectively address these issues, underscoring the significance of legislative and policy measures. It also emphasizes the importance of promoting international collaboration through multilateral initiatives, information exchange, and technical assistance to address these challenges collectively. Finally, the study offers practical solutions for preventing tax evasion and extortion, fostering equitable growth and sustainable development throughout the region.

UNDERSTANDING THE NEXUS: EXPLORING THE INTERPLAY BETWEEN TAX EVASION AND BRIBERY

A comprehensive conceptual framework is imperative to understand the complex relationship between tax evasion and bribery. In Latin America and the Caribbean, this framework investigates how tax evasion and bribery reinforce each other and the broader implications for economic, social, and political systems (Kassa, 2021). A comprehensive conceptual framework is essential for unravelling the intricate relationship between tax evasion and bribery in Latin America and the Caribbean.

This framework explores how these corrupt practices reinforce each other, creating a cycle that impacts economic stability, social equity, and political integrity. Understanding this interplay provides deeper insights into the broader implications for the region's governance and development, highlighting the need for targeted interventions to effectively address tax evasion and bribery.

To explore the effects of tax evasion and bribery, follow these steps: identify key variables (economic development, public trust, institutional integrity); develop a conceptual model of their interactions; collect and analyze quantitative and qualitative data; evaluate existing policies; propose reforms; and implement and monitor progress. This approach fosters effective policy interventions and strengthens governance.

Tax evasion is the illicit underreporting or non-payment of taxes by individuals or corporations, resulting in substantial government revenue losses. In contrast, bribery is the act of offering, giving, receiving, or procuring something of value to influence the actions of an official or other individual in a position of authority (McGee, 2023).

Bribery and tax evasion frequently occur concurrently. Businesses and individuals may bribe tax officials to mitigate their tax liabilities or evade audits and penalties. This mutual reinforcement fosters an environment where both practices thrive, rendering it challenging to address one without addressing the other (Alm, 2011). In Latin America and the Caribbean, the concurrent occurrence of bribery and tax evasion creates a deeply entrenched cycle of corruption. Businesses and individuals often resort to bribing tax officials to reduce their tax liabilities or avoid audits, leading to a mutually reinforcing dynamic that sustains both practices (Transparency International, 2019). This interconnectedness makes it challenging to combat one without addressing the other, as each practice fuels the other's persistence. As a result, this nexus undermines efforts to establish transparency, accountability, and economic fairness in the region, posing significant challenges to governance and economic development.

The prevalence of bribery undermines the efficacy of tax authorities and other institutions responsible for enforcing tax laws. In exchange for bribes, corrupt officials may neglect tax evasion, weakening the overall governance structure and cultivating a culture of impunity (McGee, 2023).

The wealthy, who possess the resources to exploit loopholes and indulge in corrupt practices, benefit disproportionately from tax evasion. It exacerbates economic inequality by placing a more significant burden on individuals who cannot evade taxes or pay bribes, eroding trust in public institutions and social cohesion (Kurauone et al., 2021). In Latin America and the Caribbean, the nexus of tax evasion and bribery disproportionately benefits the wealthy, who use their resources to exploit loopholes and engage in corrupt practices (Casas-Zamora & Carter, 2017). It exacerbates economic inequality by shifting the tax burden onto those who lack the means to evade taxes or pay bribes, undermining trust in public institutions and eroding social cohesion. Addressing this nexus is crucial for promoting economic fairness and rebuilding trust in governance.

The government's capacity to deliver critical public services is restricted by the revenue it loses due to tax evasion. Concurrently, bribery results in the inefficient allocation of resources, which further erodes the quality of services such as education, healthcare, and infrastructure, which are essential for socioeconomic development.

Latin America and the Caribbean's challenges with corruption are deeply rooted in its history. In the 16th century, Spanish and Portuguese colonizers established centralized power, exploiting indigenous labor through systems like encomienda and mita. Post-independence, leaders such as Simón Bolívar and José de San Martín faced institutional instability, while figures like Porfirio Díaz perpetuated corruption through patronage. The mid-20th century saw authoritarian regimes like Pinochet's in Chile and Argentina's junta, which entrenched corruption further. Despite democratic transitions in the 1990s, entrenched interests resisted reforms, leaving a legacy of corruption that still affects governance and tax compliance today. Wealth extraction and exploitation were the primary economic activities during the colonial era, with little consideration for equitable development. This legacy endured into the post-colonial period, when political instability, military dictatorships, and feeble institutions further entrenched corrupt practices. A system was established in which public interest was of secondary importance due to the colonial administration's emphasis on resource exploitation and wealth accumulation for the colonial powers. It created an environment conducive to corruption, as local elites frequently engaged in corrupt practices to preserve their power and fortune.

The transition to independence did not substantially alter the entrenched power dynamics. Corruption flourished in numerous newly independent states due to political instability and inadequate institutions. In certain instances, authoritarian regimes perpetuated corruption to preserve their authority, undermining public confidence in government institutions. Austerity measures and reduced public expenditure were frequently the result of the economic crises of the 1980s and 1990s, followed by structural adjustment programs imposed by international financial institutions. These circumstances exacerbated poverty and inequality, prompting individuals and businesses to resort to tax evasion and bribery as survival strategies.

The informal economy, bribery, corruption, and tax evasion are interconnected. The informal economy, which encompasses unregulated and untaxed economic activities, is substantial in numerous Latin American and Caribbean nations (Asllani & Schneider, 2024). In Latin America and the Caribbean, the informal economy significantly contributes to the nexus of tax evasion and bribery. The large scale of unregulated and untaxed economic activities within this sector facilitates tax evasion and often involves bribery to evade detection or regulation (Organization for Economic

Cooperation and Development, 2018; Vuletin, 2008). This interconnection between the informal economy, bribery, and tax evasion perpetuates a cycle of corruption, undermining economic stability and governance. Addressing these issues requires tackling the informal economy's role in evasion and bribery to improve regional transparency and fiscal integrity.

Businesses and individuals may be compelled to operate in the informal economy due to elevated levels of corruption, which allows them to operate beyond the jurisdiction of the state. It results in a decrease in the tax base and an increase in the prevalence of tax evasion, as informal sector participants frequently fail to pay taxes. Concurrently, bribery may be employed to either facilitate informal economic activities or safeguard them from law enforcement. Due to an overly burdensome regulatory framework, businesses may be encouraged to maintain an informal status. Excessive regulations and bureaucratic red tape elevate the probability of bribery as businesses attempt to circumvent these obstacles. The need for bribery can be reduced, and formalization can be encouraged by simplifying regulations and enhancing the business environment. Tax evasion and bribery are socially permissible behaviours in societies where corruption is normalized and public trust in institutions is low. The informal economy frequently operates by these social norms, perpetuating a cycle of informality and corruption.

Fostering a culture of transparency and accountability, fortifying institutions, and enhancing regulatory frameworks are all necessary components of a comprehensive strategy to address the nexus of tax evasion and bribery. Policies designed to decrease informality, such as simplifying tax procedures and enhancing access to finance, can also facilitate the integration of the informal economy into the formal sector, thereby expanding the tax base and decreasing the likelihood of corruption (De Andrade et al., 2020).

By comprehending the interplay between the informal economy, corruption, extortion, and tax evasion, policymakers can develop more effective interventions to address these pervasive issues and promote sustainable development in Latin America and the Caribbean.

ECONOMIC IMPLICATIONS: IMPACT ON GROWTH, INVESTMENT, AND FISCAL SUSTAINABILITY

Tax evasion and bribery significantly affect government revenue and budgetary health in Latin America and the Caribbean. Governments need more essential funds to finance public services and infrastructure initiatives due to the revenue loss resulting from tax evasion. Bribery exacerbates this issue by diverting resources from their intended purposes, further straining public budgets (Asllani & Schneider, 2024).

In Latin America and the Caribbean, the nexus of tax evasion and bribery critically undermines government revenue and budgetary health. Tax evasion depletes essential public services and infrastructure funds, while bribery exacerbates the problem by misdirecting resources away from their intended purposes. This combined effect severely strains public budgets, highlighting the urgent need to address both practices simultaneously to restore financial stability and support effective governance.

The government incurs substantial losses in prospective revenue when corporations and individuals evade taxes. The capacity to deliver critical services, including healthcare, education, and social welfare programs, is adversely affected by this deficit. It also restricts the government's ability to invest in infrastructure and development initiatives essential for economic growth (Rashid et al., 2022). In Latin America and the Caribbean, the nexus of tax evasion and bribery results in significant government revenue losses, as both corporations and individuals evade taxes. This revenue shortfall severely impacts the government's ability to fund critical services such as healthcare, education, and social welfare programs. Additionally, the deficit restricts investment in infrastructure and development initiatives necessary for economic growth. Addressing the intertwined issues of tax evasion and bribery is essential to restoring fiscal health and supporting sustainable development in the region.

To offset the revenue loss, governments may borrow, increasing public debt. Austerity measures, which frequently disproportionately adversely impact the most vulnerable populations, can result from the crowding out other essential expenditures by high debt levels (Nguyen & Luong, 2021).

Bribery disturbs budget allocations, as funds are frequently misdirected toward initiatives that benefit corrupt officials rather than the public good. This misallocation impedes the ability of the government to address critical requirements and reduces the overall effectiveness of government spending (Wang et al., 2020). In Latin America and the Caribbean, bribery significantly disrupts budget allocations by diverting funds away from public welfare projects and towards initiatives that benefit corrupt officials. This misallocation impairs the government's capacity to address critical needs and diminishes the overall effectiveness of government spending (Transparency International, 2019). Addressing the nexus of tax evasion and bribery is crucial, as both practices perpetuate a cycle of mismanagement and inefficiency that severely hampers economic and social development. Tax evasion and bribery undermine fiscal integrity and public trust, leading to misallocation of resources and reduced effectiveness of governance. Tackling these issues is essential for fostering a more transparent, equitable, and efficient system that supports sustainable growth and development.

Addressing the nexus of tax evasion and bribery requires strengthening legal frameworks, enhancing transparency, improving enforcement, and fostering public accountability to restore fiscal integrity and support sustainable development.

Market dynamics are distorted by the prevalence of tax evasion and bribery, which undermines economic efficiency and equitable competition. Businesses that indulge in corruption are granted an unfair advantage over those that operate transparently due to these practices, which establish an unequal playing field.

Businesses that violate tax laws and ethical standards may reduce expenses and undermine their competitors. This unjust competition can potentially drive legitimate businesses out of the market or into the informal economy (Kong et al., 2023). In Latin America and the Caribbean, the nexus of tax evasion and bribery creates an environment where businesses flout tax laws and ethical standards to gain an unfair advantage (Statista Research Department, 2024). By reducing expenses through evasion and bribery, these businesses undermine legitimate competitors, potentially driving them out of the market or pushing them into the informal economy. This unjust competition destabilizes the market, exacerbates economic inequality, and reinforces corrupt practices. Addressing tax evasion and bribery to foster a fair and transparent business environment is crucial.

Corruption can stifle innovation by prioritizing connections and bribes over merit and efficiency. Businesses prioritizing corrupt practices to secure contracts or circumvent taxes may have a reduced investment in research, development, and innovation, which are critical for long-term economic growth. Bribery can result in the selection of suboptimal suppliers and contractors, which can produce inferior products and services. This inefficiency can potentially infiltrate various sectors of the economy, thereby diminishing overall productivity and competitiveness.

Foreign direct investment (FDI) is critical in accelerating economic development, as it introduces capital, technology, and expertise. Nevertheless, foreign investors may be discouraged by an unfavourable investment climate exacerbated by tax evasion and bribery. High levels of corruption exacerbate the hazards and uncertainties associated with investment. The investment environment may need to be more predictable and attractive for foreign investors due to the potential for expropriation, unexpected costs associated with bribes, and arbitrary enforcement of laws. Investor confidence may decrease as a result of a damaged reputation. This is particularly true for countries that are notorious for corruption. This reputational risk may decrease FDI inflows as investors prioritize more transparent and stable environments.

Bribery can increase business costs by necessitating additional payments to officials and traversing complex regulatory landscapes. Foreign companies may be discouraged from entering the market or expanding their operations due to these elevated costs, which can restrict economic development opportunities (Zhou &

Peng, 2011). The nexus between tax evasion and bribery in Latin America and the Caribbean is a significant and complex issue that undermines economic development and governance. Tax evasion, facilitated by bribery, creates a cycle of corruption that weakens public institutions, reduces public revenues, and exacerbates inequality. This relationship is particularly problematic in regions like Latin America and the Caribbean, where informal economies are substantial, and corruption is often pervasive.

In many Latin American and Caribbean countries, bribery is often used to facilitate tax evasion. Businesses or individuals may offer bribes to tax officials in exchange for reduced tax liabilities, the omission of taxes owed, or the manipulation of tax records. This practice results in significant revenue losses for governments and perpetuates a culture of impunity and corruption.

The revenue losses caused by tax evasion and bribery are substantial, reducing the funds available for public services such as healthcare, education, and infrastructure. This directly impacts economic development and social welfare as governments struggle to provide essential services to their populations. In turn, the lack of adequate public services can lead to further dissatisfaction with governance and exacerbate the cycle of corruption.

The prevalence of bribery and tax evasion can act as a significant deterrent to foreign investment. As Zhou and Peng (2011) noted, bribery's additional costs and complex regulatory landscapes can discourage foreign companies from entering or expanding their regional operations. This restricts economic development opportunities, as potential investments that could stimulate growth, create jobs, and bring in new technologies are lost.

In Latin America and the Caribbean, the prevalence of bribery and tax evasion creates a complex and costly regulatory environment that deters foreign investment. As Zhou and Peng (2011) noted, these corrupt practices increase operational costs and complicate the business landscape, discouraging foreign companies from entering or expanding within the region. This reluctance restricts economic development opportunities by preventing investments that could drive growth, create jobs, and introduce new technologies. Uncovering the nexus of tax evasion and bribery is essential for addressing these barriers and fostering a more attractive and dynamic investment climate.

The nexus between tax evasion and bribery also perpetuates inequality in Latin America and the Caribbean. Wealthy individuals and corporations are often better positioned to engage in corrupt practices to evade taxes, while ordinary citizens bear the brunt of the tax burden. This unequal distribution of tax responsibilities further entrenches social and economic disparities in the region.

The interaction between tax evasion and bribery erodes the integrity of public institutions, making them less effective and more vulnerable to further corruption. When tax officials and other public servants are complicit in corrupt practices, it undermines public trust in government and reduces the effectiveness of anti-corruption efforts. Weak institutions, in turn, are less capable of enforcing tax laws and combating corruption, creating a vicious cycle that is difficult to break.

Addressing the nexus of tax evasion and bribery in Latin America and the Caribbean requires comprehensive and coordinated efforts at national and regional levels.

Enhancing the capacity of tax authorities and anti-corruption agencies to detect, investigate, and prosecute cases of tax evasion and bribery is crucial. This may involve providing better training, resources, and technology and improving transparency and accountability mechanisms.

Given the transnational nature of tax evasion and corruption, international cooperation is essential. This includes sharing information, coordinating enforcement actions, and effectively aligning legal frameworks to combat cross-border tax evasion and bribery.

Promoting a culture of corporate integrity, where businesses adhere to ethical practices and reject bribery, is vital. This can be supported through regulations, incentives, and public-private partnerships to encourage compliance with tax laws and anti-corruption standards.

Civil society organizations are critical in monitoring government actions, advocating for transparency, and holding public officials accountable. Strengthening the role of civil society in the fight against corruption and tax evasion can lead to more effective oversight and greater public awareness.

The nexus of tax evasion and bribery in Latin America and the Caribbean is a significant barrier to sustainable economic development and good governance. The region can create a more equitable, transparent, and prosperous future by addressing these intertwined challenges through comprehensive reforms and international collaboration.

To foster sustained economic development, Latin America and the Caribbean must strengthen institutions, promote transparency, and enforce reforms to counter tax evasion and bribery, ensuring a stable and equitable environment.

SOCIO-EDUCATIONAL CONSEQUENCES: DISPARITIES IN ACCESS, QUALITY, AND EQUITY

The widespread prevalence of tax evasion and bribery substantially undermines public trust in Latin American and Caribbean institutions. The confidence of citizens in the legitimacy and efficacy of public institutions is diminished when they perceive that corruption is widespread and that laws are not universally enforced. The absence of punishment for high-profile cases of tax evasion and bribery involving affluent individuals and corporations contributes to a perception of injustice and inequity. This perception has the potential to result in a significant decrease in civic engagement and participation in democratic processes, as well as pervasive disillusionment and apathy among the populace.

Decreased voluntary compliance with tax laws and other regulations may result from low trust in public institutions. Citizens may be more inclined to evade taxes if they perceive that tax revenue is being misappropriated or that they need to receive sufficient public services (Horodnic, 2018). In Latin America and the Caribbean, low trust in public institutions can significantly influence the nexus of tax evasion and bribery. When citizens perceive that tax revenue is misappropriated or that public services are inadequate, their voluntary compliance with tax laws diminishes (OECD, 2022). This erosion of trust encourages tax evasion and can drive individuals to engage in bribery to navigate a corrupt system. Addressing these issues requires rebuilding public trust through transparent governance and effective use of tax revenues to mitigate the cycle of evasion and bribery.

The social contract between the government and its citizens predates mutual obligations. In exchange for public services and effective governance, citizens pay taxes. Corruption undermines societal cohesion and weakens the sense of collective responsibility, disrupting this social contract. Tax evasion and extortion directly impact the education sector, diverting essential resources from educational infrastructure and services, compromising quality and accessibility. More funding is needed for public institutions due to the decrease in tax revenue. This leads to a need for more investment in infrastructure and technology improvements, insufficient educational materials, and inadequate facilities. The performance and outcomes of students are impacted by the inability of underfunded institutions to establish a conducive learning environment.

Bribery can misallocate educational resources, as funds are typically allocated to institutions or areas that benefit corrupt officials rather than those in genuine need. This results in discrepancies in the quality of education among various socioeconomic categories and regions (Wang et al., 2020). In Latin America and the Caribbean, bribery exacerbates educational inequalities by misallocating resources. Funds often flow to institutions or projects that benefit corrupt officials rather than those needing support. This misallocation leads to significant disparities in educational quality across different socioeconomic groups and regions. Addressing the nexus of tax evasion and bribery is crucial for ensuring educational resources are distributed equitably, promoting fair access to quality education and reducing systemic inequalities.

A shortage of qualified teachers and low morale among existing staff can result from low salaries and poor working conditions, frequently resulting from budgetary constraints. Teachers may also engage in corrupt practices, such as requesting gratuities in exchange for grades, which can further compromise educational standards. Substandard construction and maintenance of school structures may result from corruption in the procurement processes for educational infrastructure. This hurts the overall learning experience and the protection and comfort of students.

The interconnected issues of tax evasion and extortion exacerbate social inequality and exclusion by depriving marginalized groups of the quality education necessary to improve their socioeconomic status. High-quality education is frequently unavailable to impoverished and marginalized communities. These communities are the most affected by corruption, perpetuating poverty and exclusion cycles by diverting funds from public education.

Significant disparities in educational outcomes result from the inequitable distribution of educational resources. Students from affluent families who have the financial resources to pay for private education or pay bribes in exchange for improved opportunities have a distinct advantage over those who depend on underfunded public schools. The provision of high-quality education significantly influences social mobility. The potential for individuals from disadvantaged backgrounds to improve their economic situation is restricted when educational opportunities are compromised by corruption, thereby reinforcing existing social hierarchies.

The pervasive nature of corruption and the resulting educational disparities can result in disenfranchisement and hopelessness among young people. This can lead to a higher likelihood of engaging in illicit activities, reduced motivation, and lower aspirations.

The socio-educational repercussions of tax evasion and extortion are significant, as they perpetuate social inequalities and impact the quality of education and access. Civic engagement is diminished, and the erosion of public trust in institutions undermines the efficacy of governance. The potential for students to realize their complete potential is restricted by compromised educational infrastructure and resources, which also perpetuate cycles of poverty and exclusion. To resolve these concerns, it is necessary to implement comprehensive anti-corruption measures, invest in education, and implement policies designed to reduce inequality (Argentiero et al., 2021). Latin America and the Caribbean can strive for a more inclusive and equitable educational system that caters to all facets of society by addressing the underlying causes of corruption. The nexus of tax evasion and bribery in Latin America and the Caribbean has profound socio-educational repercussions, exacerbating social inequalities and limiting access to quality education (Miller & Uriegas, 2019). As tax revenues are siphoned off through corruption, public investment in educational infrastructure and resources is severely compromised. This undermines the potential for students, particularly those from marginalized communities, to realize their full potential, thereby perpetuating cycles of poverty and exclusion. Addressing this corruption through comprehensive anti-corruption measures and investments in education is essential for building a more inclusive and equitable educational system that serves all facets of society in the region.

TECHNOLOGICAL CHALLENGES: CURBING INNOVATION AND DIGITAL TRANSFORMATION

Tax evasion and bribery entrenchment significantly impeded the adoption and assimilation new technologies in Latin America and the Caribbean. These obstacles impede the region's ability to thoroughly engage in the global digital economy. The misallocation of resources intended for technological advancements is frequently the result of corruption. Bribery may need more funds for technology infrastructure and innovation, leading to insufficient investments in critical areas such as broadband connectivity, IT infrastructure, and educational technology. The prevalence of tax evasion and bribery erodes trust in both public and private institutions. This lack of trust can discourage businesses and individuals from implementing new technologies, particularly those requiring a substantial initial investment and a long-term commitment.

Technological integration can be impeded by the inclusion of bureaucratic obstacles that are the result of corruption. Companies may encounter delays in obtaining the requisite permits or licenses unless they pay bribes, discouraging them from pursuing innovative projects and investments (Alam et al., 2023).

Corruption frequently impedes the digital transformation of public services, which has the potential to improve transparency and efficiency. Inefficient public service delivery may result from underfunding or inadequately implemented digital initiatives resulting from corrupt practices. Cybersecurity and data integrity, essential for a flourishing digital economy, are at significant risk due to corruption and inadequate regulatory frameworks. Cyber-attacks are more likely to target IT systems that are underfunded and inadequately managed due to misappropriated funds. The trust in digital platforms and services can be undermined by frequent data disclosures that result from insecure systems.

In sectors such as finance, healthcare, and education, bribery can result in the manipulation or altering of data. The integrity and reliability of data systems may be compromised if corrupt officials or employees manipulate records for personal gain. Robust regulatory supervision and enforcement are essential for the successful implementation of cybersecurity. These regulatory frameworks are weakened by corruption, which facilitates the exploitation of vulnerabilities by cybercriminals.

This need for more oversight can also discourage international tech companies from investing in the region by raising concerns about data security. The formulation and implementation of effective cybersecurity strategies can be impeded by corruption. The diversion of funds intended for cybersecurity measures results in the vulnerability of critical infrastructure and reduced ability to respond to cyber threats effectively.

Corruption has a particularly detrimental impact on the entrepreneurial environment, stifling innovation and development within start-up ecosystems. Entrepreneurs may be required to pay bribes to obtain licenses, permits, or regulatory certifications, increasing the business's cost. Entrepreneurial activity may be discouraged by these supplementary expenses, which can be prohibitive for new ventures. Unlike those prepared to pay bribes, start-ups that refuse to engage in corrupt practices are disadvantaged. Innovation is stifled, and ethical business practices are discouraged by this unjust competition.

Investors are less inclined to provide funding for start-ups in regions where corruption is prevalent, as the associated risks and uncertainties are elevated. The potential impact of new ventures on the economy is restricted by the need for more investment capital, limiting their growth and scalability. In corrupt environments, talented individuals may be discouraged from pursuing entrepreneurial ventures. They may pursue opportunities in more stable and transparent regions, resulting in a brain outflow that exacerbates the local start-up ecosystem.

The suppression of innovative ideas can result from corruption, as those in authority may resist changes threatening their interests. This resistance to innovation impeded the development of new technologies and business models that could drive economic growth and enhance quality of life (Abbasi, 2020). Corruption, particularly tax evasion and bribery, stifles innovation in Latin America and the Caribbean by maintaining the status quo and resisting reforms threatening entrenched interests. Officials benefiting from corrupt systems may obstruct innovations that enhance transparency and efficiency, such as digital tax technologies or competitive business models (Moreno, 2017; Transparency International, 2017). This resistance impedes economic growth, perpetuates inequality, and limits the region's global competitiveness. By blocking advancements that could drive sustainable development and improve public sector accountability, the nexus of tax evasion and bribery severely undermines the potential for equitable and progressive economic development. Thus, the suppression of innovation, as discussed by Abbasi (2020), is intrinsically linked to the broader issues of tax evasion and bribery in Latin America and the Caribbean. Addressing this nexus is essential for breaking the cycle of corruption that stifles progress and for creating an environment where innovation can thrive, leading to more significant economic opportunities and improved social outcomes for all.

The technological challenges of tax evasion and extortion significantly impede the region's digital transformation and innovation potential. These practices impede the adoption and integration of new technologies, compromise cybersecurity and data integrity, and inhibit entrepreneurial growth. A concerted effort is necessary to address these challenges by strengthening regulatory frameworks, enhancing transparency, and fostering an environment conducive to innovation and ethical business practices. Latin America and the Caribbean can cultivate a more competitive and dynamic digital economy by addressing corruption, enabling them to realize their technological potential.

REGULATORY RESPONSES: STRENGTHENING LEGAL FRAMEWORKS AND ENFORCEMENT MECHANISMS

To counteract tax evasion and bribery in Latin America and the Caribbean, it is imperative to implement effective regulatory responses. The foundation of these endeavours is composed of robust anti-corruption measures and legislative reforms. Establishing comprehensive legislation that explicitly prohibits tax evasion and extortion is imperative. Clear definitions, severe penalties, and provisions for the recovery of illicit gains should be included in these laws. Additionally, they should address corruption in both the public and private sectors. Enforcement can be improved by establishing autonomous anti-corruption agencies authorized to investigate and prosecute corruption cases. These agencies should be adequately funded, staffed with competent professionals, and protected from political interference.

Encouraging individuals to disclose corrupt practices without fear of retaliation is facilitated by implementing robust whistleblower protection laws. Examples of such protections include anonymity guarantees, legal safeguards, and financial incentives for whistleblowers. Improving international collaboration in the fight against extortion and tax evasion is imperative. This can entail tracking and prosecuting transnational corruption cases through information exchange, joint investigations, and mutual legal assistance treaties.

Reducing opportunities for tax evasion and extortion is contingent upon transparency and accountability. Corrupt practices can be substantially discouraged by initiatives designed to improve these aspects (McGee, 2023).

Transparency may be enhanced through legislation that mandates public access to government information. This encompasses the online publication of government budgets, expenditures, and procurement contracts, which enables citizens to examine public spending. By minimizing direct contact between officials and the public, implementing e-governance solutions can reduce bureaucratic malfeasance. Transparency and efficiency are improved by digital platforms for tax filing, business registration, and public procurement. Regulation of political campaign financing and the requirement of disclosure of donations and expenditures can mitigate corruption in the political arena. Transparent political financing is instrumental in preventing the undue influence of money in politics and fostering accountability.

Accountability is promoted by promoting the active involvement of civil society organizations in monitoring government activities. These organizations can be instrumental in advocating for transparency, undertaking independent audits, and educating the public on anti-corruption initiatives. It is imperative to have a robust and independent judiciary to enforce anti-corruption legislation and ensure that offenders are held accountable. To guarantee judicial independence, it is necessary to safeguard judges from political interference, guarantee tenure security, and provide sufficient compensation. Van (2020) asserts that independent judiciaries are more capable of impartially deciding corruption cases.

In Latin America and the Caribbean, ensuring judicial independence is vital for effectively addressing the nexus of tax evasion and bribery. The judiciary can impartially adjudicate corruption cases by protecting judges from political interference, securing their tenure, and providing adequate compensation (Financier Worldwide Magazine, 2022). Previously, Van (2020) highlighted that an independent judiciary is better equipped to handle corruption cases, including those related to tax evasion and bribery, thereby reinforcing the rule of law and promoting a fairer and more transparent legal system.

The establishment of specialized anti-corruption tribunals can facilitate the resolution of corruption cases. To guarantee that the adjudication process is conducted with expertise and efficiency, these courts must be staffed by judges and prosecutors who have received training in anti-corruption laws and practices. The efficacy of corruption prosecutions can be improved by streamlining legal procedures. This encompasses the implementation of fast-track mechanisms for high-priority cases, the reduction of procedural delays, and the simplification of evidence requirements.

It is imperative to fortify the general rule of law to establish a culture of accountability. This entails the preservation of law and order, the protection of human rights, and the consistent and equitable application of laws. A robust rule of law discourages corrupt practices by increasing the probability of detection and punishment (Saha et al., 2014). In Latin America and the Caribbean, strengthening the rule of law is crucial for addressing the nexus of tax evasion and bribery. A robust legal framework that upholds law and order protects human rights, and ensures the consistent and fair application of laws can deter corrupt practices by increasing the likelihood of detection and punishment. Establishing such a culture of accountability is essential for mitigating the intertwined issues of tax evasion and bribery and promoting a more transparent and equitable regional governance system.

It is imperative to fortify legal frameworks and enforcement mechanisms to effectively address the widespread issues of tax evasion and extortion in Latin America and the Caribbean. An effective regulatory response necessitates legislative reforms, a robust, independent judiciary, and increased transparency and accountability. Governments can implement these measures to establish an environment conducive to sustainable development, restore public trust in institutions, and prohibit corruption. Corruption can be combated through these methods, which will promote economic growth, improve public services, and better the general welfare of society.

INTERNATIONAL COOPERATION: LEVERAGING MULTILATERAL INITIATIVES AND PARTNERSHIPS

International organizations and treaties are instrumental in preventing tax evasion and bribery in Latin America and the Caribbean. They establish frameworks and standards that facilitate international collaboration and direct national efforts.

The United Nations Convention against Corruption (UNCAC) is a comprehensive international treaty designed to combat corruption globally. It offers a framework for countries to enhance transparency, promote international cooperation in the struggle against corruption, and strengthen their legal and institutional frameworks. Ratification and implementation of UNCAC provisions assist countries in aligning their anti-corruption initiatives with international standards.

Organization for Economic Cooperation and Development (OECD) is an Anti-Bribery Convention that mandates signatory countries to criminalize foreign public officials' bribery and implement measures to prevent, detect, and investigate such practices. The OECD also offers guidelines for the conduct of multinational enterprises and transparency.

The Financial Action Task Force (FATF) establishes international standards to combat money laundering and terrorist financing, which are closely associated with corruption. By adhering to the Financial Action Task Force (FATF) recommendations, nations can fortify their financial systems and mitigate the potential for illicit financial flows that originate from tax evasion and bribery. The World Bank and the International Monetary Fund (IMF) provide financial and technical support to countries instituting anti-corruption reforms. They also offer governance and accountability frameworks that countries can implement to improve their anti-corruption strategies.

Robust cross-border collaboration and information exchange between countries is essential for effectively combating tax evasion and extortion. In criminal investigations, including those concerning corruption and tax evasion, Mutual Legal Assistance Treaties (MLATs) facilitate the transmission of information and evidence between various countries. International cooperation in prosecuting cross-border corruption cases can be improved by fortifying and expanding MLATs.

Automatic Exchange of Information (AEOI) agreements, such as those promoted by the OECD's Common Reporting Standard (CRS), facilitate the automatic exchange of financial account information between countries. This facilitates the more effective detection and resolution of cross-border tax evasion by tax authorities. Establishing joint investigative bodies and task forces can enhance the coordination and efficacy of cross-border investigations into corruption and tax evasion. These collaborative endeavours enable the consolidation of intelligence, expertise, and resources.

Cooperation among member states can be facilitated by regional organizations, including the Organization of American States (OAS) and the Caribbean Community (CARICOM). These organizations can assist in the coordination of regional anti-corruption initiatives, the exchange of best practices, and the harmonization of legal frameworks. The capacity of institutions and the provision of technical assistance are essential for improving countries' capacity to combat extortion and tax evasion.

International organizations can provide training programs for law enforcement officials, judges, prosecutors, and tax authorities to improve the detection, investigation, and prosecution of corruption and tax evasion cases. Forensic accounting, financial analysis, and cybercrime may be addressed during this training. It is imperative to offer technical support to enhance legal frameworks, establish robust enforcement mechanisms, and develop and execute anti-corruption strategies. Advisory services, funding, and technology transfer are all potential sources of this assistance. Implementing initiatives to fortify institutions, including financial intelligence divisions, anti-corruption agencies, and judicial bodies, is essential. These initiatives may prioritize the enhancement of operational efficiency, the promotion of interagency collaboration, and the enhancement of governance structures.

Public awareness campaigns that educate citizens about the significance of tax compliance and the detrimental effects of corruption can be supported by international organizations. Increasing awareness can contribute to establishing a culture of accountability and integrity in society (Farrar et al., 2018). In Latin America and the Caribbean, public awareness campaigns supported by international organizations play a crucial role in addressing the nexus of tax evasion and bribery (Larraín B. & Zhang, 2022). By educating citizens on the importance of tax compliance and the harmful impacts of corruption, these campaigns can foster a culture of accountability and integrity. Increasing awareness helps to challenge entrenched corrupt practices and promotes a collective effort towards transparency, thereby mitigating the intertwined issues of tax evasion and bribery in the region.

International cooperation is imperative to effectively counteract tax evasion and bribery in Latin America and the Caribbean. A strong foundation for national endeavours is established by utilizing multilateral initiatives and partnerships through international organizations and treaties. The detection and prosecution of transnational corruption cases are improved through cross-border collaboration and information exchange. At the same time, the capacity of institutions to address collaborating on these fronts countries effectively is strengthened through capacity building and technical assistance programs in a transparent, accountable, and equitable global economic environment by collaborating on these fronts.

ORGANIZATION OF AMERICAN STATES

The Inter-American Convention Against Corruption, commonly known as the OAS Convention (OAS), was adopted by the Organization of American States (OAS) on March 29, 1996, and entered into force on March 6, 1997. It marked the first international convention to combat corruption in the Western Hemisphere. The convention was significant as it established a comprehensive framework for preventing, detecting, and punishing corruption in public offices. It also sought to promote regional cooperation among member states in tackling this pervasive issue.

One of the key objectives of the OAS Convention is to promote and strengthen the development of mechanisms necessary to prevent, detect, punish, and eradicate corruption. It encourages states to adopt measures to prevent conflicts of interest, increase transparency in public administration, and ensure accountability. The convention also focuses on international cooperation, urging member states to provide mutual assistance in investigating and prosecuting acts of corruption.

As part of the OAS, the Caribbean nations are signatories to this convention. By ratifying the convention, these countries committed to implementing measures such as criminalizing bribery and other forms of corruption in the public and private sectors. They also agreed to facilitate the extradition of individuals charged with corruption-related offences and cooperate in recovering assets obtained through corrupt means.

Regarding more recent regional accords, Caribbean countries have continued to participate in various initiatives to combat corruption. For example, the Caribbean countries are part of the Caribbean Financial Action Task Force (CFATF), an organization of states and territories of the Caribbean Basin that have agreed to implement common countermeasures against money laundering, terrorist financing, and related threats to the international financial system. The CFATF also focuses on preventing and addressing corruption, particularly in the context of financial crimes.

Moreover, several Caribbean countries are part of the United Nations Convention against Corruption (UNCAC), adopted in 2003 and entered into force in 2005. This global treaty builds on regional efforts like the OAS Convention and provides a comprehensive framework for preventing and combating corruption worldwide.

Through UNCAC, Caribbean countries have access to a broader international network for cooperation and assistance in fighting corruption.

The participation of Caribbean countries in the OAS Convention and other regional and international agreements underscores their commitment to addressing the challenges of corruption, tax evasion, and bribery. These accords provide the legal and institutional frameworks necessary for effective action against corruption in the region.

RECOMMENDATIONS AND SOLUTIONS

A comprehensive and multifaceted strategy is necessary to address the widespread issues of tax evasion and extortion in Latin America and the Caribbean. The analysis of this study emphasizes the necessity of comprehensive legislative reforms to fortify legal frameworks. It is essential to implement measures to close legal loopholes, provisions for the recovery of illicit gains, and stricter penalties for offenders to effectively curtail corruption. Moreover, promoting public access to government information and implementing whistleblower protection laws is essential to cultivate a culture of integrity and reduce the likelihood of corrupt practices. This involves enhancing transparency and accountability measures. Guaranteeing impartial adjudication of corruption cases and maintaining the rule of law necessitates ensuring judicial independence.

Fostering international collaboration is essential in the fight against cross-border tax evasion, extortion, and domestic initiatives. To effectively address transnational corruption networks, it is imperative to strengthen collaboration with international organizations and neighbouring countries by facilitating information exchange, conducting joint investigations, and providing mutual legal assistance. Additionally, the socioeconomic consequences of corruption are significantly mitigated by investing in education and technology. It is imperative to allocate resources to enhance cybersecurity measures, promote entrepreneurship, and improve educational infrastructure to promote sustainable development and inclusive growth.

Another essential component of corruption prevention is the empowerment of civil society. To cultivate transparency and accountability, it is imperative to promote awareness campaigns, strengthen the capacity of civil society organizations to hold public officials accountable and encourage citizen engagement. Additionally, enforcing existing anti-corruption laws and encouraging ethical business practices is essential to establish an environment conducive to ethical behaviour in both the public and private sectors.

By implementing these exhaustive recommendations and solutions, policymakers, government officials, and stakeholders can collaborate to foster sustainable development, reduce corruption, and promote integrity throughout Latin America and the Caribbean. This collective endeavour is indispensable for establishing a future in which accountability, transparency, and equity are the norm, fostering greater prosperity and well-being for all regional residents.

DISCUSSIONS

The intricate interplay of socioeconomic factors contributing to these ubiquitous issues is revealed in the discussion of tax evasion and bribery in Latin America and the Caribbean. The historical, cultural, and institutional context that influences the prevalence of corruption in the region is a critical factor. The legacy of colonialism and authoritarian rule has enduring influenced governance structures, promoting a culture of patronage and impunity. Furthermore, the challenges of tax evasion and bribery are further exacerbated by the fertile ground provided by profoundly entrenched social inequalities and informal economies, which foster the growth of corrupt practices.

The economic consequences of corruption are significant, as they influence the investment climate, market dynamics, and revenue generation. Tax evasion perpetuates cycles of poverty and inequality by depriving governments of critical resources for infrastructure development and public services. Moreover, bribery distorts market competition, favouring well-connected elites and multinational corporations over small businesses and entrepreneurs. This exacerbates the socioeconomic challenges of the region by discouraging foreign investment and undermining economic growth.

The socio-educational repercussions of corruption are equally concerning, as they undermine public confidence in institutions and compromise educational quality and accessibility. The credibility of governments and institutions is eroded by corruption, which results in disillusionment among citizens and a deterioration of social cohesion. Furthermore, the diversion of funds intended for education to corrupt activities leads to insufficient resources and infrastructure, perpetuating disparities in educational outcomes and reinforcing social inequality.

Additionally, corruption presents substantial technological obstacles that impede digital transformation and innovation. The region's capacity to engage in the global digital economy is restricted by the need for more transparency and accountability in governance, which impedes the adoption and integration of technology. In addition, trust in digital platforms is undermined, and entrepreneurship and start-up ecosystems are impeded by cybersecurity risks resulting from corruption. These risks pose a threat to data integrity and privacy.

To address these obstacles, policymakers must implement a multifaceted strategy that enhances transparency and accountability measures, strengthens legal frameworks, and promotes international cooperation. Deterring corrupt practices and fostering good governance necessitate comprehensive legislative reforms and robust enforcement mechanisms. Additionally, the investment in education, technology, and civil society empowerment can contribute to the development of a culture of accountability and integrity, as well as the development of resilience against corruption. The international community, civil society, and governments must collaborate to combat tax evasion and extortion in Latin America and the Caribbean. The region can realize its maximum potential for sustainable development and inclusive growth by confronting corruption directly and fostering transparency and accountability.

FUTURE SCOPE OF RESEARCH

Investigating tax evasion and extortion in Latin America and the Caribbean offers a fertile foundation for future research initiatives to comprehend and resolve regional corruption. Longitudinal studies that monitor corruption trends over time can provide valuable insights into the effectiveness of anti-corruption measures implemented by governments and institutions and the evolving character of corrupt practices. The development of targeted interventions customized to specific contexts is facilitated by comparative analyses across countries and sectors, which can illuminate the diverse factors that influence corruption levels. Sector-specific research that concentrates on industries such as healthcare, construction, or natural resources can offer a more comprehensive understanding of the corruption mechanisms within these sectors, thereby influencing regulatory reforms and governance enhancements.

Additionally, the potential to improve transparency, accountability, and efficacy in the fight against corruption is present in exploring technological solutions, including blockchain and artificial intelligence. Comprehending corruption's social and cultural determinants is essential to creating strategies that encourage ethical behaviour and promote integrity. Furthermore, it is imperative to assess the efficacy of current anti-corruption policies and analyze the effects of globalization to identify areas for improvement and refine governance strategies.

Additionally, promoting cross-disciplinary collaboration among researchers from various disciplines, including sociology, economics, law, and political science, can result in a more comprehensive comprehension of corruption dynamics and streamlining interdisciplinary solutions. There are also emergent areas that require further investigation, such as the intersection of climate change with corruption and youth engagement, as they have the potential to provide innovative approaches and novel insights for addressing corruption in the region. Scholars can enhance their comprehension of corruption dynamics in Latin America and the Caribbean and create evidence-based policies and interventions to effectively combat corruption and promote integrity and accountability in the region by exploring these diverse research areas.

CONCLUSION

The profound challenges of tax evasion and bribery substantially impede the socioeconomic development of Latin America and the Caribbean. Finally, these unscrupulous practices perpetuate inequality and impede sustainable development by distorting market dynamics, compromising educational infrastructure, stifling technological innovation, and undermining public trust. A multifaceted approach is necessary to address these issues, which includes enhancing transparency and accountability, reinforcing legal frameworks and enforcement mechanisms, and guaranteeing judicial independence. Establishing independent agencies, comprehensive anti-corruption measures, and legislative reforms are essential in mitigating these pervasive issues. Fostering a culture of transparency is equally critical, and this can be achieved through public access to information, robust civil society engagement, and e-governance initiatives.

Leveraging multilateral initiatives and partnerships is essential in the international arena. Cross-border collaboration, international organizations and treaties, and information exchange are essential components of a global strategy to combat extortion and tax evasion. Technical assistance and capacity-building programs bolster these endeavours by improving the capacity of national institutions to identify, investigate, and prosecute corrupt practices. The socio-educational and technological ramifications of malfeasance underscore the urgency of action. The erosion of public trust underscores the far-reaching consequences of these issues, compromised educational infrastructure, and inhibited technological advancement. The region can establish a more sustainable, competitive, and equitable future by promoting international cooperation and implementing comprehensive reforms. Preventing tax evasion and extortion is about improving economic efficiency and governance and establishing a more equitable society where all citizens can access resources and opportunities. By uniting at both the national and international levels, Latin America and the Caribbean can surmount these obstacles, thereby cultivating an environment of inclusive growth, innovation, and integrity.

REFERENCES

Abbasi, K. (2020). COVID-19: Politicization, "corruption," and suppression of science. *BMJ (Clinical Research Ed.)*, m4425. Advance online publication. DOI: 10.1136/bmj.m4425 PMID: 33187972

Alam, T., Aftab, M., Abbas, Z., Ugli, K. M. M., & Bokhari, S. A. A. (2023). Impact of E-Government initiatives to combat corruption mediating by behavioral intention: A Quantitative analysis from emerging economies. *Sustainability (Basel)*, 15(3), 2694. DOI: 10.3390/su15032694

Alm, J. (2011). Measuring, explaining, and controlling tax evasion: Lessons from theory, experiments, and field studies. *International Tax and Public Finance*, 19(1), 54–77. DOI: 10.1007/s10797-011-9171-2

Argentiero, A., Casal, S., Mittone, L., & Morreale, A. (2021). Tax evasion and inequality: Some theoretical and empirical insights. *Economics of Governance*, 22(4), 309–320. DOI: 10.1007/s10101-021-00261-y

Asllani, A., & Schneider, F. (2024). A review of the driving forces of the informal economy and policy measures for mitigation: An analysis of six EU countries. *International Tax and Public Finance*. Advance online publication. DOI: 10.1007/s10797-024-09842-z

Casas-Zamora, K., & Carter, M. (2017). *Beyond the scandals: The changing context of corruption in Latin America*. The Dialogue. https://www.thedialogue.org/analysis/beyond-the-scandals-the-changing-context-of-corruption-in-latin-america/

De Andrade, E. M., Rodrigues, L. L., & Cosenza, J. P. (2020). Corporate behavior: An exploratory study of the Brazilian tax management from a corporate social responsibility perspective. *Sustainability (Basel)*, 12(11), 4404. DOI: 10.3390/su12114404

Farrar, J., Massey, D. W., Osecki, E., & Thorne, L. (2018). Tax fairness: Conceptual foundations and empirical measurement. *Journal of Business Ethics*, 162(3), 487–503. DOI: 10.1007/s10551-018-4001-4

Financier Worldwide Magazine. (2022, February). *Q&A: Tackling financial crime in Latin America*. https://www.financierworldwide.com/qa-tackling-financial-crime-in-latin-america

Horodnic, I. A. (2018). Tax morale and institutional theory: A systematic review. *The International Journal of Sociology and Social Policy*, 38(9/10), 868–886. DOI: 10.1108/IJSSP-03-2018-0039

Kassa, E. T. (2021). Factors influencing taxpayers' involvement in tax evasion: Evidence from Woldia City administration micro, small, and large enterprise taxpayers. *Journal of Innovation and Entrepreneurship*, 10(1), 8. Advance online publication. DOI: 10.1186/s13731-020-00142-4 PMID: 34745824

Kong, D., Zhang, Y., & Qin, N. (2023). Anti-corruption campaign and corporate tax evasion: Evidence from China. *International Tax and Public Finance*. Advance online publication. DOI: 10.1007/s10797-023-09777-x

Kumar, P. (2023). How does corruption affect innovation? - New evidence from macro-level data. *Journal of Quantitative Economics*, 21(4), 925–941. DOI: 10.1007/s40953-023-00362-x

Kurauone, O., Kong, Y., Sun, H., Famba, T., & Muzamhindo, S. (2021). Tax evasion; public and political corruption and international trade: A global perspective. *Journal of Financial Economic Policy*, 13(6), 698–729. DOI: 10.1108/JFEP-04-2020-0067

Larraín, B. F., & Zhang, P. (2022). *Improving tax policy in Latin America and the Caribbean: A balancing act*. Atlantic Council. https://www.atlanticcouncil.org/in-depth-research-reports/report/improving-tax-policy-in-lac-a-balancing-act/

McGee, R. W. (2023). The ethics of bribery: An introduction. In *Springer eBooks* (pp. 3–8). DOI: 10.1007/978-3-031-17707-1_1

Miller, B., & Uriegas, F. (2019). *Latin America's biggest corruption cases: A retrospective*. Americas Quarterly. https://www.americasquarterly.org/article/latin-americas-biggest-corruption-cases-a-retrospective/

Moreno, L. A. (2017, December 14). *How tech can fight corruption in Latin America and the Caribbean*. World Economic Forum. https://www.weforum.org/agenda/2017/12/how-technology-is-becoming-a-powerful-ally-in-the-fight-against-corruption-in-latin-america-and-the-caribbean/

Nguyen, T. N., & Luong, T. T. H. (2021). Fiscal policy, institutional quality, and public debt: Evidence from transition countries. *Sustainability (Basel)*, 13(19), 10706. DOI: 10.3390/su131910706

Organization for Economic Cooperation and Development. (2018). *Latin American and Caribbean competition forum - Session I: Informal economy in Latin America and the Caribbean: Implications for competition policy* [Conference session]. Buenos Aires, Argentina. https://one.oecd.org/document/DAF/COMP/LACF%282018%294/en/pdf

Organization for Economic Cooperation and Development (OECD). (2022). *Tax transparency in Latin America 2021: Punta del Este declaration progress report.* https://web-archive.oecd.org/temp/2022-03-10/592947-tax-transparency-in-latin-america-2021.htm

Rashid, M. H. U., Uddin, N., Haque, M. S., & Hossain, S. Z. (2022). Good governance and tax evasion: The mediating effect of socioeconomic conditions. *Asia-Pacific Journal of Regional Science*, 6(2), 759–776. DOI: 10.1007/s41685-022-00242-x

Saha, S., Gounder, R., Campbell, N., & Su, J. J. (2014). Democracy and corruption: A complex relationship. *Crime, Law, and Social Change*, 61(3), 287–308. DOI: 10.1007/s10611-013-9506-2

Statista Research Department. (2024). *Latin America & Caribbean: Tax revenue loss caused globally 2021*. Statista. https://www.statista.com/statistics/1224443/tax-evasion-avoidance-latin-america-caribbean-country/

Transparency International. (2017). *Corruption on the rise in Latin America and the Caribbean.* https://www.transparency.org/en/news/corruption-on-the-rise-in-latin-america-and-the-caribbean

Transparency International. (2019). *Latin America and the Caribbean: 10th edition - 2019.* https://www.transparency.org/en/gcb/latin-america/latin-america-and-the-caribbean-x-edition-2019

Transparency International. (2019). *Global corruption barometer: Latin America and the Caribbean 2019 - Citizens' views and opinions of corruption.* Transparency International. https://www.transparency.org/en/publications/global-corruption-barometer-latin-america-and-the-caribbean-2019

Van Dijk, F. (2020). Judicial independence and perceptions of judicial independence. In *Springer eBooks* (pp. 7–28). DOI: 10.1007/978-3-030-63143-7_2

Vuletin, G. (2008, April). *Measuring the informal economy in Latin America and the Caribbean.* International Monetary Fund. https://www.imf.org/external/pubs/ft/wp/2008/wp08102.pdf

Wang, S., Zhao, D., & Chen, H. (2020). A spatial analysis of corruption, misallocation, and efficiency. *Environmental Science and Pollution Research International*, 27(29), 36845–36856. DOI: 10.1007/s11356-020-09707-y PMID: 32577961

Zhou, J. Q., & Peng, M. W. (2011). Does bribery help or hurt firm growth around the world? *Asia Pacific Journal of Management*, 29(4), 907–921. DOI: 10.1007/s10490-011-9274-4

KEYWORDS AND DEFINITIONS

Bribery: Offering or receiving something of value to influence the actions of an official or other person in power.

Caribbean: A region consisting of the Caribbean Sea, its islands, and the surrounding coasts.

Corruption: The abuse of entrusted power for private gain, undermining fairness and justice.

Extortion: The practice of obtaining something, often money, through force, threats, or abuse of power.

International Cooperation: Collaborative efforts between countries to address global issues, including trade, security, and development.

Latin America: A region in the Americas where Romance languages (Spanish, Portuguese, French) are primarily spoken.

Regulatory Frameworks: The set of rules, laws, and guidelines designed to control and govern specific activities or industries.

Socioeconomic: Relating to the interaction between social and economic factors, influencing people's living conditions.

Tax Evasion: The illegal act of not paying taxes by underreporting income or inflating deductions.

Chapter 8

Intercultural Competence Through Collaborative Online International Learning

Jahir Lombana-Coy
https://orcid.org/0000-0002-0055-8392
Universidad del Norte, Colombia

Lorena Palacios-Chacón
https://orcid.org/0000-0003-1919-2527
Tecnológico de Monterrey, Mexico

Kathleen A. Corrales
https://orcid.org/0000-0001-6778-3925
Universidad del Norte, Colombia

Lourdes Rey-Paba
https://orcid.org/0000-0003-1553-5422
Universidad del Norte, Colombia

ABSTRACT

This chapter seeks to explore whether international business undergraduate students from two countries evidenced characteristics associated with intercultural competence after participating in a virtual exchange. The intervention was between students with equivalent thematic units who worked together to discuss and produce a collaborative video on ways companies enter into international markets. Using a mixed method approach, data were collected through professor written reflections, student focus group, written reflections, and a questionnaire. Results show that virtual

DOI: 10.4018/979-8-3693-3763-9.ch008

exchanges have a great potential to foster both discipline learning and intercultural competence, but non-disciplinary relationships are also required for these to occur. Culturally, students found similarities that facilitated interaction, fostered positive attitudes, and encouraged their own cultural recognition and that of their peers. Several implications regarding technological and pedagogical aspects are described.

INTRODUCTION

Currently, the labor market tends to focus beyond national borders, where the relationship of professionals with their international peers plays a fundamental role because working in the business world transcends the local level, where one acts, without forgetting the global level, where one thinks (Matusitz & Forrester, 2009; Tien & Talley, 2012). For this reason, higher education institutions (HEIs), and business schools specifically, are responsible for providing opportunities for their students to develop their intercultural competence (IC). The COVID-19 pandemic exacerbated this situation with the closing of borders and the difficulty of establishing links between students through traditional international mobility mechanisms and introduced unforeseen complexities for HEIs. Particularly for Latin America, this represented a challenge given the economic limitations of students, and HEIs began to look for different strategies to approach internationalization. One strategy that gained quick acceptance was carrying out collaborative online learning activities through the use of information and communication technologies (ICTs), such as videoconference services in order to enhance IC development among students.

Video conferencing has given origin to the implementation of virtual exchanges (VE) that the literature has shown to be effective in terms of IC development (Cao & Meng, 2020; Lombana et al., 2024; Luo & Gao, 2022, Rodríguez-Fuentes et al., 2022). Specifically in the world of business, VEs seem to facilitate learning about other countries, cultures, and discipline knowledge (Kang et al., 2018). According to O'Dowd (2018), VEs can be defined as a "pedagogically-structured online collaborative learning between groups of learners in different cultural contexts or geographical locations" (p. 3).

Besides enhancing IC development, VEs mirror post-pandemic global business practices and prepare students to interact in geographically distant teams promoting collaboration and the achievement of common goals (Reiter-Palmon et al., 2021). According to these authors, virtual work environments since 2020 have increased and likely will continue to increase, requiring professionals with the "ability to engage in teamwork anywhere, anytime, and with just about anyone" (p. 166). Therefore, implementing VEs in business education can contribute to developing both generic competences such as IC, teamwork, and technical savviness and specific knowledge and skills related to the business topic under study.

This chapter reports the experience of a collaborative online exchange between a group of fourth semester Colombian students and a group of seventh to ninth semester Mexican students enrolled in an undergraduate international business program from different universities. A study was carried out to explore whether these undergraduate students evidenced characteristics associated with intercultural competence (IC) after participating in the VE through collaborative learning.

Literature Review

The literature review begins with a brief description of the development of the concept of competences, with particular reference to intercultural competence within the framework of international business. It also addresses the role of ICTs as mediators of collaborative learning activities and practical application in IB education contexts.

Competences in Business Education

The concept of competences has been widely studied in business academic literature and is often divided into workplace and professional competences. McClelland (1973), one of the first to research these topics further divided them into skills, aptitudes, and knowledge. In business, specifically, there has been a historical tension between what organizational strategy scholars and human resources experts believe about competences (Le Deist & Winterton, 2005). For organizational strategists, core competences are unique and depend on the particularities and context of the company (Prahalad & Hamel, 1990), while for human resources scholars, they are generic and transferable between different jobs or roles (Levy-Leboyer, 1996; Stasz, 1997). This dichotomy has generated interest in combining generic and specific competences in business education with an emphasis on needs, time, and space for the role to be carried out (Le Deist & Winterton, 2005). Balancing both strengthens the possibility of getting a job and/or being prepared for changing environments (Bath et al., 2024). From the theoretical and practical point of view, programs should be built upon the integrative model which combines knowledge, skills, reflection, and adaptation (Carrillo Mendoza, 2015; Díaz Villavicencio, 2016; Le Deist & Winterton, 2005). Another perspective is the one from Demirkan and Spohrer (2015) who propose a T-Shape model for service innovation which includes specific competences as the vertical axis and the generic and transferable competences in the horizontal axis. In this model, students are expected to attain a deep knowledge of their specialization with a broad spectrum of general skills. A third way to integrate specific and generic competences is through the use of active and collaborative learning, often found in cases, simulations, and projects, for example (Habbal et al., 2024; Pinilla Roa, 2010). Finally, there is also a need for continuous assessment (e.g. self-/co- evaluation; projects) to give feedback on the development of competences (Moreno Olivos, 2010).

In line with this, the current labor market must focus beyond national borders, where the relationship of professionals with their international peers plays a fundamental role. Remote work has created new opportunities to hire global talent, creating the need for enhancing intercultural skills as future professionals will likely be part of global teams (Caligiuri et al., 2022). Thus, the field of business requires professionals to transcend the local level, which, although this level is where one acts, the global level is where one thinks (Matusitz & Forrester, 2009; Tien & Talley, 2012). In summary, the concept of glocal, acting locally and thinking globally, is essential in the multicultural world of today (Patel & Lynch, 2013). It is in this glocality that IC applied to the areas of economics, business, and other related fields is important. However, reaching a consensus about what IC entails is necessary but difficult since authors have defined it in different ways. Deardorff (2009) emphasizes that in order to have interculturally appropriate behavior, people should have essential attitudes and reflective skills. Furthermore, Leung et al. (2014) adds to the discussion that, on one side, IC refers to the traits, attitudes, worldviews, or abilities that are separate from each other and, on the other side, are holistic, combining all the above elements into multiple domains. Johnson et al. (2014) argue that individuals' attitudes, knowledge, and skills enhance their work capacities and successful professional performance with peers of diverse cultural origins, recognizing aspects of their own cultural environment and that of the other. An important aspect of IC is that it requires people to be aware that differences and potential challenges can exist and that these will affect intercultural interactions (Swartz et al., 2020). Taking into account these multiple ideas about IC, for this chapter we understand it as the "ability to learn, think, act, and work effectively with people from different cultures to achieve a common understanding" (Corrales et al., 2021, p. 84).

Developing Intercultural Competence in Higher Education

International business courses in higher education typically use internationalization at home (IaH) activities, which aim to provide students with an internationalized learning experience without leaving the domestic environment (Beelen & Jones, 2015). Thus, through business cases, role-play activities (Corrales et al., 2021), and conferences with visiting professors or entrepreneurs, students are provided with opportunities to approach the intercultural and international reality they will face when they graduate. Likewise, the use of second and third languages in the educational context is imperative and has become a core component for the labor market (Gazzola et al., 2019). Moreover, student international mobility is often perceived as necessary for students to immerse themselves in another culture and develop IC. However, mobility has not shown conclusive results in the development of intercultural competences, as explained by Lokkesmoe et al. (2016), and it only impacts a limited number of students mostly because the lack of financial resources or desire to travel restricts mobility for the majority of the student population. Therefore, institutions who rely on student mobility may not attain the desired development of IC. For this reason, the use of role-plays, case studies, visiting professors, and virtual exchanges has become valuable tools for fostering IC.

After the pandemic, IC development in business education has heavily relied on the use of new communication technologies to support intercultural interaction (Lombana et al., 2024; Swartz & Shrivastava, 2022). As a result, universities have increased the delivery of hybrid and online educational courses as a way to offer more accessible and flexible learning options (Bashir et al., 2021). Additionally, a rising demand for micro-credentials and online lifelong learning programs from newcomers in the educational market (e.g., Coursera) have forced traditional institutions to broaden their programs (Brown et al., 2021) and embrace new trends such as artificial intelligence (AI), data analytics, machine learning, among others. In fact, emerging empirical studies have demonstrated that AI technologies hold the potential to revolutionize how IC is taught and learned (Karakas, 2023) and support the development of this competence (Sarwari et al., 2024). For instance, AI intercultural training tools have been linked to promoting cultural awareness and intercultural communication skills (Sawari et al., 2024).

The transition to remote work has uncovered issues related to the acknowledgement of cultural difference, a lack of understanding, difficulties in reaching consensus, and a tendency to work in isolation, which have implications on trustfulness and collaboration that are essential for teamwork. Studies have shown the effectiveness of using technology to build trust and promote interculturality in different contexts such as virtual worlds since these can provide a platform for fostering empathy and encouraging positive cultural change (Ganayem et al., 2020; Garcia et al., 2023). In contrast, the rise of isolated work has affected the development of IC due to less opportunities to interact, which, then, demands the development of cultural intelligence (Mangla, 2021). Of course, new opportunities have emerged as the possibility to access global talent using remote work that enhances intercultural skills from global teams (Caligiuri et al., 2022). Norms and practices are also rewritten to make equilibrium between family and workload to create a compatible sense of empathy and understanding among cultures (Wikberg, 2023). Finally, the increasing offer for online learning platforms and virtual collaboration fosters the possibility of access to IC training and development.

While VEs are not a new pedagogical innovation, their popularity has resurged since the COVID-19 pandemic and because of the development of more effective technology. Beginning in the late 1990s in foreign language teaching, the use of VEs as a pedagogical tool has been termed in many ways, including telecollaboration, online intercultural exchange, virtual exchange, collaborative online international learning, internet-mediated intercultural foreign language education, globally networked learning environments, and e-tandem or teletandem language exchange (O'Dowd, 2018). Research on virtual exchanges has been proven to be effective for cultural exchange in a variety of educational programs (Erkens et al., 2016; Lee & Markey, 2014; Rodríguez-Fuentes et al., 2021). Furthermore, in higher education, VEs have been promoted to enhance international mobility and strengthen relationships between institutions (Zilberberg et al., 2022).

Recently, other disciplines have integrated virtual exchanges into their academic programs. Business is not the exception as research specific to this field has shown that virtual activities can be implemented successfully in the curricula (Commander et al., 2022). A study conducted by Taras et al. (2013) with 6,000 university students from 43 countries working in virtual teams demonstrated that VEs were an opportunity for business students to differentiate, accept, and appreciate cultures while they developed competences in the use of ICTs for learning. In addition, other researchers have found that collaborative virtual projects develop a global mindset, prepare students for diversity and multicultural work (García et al., 2023), and raise their comprehension of cultural differences through a group research of potential difficulties companies face when entering into foreign markets (Swartz & Shrivastava, 2021). Not only do they serve to support IC development, but they also promote business specific learning (Kang et al., 2018; Xu & Lin, 2023). For example, Kang et al. (2018) describe how students conducted consumer and competitive analyses of the fashion industry in their countries of origin and discussed their findings with an international peer.

Methodology

Following Hernández-Sampieri et al. (2014), this chapter is based on a mixed methods descriptive study since it seeks to specify profiles, properties, and characteristics of a group of students. In addition, in this project, the phenomena are observed as they occur naturally, so non-experimental design was employed. Qualitative data included professor and student reflections, student focus groups while quantitative data was obtained from the application of a survey. To analyze the results and confirm conclusions, multiple investigators and sources of data were used to triangulate the information collected (Benavides & Gómez-Restrepo, 2005; Merriam & Tisdell, 2016). The research question guiding this study was the following:

Did undergraduate students evidence characteristics associated with intercultural competence (IC) after participating in the virtual exchange (VE)?

Context and Participants

The pedagogical experience occurred in a context of a VE between Colombian (n=63) and Mexican (n=64) students and their professors (n=2). Colombian participants were fourth semester undergraduate international business students ranging from 17 to 18 years old. The Mexican students were from seventh to ninth semester, also of international business, and were between 19 to 21 years old. The experience took place in the second semesters of 2020 and 2021 (see Table 1).

Table 1. Number of Students Enrolled in the Course

	Mexico	Colombia
Second semester 2020	29	30
Second semester 2021	35	33

Note. The number of students enrolled may differ slightly from those who actually answered the instruments.

In the case of the Colombian students, they were all in their fourth semester of International Business and had already taken an introductory course in international business, one in global cultures, and one in introduction to economics and microeconomics. The experience took place as a part of the *International Business and Competitiveness* course, in which conceptual aspects of internationalization are deepened and interrelated with competitiveness. It also aims to apply these concepts in simulated business realities. Therefore, developing IC is essential for the students in this course.

In the case of the Mexican students, they ranged from seventh to ninth semester of International Business. Some of them are already working or involved in business internships while they take the course where this experience was carried out. They have broader theoretical-conceptual knowledge than that of their Colombian counterparts, and many have already completed practical activities in both simulated and real companies. The courses they have taken a range of course in their field (e.g., *Company, Culture and Business in the World, International Perspective, Geopolitics and Global Changes, Negotiation and International Marketing Techniques,* N*egotiation and Intercultural Communication*, among others).

To introduce the VE, professors described the specific discipline learning outcome and asked for consent from the participants to use their data for this research project. The VE focused on learning about the forms of entry of businesses into international markets, including the definition of the concepts, advantages and disadvantages of each, how to use this information for entrepreneurs to make informed decisions. The courses also include learning outcomes related to critical thinking, decision-making, ethics, global perspective, effective communication, collaborative work, and the capacity to recognize how multicultural and multidisciplinary differences impact the same situation.

Furthermore, the professors explained the guidelines of the VE to clarify (i) participation policies; (ii) recommended resources (*Slack* for interactions between students and students and teachers, *Zoom/Google Meet* for interactions among students, *Google Sites* to present instructions and to upload the assignments; and *Padlet* for the icebreaker activity); (iii) assessment; and (iv) the description of the activities.

During the implementation of the VE, some adjustments to the icebreaker were made. In 2020, professors asked students to only do the first icebreaker. In 2021, the students completed three icebreakers. Table 2 shows the main stages of the virtual experience.

Table 2. Stages of the VE

Stage	Description
Icebreaker	The objective of this activity is for students to meet each other and begin to get to know both the local and international peers. For the experience in 2020, students created a video about their personal interests and knowledge of the concept of internationalization and uploaded it to Padlet (they used Powtoon, Zoom, and other apps as support). For the 2021 version, in addition to the presentation in Padlet, the icebreaker included a synchronous meeting ("Netflix Party") to watch and analyze a movie. A third icebreaker ("Meet your Multicultural Team") included students meeting in smaller groups (six to eight students of both nationalities) to present themselves and report what they already "knew" about the other country. Students then discussed what the other members presented.
Preliminary research activity	Professors established smaller groups with only local students (6 groups per country) to research an assigned form of internationalization (exports, licensing, franchising, turnkey projects, foreign direct investment by co-participation, and foreign direct investment by absolute ownership). As part of this research, they needed to write a text where they defined the concept and listed five advantages and five disadvantages of their assigned topic. At the end of the activity, professors provided feedback on this assignment.
Research activity by intercultural groups	Professors randomly divided the students into 12 new groups, which included local and international peers. In these groups, and based on the feedback from the previous activity, students reviewed the definitions of each type of internationalization. Then six of the groups worked together to list 10 advantages of an assigned type of internationalization and the other six groups listed 10 disadvantages. Finally, students collaborated to create a video and a short written report where they defined the form of internationalization assigned and listed its advantages and disadvantages. Again, students received feedback on their work.
Reflection and Evaluation	In this stage, students were assessed on the concepts, advantages, and disadvantages of the different types of internationalization. They also wrote a reflection on the intercultural experience. This was reinforced with a synchronous focus group with the students to explore opportunities for improvement of the VE, both for discipline and intercultural aspects.

Data Collection Techniques

As reported earlier, several instruments were used to collect data. First, students answered an intercultural competence questionnaire based on Cano and Ricardo (2014) and validated as reported in Corrales et al. (2021) at the end of the VE. The questionnaire sought to examine students' perceptions regarding their intercultural competence resulting from the intervention.

Table 3. Codification based on statements related to factors and dimensions of intercultural competence

	Factors			
Dimensions	**Intercultural effectiveness**	**Willingness to learn from and adapt to other cultures**	**Openness to other cultures**	**Awareness of diversity**
Attitudes	1. I can identify the culture to which I belong and the meaning of belonging to it. 2. I can identify beliefs and attitudes from other cultures. 3. I can appreciate positive aspects of my own culture, heritage and recognize how these can help me understand cultural differences. 5. I can identify attitudes, beliefs and values that show my respect and appreciation towards other cultures. 6. I can identify attitudes, beliefs and values that prevent me from respecting or appreciating other cultures.		4. I consider it necessary to know about other cultures and be sensitive to them. 7. I will try to correct attitudes and beliefs that prevent me from respecting and appreciating differences with other ethnic groups and cultures.	16. I recognize that I have stereotypes (pre-established ideas) about people who belong to a cultural group different from my own. 17. I can give examples of how my stereotypes—pre-established ideas—can affect my relationships with other people.

continued on following page

Table 3. Continued

	Factors			
Dimensions	**Intercultural effectiveness**	**Willingness to learn from and adapt to other cultures**	**Openness to other cultures**	**Awareness of diversity**
Knowledge	8. I know my cultural heritage, for example, ethnic group, language and the history of my ancestors. 9. I can identify at least 5 characteristics of my own culture and explain how these affect my relationship with people in my own culture and that of others. 10. I can identify commonalities with other cultures that help me respect and value them.	12. When I interact with people from other cultures, I try to learn as much as you can from them to avoid behaviors that can lead to discrimination. 13. When I interact with people from other cultures, I can recognize behaviors that lead to discrimination.		11. I can describe a situation in which I have offended someone by: racism, prejudice, discrimination, and/or stereotypes.
Skills		14. I can relate to people from different backgrounds cultures and maintain a dialogue about cultural differences and preferences. 15. I stay well connected with individuals who belong to a cultural group different from my own, and I participate in an open dialogue that gives feedback on my behavior. 18. I can set a positive example or negative emotional reactions to other cultural groups and how they influence my behavior.		

Note. Adapted from Corrales et al. (2021)

The questionnaire contained 18 statements to which students responded using a Likert-type scale ranging from 1 (strongly disagree) to 4 (strongly agree). The statements were categorized into attitudes, knowledge, and skills and also into four factors according to the model derived from the study by Corrales et al. (2021; see Table 3: *Intercultural effectiveness* (i.e., recognition of one's own culture, compared to the cultural perspective of others), *Willingness to learn from and adapt to other cultures* (i.e., choosing appropriate patterns of behavior and communication in intercultural interaction), *Openness to other cultures* (i.e., receptivity to other perspectives, without judging and respecting other points of view), and *Awareness of diversity* (i.e., recognizing the uniqueness of oneself and others)).

Additionally, qualitative data was obtained from: (i) professor written reflections about the results of the VE; (ii) student written reflections reporting lessons learned from the experience; and (iii) a focus group including both the Colombian and Mexican students. The guiding questions for this focus group were:

- What was the easiest part of the experience?
- What was the hardest part of the experience?
- What surprised you during the experience?
- What learning outcomes do you highlight?
- What similarities and differences did you find when working in teams with Mexicans, Colombians, and between Colombians and Mexicans?
- What cultural similarities and differences did you find between Colombians and Mexicans?

Data Analysis

Data from the student reflections, focus groups, and professor reflections were analyzed following the procedures of thematic analysis (Nowell et al., 2017). For student reflections and focus groups, each researcher initially reviewed the data individually using the *a priori* codes for qualitative analysis shown in Table 4. As is typical of qualitative analyses, other categories emerged such as teamwork and discipline learning. Student responses in the focus group were labeled by the year, and the turn was numbered (i.e., year, turn; 2020-66). Regarding reflections, students were numbered and labeled with their country of origin (i.e., number Country [Col, Mex]; 8 Col). Using the *a priori* and emerging codes, we were able to make connections between the IC dimensions and the factors of interculturality. Then, researchers discussed the coding to reach a consensus about the final categories using AtlasTi Web v.9 and MS Excel software. The findings of both instruments were combined in the results section.

Table 4. Codes for Qualitative Analysis

Intercultural Effectiveness	**Willingness to learn from and adapt to other cultures**	**Openness to other cultures**	**Awareness of diversity**
Attitude- Intercultural Effectiveness		Attitude- Openness to other cultures	Attitude- Awareness of diversity
Knowledge – Intercultural Effectiveness	Knowledge- Willingness to learn from and adapt to other cultures		Knowledge- Awareness of diversity
	Skills- Willingness to learn from and adapt to other cultures		

In the case of the professor reflections, the researchers reviewed the data to identify emerging themes. These codes resulted by identifying "interesting aspects in the data items that may form the basis of themes across the data set" (Nowell et al., 2017, p. 6).

When analyzing the questionnaire applied after the VE, the researchers reviewed the average of each statement to explore student perceptions in relation to their intercultural competence. Within the Lickert-type scale of one to four, researchers established that above two (i.e., agree and strongly agree) showed a trend towards a positive perception while below two, a negative trend (i.e., agree and strongly disagree).

Results

This section describes the results from the three analyses: professor reflections, student reflections and interviews, and the student questionnaire.

Professor Reflections

The professors participating in the VE wrote reflections, giving their perceptions of the activities and their impact on students. Professors reported that of the three icebreaker activities, only the "Netflix Party" and the "Meet your Multicultural Team" allowed for interaction, with the last activity being the most useful because students were guided to discuss what they knew about one country or another and confirm these aspects to see if their initial perception was true or false. They also reported that they observed intercultural interaction and a recognition of the differences between students from the two countries. Professors even cited that their students mentioned that the experience "made things much easier, and…it was the detonating element for the experience" and that "it was too short."

Teachers also reported in their reflections about the themes that emerged during the interaction of the 12 groups of the third icebreaker (see Figure 1). Findings showed that they touched on topics such as food, music, television, and even social problems.

Figure 1. Topics of Discussion in "Meet your Multicultural Team" Activity

In their reflection, professors also assessed the pertinence of the ICT tools used in the different activities. While professors recommended using Slack to meet asynchronously, students felt it was an ineffective way to complete the assigned task. The professors reported that Slack was only used to exchange phone numbers so they could connect with a tool that students felt more comfortable with, such as WhatsApp.

Another finding in the professor reflections is students' capacity to use problem-solving skills. In this particular experience, the teachers intervened little in the development of the activity because of the virtual nature of the interaction. Professors reported that students were able to autonomously solve problems that arose within the groups. When intra-group problems occurred, teachers, rather than imposing decisions, motivated the members of the groups to reach a consensus and find solutions.

A final aspect that teachers mentioned was related to the stage of the VE in which students had to create videos. They observed that the videos evidenced the depth of discipline learning that occurred due to the VE. Additionally, the videos showed diversity and creativity in the ways of approaching the topic, which professors linked to previous student preparation and the creation of rapport within the members of their group resulting from the icebreaker activities. They felt that students created a connection with each other and generated a feeling of responsibility and commitment towards each other. Since professors saw their students' first assignment after collaborating in a group with only local students and then again after their intercultural work, they observed a substantial positive change in discipline learning through a better use of concepts, economic jargon, and research skills.

Student Reflections and Focus Group

This section is based on the combined analysis of the student reflections and focus group at the end of the VE. In terms of **intercultural attitudes-effectiveness,** students reported reaching consensus and adapting in their intercultural teams. Students mentioned that "since we were not always available at the same times, we had to reach an agreement" (2020-38), adapt in order to "appreciate the differences that exist within our cultures and motivate us to show our best self" (2020-66), and "diversify ways of thinking, especially with people from other countries" (2021-26).

Data also demonstrated that students believed that **attitudes-openness towards other cultures** emerges from an environment of trust "because when one is in a very rigid environment, it can inhibit ideas and keep us from expressing certain things. Sometimes even good ideas are inhibited" (8 Col). Students felt this openness can be more complex if there are obstacles such as "differences due to geographical distance" (14 Mex), even if they all speak the same language since "even speaking Spanish can cause confusion" (2020-5). Thus, they said that once those obstacles are overcome, "having a perspective of someone from another culture can be very enriching since you can get a better view of the situation or things that you had not thought of" (2021-66). They link this appreciation to an awareness and openness towards cultural diversity, pointing out that this diversity may include not only national culture but also personal characteristics. One student indicated that her issues stemmed more from "personality than from nationality" (12 Col) because, as another student reported, "their culture is more similar than we thought" (4 Mex). However, findings showed students were aware of the differences and were careful to when "us[ing] jargon since this can cause confusion when communicating, and if it is used, they must be explained so that all members of the group can understand" (2020-27). It is in the "'knowing how to speak' to make oneself understood where confusion or misunderstandings do not occur" (2020-61), where interactions are facilitated because "in a group, there may be different personalities and tastes, so unity and good coexistence can exist" (2021-13). As a result, several students recommended that people:

"never take for granted stereotypes we have about other cultures. Although the cultures are similar, realize that each has different elements that are key when negotiating. Be aware that your way of doing things is not necessarily the right way for the other culture." (2021-86)

Findings on **knowledge about cultural effectiveness** focus on aspects such as knowing the others' "customs, traditions and native words" (2020-44) and "noticing several similarities and some cultural differences" (2020-53). These aspects may support discipline learning because "other cultures can enrich the content of the activity; and multicultural teams allow for greater vision and scope in projects" (2021-73).

In addition to this effectiveness, traits of **attitude of willingness to learn and adapt to other cultures** were identified in students. This was observed especially in the icebreaker activities. Students reported that "the first encounter made things much easier, and from the small groups, it was like the detonating element for the experience" (3 Col). Others found that "opinions can vary more than one expects, although it does not mean that they cannot be discussed and understood" (2020-99). It can be inferred from the data that although there is a willingness to learn and adapt to other cultures, this category is not as explicit in students as the others. Something similar happened with the factor of **knowledge of cultural diversity**. Students explicitly recognized cultural diversity when they mentioned that "the stereotype of the Colombian/Mexican is that we leave everything for the last minute" (15 Col) or that language "made an impression on me in some words we mentioned, even though we spoke the same language" (2020-24). In the end, students seemed to have understood that "differences in nationality and location are not a great impediment when you want to collaborate" (2021-71).

Finally, in the factor referring to the **skill of willingness to learn and adapt to other cultures**, students listed aspects such as: (i) "active listening: many times Mexicans can talk more than listen, and in these activities, it was important to listen to understand what our classmates wanted to say" (2020-36), (ii) "new ways of working as a team to establish clear communication" (2020-50), and (iii) "formality when communicating with different people" (2021-23). Additionally, students discussed debunking some of the stereotypes of Latino culture, such as procrastination. One student said that they "are able to work and achieve objectives in a timely manner if [they] organize well and focus from the beginning" (2021-79).

From this experience, additional categories emerged outside of those originally identified from the literature: (i) **teamwork** and (ii) **disciplinary learning**. Regarding **teamwork**, this was clearly an important element since it appeared in the data collected from the instruments. Beyond the cultural aspect, teamwork in times of pandemic depended on the use of technological tools, and students taught each other how to use new ones. This was confirmed when one student stated that "it was very good because since we usually use different platforms, we could explain how to use them and vice versa" (9 Mex). Besides collaborating with each other with the ICTs, students reported that trust was an important part of teamwork. An example of this is when students said: "working with a team you do not know implies some uncertainty since the way the other person works is new" (2020-83), so it is "very important to build a good relationship" (2021-83). Among the challenges of teamwork, students highlighted that "it is very difficult to work simultaneously with a large team that is in another country" (2021-62) and that for effective teamwork, "punctuality is extremely important" (2021-84). Other lessons learned included their belief that it was essential "to organize, create schedules, assign roles, and get to know colleagues before carrying out everything effectively" (2021- 75). In this sense, a student emphasized that "*bonding* is essential to be able to move from 'groups' to 'teams'" (2021-9).

As for **discipline learning**, researchers confirmed that the topics studied—the forms of entry—were evident in the student reflections and interviews. Students emphasized that before the VE, they knew "the general definition but had not started to analyze the advantages and disadvantages" (5 Mex), and they learned "the ways of entering foreign markets, the ways to segment the population, as well as the ways to approach these segments" (2021-29).

Student Questionnaire

This section is based on the responses to the questionnaire on intercultural competence. Results of the analysis of the data showed that the averages of all the statements were above 3 (agree), except for Statement 11 (*I can identify points in common with other cultures that help me respect and value them*) which in 2020 was slightly below (see Figures 2 and 3).

Figure 2. Average of Statements (2020)

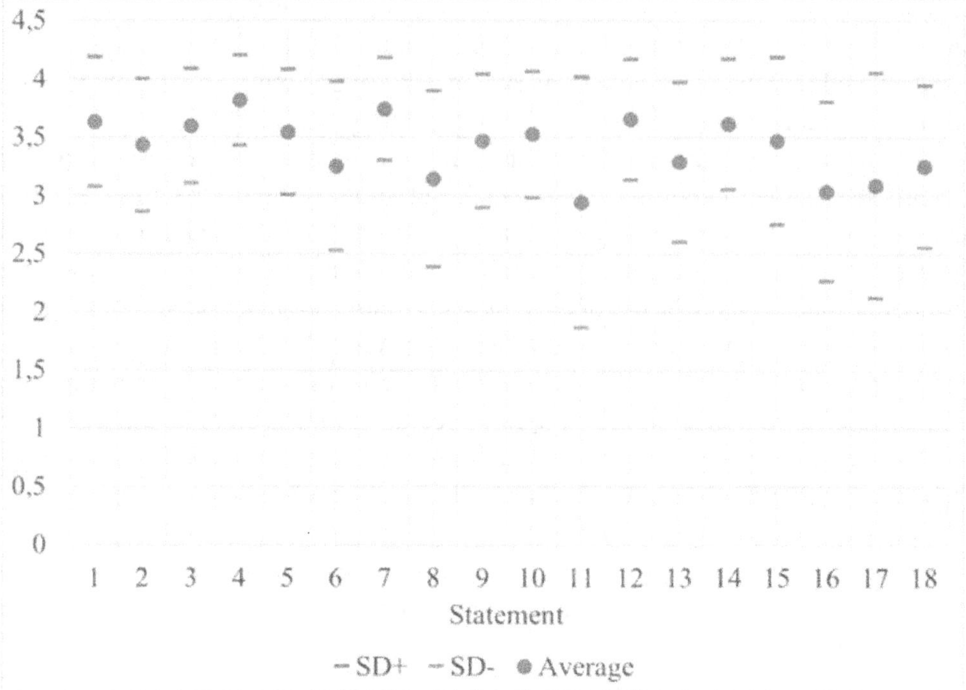

Figure 3. Average of Statements (2021)

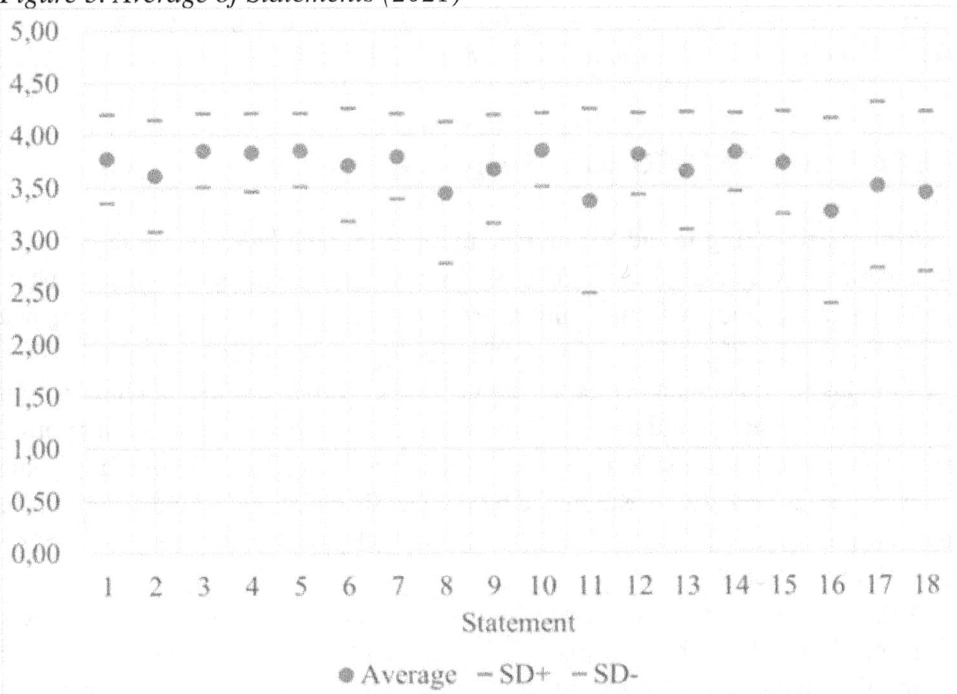

In 2020, the perceptions of students on Statements 4 (*I consider it necessary to know other cultures and be sensitive to them*) and 7 (*I commit myself to correct attitudes and beliefs that do not allow me to respect or value the differences of other ethnic and cultural groups*) stood out for their high level of agreement. Both of these fall within the category of **attitudes and openness to other cultures**. In 2021, these two (Statements 4 and 7) continue to be high, but two other statements also scored high in the category of **attitude-intercultural effectiveness**: 3, (*I am able to appreciate the positive aspects of my own cultural heritage and recognize that they help me understand cultural differences*) and 5 (*I can identify the attitudes, beliefs, and values that demonstrate my respect and appreciation towards other cultures*). The second highest category in 2021 was **knowledge-intercultural effectiveness** which included two statements: 10 (*I can identify commonalities with other cultures that help me respect and value them*) and **skills-willingness to learn from and adapt to other cultures**: 14 (*I can relate to people from different cultural contexts and maintain a dialogue about cultural differences and preferences*).

The results showed that the lowest aspect in both years to be in **knowledge about cultural diversity** with Statement 11 (*I can describe a situation in which I have offended someone for any of these causes: racism, prejudice, discrimination* *and stereotypes*), although, in 2021, we found **attitude towards cultural diversity** to also be low (Statement 16 - *I recognize that I have stereotypes -pre-established ideas- about some people who are different from my cultural group*).

DISCUSSION AND CONCLUSION

After participating in the VE, university international business professors and students from two different countries perceived that students showed some characteristics associated with intercultural competence as a result of the experience (Machwate et al., 2021; Varo Varo, 2021; Rodríguez-Fuentes et al., 2022). One aspect to take into account is that the countries the students were from have a high orientation to affective intercultural communication, which could have supported favorable student behavior during the VE (Machwate et al., 2021). In the case of this experience, this aspect is strengthened by the fact that students' countries of origin share historical, socio-cultural, and linguistic backgrounds, possibly facilitating more fluid interactions.

Although the learning of discipline knowledge is one of the most essential aspects of any educational experience, this VE showed that to attain the content objectives in virtual exchanges, students needed to create first a space of mutual cultural and personal recognition and understanding, regardless of nationality. This confirms the holistic vision proposed by Le Deist and Winterton (2005) that advocates the importance of both hard and soft skills to be successful in the professional environment. In relation to the above, in this particular study, it was necessary that students of both cultures build a level of closeness by recognizing similarities and differences in language, music, gastronomy, etc., which facilitated the understanding of discipline-related global issues (Vargas-Madriz, 2018). Furthermore, the VE gave students the opportunity to go beyond superficial information and learn about the human beings in the experience. It also allowed students to use a global perspective to apply their attitudes, skills, and knowledge to a local context. Therefore, they had to combine both the discipline and their own cultural experience and that of the other. As Johnson et al. (2014) propose, it is hoped that this application of global thinking will result in successful behavior in professional multicultural environments.

In addition, results showed a predominance of **attitudinal** aspects. The students had an **attitude of openness** towards their peers from the other country (O'Dowd, 2021) that was motivated, as they expressed, by the trust and closeness created in the icebreaker activities, which showed a great difference between the intervention of 2020 compared to 2021. This indicates that students consider that participating in the VEs gives them not only the opportunity to learn about their partner as a person but also gain access to the cultural and social aspects of their partner's context. Furthermore, students showed a strong **attitude of awareness of cultural diversity** which can support further development of attitudes and encourage positive cross-cultural interactions by remaining sensitive to the difference. However, according to the analysis, there were still aspects of **knowledge** in that same factor which students perceived as insufficient. This can be related to what Deardorff (2011) says about the evolution of intercultural competence being a process that takes time to develop. Kohli Bagwe and Haskollar (2020) also support the idea that the longer the intercultural experience takes, the more IC can be developed. In the case of this experience, students only interacted for a few weeks. Therefore, to attain more conclusive results in terms of IC development, VEs may require more time.

Additionally, in the category of **skills of willingness to learn from and adapt to other cultures**, interaction mediated through ICTs played a fundamental role. The students recognized that the technological tools facilitated the activity, but they moved from those suggested by the teachers toward those that they already felt comfortable using. Finding the right tool to engage students is a challenge. Sharma (2023) suggests ICT tools in VEs should help students to construct ideas, collaborate with peers, and create original work as this can facilitate interaction and enhance the possibility to learn from and adapt to other cultures. This is in line with what Abdel-Kader (2020) and O'Dowd (2018) argue when they suggest that new technologies should foster communication between learners in different parts of the world in real-time. However, some scholars (Ruben et al., 2021) argue that the use of ICT could hinder interpersonal communication skills since non-verbal communication signals are also important for the cultural exchange. Moreover, anecdotal evidence has shown that hyperconnectivity may increase the possibility of students suffering stress and anxiety, affecting critical thinking and engagement to learning (Anderson & Rianie, 2018). Additionally, the overwhelming amount of information could lead to misinformation and loss of authenticity in the cultural exchange (Isachenko, 2018). In the case of this experience, as students had the opportunity to choose the ICT tools they were most familiar with, these negative aspects seemed to have been mitigated.

Furthermore, from the emerging categories, both **teamwork** and **discipline knowledge** appeared often in the students' reflections and interviews which can be related to the nature of virtual exchanges that promote cooperative work and content learning. This could be observed as students took on leadership roles to ensure that the work was carried out evenly by the members of the team. A practical example of the benefits of teamwork resulting from virtual exchanges was found in Buko et al.'s (2022) study which analyzed the results of 250 students' pre- and post-exchanges. The findings suggest that teamwork was a principal factor in their development of knowledge, skills, and attitudes related to the experience. Besides teamwork, Fonseca et al. (2021) argue that interdisciplinary VEs with people of different backgrounds offer the possibility to foster cultural diversity and enhance the creation of knowledge.One of the aspects that the professors expected and encouraged in an explicit way was the development of creative presentations as the final product of the VE to avoid using traditional presentation tools such as PowerPoint and Powtoon, although they were not banned, so the final product was innovative and pleasant to the viewer. While studies on innovation and creativity in virtual teams is incipient in the literature (Reiter-Palmon, 2021), in this experience, the professors were pleasantly surprised by the quality and creativity of the audiovisual products, evidencing students' artistic talents that surely would not have been visible if this type of initiative did not exist.

Finally, findings showed clear student and teacher learning from the VE. For the students, a seed of intercultural openness was laid. For many of them, it was their first academic relationship with people from other countries in contexts different from vacation or social interactions. Therefore, they learned how to establish relationships, build trust, and work together towards a common goal using ICTs, which is an essential part of virtual teams now and most likely even more important in the future work setting of these students (Reiter-Palmon, 2021). For teachers, implementing the VE was a process of continuous learning where they had the opportunity to make decisions to improve the experience. This was seen when professors decided to make adjustments to the icebreakers in 2021 version of the VE. As Rodríguez-Fuentes et al. (2022) suggests, through VEs, instructors can develop new skills as they negotiate with their teaching partner from a different culture and learn from their own students and those of their partner.

Implications and Recommendations

Because of the experience gained from the COVID-19 pandemic, working virtually in education and professional contexts most likely will only continue to grow, especially as online communication technologies innovate and evolve. Thus, incorporating VEs in business education not only can give students experience working collaboratively online but also can provide diverse opportunities to enhance IC and develop 21st century skills (Adbel-Kadel, 2020). Therefore, from this experience, we offer several suggestions for those interested in implementing VEs and highlight some challenges that emerged while providing possible solutions for them.

First, one important aspect to consider when implementing this type of experience relates to choosing a partner institution to work with since communication is essential between professors. From our experience, VEs seem to be most successful with institutions that have worked well together previously or with professors who already have some type of professional or personal relationship, as in the case of this study. This is true because, to design the VE activity, course content and student learning outcomes should be discussed to find common aspects, to agree on the type of activities, and to set the timeline to develop them. Furthermore, professors should maintain contact with both students and the other professor throughout the experience to ensure successful troubleshooting and completion of the VE activities.

Another aspect to keep in mind is the use of technology. ICTs require the connection to be easy for the emitter, transmitter, and receiver. Although in this study, the institutions guaranteed a good level of connectivity, student individual connection was problematic and caused challenges for them when completing the activities. Thus, professors should ensure that students have technical support to back the methodological aspects of the VE.

A third aspect relates to the flexibility that professors should have with these types of experiences. It is essential that teachers keep an open mind since they may need to adapt not only the initial activities but also the selection of ICT tools to use as the experience is developing. As in this VE, it is possible that communication technology may need to change to those that are more student-friendly and well-known to them. For example, initially, professors suggested using *Slack* to provide a secure platform for data protection, but students ignored this and quickly moved their interactions to their everyday social networks (e.g., WhatsApp, Instagram, TikTok). This implies that professors must be willing to sacrifice some control (e.g., allowing students to choose which ICTs to use) in order to increase interaction and, hopefully, facilitate both content learning and IC development in the students.

A further aspect to consider is the length of the project which could have implications for both IC development and discipline learning. It is possible that longer projects can generate greater trust between the students and, therefore, have better results in these two areas. Yet, at the same time, longer projects may affect student motivation and decrease interest in the VE. Similar to Rodríguez-Fuentes et al.'s (2022) experience, with each iteration, managing logistics, curricular alignment, and activities have become easier even though we have made several changes. In our first experience, we implemented a limited number of activities in a shorter timeframe and realized that they were insufficient while in the second, we were too ambitious. The VE reported in this chapter details what we found to be the most effective for student engagement and learning. Therefore, professors should consider both the length of time and the number of activities when designing a VE.

Turning to challenges, the professors observed students who did not contribute to the completion of the activities and took advantage of their peer' work, which we have termed "*free riders.*" This is something that goes beyond the control of the professors even in the face-to-face modality. In this case, self-assessment and co-evaluation tools could be used to make the contribution of each individual in the team visible. This is an aspect that we are considering implementing in future iterations.

Additionally, student age difference was a sensitive issue when implementing the VE as students evidenced different levels of maturity or responsibility during the collaboration. Furthermore, students identified that finding synchronous moments to interact was the biggest challenge to complete the tasks of the VE and they had some difficulty in following instructions even though they were uploaded in the learning management system. These aspects require that professors clarify their responsibilities in the VE. The idea is that the role of the professor is not to solve technical problems or conflicts with group schedules but rather to facilitate student intercultural interaction and learning. From our experience, the professor tends to try to solve these logistical and technical problems instead of focusing on the pedagogical needs of the experience.

As a final thought, this study confirms that VEs have a great potential to foster both discipline learning and intercultural competence. This is true especially because students have the opportunity to interact with international peers to learn and apply course content at both the global and local levels. One of the main gains of VEs is that they promote relationship building between students since they facilitate getting to know each other by discussing general aspects resembling face-to-face interaction (i.e., family relationships, political views, cultural customs, values). The findings of this study also demonstrated that VEs open doors to dynamize the learning process in the 21st century and provide opportunities for internationalization at home of universities, guiding students on the path of becoming more open towards others.

REFERENCES

Adbel-Kadel, M. (2020, April 14). Harnessing technology for global education. *Inside Higher Education*. Retrieved from https://www.insidehighered.com/views/2020/04/14/colleges -should-develop-more-virtual-exchange-programs-maintain-and-increase-global

Anderson, J., & Rainie, L. (2018). *The future of well-being in a tech-saturated world*. Pew Research Center. https://assets.pewresearch.org/wp-content/uploads/sites/14/2018/04/14154552/PI_2018.04.17_Future-of-Well-Being_FINAL.pdf

Bashir, A., Bashir, S., Rana, K., Lambert, P., & Vernallis, A. (2021). Post-COVID-19 adaptations; The shifts towards online learning, hybrid course delivery and the implications for biosciences courses in the higher education setting. *Frontiers in Education*, 6(711619), 711619. https://www.frontiersin.org/journals/education/articles/10.3389/feduc.2021.711619. DOI: 10.3389/feduc.2021.711619

Bath, D., Smith, C., Stein, S., & Swann, R. (2004). Beyond mapping and embedding graduate attributes: Bringing together quality assurance and action learning to create a validated and living curriculum. *Higher Education Research & Development*, 23(3), 313–328. DOI: 10.1080/0729436042000235427

Beelen, J., & Jones, E. (2015). Redefining internationalization at home. In Curaj, A., Matei, L., Pricopie, R., Salmi, J., & Scott, P. (Eds.), *The European Higher Education Area*. Springer., DOI: 10.1007/978-3-319-20877-0_5

Benavides, M., & Gómez-Restrepo, C. (2005). Methods in qualitative research: Triangulation. *Revista Colombiana de Psiquiatría*, XXXIV(1), 118–124. https://www.redalyc.org/pdf/806/80628403009.pdf

Brown, M., Nic Giolla Mhichil, M., Beirne, E., & Mac Lochlainn, C. (2021). The global micro-credential landscape: Charting a new credential ecology for lifelong learning. *Journal of Learning for Development*, 8(2), 228–254. DOI: 10.56059/jl4d.v8i2.525

Buko, S., Knappitsch, E., Zinenko, A., & Covarrubias-Venegas, B. (2022). *The global case study challenge: A virtual exchange developing global work competencies*. Retrieved September 1, 2024 from https://www.academia.edu/105843026/The_Global_Case_Study_Challenge_A_Virtual_Exchange _Developing_Global_Work_Competencies

Caligiuri, P., De Cieri, H., Minbaeva, D., Verbeke, A., & Zimmermann, A. (2022). International HRM insights for navigating the COVID-19 pandemic: Implications for future research and practice. In Mithani, M. A., Narula, R., Surdu, I., & Verbeke, A. (Eds.), *Crises and disruptions in International Business. JIBS special collections.* Palgrave Macmillan., DOI: 10.1007/978-3-030-80383-4_17

Cano, J., & Ricardo, C. (2014). *Survey for the analysis of intercultural competence* [Internal document]. Universidad del Norte.

Cao, C., & Meng, Q. (2020). Effects of online and direct contact on Chinese international students' social capital in intercultural networks: Testing moderation of direct contact and mediation of global competence. *Higher Education*, 80(4), 625–643. DOI: 10.1007/s10734-020-00501-w

Carrillo Mendoza, G. (Ed.). (2015). *El currículo por competencias en la educación superior: Ponencias y debate* [Competence curriculum in higher education: Presentations and debate]. I Encuentro Internacional Universitario, Lima, Peru. https://cdn02.pucp.education/academico/2015/09/01094909/curriculo_competencias.pdf

Commander, N. E., Schloer, W. F., & Cushing, S. T. (2022). Virtual exchange: A promising high-impact practice for developing intercultural effectiveness across disciplines. *Journal of Virtual Exchange*, 5, 1–19. DOI: 10.21827/jve.5.37329

Corrales, K. A., Lombana-Coy, J., & Rey-Paba, L. (2021). Fostering global competence in international business students on a Latin American campus. *Journal of Teaching in International Business*, 32(1), 81–101. DOI: 10.1080/08975930.2021.1906381

Deardorff, D. K. (Ed.). (2009). *The SAGE handbook of intercultural competence.* SAGE. DOI: 10.4135/9781071872987

Deardorff, D. K. (2011). Assessing intercultural competence. *New Directions for Institutional Research*, 2011(149), 65–79. DOI: 10.1002/ir.381

Demirkan, H., & Spohrer, J. (2015). T-Shaped innovators: Identifying the right talent to support service innovation. *Research Technology Management*, 58(5), 12–15. DOI: 10.5437/08956308X5805007

Díaz Villavicencio, C. (Ed.). (2016). Las competencias genéricas en la educación superior: Ponencias y conversatorio [Generic competences in higher education: Presentations and panels. II Encuentro Internacional Universitario, Lima, Peru. https://cdn02.pucp.education/academico/2016/06/24194836/II_EncuentroInt _competencias_generi cas_en_edusup.pdf

Erkens, M., Bodemer, D., & Hoppe, H. U. (2016). Improving collaborative learning in the classroom: Text mining based grouping and representing. *International Journal of Computer-Supported Collaborative Learning*, 11(4), 387–415. DOI: 10.1007/s11412-016-9243-5

Fonseca, P., Julian, K., Hulme, W., Martins, M. D. L., & Brautlacht, R. (2021). The multi-disciplinary approach to an interdisciplinary virtual exchange. In M. Satar (Ed.), *Virtual exchange: Towards digital equity in internationalisation* (pp. 41-49). Research-publishing.net. DOI: 10.14705/rpnet.2021.53.1288

Ganayem, A., Hoter, E., & Shonfeld, M. (2020). Lessons learned from 15 years of multicultural online collaborative learning in Israel. In Hunter, W. J., & Austin, R. S. P. (Eds.), *Blended and online learning for global citizenship: New technologies and opportunities for intercultural education* (pp. 32–50). Routledge. DOI: 10.4324/9780367821661-3

García, F., Smith, S., Burger, A., & Helms, M. (2023). Increasing global mindset through collaborative online international learning (COIL): Internationalizing the undergraduate international business class. *Journal of International Education in Business*, 16(2), 184–203. DOI: 10.1108/JIEB-08-2022-0054

Gazzola, M., Wickström, B. A., & Templin, T. (2019). Language skills, the labour market, and socioeconomic integration. *Empirica*, 46(4), 617–623. DOI: 10.1007/s10663-019-09463-4

Habbal, F., Kolmos, A., Hadgraft, R. G., Holgaard, J. E., & Reda, K. (2024). *Reshaping engineering education*. Springer., DOI: 10.1007/978-981-99-5873-3

Hernández-Sampieri, R., Fernández, C., & Baptista, P. (2014). *Research methodology* (6th ed.). McGraw Hill.

Isachenko, N. (2018). The role of information and informational and communication technologies in modern society. *Utopía y Praxis Latinoamericana*, 23(82), 361–367. DOI: 10.5281/zenodo.1512122

Johnson, D. W., Johnson, R. T., & Smith, K. A. (2014). Co-operative learning: Improving university instruction by basing practice on validated theory. *Journal on Excellence in College Teaching*, 25(3&4), 85–118. https://celt.miamioh.edu/ojs/index.php/JECT/issue/view/64

Kang, J. H., Kim, S. Y., Jang, S., & Koh, A.-R. (2018). Can college students' global competence be enhanced in the classroom? The impact of cross- and inter-cultural online projects. *Innovations in Education and Teaching International*, 55(6), 683–693. DOI: 10.1080/14703297.2017.1294987

Karakas, A. (2023). Breaking down barriers with artificial intelligence (ai): Cross-cultural communication in foreign language education. In Kartal, G. (Ed.), *Transforming the Language Teaching Experience in the Age of AI* (pp. 215–233). IGI Global., DOI: 10.4018/978-1-6684-9893-4.ch012

Kohli Bagwe, T., & Haskollar, E. (2020). Variables impacting intercultural competence: A systematic literature review. *Journal of Intercultural Communication Research*, 49(4), 346–371. DOI: 10.1080/17475759.2020.1771751

Le Deist, F. D., & Winterton, J. (2005). What is competence? *Human Resource Development International*, 8(1), 27–46. DOI: 10.1080/1367886042000338227

Lee, L., & Markey, A. (2014). A study of learners' perceptions of online intercultural exchange through web 2.0 technologies. *ReCALL*, 26(3), 281–297. DOI: 10.1017/S0958344014000111

Leung, K., Ang, S., & Tan, M. L. (2014). Intercultural competence. *Annual Review of Organizational Psychology and Organizational Behavior*, 1(1), 489–519. DOI: 10.1146/annurev-orgpsych-031413-091229

Levy-Leboyer, C. (1996). *La gestion des compétences*. Les Editions d'Organisation.

Lokkesmoe, K. J., Kuchinke, K. P., & Ardichvili, A. (2016). Developing cross-cultural awareness through foreign immersion programs: Implications of university study abroad research for global competency development. *European Journal of Training and Development*, 40(3), 155–170. DOI: 10.1108/EJTD-07-2014-0048

Lombana-Coy, J., Corrales, K. A., & Rey-Paba, L. (2024). Teaching business through online intercultural exchanges: A method to develop global competence. In Blair, J., & Robles, M. (Eds.), *Effective methods for teaching business related topics: During and post crisis* (Vol. 1, pp. 163–176). National Business Education Association.

Luo, H., & Gao, P. (2022). Intercultural learning through Chinese-American telecollaboration: Results of a song sharing project. *Computer Assisted Language Learning*, 37(1-2), 85–113. DOI: 10.1080/09588221.2022.2026405

Machwate, S., Bendaoud, R., Henze, J., Berrada, K., & Burgos, D. (2021). Virtual exchange to develop cultural, language, and digital competencies. *Sustainability (Basel)*, 13(11), 5926. Advance online publication. DOI: 10.3390/su13115926

Mangla, N. (2021). Working in a pandemic and post-pandemic period – Cultural intelligence is the key. *International Journal of Cross Cultural Management*, 21(1), 53–69. DOI: 10.1177/14705958211002877

Matusitz, J., & Forrester, M. (2009). Successful glocalization practices: The case of Seiyu in Japan. *Journal of Transnational Management*, 14(2), 155–176. DOI: 10.1080/15475770903028696

McClelland, D. (1973). Testing for competence rather than for 'intelligence.'. *The American Psychologist*, 28(1), 1–14. https://psycnet.apa.org/doi/10.1037/h0034092. DOI: 10.1037/h0034092 PMID: 4684069

Merriam, S. B., & Tisdell, E. J. (2016). *Qualitative research. A guide to design an implementation*. Jossey-Bass.

Moreno Olivos, T. (2010). El currículo por competencias en la universidad: Más ruido que nueces [The competence curriculum at the university: More sound than nuts]. *Revista de la Educación Superior*, 39(2), 77–90. https://desarrollocurricular.uantof.cl/wp-content/uploads/2024/01/Moreno-Olivos-T.-2010.-El-curriculo-por-competencias-en-la-universidad-mas-ruido-que-nueces.pdf

Nowell, L. S., Norris, J. M., White, D. E., & Moules, N. J. (2017). Thematic analysis: Striving to meet the trustworthiness criteria. *International Journal of Qualitative Methods*, 16(1), 1–13. DOI: 10.1177/1609406917733847

O'Dowd, R. (2018). A transnational model of virtual exchange for global citizenship education. Revised version of a plenary address given at the Sixth International Conference on the Development and Assessment of Intercultural Competence: *Intercultural Competence and Mobility: Virtual and Physical*. January 25-28, 2018, University of Arizona, USA.

O'Dowd, R. (2021). What do students learn in virtual exchange? A qualitative content analysis of learning outcomes across multiple exchanges. *International Journal of Educational Research*, 109, 11–13. DOI: 10.1016/j.ijer.2021.101804

Patel, F., & Lynch, H. (2013). Glocalization as an alternative to internationalization in higher education: Embedding positive glocal learning perspectives. *International Journal on Teaching and Learning in Higher Education*, 25(2), 223–230. https://www.isetl.org/ijtlhe/ijtlhe-issue.php?v=25&n=2&y=2013

Pinilla Roa, A. E. (2010). Competencias en educación universitaria1. *Revista EDU-CyT, 2*, 1-18. https://bibliotecadigital.univalle.edu.co/server/api/core/bitstreams/0c0a4944-35dc-4b66-bbaf-4b60cbcb8e06/content

Prahalad, C. K., & Hamel, G. (1990). The core competence of the corporation. *Harvard Business Review*, (May-June), 79–91.

Reiter-Palmon, R., Kramer, W., Allen, J., Murugavel, V., & Leone, S. (2021). Creativity in virtual teams: A review and agenda for future research. *Creativity. Theories – Research - Applications, 8*(1) 165-188. DOI: 10.2478/ctra-2021-0011

Rodríguez-Fuentes, R. A., Corrales, K. A., Rey Paba, L., & Rosado-Mendinueta, N. (2022). Promoting communicative and intercultural competence development through virtual exchanges. In Allen, M., Ene, E., & McIntosh, K. (Eds.), *Building internationalized spaces: Second language perspectives on developing language and cultural exchange programs in higher education* (pp. 79–100). University of Michigan Press., https://www.press.umich.edu/11762571/building_internationalized_spaces

Ruben, M. A., Stosic, M. D., Correale, J., & Blanch-Hartigan, D. (2021). Is technology enhancing or hindering interpersonal communication? A framework and preliminary results to examine the relationship between technology use and nonverbal decoding skill. *Frontiers in Psychology*, 11, 611670. DOI: 10.3389/fpsyg.2020.611670 PMID: 33519627

Sarwari, A. Q., Javed, M. N., Mohd Adnan, H., & Abdul Wahab, M. N. (2024). Assessment of the impacts of artificial intelligence (AI) on intercultural communication among postgraduate students in a multicultural university environment. *Scientific Reports*, 14(1), 13849. DOI: 10.1038/s41598-024-63276-5 PMID: 38879546

Sharma, S. (2023, July 5). *Supporting student engagement with technology*. Edutopia. Retrieved September 22, 2024, from https://www.edutopia.org/article/using-technology-support-student-engagement/

Stasz, C. (1997). Do employers need the skills they want? Evidence from technical work. *Journal of Education and Work*, 10(3), 205–233. DOI: 10.1080/1363908970100301

Swartz, S., Barbosa, B., & Crawford, I. (2020). Building intercultural competence through virtual team collaboration across global classrooms. *Business and Professional Communication Quarterly*, 83(1), 57–79. DOI: 10.1177/2329490619878834

Swartz, S., & Shrivastava, A. (2022). Stepping up the game–meeting the needs of global business through virtual team projects. *Higher Education. Skills and Work-Based Learning*, 12(2), 346–368. DOI: 10.1108/HESWBL-02-2021-0037

Taras, , Caprar, D. V., Rottig, D., Sarala, R. M., Zakaria, N., Zhao, F., Jiménez, A., Wankel, C., Lei, W. S., Minor, M. S., Bryła, P., Ordeñana, X., Bode, A., Schuster, A., Vaiginiene, E., Froese, F. J., Bathula, H., Yajnik, N., Baldegger, R., & Huang, V. Z. (2013). A global classroom? Evaluating the effectiveness of global virtual collaboration as a teaching tool in management education. *Academy of Management Learning & Education*, 12(3), 414–435. DOI: 10.5465/amle.2012.0195

Tien, C. Y., & Talley, P. (2012). Think globally, act locally: 'Glocalization' in Taiwanese higher education. *International Journal of Business and Social Science*, 3(15), 124–130. https://www.ijbssnet.com/journals/Vol_3_No_15_August_2012/16.pdf

Vargas-Madriz, L. F. (2018). Experiences of online closeness in virtual learning environments (VLEs). *The Indo-Pacific Journal of Phenomenology*, 18(2), 1–14. DOI: 10.1080/20797222.2018.1507350

Varo Varo, A. (2021). Fostering intercultural competence through videoconference exchange: Using an external provider to match learners with trained native speakers and administer video calls. *Journal of Virtual Exchange*, 4, 1–13. DOI: 10.21827/jve.4.35981

Wikberg, K. (2023). Family-friendly policies and practices: Scoping review (Master's thesis, Metropolia Ammattikorkeakoulu). https://www.theseus.fi/bitstream/handle/10024/809553/Wikberg_Katja.pdf? sequence=2&isAllowed=y

Xu, H., & Lin, Y. (2023). Using collaborative online international learning to increase student success in a quantitative business core course: Using COIL to increase student success in a quantitative business core course. In *ICDEL '23: Proceedings of the 8th International Conference on Distance Education and Learning* (pp. 185-189). Association for Computing Machinery. doi:DOI: 10.1145/3606094.3606148

Zilberberg, L. E., & Krimphove, J. (2022). Virtual exchange contributions to the development of intercultural competence: A Brazilian higher education institutions' perspective. *Actualidades Investigativas en Educación*, 22(1), 312–336. DOI: 10.15517/aie.v22i1.47481

ADDITIONAL READING

de Hei, M., Tabacaru, C., Sjoer, E., Rippe, R., & Walenkamp, J. (2020). Developing intercultural competence through collaborative learning in international higher education. *Journal of Studies in International Education*, 24(2), 190–211. DOI: 10.1177/1028315319826226

Guth, S., & Helm, F. (Eds.). (2010). *Telecollaboration 2.0: Language, literacies, and intercultural learning in the 21st century*. Peter Lang. DOI: 10.3726/978-3-0351-0013-6

Hackett, S., Janssen, J., Beach, P., Perreault, M., Beelen, J., & Van Tartwijk, J. (2023). The effectiveness of Collaborative Online International Learning (COIL) on intercultural competence development in higher education. *International Journal of Educational Technology in Higher Education*, 20(5), 5. Advance online publication. DOI: 10.1186/s41239-022-00373-3 PMID: 36713634

Helm, F. (2015). The practices and challenges of telecollaboration in higher education in Europe. *Language Learning & Technology*, 19(2), 197–217. 10125/44424

Liu, Y., & Shirley, T. (2021). Without crossing a border: Exploring the impact of shifting study abroad online on students' learning and intercultural competence development during the COVID-19 pandemic. *Online Learning : the Official Journal of the Online Learning Consortium*, 25(1), 182–194. DOI: 10.24059/olj.v25i1.2471

Müller-Hartmann, A., & O'Dowd, R. (2017). *A training manual on telecollaboration for teachers*. Telecollaboration.org

O'Dowd, R., & Lewis, T. (Eds.). (2016). *Online intercultural exchange: Policy, pedagogy, practice*. Routledge. DOI: 10.4324/9781315678931

Rey, L., Corrales, K., & Lombana, J. (2022). *Internacionalización de la educación superior.* Editorial Universidad del Norte. https://editorial.uninorte.edu.co/gpd-internacionalizacion-de-la-educacion-superior-9789587894653-637c0c54c4931.html

Schenker, T. (2012). Intercultural competence and cultural learning through telecollaboration. *CALICO Journal*, 29(3), 449–470. DOI: 10.11139/cj.29.3.449-470

Thorne, S. L. (2003). Artifacts and cultures-of-use in intercultural communication. *Language Learning & Technology*, 7(2), 38–67. 10125/25200

KEY TERMS AND DEFINITIONS

Collaborative Online International Learning (COIL): A model of virtual exchange used in educational settings to promote intercultural learning and international collaboration without physical mobility.

Internationalization at Home (IaH): The process of offering students an internationalized learning experience through online interactions and collaborative projects without leaving their home country

Intercultural Competence (IC): The ability to effectively interact, communicate, and work with people from different cultural backgrounds, developed through both attitudes and skills.

Information and Communication Technology (ICT): The use of technological tools, such as Zoom, Slack, and Google Sites, to facilitate cross-cultural collaboration and communication in virtual learning environments.

Virtual Exchange (VE): A pedagogically-structured online collaboration between learners from different cultural or geographical contexts aimed at enhancing intercultural competence and fostering global collaboration.

Compilation of References

Abasolo, A. E. (1991). Un análisis empírico de los determinantes de la especialización productiva y comercial de Euskadi. *Ekonomiaz: Revista vasca de economía*, (21), 210-226.

Abbasi, K. (2020). COVID-19: Politicization, "corruption," and suppression of science. *BMJ (Clinical Research Ed.)*, m4425. Advance online publication. DOI: 10.1136/bmj.m4425 PMID: 33187972

Abdulla, H. (February 14, 2024) Data points to 2023 as turning point in US apparel nearsourcing, *JustStyle News*. https://www.just-style.com/features/data-points-to-2023-as-turning-point-in-us-apparel-nearsourcing/

Abdullah, A. B. M., Murad, M. W., & Ahmed, E. (2022). Social protection transfers: Types, impacts, and experiences. In *Encyclopedia of the UN sustainable development goals* (pp. 1–11). DOI: 10.1007/978-3-319-71060-0_89-1

Abdullah, S. N. (2014). The causes of gender diversity in Malaysian large firms. *The Journal of Management and Governance*, 18(4), 1137–1159. DOI: 10.1007/s10997-013-9279-0

Abdullah, S. N., Ismail, K. N. I. K., & Nachum, L. (2016). Does having women on boards create value? The impact of societal perceptions and corporate governance in emerging markets: Women on Boards. *Strategic Management Journal*, 37(3), 466–476. DOI: 10.1002/smj.2352

Aboh, E., & deGraff, M. (2017). A null theory of creole formation based on universal grammar. In Roberts, I. (Ed.), *The Oxford handbook of universal grammar* (pp. 401–467)., DOI: 10.1093/oxfordhb/9780199573776.013.18

Adams, R. B., & Ferreira, D. (2009). Women in the boardroom and their impact on governance and performance. *Journal of Financial Economics*, 94(2), 291–309. DOI: 10.1016/j.jfineco.2008.10.007

Adbel-Kadel, M. (2020, April 14). Harnessing technology for global education. *Inside Higher Education*. Retrieved from https://www.insidehighered.com/views/2020/04/14/colleges -should-develop-more-virtual-exchange-programs-maintain-and-increase-global

Afonso, W. B. (2017). Citizens engaging government: Participatory budgeting in Greensboro, North Carolina. *Public Administration Quarterly*, 41(1), 7–42. DOI: 10.1177/073491491704100102

Agbude, E. (2023). Changes In Export Trade Relationship Between Vietnam and the US. Norwegian University of Life Sciences. School of Economics and Business (HH). Postboks 5003 No. 1432. Norway, pp. 1-55.

Aguilera, R. V., & Jackson, G. (2003). The cross-national diversity of corporate governance: Dimensions and determinants. *Academy of Management Review*, 28(3), 447–465. DOI: 10.2307/30040732

Alam, T., Aftab, M., Abbas, Z., Ugli, K. M. M., & Bokhari, S. A. A. (2023). Impact of E-Government initiatives to combat corruption mediating by behavioral intention: A Quantitative analysis from emerging economies. *Sustainability (Basel)*, 15(3), 2694. DOI: 10.3390/su15032694

Al-Asfour, F., & McGee, R. W. (2024). Tax evasion and tax compliance: What have we learned from the 100 most cited studies? In R. W. McGee & J. Shopovski (Eds.), *The ethics of tax evasion, Volume 2: New perspectives in theory and practice.* Springer (in press). Preprint available at *SSRN*: https://ssrn.com/abstract=4709193

Alesina, A., & Dollar, D. (2000). Who gives foreign aid to whom and why? *Journal of Economic Growth*, 5(1), 33–63. DOI: 10.1023/A:1009874203400

Alm, J. (2011). Measuring, explaining, and controlling tax evasion: Lessons from theory, experiments, and field studies. *International Tax and Public Finance*, 19(1), 54–77. DOI: 10.1007/s10797-011-9171-2

Anderson, J., & Rainie, L. (2018). *The future of well-being in a tech-saturated world.* Pew Research Center. https://assets.pewresearch.org/wp-content/uploads/sites/14/2018/04/14154552/PI_2018.04.17_Future-of-Well-Being_FINAL.pdf

Antigua Orden Dominicana. (n.d.). Home [Facebook page]. Antigua Orden Dominicana. Retrieved June 10, 2024 from https://www.facebook.com/Antiguaordendominicana1844

Argentiero, A., Casal, S., Mittone, L., & Morreale, A. (2021). Tax evasion and inequality: Some theoretical and empirical insights. *Economics of Governance*, 22(4), 309–320. DOI: 10.1007/s10101-021-00261-y

Ashby, A. (2016). From global to local: Reshoring for sustainability. *Operations Management Research : Advancing Practice Through Research*, 9(3-4), 75–88. DOI: 10.1007/s12063-016-0117-9

Asllani, A., & Schneider, F. (2024). A review of the driving forces of the informal economy and policy measures for mitigation: An analysis of six EU countries. *International Tax and Public Finance*. Advance online publication. DOI: 10.1007/s10797-024-09842-z

Associated Press. (2024, April 9). "Panama Papers" trial commences. *Wall Street Journal*, CCLXXXIII(83), A6.

Associated Press. (2024, May 21). ¿Que sigue en las restricciones migratorias a los Haitianos en República Dominicana? *Voz de America.*https://www.vozdeamerica.com/a/que-sigue-en-las-restricciones-migratorias-a-los-haitianos-en-republica-dominicana/7620661.html#comments

Atiles, J. (2024a). Anti-corruption markets: Law, public procurement, and the colonial regime of permission in Puerto Rico. *Journal of White Collar and Corporate Crime*, 5(2), 95–104. DOI: 10.1177/2631309X241234354

Atiles, J. (2024b). Crimes of the powerful in Latin America and the Caribbean: Toward a research agenda. *Sociology Compass*, 18(2), e13172. DOI: 10.1111/soc4.13172

Aydin-Cakir, A., & Ilter Akarcay, E. (2024, March 13). When do the governments attack the judiciary? The explanatory power of corruption. Available at *SSRN*: https://ssrn.com/abstract=4757545 DOI: 10.2139/ssrn.4757545

Badur, M. M., Yılmaz, E., & Sensoy, F. (2024). Do corruption and inequality shape sustainable development? Evidence from the post-Soviet countries. *International Journal of Social Economics*, 51(1), 115–132. DOI: 10.1108/IJSE-01-2023-0065

Bailey, D., & De Propris, L. (2014). Manufacturing reshoring and its limits: The UK automotive case. *Cambridge Journal of Regions, Economy and Society*, 7(3), 379–395. DOI: 10.1093/cjres/rsu019

Balaguer, J. (1970). *Centinela de la frontera.* (n.p.).

Balaguer, J. (1983). *La isla al revés: Haití y el destino dominicano*. Librería Dominicana.

Balassa, B. (1965). Trade Liberalization and "Revealed" Comparative Advantage. *Manchester School*, 33(2), 99–123. DOI: 10.1111/j.1467-9957.1965.tb00050.x

Barbieri, P., Ciabuschi, F., Fratocchi, L., & Vignoli, M. (2018). What do we know about manufacturing reshoring? *Journal of Global Operations and Strategic Sourcing*, 11(1), 79–122. DOI: 10.1108/JGOSS-02-2017-0004

Bardos, P. R. (Ed.). (Nov. 2017). *A Centennial History of the USITC*. United States International Trade Commission.

Bashir, A., Bashir, S., Rana, K., Lambert, P., & Vernallis, A. (2021). Post-COVID-19 adaptations; The shifts towards online learning, hybrid course delivery and the implications for biosciences courses in the higher education setting. *Frontiers in Education*, 6(711619), 711619. https://www.frontiersin.org/journals/education/articles/10.3389/feduc.2021.711619. DOI: 10.3389/feduc.2021.711619

Bath, D., Smith, C., Stein, S., & Swann, R. (2004). Beyond mapping and embedding graduate attributes: Bringing together quality assurance and action learning to create a validated and living curriculum. *Higher Education Research & Development*, 23(3), 313–328. DOI: 10.1080/0729436042000235427

Beelen, J., & Jones, E. (2015). Redefining internationalization at home. In Curaj, A., Matei, L., Pricopie, R., Salmi, J., & Scott, P. (Eds.), *The European Higher Education Area*. Springer., DOI: 10.1007/978-3-319-20877-0_5

Bem, S. L. (1981). Gender schema theory: A cognitive account of sex typing. *Psychological Review*, 88(4), 354–364. DOI: 10.1037/0033-295X.88.4.354

Benavides, M., & Gómez-Restrepo, C. (2005). Methods in qualitative research: Triangulation. *Revista Colombiana de Psiquiatría*, XXXIV(1), 118–124. https://www.redalyc.org/pdf/806/80628403009.pdf

Benson, D., & Gong, Y. (2022). Aiding and Abetting: Is donor Official Development Assistance competition greatest in sectors key to Chinese interest? *Williamsburg, VA: AidData at William & Mary., Working Pa*(121).

Benstead, A. V., Stevenson, M., & Hendry, L. C. (2017). Why and how do firms reshore? A contingency-based conceptual framework. *Operations Management Research : Advancing Practice Through Research*, 10(3-4), 85–103. DOI: 10.1007/s12063-017-0124-5

Benton, R. A. (2021). Women in the inner circle: Gender and director networks after the fracturing of the corporate elite. *Organization Science*, 32(6), 1492–1522. DOI: 10.1287/orsc.2021.1433

Berglez, P., & Gearing, A. (2018). The Panama and Paradise Papers. The rise of a global fourth estate. *International Journal of Communication*, 12, 4573–4592. https://ijoc.org/index.php/ijoc/article/view/9141/2501

Bertrand, M., & Schoar, A. (2006). The role of family in family firms. *The Journal of Economic Perspectives*, 20(2), 73–96. DOI: 10.1257/jep.20.2.73

Bhambri, S. (2015). Product Life Cycle. *International Journal of Business and Management*, II(1), 1–5.

Bhuiyan, S. (2023). The Pandora Papers opens up Pandora's Box: Integrity in crisis. *Public Integrity*, 25(2), 245–256. DOI: 10.1080/10999922.2022.2035945

Bobba, M., & Powell, A. (2006). Multilateral intermediation of foreign aid: what is the trade-off for donor countries? *Vol. Working Pa* (Issue 594). Inter-American Development Bank, Research Department, Washington, DC.

Boese, H. K. (2022). Nou bouke – we are tired: Human security as a tool for foreign aid in Haiti. [Bachelor's thesis, University of Arizona, Tucson, USA]. http://hdl.handle.net/10150/665729

Boffelli, A., Orzes, G., & Dotti, S. (2018). "How to reshore": Some evidence from the apparel industry. *IEEE Engineering Management Review*, 46(4), 122–127. DOI: 10.1109/EMR.2018.2886183

Borja Reyes, N. E. (2019). Las ventas desde una perspectiva del ciclo de vida del producto (Bachelor's thesis, Universidad Técnica de Ambato. Facultad de Ciencias Administrativas. Carrera Organización de Empresas).

Bossavie, L., & Kanninen, O. (2018). *What explains the gender gap reversal in education? Theory and evidence* (Policy Research Working Paper No. 8303). World Bank. https://openknowledge.worldbank.org/handle/10986/29213

Bourguignon, F., & Platteau, J.-P. (2015). The hard challenge of aid coordination. *World Development*, 69, 86–97. DOI: 10.1016/j.worlddev.2013.12.011

Brain, S., & Oyadeyi, O. (2024). Funding crime online: Cybercrime and its links to organised crime in the Caribbean. *The Commonwealth Cybercrime Journal, 1*(1), 84–110. https://thecommonwealth.org/publications/commonwealth-cybercrime-journal-volume-1/funding-crime-online-cybercrime-and-its-links-organised-crime-caribbean#:~:text=Organised%20crime

Brammer, S., Millington, A., & Pavelin, S. (2007). Gender and ethnic diversity among UK corporate boards. *Corporate Governance*, 15(2), 393–403. DOI: 10.1111/j.1467-8683.2007.00569.x

Bräutigam, D. (2011). Aid 'with Chinese characteristics': Chinese foreign aid and development finance meet the OECD-DAC aid regime. *Journal of International Development*, 23(5), 752–764. DOI: 10.1002/jid.1798

Bray, C., & Reed, S. (2018, January 3). Petrobras of Brazil to Pay $2.95 Billion Over Corruption Scandal. *New York Times.*https://www.nytimes.com/2018/01/03/business/dealbook/brazil-petrobras-corruption-scandal.html

Brown, M., Nic Giolla Mhichil, M., Beirne, E., & Mac Lochlainn, C. (2021). The global micro-credential landscape: Charting a new credential ecology for lifelong learning. *Journal of Learning for Development*, 8(2), 228–254. DOI: 10.56059/jl4d.v8i2.525

Buko, S., Knappitsch, E., Zinenko, A., & Covarrubias-Venegas, B. (2022). *The global case study challenge: A virtual exchange developing global work competencies*. Retrieved September 1, 2024 from https://www.academia.edu/105843026/The_Global_Case_Study_Challenge_A_Virtual_Exchange _Developing_Global_Work_Competencies

Burke, R. (1999). Women on Canadian corporate boards of directors: Getting the numbers right! *Corporate Governance*, 7(4), 374–378. DOI: 10.1111/1467-8683.00167

Bustamante, V. (2022). De Vuelta a casa: La política de Reshoring del Gobierno de Estados Unidos. Universidad Pontificia de Madrid, Facultad de Ciencias Económicas y Empresariales. Junio 2022, pp. 1-57.

Cachanosky, N., & Padilla, A. (2020). A panel data analysis of Latin American populism. *Constitutional Political Economy*, 31(3), 329–343. DOI: 10.1007/s10602-020-09302-w

Calder, B. (1984). *The impact of intervention.* University of Texas Press.

Caligiuri, P., De Cieri, H., Minbaeva, D., Verbeke, A., & Zimmermann, A. (2022). International HRM insights for navigating the COVID-19 pandemic: Implications for future research and practice. In Mithani, M. A., Narula, R., Surdu, I., & Verbeke, A. (Eds.), *Crises and disruptions in International Business. JIBS special collections*. Palgrave Macmillan., DOI: 10.1007/978-3-030-80383-4_17

Campbell, J. L. (2007). Why would corporations behave in socially responsible ways? An institutional theory of corporate social responsibility. *Academy of Management Review*, 32(3), 946–967. DOI: 10.5465/amr.2007.25275684

Campos-Herrera, G., & de Reguero, S. U. (2019). Populism in Latin America: Past, present, and future [Review of The Resurgence of Populism in Latin America; Political Communication and Leadership: Mimetisation, Hugo Chávez and the Construction of Power and Identity; From Fascism to Populism in History; Revolutionizing Repertoires: The Rise of Populist Mobilization in Peru, by R. R. Barr, E. Block, F. Finchelstein, & R. S. Jansen]. *Latin American Politics and Society*, 61(1), 148–159. https://www.jstor.org/stable/26779154. DOI: 10.1017/lap.2018.63

Campos, N., Engel, E., Fischer, R. D., & Galetovic, A. (2021). The ways of corruption in infrastructure: Lessons from the Odebrecht case. *The Journal of Economic Perspectives*, 35(2), 171–190. https://pubs.aeaweb.org/doi/pdfplus/10.1257/jep.35.2.171. DOI: 10.1257/jep.35.2.171

Canals, J. (1994). *La internacionalización de la empresa*. McGraw-Hill.

Cano, J., & Ricardo, C. (2014). *Survey for the analysis of intercultural competence* [Internal document]. Universidad del Norte.

Cao, C., & Meng, Q. (2020). Effects of online and direct contact on Chinese international students' social capital in intercultural networks: Testing moderation of direct contact and mediation of global competence. *Higher Education*, 80(4), 625–643. DOI: 10.1007/s10734-020-00501-w

Cao, H., & Folan, P. (2011). *Product Life Cycle: the evolution of a paradigm and literature review from 1950-2009*. Department of Industrial Engineering, Tsinghua University.

Carlos Herrera, L., Montenegro, M., & Torres–Lista, V. (2020). *The'two Chinas' and Panama: an historical review of Panamanian relations with the People's Republic of China and Taiwan, 1903–2017*.

Carrasco, A., Francoeur, C., Labelle, R., Laffarga, J., & Ruiz-Barbadillo, E. (2015). Appointing women to boards: Is there a cultural bias? *Journal of Business Ethics*, 129(2), 429–444. DOI: 10.1007/s10551-014-2166-z

Carrillo Mendoza, G. (Ed.). (2015). *El currículo por competencias en la educación superior: Ponencias y debate* [Competence curriculum in higher education: Presentations and debate]. I Encuentro Internacional Universitario, Lima, Peru. https://cdn02.pucp.education/academico/2015/09/01094909/curriculo_competencias.pdf

Carrón, H. (2013). Borrando la huella africana: La sentencia 168-13 del Tribunal Constitucional Dominicano y la identidad nacional. *Afro-Hispanic Review, 32*(2), 27-40. https://www.jstor.org/stable/24585141

Carter, D. A., Simkins, B. J., & Simpson, W. G. (2003). Corporate governance, board diversity, and firm value. *Financial Review*, 38(1), 33–53. DOI: 10.1111/1540-6288.00034

Casas-Zamora, K., & Carter, M. (2017). *Beyond the scandals: The changing context of corruption in Latin America*. The Dialogue. https://www.thedialogue.org/analysis/beyond-the-scandals-the-changing-context-of-corruption-in-latin-america/

Casey, M. (2023) Black activists take on Dominican government and society in quest for justice and recognition. *Cronkite Borderlands Project*. https://cronkitenews.azpbs.org/2023/09/15/black-activists-dominican-government-justice-and-recognition/

Castro-Gonzáles, S., Espina, M., & Tinoco-Egas, R. (2017). Strategies and competitiveness for emerging countries: A comparative study among three South-American countries. *International Journal of Emerging Markets.*, 12(1), 125–139. DOI: 10.1108/IJoEM-12-2014-0222

Central Romana. (n.d.). *History*. Retrieved June 5, 2024 from https://centralromana.com.do/memorias/?lang=en

Cerf, M. E. (2023). The social-education-economy-health nexus, development and sustainability: Perspectives from low- and middle-income and African countries. *Discover Sustainability*, 4(1), 37. Advance online publication. DOI: 10.1007/s43621-023-00153-7

Chandy, L. (2011). It's complicated: The challenge of implementing the Paris Declaration on aid effectiveness. *Global Economy and Development at Brookings Blog, 22*.

Chebli, M., & Saidi, K. (2024). Economic growth in middle-income countries: The role of political stability and foreign direct investment. *Journal of Quantitative Economics*, 22(3), 641–665. DOI: 10.1007/s40953-024-00394-x

Chen, G., Crossland, C., & Huang, S. (2016). Female board representation and corporate acquisition intensity. *Strategic Management Journal*, 37(2), 303–313. DOI: 10.1002/smj.2323

Childers, T. B. (2023). The role of anti-Haitian racism in Dominican mass deportation policy. *Georgetown Journal of International Affairs*, 24(1), 107–113. DOI: 10.1353/gia.2023.a897708

Chi-Loi, C. (2017). Dinámica de las relaciones comerciales Vietnam-Estados Unidos desde una perspectiva comparada revelada. *Revista de Estudios Estrategicos.*, 4, 59–79.

Chizema, A., Kamuriwo, D. S., & Shinozawa, Y. (2015). Women on corporate boards around the world: Triggers and barriers. *The Leadership Quarterly*, 26(6), 1051–1065. DOI: 10.1016/j.leaqua.2015.07.005

Choudhary, N. A., Ramkumar, M., Schoenherr, T., Rana, N. P., & Dwivedi, Y. K. (2023). Does reshoring affect the resilience and sustainability of supply chain networks? The cases of Apple and Jaguar Land Rover. *British Journal of Management*, 34(3), 1138–1156. DOI: 10.1111/1467-8551.12614

Ciccariello-Maher, G. (2020). Populism, universalism, and democracy in Latin America. In L. K. Jenco, M. Idris, & M. C. Thomas (Eds.), *The Oxford handbook of comparative political theory* (online edn). Oxford Academic. DOI: 10.1093/oxfordhb/9780190253752.013.16

Cirera, X., & Lakshman, R. W. D. (2017). The impact of export processing zones on employment, wages and labour conditions in developing countries: Systematic review. *Journal of Development Effectiveness*, 9(3), 344–360. DOI: 10.1080/19439342.2017.1309448 PMID: 30363912

Civicus.org. (2020, August 13). *Dominican Republic: We are part of a global anti-racist movement*. Retrieved June 6, 2024, from https://www.civicus.org/index.php/media-resources/news/interviews/4562-dominican-republic-we-are-part-of-a-global-anti-racist-movement

Clist, P. (2011). 25 years of aid allocation practice: Whither selectivity? *World Development*, 39(10), 1724–1734. DOI: 10.1016/j.worlddev.2011.04.031

Commander, N. E., Schloer, W. F., & Cushing, S. T. (2022). Virtual exchange: A promising high-impact practice for developing intercultural effectiveness across disciplines. *Journal of Virtual Exchange*, 5, 1–19. DOI: 10.21827/jve.5.37329

Contractor, F. J., Kumar, V., Kundu, S. K., & Pedersen, T. (Eds.). (2011). *Global Outsourcing and Offshoring: An Integrated Approach to Theory and Corporate Strategy*. Cambridge University Press.

Córdoba Ramírez, T. M. (2005). *The significance of Costa Rica in Taiwan's diplomacy and the competition from Beijing*.

Coriat, A. (2017, August 7). Panama expects juicy investments from China. *El Siglo*, 1–1.

Corrales, J., & Penfold, M. (2015). *Dragon in the Tropics: Hugo Chávez and the Political Economy of Revolution in Venezuela*. Brookings Institution Press.

Corrales, K. A., Lombana-Coy, J., & Rey-Paba, L. (2021). Fostering global competence in international business students on a Latin American campus. *Journal of Teaching in International Business*, 32(1), 81–101. DOI: 10.1080/08975930.2021.1906381

Correa, M. A. (2021). México y el regionalismo norteamericano. Del tlcan alt-mec. En Molano, G y Briceño, J. (Ed.) *El regionalismo en América Latina después de la Post-Hegemonía. Centro de Investigaciones sobre América Latina y el Caribe.* Universidad Autónoma de México. (pp. 15-30). México.

Council on Foreign Relations. (2022, September 7). Mexico's Long War: Drugs, crime, and the cartels: Violence continues to rage more than a decade after the Mexican government launched a war against drug cartels. https://www.cfr.org/backgrounder/mexicos-long-war-drugs-crime-and-cartels

Cumming, D., Leung, T. Y., & Rui, O. (2015). Gender diversity and securities fraud. *Academy of Management Journal*, 58(5), 1571–1593. DOI: 10.5465/amj.2013.0750

Custer, S., Dreher, A., Elston, T. B., Fuchs, A., Ghose, S., Lin, J., Malik, A., Parks, B. C., Russell, B., & Solomon, K. (2023). *Tracking Chinese development finance: An application of AidData's TUFF 3.0 methodology*. AidData.

da Costa Silva, P. H., Coimbra, L. W. P., & Monteiro, V. S. (2023). FIFA World Cup and corruption: an analysis by the Synthetic Control Method applied to the host countries from 2006 to 2014. *Espacio abierto: cuaderno venezolano de sociología, 32*(3), 51–75. Available at Dialnet-FIFAWorldCupAndCorruptionAnAnalysisBy-TheSyntheticC-9076835.pdf

Da Ros, L., & Gehrke, M. (2024). Convicting politicians for corruption: The politics of criminal accountability. *Government and Opposition*, 59(3), 951–975. Advance online publication. DOI: 10.1017/gov.2023.48

de Abreu, M. C. S., Soares, R. A., Daniel-Vasconcelos, V., & Crisóstomo, V. L. (2023). Does board diversity encourage an environmental policy focused on resource use, emission reduction and innovation? The case of companies in Latin America. *Corporate Social Responsibility and Environmental Management*, 30(3), 1161–1176. DOI: 10.1002/csr.2411

De Andrade, E. M., Rodrigues, L. L., & Cosenza, J. P. (2020). Corporate behavior: An exploratory study of the Brazilian tax management from a corporate social responsibility perspective. *Sustainability (Basel)*, 12(11), 4404. DOI: 10.3390/su12114404

De Backer, K., Menon, C., Desnoyers-James, I., & Moussiegt, L. (2016). Reshoring: Myth or reality? https://www.jstor.org/stable/155557

De La Torre, C. (2014). Populism in Latin American politics. In *Research in political sociology* (pp. 79–100). DOI: 10.1108/S0895-993520140000022003

De la Torre, C. (2017). Populism in Latin America. In C. Rovira Kaltwasser, P. A. Taggart, P. O. Esponda, & M. M. T. (Eds.), *The Oxford handbook of populism* (pp. 115-139). Oxford University Press. DOI: 10.1093/oxfordhb/9780198803560.013.8

De La Torre, C. (2023). Messianic and autocratic populism's waves in the recent history of the Americas: Continuities, twists, and rupture. In A. Akande (Ed.), *U.S. democracy in danger*. Springer Studies on Populism, Identity Politics and Social Justice. Springer, Cham. DOI: 10.1007/978-3-031-36099-2_16

De La Torre, C. (2018). Populism revived: Donald Trump and the Latin American leftist populists. *The Americas*, 75(4), 733–753. DOI: 10.1017/tam.2018.39

Deardorff, D. K. (2011). Assessing intercultural competence. *New Directions for Institutional Research*, 2011(149), 65–79. DOI: 10.1002/ir.381

Deardorff, D. K. (Ed.). (2009). *The SAGE handbook of intercultural competence*. SAGE. DOI: 10.4135/9781071872987

Deephouse, D. L., Newburry, W., & Soleimani, A. (2016). The effects of institutional development and national culture on cross-national differences in corporate reputation. *Journal of World Business*, 51(3), 463–473. DOI: 10.1016/j.jwb.2015.12.005

Del Monte, F. M. (1885). *Las vírgenes de Galindo.* https://curiosity.lib.harvard.edu/latin-american-pamphlet-digital-collection/catalog/43-990061373890203941

Deloitte. (2024). *Women in the boardroom: a global perspective*. Deloitte Global Boardroom Program, Eight Edition.

Demirkan, H., & Spohrer, J. (2015). T-Shaped innovators: Identifying the right talent to support service innovation. *Research Technology Management*, 58(5), 12–15. DOI: 10.5437/08956308X5805007

DeRose, L. F., Huarcaya, G., & Salazar-Arango, Á. (2018). Father absence and the reverse gender gap in Latin America. *Journal of Family Issues*, 39(13), 3508–3534. DOI: 10.1177/0192513X18783802

Desender, K. A., Castro, C. E., & Escamilla de León, S. A. (2011). Earnings management and cultural values: Earnings management and cultural values. *American Journal of Economics and Sociology*, 70(3), 639–670. DOI: 10.1111/j.1536-7150.2011.00786.x

Desender, K. A., LópezPuertas-Lamy, M., Pattitoni, P., & Petracci, B. (2020). Corporate social responsibility and cost of financing—The importance of the international corporate governance system. *Corporate Governance*, 28(3), 207–234. DOI: 10.1111/corg.12312

Desender, K., & Epure, M. (2021). The pressure behind corporate social performance: Ownership and institutional configurations. *Global Strategy Journal*, 11(2), 210–244. DOI: 10.1002/gsj.1390

Deutscher, E., & Fyson, S. (2008). Improving the effectiveness of aid. *Finance & Development*, 45(003).

Díaz Villavicencio, C. (Ed.). (2016). Las competencias genéricas en la educación superior: Ponencias y conversatorio [Generic competences in higher education: Presentations and panels. II Encuentro Internacional Universitario, Lima, Peru. https://cdn02.pucp.education/academico/2016/06/24194836/II_EncuentroInt _competencias_generi cas_en_edusup.pdf

Dikler, J. (2021). Reshoring: An overview, recent trends, and predictions for the future. *KIEP Research Paper, World Economy Brief*, 21-35.

Dominican Republic. (1989). In P. W. Goetz (ed.). *The New Encyclopaedia Britannica* (29, pp. 753-758). Chicago. @el_meneoTV (2024, February 21). *Dijeron la orden! Los Haitianos tienen 7 dias para abandonar todos La República Dominicana* [Video]. YouTube. Retrieved June 5, 2024, from https://www.youtube.com/watch ?v=q84GXB7xBws&t=219s

Dreher, A., & Fuchs, A. (2015). Rogue aid? An empirical analysis of China's aid allocation. *The Canadian Journal of Economics. Revue Canadienne d'Economique*, 48(3), 988–1023. DOI: 10.1111/caje.12166

Duncan, C. M., & Ulrich-Schad, J. D. (2021). Marginalization of rural communities in the U.S. *Investing in rural prosperity*. Federal Reserve Bank of St. Louis. https://www.ipp.gov/-/media/project/frbstl/stlouisfed/files/pdfs/community-development/investing-rural/chapters/chapter03.pdf

Duncan, D., & Peter, K. S. (2016). Unequal inequalities: Do progressive taxes reduce income inequality? *International Tax and Public Finance*, 23(4), 762–783. DOI: 10.1007/s10797-016-9412-5

Dunkerley, J. (2013). The Bolivian revolution at 60: Politics and historiography. *Journal of Latin American Studies*, 45(2), 325–350. DOI: 10.1017/S0022216X13000382

Dunning, J. H. (1988). The Eclectic Paradigm of International Production: A Restatement and Some Possible Extensions. *Journal of International Business Studies*, 19(Spring), 1–31. DOI: 10.1057/palgrave.jibs.8490372

Dunning, J. H. (1995). Reappraising the Eclectic Paradigm in an Age of Alliance Capitalism. *Journal of International Business Studies*, 26(3), 461–491. DOI: 10.1057/palgrave.jibs.8490183

Eagly, A. H., & Carli, L. L. (2007). *Through the labyrinth: The truth about how women become leaders*. Harvard Business School Press.

Earthrights. (n.d.). Doe v. Chiquita Brands International: Banana Giant Chiquita Paid Terrorist Group for Security. https://earthrights.org/case/doe-v-chiquita-brands-international/

Egger, P., & Winner, H. (2006). How corruption influences foreign direct investment: A panel data study. *Economic Development and Cultural Change*, 54(2), 459–486. DOI: 10.1086/497010

El-Hage, J. (2019, November 4). Shaking the Latin American equilibrium: The Petrobras & Odebrecht corruption scandals. *Fordham Journal of Corporate & Financial Law* [Blog]. https://news.law.fordham.edu/jcfl/2019/11/04/shaking-the-latin-american-equilibrium-the-petrobras-odebrecht-corruption-scandals/

Elliott, S., & Reid, M. (2019). Low-income Black mothers parenting adolescents in the mass incarceration era: The long reach of criminalization. *American Sociological Review*, 84(2), 197–219. DOI: 10.1177/0003122419833386

Ellis, R. E. (2014). Costa Rica at a Crossroads in Courtship with Beijing. *China Brief*, 14, 10–13.

El-Sahli, Z., & Gullstrand, J. (2023). Why reshore? Evidence from Swedish firms. *Economics Letters*, 227, 111116. DOI: 10.1016/j.econlet.2023.111116

Erkens, M., Bodemer, D., & Hoppe, H. U. (2016). Improving collaborative learning in the classroom: Text mining based grouping and representing. *International Journal of Computer-Supported Collaborative Learning*, 11(4), 387–415. DOI: 10.1007/s11412-016-9243-5

Estrella, A. (2024). Dominican Republic's neofascist paramilitaries double down on right-wing repression: New expressions of ultranationalist violence censoring Black women and migrants harken back to the Trujillo dictatorship. Anyone deemed a threat to Dominican values is a potential target. *NACLA Report on the Americas*, 56(1), 42–49. https://www.tandfonline.com/doi/full/10.1080/10714839.2024.2323399?casa_token=S1wJuIhdWEAAAAA:xlu5XU0aMmQf1P_Y59GOadrBVCBEpDIcrDsvzcCp8MAc6q90lIi3OjGkXqWkuEX5YbWYfzBbZ9qOSg. DOI: 10.1080/10714839.2024.2323399

Fainshmidt, S., Judge, W. Q., Aguilera, R. V., & Smith, A. (2018). Varieties of institutional systems: A contextual taxonomy of understudied countries. *Journal of World Business*, 53(3), 307–322. DOI: 10.1016/j.jwb.2016.05.003

Fang, Y. X., Gill, S. S., Kunasekaran, P., Rosnon, M. R., Talib, A. T., & Aziz, A. A. (2022). Digital divide: An inquiry on the native communities of Sabah. *Societies (Basel, Switzerland)*, 12(6), 148. DOI: 10.3390/soc12060148

Farag, H., & Mallin, C. (2016). The impact of the dual board structure and board diversity: Evidence from Chinese initial public offerings (IPOs). *Journal of Business Ethics*, 139(2), 333–349. DOI: 10.1007/s10551-015-2649-6

Farrar, J., Massey, D. W., Osecki, E., & Thorne, L. (2018). Tax fairness: Conceptual foundations and empirical measurement. *Journal of Business Ethics*, 162(3), 487–503. DOI: 10.1007/s10551-018-4001-4

Faust, J., Grävingholt, J., & Ziaja, S. (2015). Foreign aid and the fragile consensus on state fragility. *Journal of International Relations and Development*, 18(4), 407–427. DOI: 10.1057/jird.2013.23

Feigenblatt, O. F. von. (2021). A case study on diplomatic competition between the People's Republic of China and the Republic of China (Taiwan): The experience of the Republic of Costa Rica from 1995 to 2010. *Dilemas Contemporáneos: Educación, Política y Valores, 9*(SPE1).

Feitlowitz, M. (2019). *A lexicon of terror: Argentina and the legacies of torture*. Oxford University Press., https://global.oup.com/academic/product/a-lexicon-of-terror-9780199744695?cc=us&lang=

Fernando, G. A., & Antoine, M. (2022). The network structure of global tax evasion evidence from the Panama Papers. *Journal of Economic Behavior & Organization*, 197, 660–684. DOI: 10.1016/j.jebo.2022.03.024

Ferreira, M., Pinto, C., Serra, F., & Santos, J. (2013). A Bibliometric Study of John Dunning's Contribution to International Business Research. *Revista Brasileira de Gestão de Negócios*, 15(46), 56–75. DOI: 10.7819/rbgn.v15i46.1163

Fiber2Fashion. (May 17, 2024) UFLPA's impact on US textile imports: A shift in global trade dynamics. https://www.fibre2fashion.com/news/printstory.aspx?news_Id=295371

Filiau, A. (2023). *Hope for the future: Key informants' perspectives on HIV prevention in Dominican Republic batey communities* [Doctoral dissertation, UMass Chan Medical School]. https://repository.escholarship.umassmed.edu/handle/20.500.14038/52149

Financier Worldwide Magazine. (2022, February). *Q&A: Tackling financial crime in Latin America*. https://www.financierworldwide.com/qa-tackling-financial-crime-in-latin-america

Finley-Brook, M. (2018). CAFTA-DR: diverging trajectories and uneven development. In Handbook of International Trade Agreements (pp. 166-180). Routledge.

Florido, A., Janse, A. M., & Rampton, R. (2022, May 12). In Puerto Rico, the arrests of elected officials worsen trust in government. https://www.npr.org/2022/05/12/1098585366/in-puerto-rico-the-arrests-of-elected-officials-worsen-trust-in-government

Foerstl, K., Kirchoff, J. F., & Bals, L. (2016). Reshoring and insourcing: Drivers and future research directions. *International Journal of Physical Distribution & Logistics Management*, 46(5), 492–515. DOI: 10.1108/IJPDLM-02-2015-0045

Fonseca, P., Julian, K., Hulme, W., Martins, M. D. L., & Brautlacht, R. (2021). The multi-disciplinary approach to an interdisciplinary virtual exchange. In M. Satar (Ed.), *Virtual exchange: Towards digital equity in internationalisation* (pp. 41-49). Research-publishing.net. DOI: 10.14705/rpnet.2021.53.1288

Forsythe, M. (2017, November 5). Paradise Papers shine light on where the elite keep their money. *The New York Times*. https://www.nytimes.com/2017/11/05/world/paradise-papers.html

Fratocchi, L., Ancarani, A., Barbieri, P., Di Mauro, C., Nassimbeni, G., Sartor, M., Vignoli, M., & Zanoni, A. (2016). Motivations of manufacturing reshoring: An interpretative framework. *International Journal of Physical Distribution & Logistics Management*, 46(2), 98–127. DOI: 10.1108/IJPDLM-06-2014-0131

Freeman, C. P. (2019). Constructive Engagement? The US and the AIIB. *Global Policy*, 10(4), 667–676. DOI: 10.1111/1758-5899.12764

Fuchs, A., Nunnenkamp, P., & Öhler, H. (2015). Why donors of foreign aid do not coordinate: The role of competition for export markets and political support. *World Economy*, 38(2), 255–285. DOI: 10.1111/twec.12213

Ganayem, A., Hoter, E., & Shonfeld, M. (2020). Lessons learned from 15 years of multicultural online collaborative learning in Israel. In Hunter, W. J., & Austin, R. S. P. (Eds.), *Blended and online learning for global citizenship: New technologies and opportunities for intercultural education* (pp. 32–50). Routledge. DOI: 10.4324/9780367821661-3

García, F., Smith, S., Burger, A., & Helms, M. (2023). Increasing global mindset through collaborative online international learning (COIL): Internationalizing the undergraduate international business class. *Journal of International Education in Business*, 16(2), 184–203. DOI: 10.1108/JIEB-08-2022-0054

García-Peña, L. G. (2016). *The borders of dominicanidad: Race, nation, and archives of contradiction*. Duke University Press.

Garside, J. (2016, September 21). Bahamas files leaks expose politicians' offshore links. *The Guardian*.https://www.theguardian.com/business/2016/sep/21/leaked-bahamas-files-expose-politicians-offshore-links

Gazzola, M., Wickström, B. A., & Templin, T. (2019). Language skills, the labour market, and socioeconomic integration. *Empirica*, 46(4), 617–623. DOI: 10.1007/s10663-019-09463-4

Gereffi, G., Lim, H.-C., & Lee, J. (2021). Trade policies, firm strategies, and adaptive reconfigurations of global value chains. *Journal of International Business Policy*, 4(4), 506–522. DOI: 10.1057/s42214-021-00102-z

Gomez, D., Aparicio, S., & Urbano, D. (2023). Entrepreneurial activity and economic growth: A literature review. In *Springer eBooks* (pp. 13–39). DOI: 10.1007/978-3-031-34386-5_2

Gossel, S. (2024). FDI and inequality in Sub-Saharan Africa: Does democracy matter? *International Journal of Emerging Markets*, 19(1), 33–55. DOI: 10.1108/IJOEM-03-2021-0321

Grenoble, L. (2021). Language shift. In Aronoff, M. (Ed.), *Oxford Encyclopedia of Linguistics*., DOI: 10.1093/acrefore/9780199384655.013.347

Grigera, J. (2017). Populism in Latin America: Old and new populisms in Argentina and Brazil. *International Political Science Review / Revue Internationale de Science Politique, 38*(4), 441–455. https://www.jstor.org/stable/26940303

Grosvold, J., & Brammer, S. (2011). National institutional systems as antecedents of female board representation: An empirical study. *Corporate Governance*, 19(2), 116–135. DOI: 10.1111/j.1467-8683.2010.00830.x

Grosvold, J., Rayton, B., & Brammer, S. (2016). Women on corporate boards: A comparative institutional analysis. *Business & Society*, 55(8), 1157–1196. DOI: 10.1177/0007650315613980

Guerra-Sánchez, A. J. I. (2016). El crimen de las vírgenes de Galindo. *Historia dominicana en graficas*. Retrieved June 6, 2024, from https://historiadominicanaengraficas.blogspot.com/2016/06/el-crimen-de-las-virgenes-de-galindo.html?view=flipcard

Guilamo, D. (2018). Dominican attitudes toward Haitian immigrants following the 2010 earthquake and before the 2013 sentencing. *The Journal of Pan African Studies*, 12(4), 488–509. https://www.jpanafrican.org/docs/vol12no4/12.4-14-Guilamo.pdf

Guild, J. (2023, June 27). Is Indonesia's New High-Speed Rail Line Worth It? *The Diplomat*, 1–1. https://thediplomat.com/2023/06/is-indonesias-new-high-speed-rail-line-worth-it/

Guiso, L., Sapienza, P., & Zingales, L. (2006). Does culture affect economic outcomes? Social Science Research Network. CEPR Discussion Paper No. 5505.

Guldiken, O., Mallon, M. R., Fainshmidt, S., Judge, W. Q., & Clark, C. E. (2019). Beyond tokenism: How strategic leaders influence more meaningful gender diversity on boards of directors. *Strategic Management Journal*, 40(12), 2024–2046. DOI: 10.1002/smj.3049

Gutierrez, B. N., & Peoples, C. D. (2024). The Foreign Corrupt Practices Act (FCPA) as a symbolic policy in the broader "Anti-Corruption Movement": A case study of Latin American prosecutions. *Journal of White Collar and Corporate Crime*, 5(2), 85–94. DOI: 10.1177/2631309X241234358

Habbal, F., Kolmos, A., Hadgraft, R. G., Holgaard, J. E., & Reda, K. (2024). *Reshaping engineering education*. Springer., DOI: 10.1007/978-981-99-5873-3

Hafiyer Al Halim, T. H. A. (2021). Two-Level Games Theory in Panama–Taiwan Diplomatic Relations. *Asia-Pacific Research in Social Sciences and Humanities Universitas Indonesia Conference (APRISH 2019)*, 147–153.

Haitian unification period (1822-1844): Towards a Dominican perspective. *Cleveland State Law Review, 52*(1), 63-78. https://engagedscholarship.csuohio.edu/clevstlrev/vol52/iss1/5/

Henochsberg, S. (2016). Public debt and slavery: The case of Haiti (1760-1915). [Master's thesis, Paris School of economics.] http://piketty.pse.ens.fr/files/Henochsberg2016.pdf

Hernández-Sampieri, R., Fernández, C., & Baptista, P. (2014). *Research methodology* (6th ed.). McGraw Hill.

Highway Motion. (2024, April 6). *Avenida Independencia* [Video]. YouTube. Accessed June 6, 2024 at https://www.youtube.com/watch?v=nylP7oGktlQ&t=587s

Hillman, A. J., Shropshire, C., & Cannella, A. A.Jr. (2007). Organizational predictors of women on corporate boards. *Academy of Management Journal*, 50(4), 941–952. DOI: 10.5465/amj.2007.26279222

Hoang, K. K. (2022). *Spiderweb capitalism: How global elites exploit frontier markets*. Princeton University Press.

Hofstede, G. (1980). *Culture's consequences: international differences in work related values*. Sage.

Hofstede, G. (2001). *Culture's Consequences: Comparing Values, Behaviors, Institutions, and Organizations Across Nations* (2nd ed.). Sage.

Horodnic, I. A. (2018). Tax morale and institutional theory: A systematic review. *The International Journal of Sociology and Social Policy*, 38(9/10), 868–886. DOI: 10.1108/IJSSP-03-2018-0039

Human Rights Watch. (2020). *Venezuela: Government use of digital surveillance to target critics*. Human Rights Watch. https://www.hrw.org/world-report/2020/country-chapters/venezuela

Humphrey, C., & Michaelowa, K. (2019a). China in Africa: Competition for traditional development finance institutions? *World Development*, 120, 15–28. DOI: 10.1016/j.worlddev.2019.03.014

Husband, L. (13 March, 2024) Honduras biggest winner of US apparel nearshoring drive in January 2024. *Investment Monitor*.

Husted, B. W., & de Sousa-Filho, J. M. (2019). Board structure and environmental, social, and governance disclosure in Latin America. *Journal of Business Research*, 102, 220–227. DOI: 10.1016/j.jbusres.2018.01.017

Isachenko, N. (2018). The role of information and informational and communication technologies in modern society. *Utopía y Praxis Latinoamericana*, 23(82), 361–367. DOI: 10.5281/zenodo.1512122

Jansen, S. (2013). Language maintenance and language loss in marginalized communities: The case of the bateyes in the Dominican Republic. *International Journal of the Sociology of Language*, 2013(221), 77–100. https://www.degruyter.com/document/doi/10.1515/ijsl-2013-0024/html. DOI: 10.1515/ijsl-2013-0024

Jaskolka-Brown, A. (2022). Haitians In the Dominican Republic: Marginalization and its relationship with public health. *The Macksey Journal, 3*(1).

Jha, S., & Awaate, S. (2024). Offshore FDI, tax havens, and productivity: A network analysis. *Global Strategy Journal*, 14(2), 350–382. DOI: 10.1002/gsj.1466

Johnson, D. W., Johnson, R. T., & Smith, K. A. (2014). Co-operative learning: Improving university instruction by basing practice on validated theory. *Journal on Excellence in College Teaching*, 25(3&4), 85–118. https://celt.miamioh.edu/ojs/index.php/JECT/issue/view/64

Joo, S. J., Chik, A., & Djonov, E. (2024). From my parents' language to my language: Understanding language ideologies of young Australian Korean heritage language learners at the primary and secondary school level. *Journal of Multilingual and Multicultural Development*, 45(2), 147–160. DOI: 10.1080/01434632.2020.1871359

Kang, H., Cheng, M., & Gray, S. J. (2007). Corporate governance and board composition: Diversity and independence of Australian boards. *Corporate Governance*, 15(2), 194–207. DOI: 10.1111/j.1467-8683.2007.00554.x

Kang, J. H., Kim, S. Y., Jang, S., & Koh, A.-R. (2018). Can college students' global competence be enhanced in the classroom? The impact of cross- and inter-cultural online projects. *Innovations in Education and Teaching International*, 55(6), 683–693. DOI: 10.1080/14703297.2017.1294987

Karakas, A. (2023). Breaking down barriers with artificial intelligence (ai): Cross-cultural communication in foreign language education. In Kartal, G. (Ed.), *Transforming the Language Teaching Experience in the Age of AI* (pp. 215–233). IGI Global., DOI: 10.4018/978-1-6684-9893-4.ch012

Kassa, E. T. (2021). Factors influencing taxpayers' involvement in tax evasion: Evidence from Woldia City administration micro, small, and large enterprise taxpayers. *Journal of Innovation and Entrepreneurship*, 10(1), 8. Advance online publication. DOI: 10.1186/s13731-020-00142-4 PMID: 34745824

Kayyali, Y., Mair, S. & Seifert, R. (2023). A machine learning-based framework for forecasting sales of new products with short life cycles using deep neural networks. *International Journal of Forecasting*. Vol. 39, issue 2023, pp. 1874–1894

Keefer, P., & Roseth, B. (2024). Transparency and grand corruption: Lessons from the Colombia school meals program. *Journal of Comparative Economics*, 52(2), 445–462. DOI: 10.1016/j.jce.2024.02.003

Kejriwal, M., & Dang, A. (2020). Structural studies of the global networks exposed in the Panama papers. *Applied Network Science*, 5(1), 63. Advance online publication. DOI: 10.1007/s41109-020-00313-y

Kendall, N., & Thangaraj, M. (2013). Ethnography. In *Reviewing qualitative research in the social sciences* (pp. 82–107). Routledge.

Khalid, A. M. (2024). Does corruption hinder foreign direct investment and growth in Asia and beyond? The grabbing versus the helping hand revisited. In Teramura, N., Nottage, L., & Jetin, B. (Eds.), *Corruption and illegality in Asian investment arbitration* (pp. 39–67). DOI: 10.1007/978-981-99-9303-1_2

Kilama, E. G. (2016). Evidences on donors competition in Africa: Traditional donors versus China. *Journal of International Development*, 28(4), 528–551. DOI: 10.1002/jid.3198

Kinkel, S. (2012). Trends in production relocation and backshoring activities: Changing patterns in the course of the global economic crisis. *International Journal of Operations & Production Management*, 32(6), 696–720. DOI: 10.1108/01443571211230934

Knack, S., Rogers, H. F., & Eubank, N. (2010). *Aid quality and donor rankings*. The World Bank. DOI: 10.1596/1813-9450-5290

Knippen, J. M., Shen, W., & Zhu, Q. (2019). Limited progress? The effect of external pressure for board gender diversity on the increase of female directors. *Strategic Management Journal*, 40(7), 1123–1150. DOI: 10.1002/smj.3014

Koenigstorfer, J. (2024). Corruption in connection to major sport events. In Solberg, H. A., Storm, R. K., & Swart, K. (Eds.), *Research handbook on major sporting events* (pp. 591–606). Edward Elgar Publishing. DOI: 10.4337/9781800885653.00057

Kohli Bagwe, T., & Haskollar, E. (2020). Variables impacting intercultural competence: A systematic literature review. *Journal of Intercultural Communication Research*, 49(4), 346–371. DOI: 10.1080/17475759.2020.1771751

Kong, D., Zhang, Y., & Qin, N. (2023). Anti-corruption campaign and corporate tax evasion: Evidence from China. *International Tax and Public Finance*. Advance online publication. DOI: 10.1007/s10797-023-09777-x

Konrad, A. M., Kramer, V., & Erkut, S. (2008). Critical mass: The impact of three or more women on corporate boards. *Organizational Dynamics*, 37(2), 145–164. DOI: 10.1016/j.orgdyn.2008.02.005

Kragelund, P. (2011). Back to BASICs? The rejuvenation of non-traditional donors' development cooperation with Africa. *Development and Change*, 42(2), 585–607. DOI: 10.1111/j.1467-7660.2011.01695.x

Kragelund, P. (2012). The Revival of Non-Traditional State Actors' Interests in Africa: Does it Matter for Policy Autonomy? *Development Policy Review*, 30(6), 703–718. DOI: 10.1111/j.1467-7679.2012.00595.x

Kragelund, P. (2014). 'Donors go home': Non-traditional state actors and the creation of development space in Zambia. *Third World Quarterly*, 35(1), 145–162. DOI: 10.1080/01436597.2014.868994

Kragelund, P. (2015a). Towards convergence and cooperation in the global development finance regime: Closing Africa's policy space? *Cambridge Review of International Affairs*, 28(2), 246–262. DOI: 10.1080/09557571.2014.974141

Kubin, E., & Von Sikorski, C. (2021). The role of (social) media in political polarization: A systematic review. *Annals of the International Communication Association*, 45(3), 188–206. DOI: 10.1080/23808985.2021.1976070

Kumar, P. (2023). How does corruption affect innovation? - New evidence from macro-level data. *Journal of Quantitative Economics*, 21(4), 925–941. DOI: 10.1007/s40953-023-00362-x

Kurauone, O., Kong, Y., Sun, H., Famba, T., & Muzamhindo, S. (2021). Tax evasion; public and political corruption and international trade: A global perspective. *Journal of Financial Economic Policy*, 13(6), 698–729. DOI: 10.1108/JFEP-04-2020-0067

Kurien, A., Fevrin, W. L., & Di Vicenz, S. (2024). Haiti: It's time to strengthen homegrown solutions. *Christian Aid*. https://coilink.org/20.500.12592/ht76pq6

Lagunes, P. F., & Svejnar, E. (Eds.). (2020). *Corruption and the Lava Jato scandal in Latin America*. Routledge., DOI: 10.4324/9781003024286

Larraín, B. F., & Zhang, P. (2022). *Improving tax policy in Latin America and the Caribbean: A balancing act*. Atlantic Council. https://www.atlanticcouncil.org/in-depth-research-reports/report/improving-tax-policy-in-lac-a-balancing-act/

Lawson, M. L. (2013). *Foreign aid: international donor coordination of development assistance*. Congressional research service Washington, DC.

Le Deist, F. D., & Winterton, J. (2005). What is competence? *Human Resource Development International*, 8(1), 27–46. DOI: 10.1080/1367886042000338227

Lebovic, J. H. (2005). Donor positioning: Development assistance from the US, Japan, France, Germany, and Britain. *Political Research Quarterly*, 58(1), 119–126. DOI: 10.1177/106591290505800111

Lee, L., & Markey, A. (2014). A study of learners' perceptions of online intercultural exchange through web 2.0 technologies. *ReCALL*, 26(3), 281–297. DOI: 10.1017/S0958344014000111

Lefebvre, C. (2008). On the principled nature of the respective contributions of substrate and superstrate to a creole's lexicon. In Michaelis, S. (Ed.), *Roots of creole structure: Weighing the contribution of substrates and superstrates* (pp. 197–224). John Benjamins. DOI: 10.1075/cll.33.11lef

Leffert, M. (2007). *Costa Rica Boots Taiwan*. Welcomes China In Diplomatic Switch.

Lemons, M. A., & Parzinger, M. (2007). Gender schemas: A cognitive explanation of discrimination of women in technology. *Journal of Business and Psychology*, 22(1), 91–98. DOI: 10.1007/s10869-007-9050-0

Leung, K., Ang, S., & Tan, M. L. (2014). Intercultural competence. *Annual Review of Organizational Psychology and Organizational Behavior*, 1(1), 489–519. DOI: 10.1146/annurev-orgpsych-031413-091229

Levitsky, S., & Roberts, K. M. (2011). *The Resurgence of the Latin American Left*. Johns Hopkins University Press. https://www.press.jhu.edu/books/title/10244/resurgence-latin-american-left

Levy-Leboyer, C. (1996). *La gestion des compétences*. Les Editions d'Organisation.

Lewellyn, K. B., & Bao, S. (2017). The role of national culture and corruption on managing earnings around the world. *Journal of World Business*, 52(6), 798–808. DOI: 10.1016/j.jwb.2017.07.002

Lewellyn, K. B., & Muller-Kahle, M. I. (2020). The corporate board glass ceiling: The role of empowerment and culture in shaping board gender diversity. *Journal of Business Ethics*, 165(2), 329–346. DOI: 10.1007/s10551-019-04116-9

Liao, J. C., & Katada, S. N. (2021). Geoeconomics, easy money, and political opportunism: The perils under China and Japan's high-speed rail competition. *Contemporary Politics*, 27(1), 1–22. DOI: 10.1080/13569775.2020.1816626

Licht, A., Goldschmidt, C., & Schwartz, S. H. (2005). Culture, law, and corporate governance. *International Review of Law and Economics*, 25(2), 229–255. DOI: 10.1016/j.irle.2005.06.005

Li, H. (2005). Rivalry between Taiwan and the PRC in Latin America. *Journal of Chinese Political Science*, 10(2), 77–102. DOI: 10.1007/BF02877029

Lokkesmoe, K. J., Kuchinke, K. P., & Ardichvili, A. (2016). Developing cross-cultural awareness through foreign immersion programs: Implications of university study abroad research for global competency development. *European Journal of Training and Development*, 40(3), 155–170. DOI: 10.1108/EJTD-07-2014-0048

Lombana-Coy, J., Corrales, K. A., & Rey-Paba, L. (2024). Teaching business through online intercultural exchanges: A method to develop global competence. In Blair, J., & Robles, M. (Eds.), *Effective methods for teaching business related topics: During and post crisis* (Vol. 1, pp. 163–176). National Business Education Association.

Lopez-Claros, A., & Lynch, I. J. (2024). Combatting corruption to advance good governance: Exploring options for an International Anti-Corruption Court. In Falk, R., & Lopez-Claros, A. (Eds.), *Global governance and international cooperation* (pp. 428–443). Routledge India. DOI: 10.4324/9781032699028-29

Lovaton, R. L. (1953). *Boletin del archivo de la nación*. Editora Montalvo.

Lubatkin, M. H., Lane, P. J., Collin, S. O., & Very, P. (2007). An embeddedness framing of governance and opportunism: Towards a cross-nationally accommodating theory of agency. *Journal of Organizational Behavior*, 28(1), 43–58. DOI: 10.1002/job.402

Luo, H., & Gao, P. (2022). Intercultural learning through Chinese-American telecollaboration: Results of a song sharing project. *Computer Assisted Language Learning*, 37(1-2), 85–113. DOI: 10.1080/09588221.2022.2026405

Machwate, S., Bendaoud, R., Henze, J., Berrada, K., & Burgos, D. (2021). Virtual exchange to develop cultural, language, and digital competencies. *Sustainability (Basel)*, 13(11), 5926. Advance online publication. DOI: 10.3390/su13115926

Madrid, F. (2014). A comparative analysis of the health status of children under 5 years of age in the Dominican Republic and Dominican bateyes. [Master's thesis, Georgia State University]

Madsen, S. R., & Wilson, I. K. (2012). Humanistic theory of learning: Maslow. In *Springer eBooks* (pp. 1471–1474). DOI: 10.1007/978-1-4419-1428-6_1022

Manescu, D. M. (2022). Pandora Papers and the latest European efforts to combat money laundering, tax evasion and tax avoidance. *Technium Social Sciences Journal*, 27, 384–390. DOI: 10.47577/tssj.v27i1.5668

Mangla, N. (2021). Working in a pandemic and post-pandemic period – Cultural intelligence is the key. *International Journal of Cross Cultural Management*, 21(1), 53–69. DOI: 10.1177/14705958211002877

Marquez-Cardenas, V., Gonzalez-Ruiz, J. D., & Duque-Grisales, E. (2022). Board gender diversity and firm performance: Evidence from Latin America. *Journal of Sustainable Finance & Investment*, 12(3), 785–808. DOI: 10.1080/20430795.2021.2017256

Martínez, S. (2007). *Decency and excess: Global aspirations and material deprivation on a Caribbean sugar plantation*. Routledge.

Mastella, M., Vancin, D., Perlin, M., & Kirch, G. (2021). Board gender diversity: Performance and risk of Brazilian firms. *Gender in Management*, 36(4), 498–518. DOI: 10.1108/GM-06-2019-0088

Matusitz, J., & Forrester, M. (2009). Successful glocalization practices: The case of Seiyu in Japan. *Journal of Transnational Management*, 14(2), 155–176. DOI: 10.1080/15475770903028696

McClelland, D. (1973). Testing for competence rather than for 'intelligence.'. *The American Psychologist*, 28(1), 1–14. https://psycnet.apa.org/doi/10.1037/h0034092. DOI: 10.1037/h0034092 PMID: 4684069

McCloud, N., Delgado, M. S., & Jin, M. (2023). Foreign capital inflows, exchange rates, and government stability. *Empirical Economics*. Advance online publication. DOI: 10.1007/s00181-023-02490-y

McGee, R. W. (2023). The ethics of bribery: An introduction. In *Springer eBooks* (pp. 3–8). DOI: 10.1007/978-3-031-17707-1_1

McGee, R. W. (2023, November 14). Studies in tax evasion: A bibliography. Available at *SSRN*: https://ssrn.com/abstract=4632770

Merriam, S. B., Johnson-Bailey, J., Lee, M.-Y., Kee, Y., Ntseane, G., & Muhamad, M. (2001). Power and positionality: Negotiating insider/outsider status within and across cultures. *International Journal of Lifelong Education*, 20(5), 405–416. DOI: 10.1080/02601370120490

Merriam, S. B., & Tisdell, E. J. (2016). *Qualitative research. A guide to design an implementation*. Jossey-Bass.

Miller, B., & Uriegas, F. (2019). *Latin America's biggest corruption cases: A retrospective.* Americas Quarterly. https://www.americasquarterly.org/article/latin-americas-biggest-corruption-cases-a-retrospective/

Mohammed, K. (2022). Reparations to the Caribbean could break the cycle of corruption – and China's grip. *The Guardian.*https://www.theguardian.com/global-development/2022/jan/25/reparations-caribbean-cycle-of-corruption-china

Molano, G., & Briceño, J. (2021). Introducción: el regionalismo post-hegemónico. En Molano, G y Briceño, J. (Ed.) El regionalismo en América Latina después de la Post-Hegemonía. Centro de Investigaciones sobre América Latina y el Caribe. Universidad Autónoma de México. (pp. 15-30). México

Moran, T. (2000). The product cycle model of foreign direct investment and developing country welfare. *Journal of International Management*, 6, 297–311. DOI: 10.1016/S1075-4253(00)00031-4

Moreno Olivos, T. (2010). El currículo por competencias en la universidad: Más ruido que nueces [The competence curriculum at the university: More sound than nuts]. *Revista de la Educación Superior*, 39(2), 77–90. https://desarrollocurricular.uantof.cl/wp-content/uploads/2024/01/Moreno-Olivos-T.-2010.-El-curriculo-por-competencias-en-la-universidad-mas-ruido-que-nueces.pdf

Moreno, L. A. (2017, December 14). *How tech can fight corruption in Latin America and the Caribbean.* World Economic Forum. https://www.weforum.org/agenda/2017/12/how-technology-is-becoming-a-powerful-ally-in-the-fight-against-corruption-in-latin-america-and-the-caribbean/

Moreno-Gómez, J., Lafuente, E., & Vaillant, Y. (2018). Gender diversity in the board, women's leadership and business performance. *Gender in Management*, 33(2), 104–122. DOI: 10.1108/GM-05-2017-0058

Morgan, N. T. (1987). *Language maintenance and shift among Haitians in the Dominican Republic* (Order No. 8808137) [Doctoral dissertation, University of New Mexico]. ProQuest Dissertations and Theses Global.

Mota Prado, M., & De Assis Machado, M. R. (2021). Using criminal law to fight corruption: The potential, risks, and limitations of Operation Car Wash (Lava Jato). *The American Journal of Comparative Law*, 69(4), 834–879. DOI: 10.1093/ajcl/avac008

Moya Pons, F. (1992). *Empresarios en Conflicto: Politicas de Industrializacion y Sustitucion de Importaciones en la Republica Dominicana.* Fondo para el Avance de las Ciencias Sociales.

Mulder, P. (2012). Ciclo de Vida de un Producto. Recuperado [insertar la fecha] de toolshero: https://www.toolshero.es/mercadeo/ciclo-de-vida-de-un-producto/

Murray, I., & Bernotavicius, C. (2024). *Stabilizing Haiti: A Guide for Policymakers*. Texas National Security Review.

Nanos, E. (2022, September 7). Federal appeals court [11th Circuit] resurrects major lawsuit against Chiquita for funding Colombian terrorist organization. https://lawandcrime.com/federal-court/federal-appeals-court-resurrects-major-lawsuit-against-chiquita-banana-for-funding-colombian-terrorist-organization/

Narula, R., & Verbeke, A. (2015). Making internalization theory good for practice: The essence of Alan Rugman's contributions to international business. *Journal of World Business*, 50(4), 612–622. DOI: 10.1016/j.jwb.2015.08.007

Nekhili, M., & Gatfaoui, H. (2013). Are demographic attributes and firm characteristics drivers of gender diversity? Investigating women's positions on French boards of directors. *Journal of Business Ethics*, 118(2), 227–249. DOI: 10.1007/s10551-012-1576-z

Nguyen, T. N., & Luong, T. T. H. (2021). Fiscal policy, institutional quality, and public debt: Evidence from transition countries. *Sustainability (Basel)*, 13(19), 10706. DOI: 10.3390/su131910706

Nicholls, C., & Mendonca, D. (2024, June 29). Panama court acquits 28 implicated in Panama Papers and Operation Car Wash scandals. https://www.cnn.com/2024/06/29/americas/operation-car-wash-panama-papers-acquittals-intl/index.html

Noack, R. (2017, November 6). Leaked documents reveal financial habits of Queen Elizabeth and Trump officials. *The Washington Post.*https://www.washingtonpost.com/news/worldviews/wp/2017/11/06/paradise-papers-reveal-how-the-wealthy-and-even-the-politicians-are-still-hiding-their-wealth-from-the-taxman/

Noked, N. (2023, July 1). Ending the crypto tax haven. *Harvard Business Law Review, 15* (in press). Available at *SSRN*: https://ssrn.com/abstract=4618310 DOI: 10.2139/ssrn.4618310

North, D. C. (1990). *Institutions, Institutional Change, and Economic Performance*. Harvard University Press. DOI: 10.1017/CBO9780511808678

Nowell, L. S., Norris, J. M., White, D. E., & Moules, N. J. (2017). Thematic analysis: Striving to meet the trustworthiness criteria. *International Journal of Qualitative Methods*, 16(1), 1–13. DOI: 10.1177/1609406917733847

Nunnenkamp, P., Öhler, H., & Thiele, R. (2013). Donor coordination and specialization: Did the Paris Declaration make a difference? *Review of World Economics*, 149(3), 537–563. DOI: 10.1007/s10290-013-0157-2

O'Donovan, J., Wagner, H. F., & Zeume, S. (2019). The value of offshore secrets: Evidence from the Panama Papers. *Review of Financial Studies*, 32(11), 4117–4155. DOI: 10.1093/rfs/hhz017

O'Dowd, R. (2018). A transnational model of virtual exchange for global citizenship education. Revised version of a plenary address given at the Sixth International Conference on the Development and Assessment of Intercultural Competence: *Intercultural Competence and Mobility: Virtual and Physical*. January 25-28, 2018, University of Arizona, USA.

O'Dowd, R. (2021). What do students learn in virtual exchange? A qualitative content analysis of learning outcomes across multiple exchanges. *International Journal of Educational Research*, 109, 11–13. DOI: 10.1016/j.ijer.2021.101804

Oakley, J. G. (2000). Gender-based barriers to senior management positions: Understanding the scarcity of female CEOs. *Journal of Business Ethics*, 27(4), 321–334. DOI: 10.1023/A:1006226129868

OECD. (2019). *Geographical Distribution of Financial Flows to Developing Countries 2019*. OECD., DOI: 10.1787/fin_flows_dev-2019-en-fr

Oficina Nacional de Estadística. (2018). *ENI-2017: Segunda encuesta nacional de Inmigrantes*. https://www.one.gob.do/publicaciones/2018/segunda-encuesta-nacional-de-inmigrantes-en-la-republica-dominicana-eni-2017-informe-general/

Oficina Nacional de Estadística. (2024). *Extranjeros deportados por año, según nacionalidad, 2021-2023*. https://one.gob.do/datos-y-estadisticas/temas/estadisticas-demograficas/migracion/

Olivié, I., & Pérez, A. (2016). Why don't donor countries coordinate their aid? A case study of European donors in Morocco. *Progress in Development Studies*, 16(1), 52–64. DOI: 10.1177/1464993415608082

Organisation for Economic Co-operation and Development. (n.d.). Retrieved May 23, 2024, from https://www.oecd.org/about/members-and-partners/

Organización de los Estados Americanos (OEA). (1995). Seminario interamericano de infraestructura de transporte como factor de integración. Departamento de Desarrollo regional y medio ambiente. Secretaría ejecutiva para asuntos económicos y sociales. Washington, D.C.

Organization for Economic Cooperation and Development (OECD). (2022). *Tax transparency in Latin America 2021: Punta del Este declaration progress report.* https://web-archive.oecd.org/temp/2022-03-10/592947-tax-transparency-in-latin-america-2021.htm

Organization for Economic Cooperation and Development. (2018). *Latin American and Caribbean competition forum - Session I: Informal economy in Latin America and the Caribbean: Implications for competition policy* [Conference session]. Buenos Aires, Argentina. https://one.oecd.org/document/DAF/COMP/LACF%282018%294/en/pdf

Ortiz Casillas, S. (2024). Book review: Kimberley Kay Hoang, Spiderweb Capitalism: How Global Elites Exploit Frontier Markets. *Administrative Science Quarterly*, 69(1), NP18–NP20. DOI: 10.1177/00018392231213822

Papada, E., Nord, M., & Lindberg, S. I. (2022, December). Can democracy limit corruption? V-Dem Institute, V-Dem Policy Brief No. 36. Available at *SSRN*: https://ssrn.com/abstract=4787135

Patel, F., & Lynch, H. (2013). Glocalization as an alternative to internationalization in higher education: Embedding positive glocal learning perspectives. *International Journal on Teaching and Learning in Higher Education*, 25(2), 223–230. https://www.isetl.org/ijtlhe/ijtlhe-issue.php?v=25&n=2&y=2013

Pedroletti, D., & Ciabuschi, F. (2023). Reshoring: A review and research agenda. *Journal of Business Research*, 164, 114005. DOI: 10.1016/j.jbusres.2023.114005

Pénson, C. N. (1891). *Cosas añejas*. https://archive.org/details/cosas-anejas

Perelman, M. (2024). Living with inflation in Argentina. *Current History (New York, N.Y.)*, 123(850), 50–55. DOI: 10.1525/curh.2024.123.850.50

Pereyra, E. (2020, April 16). Las vírgenes de Galindo: Estremecedor relato de César Nicolás Penson. *Diario Libre*. Retrieved June 6, 2024, from https://www.diariolibre.com/revista/cultura/las-virgenes-de-galindo-estremecedor-relato-de-cesar-nicolas-penson-KO18168345

Phillips, A. (2008). Haiti, France and the independence debt of 1825. *Canada Haiti Action Network, 24*. https://canada-haiti.ca/sites/default/files/Haiti,%20France%20and%20the%20Independence%20Debt%20of%2018250.pdf

Pinilla Roa, A. E. (2010). Competencias en educación universitaria1. *Revista EDU-CyT, 2*, 1-18. https://bibliotecadigital.univalle.edu.co/server/api/core/bitstreams/0c0a4944-35dc-4b66-bbaf-4b60cbcb8e06/content

Pinto, A. C. (2020). Brazil in the era of fascism: The "New State" of Getúlio Vargas. In *Springer eBooks* (pp. 235–256). DOI: 10.1007/978-3-030-46831-6_11

Pohlmann, M., Valarini, E., Trombini, M., & Jorge, M. (2019). Systemic corruption in Brazil: An autopsy of the Odebrecht case. *Journal of Self-regulation and Regulation*, 5, 55–78. https://journals.ub.uni-heidelberg.de/index.php/josar/article/download/69286/62621

Pontes, J., & Anselmo, M. (2022). *Operation Car Wash: Brazil's institutionalized crime and the inside story of the biggest corruption scandal in history*. Bloomsbury Publishing. DOI: 10.5040/9781350265646

Pooler, M. (2024, May 22). Brazil's supreme court overturns 'Car Wash' corruption convictions [of José Dirceu, Marcelo Odebrecht]: Reversal of high-profile rulings comes as country backtracks on graft probe. *Financial Times*. https://www.ft.com/content/c0d84b0f-1f0b-40d0-8ebe-8bf6c60b4fbe

Portugal, M. A., & Alves de Moraes, E. (2024). Operation Car Wash: Uncovering corruption pathways in the Brazilian construction industry through bid law blind spots. *Public Integrity*, 1–19. Advance online publication. DOI: 10.1080/10999922.2024.2316492

Post, C., & Byron, K. (2015). Women on boards and firm financial performance: A meta-analysis. *Academy of Management Journal*, 58(5), 1546–1571. DOI: 10.5465/amj.2013.0319

Powell, J., & Findley, M. G. (2012). *The swarm principle? A sub-national spatial analysis of donor coordination in sub-saharan Africa*. Mimeo, mimeo.

Prahalad, C. K., & Hamel, G. (1990). The core competence of the corporation. *Harvard Business Review*, (May-June), 79–91.

PwC Report (2022). ESG-Focused Institutional Investment Seen Soaring 84% to US$33.9 Trillion in 2026, Making up 21.5% of Assets under Management.

Quinn, B. (2013, June 15). Offshore Leaks app puts secret users of tax havens in the public eye. *The Guardian*.https://www.theguardian.com/technology/2013/jun/15/database-app-icij-tax-havens

Ramírez-Cendrero, J. M., & Paz, M. J. (2017). Oil fiscal regimes and national oil companies: A comparison between Pemex and Petrobras. *Energy Policy*, 101, 473–483. DOI: 10.1016/j.enpol.2016.11.009

Rashid, M. H. U., Uddin, N., Haque, M. S., & Hossain, S. Z. (2022). Good governance and tax evasion: The mediating effect of socioeconomic conditions. *Asia-Pacific Journal of Regional Science*, 6(2), 759–776. DOI: 10.1007/s41685-022-00242-x

Reiter-Palmon, R., Kramer, W., Allen, J., Murugavel, V., & Leone, S. (2021). Creativity in virtual teams: A review and agenda for future research. *Creativity. Theories – Research - Applications, 8*(1) 165-188. DOI: 10.2478/ctra-2021-0011

Remache Lopez, A. A. (2024). *Political corruption: An explanation for Latin American migration*. [Master's thesis, Harvard University Division of Continuing Education]. https://nrs.harvard.edu/URN-3:HUL.INSTREPOS:37378447

Ricee, S. (2022). *Marginalized communities: Addressing inequality and fostering inclusion for all.* Diversity for Social Impact. https://diversity.social/marginalized-communities/

Rodríguez-Fuentes, R. A., Corrales, K. A., Rey Paba, L., & Rosado-Mendinueta, N. (2022). Promoting communicative and intercultural competence development through virtual exchanges. In Allen, M., Ene, E., & McIntosh, K. (Eds.), *Building internationalized spaces: Second language perspectives on developing language and cultural exchange programs in higher education* (pp. 79–100). University of Michigan Press., https://www.press.umich.edu/11762571/building_internationalized_spaces

Rogers, R., Malancharuvil-Berkes, E., Mosley, M., Hui, D., & Joseph, G. O. (2005). Critical discourse analysis in education: A review of the literature. *Review of Educational Research*, 75(3), 365–416. DOI: 10.3102/00346543075003365

Rontos, K., Syrmali, M. E., Salvati, L., & Vavouras, I. (2024). Competitiveness, corruption, and income inequalities: Approaching the 'Janus' face of development with simultaneous equation modelling. *Quality & Quantity*, 58(1), 343–364. DOI: 10.1007/s11135-023-01644-5

Roulston, K. (2010). Reflective interviewing: A guide to theory and practice. *Reflective Interviewing*, 1–216.

Ruben, M. A., Stosic, M. D., Correale, J., & Blanch-Hartigan, D. (2021). Is technology enhancing or hindering interpersonal communication? A framework and preliminary results to examine the relationship between technology use and nonverbal decoding skill. *Frontiers in Psychology*, 11, 611670. DOI: 10.3389/fpsyg.2020.611670 PMID: 33519627

Rubin, H. J., & Rubin, I. S. (2005). *Continuing the design: Making the research credible*. Qualitative Interviewing.

Runde, D. F., Bandura, R., & Hardman, A. (April 16, 2024) Expanding workforce development to enable nearshoring in the Northern Triangle. Washington DC: Center for Strategic and International Studies. https://www.csis.org/analysis/expanding-workforce-development-enable-nearshoring-northern-triangle

Saeed, A., Sameer, M., Raziq, M. M., Salman, A., & Hammoudeh, S. (2019). Board gender diversity and organizational determinants: Empirical evidence from a major developing country. *Emerging Markets Finance & Trade*, 55(8), 1803–1820. DOI: 10.1080/1540496X.2018.1496421

Sagás, E. (2000). *Race and politics in the Dominican Republic*. University Press of Florida.

Saha, S., Gounder, R., Campbell, N., & Su, J. J. (2014). Democracy and corruption: A complex relationship. *Crime, Law, and Social Change*, 61(3), 287–308. DOI: 10.1007/s10611-013-9506-2

Sallaberry, J. D., Quaesner, L. S., Costa, M. C., & Flach, L. (2020). Measurement of damage from corruption in Brazil. *Journal of Financial Crime*, 27(4), 1239–1239. DOI: 10.1108/JFC-04-2020-0057

Sarwari, A. Q., Javed, M. N., Mohd Adnan, H., & Abdul Wahab, M. N. (2024). Assessment of the impacts of artificial intelligence (AI) on intercultural communication among postgraduate students in a multicultural university environment. *Scientific Reports*, 14(1), 13849. DOI: 10.1038/s41598-024-63276-5 PMID: 38879546

Sato, J., Shiga, H., Kobayashi, T., & Kondoh, H. (2011). "Emerging donors" from a recipient perspective: An institutional analysis of foreign aid in Cambodia. *World Development*, 39(12), 2091–2104. DOI: 10.1016/j.worlddev.2011.04.014

Schmal, F., Sasse, K. S., & Watrin, C. (2023). Trouble in paradise? Disclosure after tax haven leaks. *Journal of Accounting, Auditing & Finance*, 38(3), 706–727. DOI: 10.1177/0148558X20986348

Schwindt-Bayer, L. A., & Tavits, M. (2016). *Clarity of responsibility, accountability, and corruption*. DOI: 10.1017/CBO9781316412404

Scott, W. R. (2001). *Institutions and organizations*. Thousands Oaks: Sage.

Sealy, R., Vinnicombe, S., & Doldor, E. (2009). *Female FTSE index and report 2009*. Cranfield University.

Shakeel, M. D., & Maranto, R. (2021). Introduction to the special issue: Elitism, populism, and school choice. *Journal of School Choice*, 15(1), 10–17. DOI: 10.1080/15582159.2021.1883901

Sharma, S. (2023, July 5). *Supporting student engagement with technology*. Edutopia. Retrieved September 22, 2024, from https://www.edutopia.org/article/using-technology-support-student-engagement/

Shiel, F., & Chavkin, S. (2019, June 25). Bribery Division: What is Odebrecht? Who is involved? International Consortium of Investigative Journalists (ICIJ). https://www.icij.org/investigations/bribery-division/bribery-division-what-is-odebrecht-who-is-involved/

Shi, G., Chan, K. K., & Lin, X. (2022). A systematic review of digital citizenship empirical studies for practitioners. *Education and Information Technologies*, 28(4), 3953–3975. DOI: 10.1007/s10639-022-11383-z

Silverio, R. (2013, October 13). Protests hit Dominican Republic's expulsion of Haitians. *Workers World.* Retrieved June 3, 2024, from https://www.workers.org/2013/10/11266/

Simmons, D. (2010). Structural violence as social practice: Haitian agricultural workers, anti-Haitianism, and health in the Dominican Republic. *Human Organization*, 69(1), 10–18. DOI: 10.17730/humo.69.1.8271r0j17372k765

Sirkin, H. L., Rose, J., & Choraria, R. (2014). *Honing US manufacturing's competitive edge*. Boston Consulting Group.

Smith, E. (2020). *Livelihoods in the balance: Haitians, Haitian-Dominicans and precarious work in the Dominican Republic*. [Master's Thesis, Pennsylvania State University]. https://etda.libraries.psu.edu/catalog/18182ees238

Snider, L. (2024). Globalized tax evasion and corruption: Two steps forward, one step back. *Journal of White Collar and Corporate Crime*, 5(2), 113–121. DOI: 10.1177/2631309X241236202

Soiney, M. (2023). The weaponization of language against ethnic Haitians in the Dominican Republic. *Tensões Mundiais, 19*(39), 157-181. https://revistas.uece.br/index.php/tensoesmundiais/article/view/10135/9071

Springer, Singapore. https://link.springer.com/chapter/10.1007/978-981-99-9303-1_2

Stack, L., Erlanger, S., Rousseau, B., Forsythe, M., MacFarquhar, N., & Castle, S. (2016, April 4). What are the Panama Papers? *The New York Times.*https://www.nytimes.com/2016/04/05/world/panama-papers-explainer.html

Starr, C., & Zurbriggen, E. L. (2017). Sandra Bem's gender schema theory after 34 years: A review of its reach and impact. *Sex Roles*, 76(9-10), 566–578. DOI: 10.1007/s11199-016-0591-4

Stasz, C. (1997). Do employers need the skills they want? Evidence from technical work. *Journal of Education and Work*, 10(3), 205–233. DOI: 10.1080/1363908970100301

Statista Research Department. (2024). *Latin America & Caribbean: Tax revenue loss caused globally 2021*. Statista. https://www.statista.com/statistics/1224443/tax-evasion-avoidance-latin-america-caribbean-country/

Statista Research Department. (2024, February 2). Largest enablers of tax avoidance and tax evasion in Latin America and the Caribbean in 2021 (in million U.S. dollars). https://www.statista.com/statistics/1224443/tax-evasion-avoidance-latin-america-caribbean-country/

Statista Research Department. (2024, March 1). Corruption in Latin America – statistics & facts. https://www.statista.com/topics/6468/corruption-in-latin-america/#topicOverview

Steinwand, M. C. (2015). Compete or coordinate? Aid fragmentation and lead donorship. *International Organization*, 69(2), 443–472. DOI: 10.1017/S0020818314000381

Swanson, A. (2017, June 1). The ultra-rich are hiding way more money overseas than anyone realized. *The Washington Post*. https://www.washingtonpost.com/news/wonk/wp/2017/06/01/researchers-are-figuring-out-just-how-much-wealth-the-super-rich-are-hiding-overseas/

Swartz, S., Barbosa, B., & Crawford, I. (2020). Building intercultural competence through virtual team collaboration across global classrooms. *Business and Professional Communication Quarterly*, 83(1), 57–79. DOI: 10.1177/2329490619878834

Swartz, S., & Shrivastava, A. (2022). Stepping up the game–meeting the needs of global business through virtual team projects. *Higher Education. Skills and Work-Based Learning*, 12(2), 346–368. DOI: 10.1108/HESWBL-02-2021-0037

Swedlund, H. J. (2013). From donorship to ownership? Budget support and donor influence in Rwanda and Tanzania. *Public Administration and Development*, 33(5), 357–370. DOI: 10.1002/pad.1665

Swedlund, H. J. (2017). Is China eroding the bargaining power of traditional donors in Africa? *International Affairs*, 93(2), 389–408. DOI: 10.1093/ia/iiw059

Taras, , Caprar, D. V., Rottig, D., Sarala, R. M., Zakaria, N., Zhao, F., Jiménez, A., Wankel, C., Lei, W. S., Minor, M. S., Bryła, P., Ordeñana, X., Bode, A., Schuster, A., Vaiginiene, E., Froese, F. J., Bathula, H., Yajnik, N., Baldegger, R., & Huang, V. Z. (2013). A global classroom? Evaluating the effectiveness of global virtual collaboration as a teaching tool in management education. *Academy of Management Learning & Education*, 12(3), 414–435. DOI: 10.5465/amle.2012.0195

Tate, W. L. (2014). Offshoring and reshoring: US insights and research challenges. *Journal of Purchasing and Supply Management*, 20(1), 66–68. DOI: 10.1016/j.pursup.2014.01.007

Teagarden, M. B., & Schotter, A. (2010, November 11). *Blood Bananas: Chiquita in Colombia*. Harvard Business School Publishing. TB0245-PDF-ENG

Teichman, J. (2022). Class and race in Latin America's left-populist politics. *Race & Class*, 64(2), 55–74. DOI: 10.1177/03063968221103073

Terjesen, S., Sealy, R., & Singh, V. (2009). Women directors on corporate boards: A review and research agenda. *Corporate Governance*, 17(3), 320–337. DOI: 10.1111/j.1467-8683.2009.00742.x

Thaler, K. M., & Mosinger, E. (2022). Nicaragua: Doubling Down on Dictatorship. *Journal of Democracy*, 33(2), 133–146. DOI: 10.1353/jod.2022.0023

The Boston Consulting Group (BCG). (2011). *Made In America Again*. Why Manufacturing Will Return to the U.S.

The Boston Consulting Group (BCG). (2013). *Behind the American Export Surge: The U.S. as One of the Developed World's Lowest-Cost Manufacturers.*

The Boston Consulting Group (BCG). (2014). *The Shifting Economics of Global Manufacturing*. How Cost Competitiveness Is Changing Worldwide.

Tien, C. Y., & Talley, P. (2012). Think globally, act locally: 'Glocalization' in Taiwanese higher education. *International Journal of Business and Social Science*, 3(15), 124–130. https://www.ijbssnet.com/journals/Vol_3_No_15_August_2012/16.pdf

Transparency International (T.I.). (2018, February 21). Perceptions remain unchanged despite progress in the Americas: Regional analysis by Alejandro Urizar and Luciana Torchiaro. https://www.transparency.org/en/news/perceptions-remain-unchanged-despite-progress-in-the-americas

Transparency International (T.I.). (n.d.). Our Work in Puerto Rico. Retrieved May 23, 2024, from https://www.transparency.org/en/countries/puerto-rico

Transparency International. (2017). *Corruption on the rise in Latin America and the Caribbean.* https://www.transparency.org/en/news/corruption-on-the-rise-in-latin-america-and-the-caribbean

Transparency International. (2019). Global Corruption Barometer: Latin America & the Caribbean 2019: Citizens' views and experiences of corruption. https://www.transparency.org/en/gcb/latin-america/latin-america-and-the-caribbean-x-edition-2019

Transparency International. (2019). *Global corruption barometer: Latin America and the Caribbean 2019 - Citizens' views and opinions of corruption.* Transparency International. https://www.transparency.org/en/publications/global-corruption-barometer-latin-america-and-the-caribbean-2019

Transparency International. (2019). *Latin America and the Caribbean: 10th edition - 2019.* https://www.transparency.org/en/gcb/latin-america/latin-america-and-the-caribbean-x-edition-2019

Transparency International. (2024, January 30). CPI 2023 for the Americas: Lack of independent judiciary hinders the fight against corruption. Luciana Torchiaro, Regional Advisor for the Americas. https://www.transparency.org/en/news/cpi-2023-americas-lack-independent-judiciary-hinders-fight-against-corruption

Türk, V. (2022). *Comment by UN High Commissioner for Human Rights Volker Türk on deportation of Haitians from Dominican Republic.*https://www.ohchr.org/en/press-releases/2022/11/comment-un-high-commissioner-human-rights-volker-turk-deportation-haitians

U.S. Department of Justice, Press Release 16-1515. (2016, December 21). Odebrecht and Braskem plead guilty and agree to pay at least $3.5 billion in global penalties to resolve largest foreign bribery case in history. https://www.justice.gov/opa/pr/odebrecht-and-braskem-plead-guilty-and-agree-pay-least-35-billion-global-penalties-resolve

U.S. Department of Justice, Press Release 18-1258. (2018, September 27). Petróleo Brasileiro S.A. – Petrobras agrees to pay more than $850 million for FCPA violations. https://www.justice.gov/opa/pr/petr-leo-brasileiro-sa-petrobras-agrees-pay-more-850-million-fcpa-violations

U.S. Governmental Accountability Office (GAO). (2023, July 10). Venezuela: Illicit financial flows and U.S. efforts to disrupt them. GAO-23-105668. https://www.gao.gov/products/gao-23-105668

Udokporo, C. K. (2021). Understanding the Stages of the Product Life Cycle. In *Product Life Cycle-Opportunities for Digital and Sustainable Transformation.* IntechOpen. DOI: 10.5772/intechopen.99036

United Nations. (2022). *Human development index.* https://hdr.undp.org/data-center/human- development-index#/indicies/HDI

United Nations. (n.d.). *International day for the elimination of violence against women 25 November.* https://www.un.org/en/observances/ending-violence-against-women-day/background

Urcuyo, C. (2021, June 19). Despite U.S. Pressure, China's Presence in Central America is Growing. *Latinoamérica21*, 1–1.

Valdman, H. (2015). *Haitian Creole: Structure, Variation, Status, Origin.* Equinox.

Van Dijk, F. (2020). Judicial independence and perceptions of judicial independence. In *Springer eBooks* (pp. 7–28). DOI: 10.1007/978-3-030-63143-7_2

van Slageren, J., & Rooduijn, M. (2023). The education divide and support for populists. In M. Gangl & others (Eds.), *The Oxford handbook of social stratification* (online edn). Oxford Academic. DOI: 10.1093/oxfordhb/9780197539484.013.48

Vargas-Madriz, L. F. (2018). Experiences of online closeness in virtual learning environments (VLEs). *The Indo-Pacific Journal of Phenomenology*, 18(2), 1–14. DOI: 10.1080/20797222.2018.1507350

Varo Varo, A. (2021). Fostering intercultural competence through videoconference exchange: Using an external provider to match learners with trained native speakers and administer video calls. *Journal of Virtual Exchange*, 4, 1–13. DOI: 10.21827/jve.4.35981

Vassilakopoulou, P., & Hustad, E. (2021). Bridging digital divides: A literature review and research agenda for information systems research. *Information Systems Frontiers*, 25(3), 955–969. DOI: 10.1007/s10796-020-10096-3 PMID: 33424421

Vega, W. B. (1994). *Los documentos básicos de la historia dominicana.* (n.p.).

Venator-Santiago, C. R. (2005). Race, nation-building and legal transculturation during the

Venator-Santiago, C. R. (2011). When literature becomes law: Clarifying Cesar Nicolas Penson's rendition of the case about the prisoners of Galindo. *Rev. Juridica U. Inter. PR, 46*, 759-766. https://heinonline.org/HOL/Page?handle=hein.journals/vjuriprc46&id=825&collection=journals&index=

Verbeke, A., & Kano, L. (2016). An internalization theory perspective on the global and regional strategies of multinational enterprises. *Journal of World Business*, 51(1), 83–92. DOI: 10.1016/j.jwb.2015.08.014

Vernon, R. (1966). International investment and international trade in the product cycle. In *International economic policies and their theoretical foundations* (pp. 415–435). Academic Press.

Vertinsky, I., Kuang, Y., Zhou, D., & Cui, V. (2023). The political economy and dynamics of bifurcated world governance and the decoupling of value chains: An alternative perspective. *Journal of International Business Studies*, 54(7), 1–27. DOI: 10.1057/s41267-023-00597-z PMID: 36743261

Vittadini Andres, S. N. (2024). Moral and cultural perspectives of tax evasion in Latin America. In R. W. McGee & J. Shopovski (Eds.). *The ethics of tax evasion, Volume 2: New perspectives in theory and practice.* Springer (in press). Preprint available at *SSRN*: https://ssrn.com/abstract=4686864

Voigt, S., & Gutmann, J. (2015). On the wrong side of the law – Causes and consequences of a corrupt judiciary. *International Review of Law and Economics*, 43, 156–166. DOI: 10.1016/j.irle.2014.04.005

Voss, B. L., Carter, D. B., & Warren, R. (2023). A car wash: Post-truth politics, Petrobras and ethics of the real. *Accounting, Auditing & Accountability Journal*, 36(2), 437–463. DOI: 10.1108/AAAJ-03-2020-4460

Vuletin, G. (2008, April). *Measuring the informal economy in Latin America and the Caribbean*. International Monetary Fund. https://www.imf.org/external/pubs/ft/wp/2008/wp08102.pdf

Wajner, D. F. (2021). Exploring the foreign policies of populist governments: (Latin) America First. *Journal of International Relations and Development*, 24(3), 651–680. DOI: 10.1057/s41268-020-00206-8

Walker, A. (2019). All spirits are roused: The 1822 antislavery revolution in Haitian Santo Domingo. *Slavery & Abolition, 40*(3), 583-605. https://ww w.tandfonline .com/doi/abs/10.1080/0144039X.2019.1565438

Wallen, F., & Wiberg, M. (2018). *Growing Protectionism After the Financial Crisis: What is the evidence?* Institute of Economic Affairs.

Walshe Roussel, L. (2013). The changing donor landscape in Nicaragua: Rising competition enhances ownership and fosters cooperation. *Journal of International Development*, 25(6), 802–818. DOI: 10.1002/jid.2932

Wang, S., Zhao, D., & Chen, H. (2020). A spatial analysis of corruption, misallocation, and efficiency. *Environmental Science and Pollution Research International*, 27(29), 36845–36856. DOI: 10.1007/s11356-020-09707-y PMID: 32577961

Ward, H., & Brown, S. (2024). Beyond intervention: Sustainable solutions for Haiti's security needs. *GNSI Decision Brief.* https://digitalcommons.usf.edu/gnsi_decision_briefs/13/

Watters, R. (2021). The economic crisis and the Chávez presidency. In *Springer eBooks* (pp. 223–251). DOI: 10.1007/978-3-030-65033-9_10

Weitzman, A., Caudillo, M., & Levy, E. J. (2024). Hybrid interpersonal violence in Latin America: Patterns and causes. *Annual Review of Criminology*, 7(1), 163–186. DOI: 10.1146/annurev-criminol-022422-014603 PMID: 38304058

Weyland, K. (2001). Clarifying a contested concept: Populism in the study of Latin American politics. *Comparative Politics*, 34(1), 1–22. DOI: 10.2307/422412

Wikberg, K. (2023). Family-friendly policies and practices: Scoping review (Master's thesis, Metropolia Ammattikorkeakoulu). https://www.theseus.fi/bitstream/handle/10024/809553/Wikberg_Katja.pdf? sequence=2&isAllowed=y

Williamson, J. (2003). The Washington consensus and beyond. *Economic and Political Weekly*, 38(15), 1475–1481. https://www.jstor.org/stable/4413431

Williams, R. M. (1970). *American society: A sociological interpretation*. Knopf.

Winter, B. (2017). Brazil's never-ending corruption crisis: Why radical transparency is the only fix. *Foreign Affairs*, 96(3), 87–94. https://www.jstor.org/stable/44823734

Winters, M. S. (2012). The obstacles to foreign aid harmonization: Lessons from decentralization support in Indonesia. *Studies in Comparative International Development*, 47(3), 316–341. DOI: 10.1007/s12116-012-9114-7

Winters, M. S., & Martinez, G. (2015). The role of governance in determining foreign aid flow composition. *World Development*, 66, 516–531. DOI: 10.1016/j.worlddev.2014.09.020

Wolf, M. L. (2014, July 23). The case for an International Anti-Corruption Court. Brookings Institution. https://www.brookings.edu/articles/the-case-for-an-international-anti-corruption-court/

Wolf, M. L., Goldstone, R. J., & Rotberg, R. I. (2022, August 24). The progressing proposal for an International Anti-Corruption Court. American Academy of Arts and Sciences. https://www.amacad.org/publication/proposal-international-anti-corruption-court

Wolf, M. L. (2018). The world needs an International Anti-Corruption Court. *Daedalus*, 147(3), 144–156. https://www.jstor.org/stable/48563086. DOI: 10.1162/daed_a_00507

World Bank. (2018). *Annual Report 2018*. World Bank. https://documents1.worldbank.org/curated/en/630671538158537244/pdf/The-World-Bank-Annual-Report-2018.pdf

World Bank. (2019). *Implementation completion and results report: IBRD 7841-BR on a loan in the amount of US$200 million to the Federative Republic of Brazil for the second Bolsa Família project* (Report No. ICR00004576). Social Protection and Jobs Global Practice, Latin America and the Caribbean Region. https://documents1.worldbank.org/curated/en/578141568314136393/pdf/Brazil-Second-Bolsa-Familia-Project.pdf

World Bank. (2020). *Doing Business 2020.*

World Bank. (2021). [The World Bank.]. *World Development Indicators*, •••, 2021.

World Bank. (2022). *Educational underachievement among boys and men.* World Bank. https://documents1.worldbank.org/curated/en/111041644611110155/pdf/Educational-Underachievement-Among-Boys-and-Men.pdf

World Economic Forum. (2016, June 15). Corruption in Latin America is skyrocketing. Here's why that's good news. https://www.weforum.org/agenda/2016/06/corruption-in-latin-america/

World Justice Project. (2023). *Corruption in the Caribbean: Insights from the General Public 2022*. Washington, DC. https://worldjusticeproject.org/sites/default/files/documents/Corruption-in-the-Caribbean-report-v4.pdf

Wu, T., Delios, A., Chen, Z., & Wang, X. (2023). Rethinking corruption in international business: An empirical review. *Journal of World Business*, 58(2), 101410. DOI: 10.1016/j.jwb.2022.101410

Xu, H., & Lin, Y. (2023). Using collaborative online international learning to increase student success in a quantitative business core course: Using COIL to increase student success in a quantitative business core course. In *ICDEL '23: Proceedings of the 8th International Conference on Distance Education and Learning* (pp. 185-189). Association for Computing Machinery. doi:DOI: 10.1145/3606094.3606148

Yahyaoui, I. (2024). How corruption mitigates the effect of FDI on economic growth? *Journal of the Knowledge Economy*, 15(1), 1344–1362. DOI: 10.1007/s13132-023-01098-y

Yansura, J., Mavrellis, C., Kumar, L., & Helms, C. (2021, October 15). Financial crime in Latin America and the Caribbean: Understanding country challenges and designing effective technical responses. Global Financial Integrity. https://gfintegrity.org/report/financial-crime-in-latin-america-and-the-caribbean/

Yao, T. (2023). Antecedents of top management team and board gender diversity: A review and an agenda for research. *Corporate Governance*, 31(1), 227–248. DOI: 10.1111/corg.12495

Ylönen, M., Raudla, R., & Babic, M. (2024). From tax havens to cryptocurrencies: Secrecy-seeking capital in the global economy. *Review of International Political Economy*, 31(2), 563–588. DOI: 10.1080/09692290.2023.2232392

Zattoni, A., Leventis, S., Van Ees, H., & De Masi, S. (2023). Board diversity's antecedents and consequences: A review and research agenda. *The Leadership Quarterly*, 34(1), 101659. DOI: 10.1016/j.leaqua.2022.101659

Zeitz, A. (2020). Emulation or Differentiation? China's Development Finance and Traditional Donor Aid in Developing Countries. *The Review of International Organizations*, 16(4), 933–938. DOI: 10.1007/s11558-021-09429-x

Zhai, W., Sun, S., & Zhang, G. (2016). Reshoring of American manufacturing companies from China. *Operations Management Research : Advancing Practice Through Research*, 9(3-4), 62–74. DOI: 10.1007/s12063-016-0114-z

Zhou, J. Q., & Peng, M. W. (2011). Does bribery help or hurt firm growth around the world? *Asia Pacific Journal of Management*, 29(4), 907–921. DOI: 10.1007/s10490-011-9274-4

Zilberberg, L. E., & Krimphove, J. (2022). Virtual exchange contributions to the development of intercultural competence: A Brazilian higher education institutions' perspective. *Actualidades Investigativas en Educación*, 22(1), 312–336. DOI: 10.15517/aie.v22i1.47481

Zucker, L. (1983). Organizations as institutions. In Bacharach, S. (Ed.), *Research in the sociology of organizations* (Vol. 2, pp. 1–47). JAI Press.

Zysman-Quirós, D. (2019). White-collar crime in South and Central America: Corporate-state crime, governance, and the high impact of the Odebrecht corruption case. In Rorie, M. L. (Ed.), *The handbook of white-collar crime* (pp. 363–380). John Wiley., DOI: 10.1002/9781118775004.ch23

Related References

To continue our tradition of advancing information science and technology research, we have compiled a list of recommended IGI Global readings. These references will provide additional information and guidance to further enrich your knowledge and assist you with your own research and future publications.

Abdul Razak, R., & Mansor, N. A. (2021). Instagram Influencers in Social Media-Induced Tourism: Rethinking Tourist Trust Towards Tourism Destination. In M. Dinis, L. Bonixe, S. Lamy, & Z. Breda (Eds.), *Impact of New Media in Tourism* (pp. 135-144). IGI Global. https://doi.org/10.4018/978-1-7998-7095-1.ch009

Abir, T., & Khan, M. Y. (2022). Importance of ICT Advancement and Culture of Adaptation in the Tourism and Hospitality Industry for Developing Countries. In Ramos, C., Quinteiro, S., & Gonçalves, A. (Eds.), *ICT as Innovator Between Tourism and Culture* (pp. 30–41). IGI Global. https://doi.org/10.4018/978-1-7998-8165-0.ch003

Abtahi, M. S., Behboudi, L., & Hasanabad, H. M. (2017). Factors Affecting Internet Advertising Adoption in Ad Agencies. *International Journal of Innovation in the Digital Economy*, 8(4), 18–29. DOI: 10.4018/IJIDE.2017100102

Aburezeq, I. M., & Dweikat, F. F. (2017). Cloud Applications in Language Teaching: Examining Pre-Service Teachers' Expertise, Perceptions and Integration. *International Journal of Distance Education Technologies*, 15(4), 39–60. DOI: 10.4018/IJDET.2017100103

Acharjya, B., & Das, S. (2022). Adoption of E-Learning During the COVID-19 Pandemic: The Moderating Role of Age and Gender. *International Journal of Web-Based Learning and Teaching Technologies*, 17(2), 1–14. https://doi.org/10.4018/IJWLTT.20220301.oa4

Adams, J. L., & Thomas, S. K. (2022). Non-Linear Curriculum Experiences for Student Learning and Work Design: What Is the Maximum Potential of a Chat Bot? In Ramlall, S., Cross, T., & Love, M. (Eds.), *Handbook of Research on Future of Work and Education: Implications for Curriculum Delivery and Work Design* (pp. 299–306). IGI Global. https://doi.org/10.4018/978-1-7998-8275-6.ch018

Adera, B. (2017). Supporting Language and Literacy Development for English Language Learners. In Keengwe, J. (Ed.), *Handbook of Research on Promoting Cross-Cultural Competence and Social Justice in Teacher Education* (pp. 339–354). Hershey, PA: IGI Global. DOI: 10.4018/978-1-5225-0897-7.ch018

Afenyo-Agbe, E., & Mensah, I. (2022). Principles, Benefits, and Barriers to Community-Based Tourism: Implications for Management. In Mensah, I., & Afenyo-Agbe, E. (Eds.), *Prospects and Challenges of Community-Based Tourism and Changing Demographics* (pp. 1–29). IGI Global. DOI: 10.4018/978-1-7998-7335-8.ch001

Agbo, V. M. (2022). Distributive Justice Issues in Community-Based Tourism. In Mensah, I., & Afenyo-Agbe, E. (Eds.), *Prospects and Challenges of Community-Based Tourism and Changing Demographics* (pp. 107–129). IGI Global. https://doi.org/10.4018/978-1-7998-7335-8.ch005

Agrawal, S. (2017). The Impact of Emerging Technologies and Social Media on Different Business(es): Marketing and Management. In Rishi, O., & Sharma, A. (Eds.), *Maximizing Business Performance and Efficiency Through Intelligent Systems* (pp. 37–49). Hershey, PA: IGI Global. DOI: 10.4018/978-1-5225-2234-8.ch002

Ahamer, G. (2017). Quality Assurance for a Developmental "Global Studies" (GS) Curriculum. In I. Management Association (Ed.), *Educational Leadership and Administration: Concepts, Methodologies, Tools, and Applications* (pp. 438-477). Hershey, PA: IGI Global. https://doi.org/DOI: 10.4018/978-1-5225-1624-8.ch023

Ahamer, G. (2017). Quality Assurance for a Developmental "Global Studies" (GS) Curriculum. In I. Management Association (Ed.), *Educational Leadership and Administration: Concepts, Methodologies, Tools, and Applications* (pp. 438-477). Hershey, PA: IGI Global. https://doi.org/DOI: 10.4018/978-1-5225-1624-8.ch023

Ahmad, A., & Johari, S. (2022). Georgetown as a Gastronomy Tourism Destination: Visitor Awareness Towards Revisit Intention of Nasi Kandar Restaurant. In Valeri, M. (Ed.), *New Governance and Management in Touristic Destinations* (pp. 71–83). IGI Global. https://doi.org/10.4018/978-1-6684-3889-3.ch005

Akayoğlu, S., & Seferoğlu, G. (2019). An Analysis of Negotiation of Meaning Functions of Advanced EFL Learners in Second Life: Negotiation of Meaning in Second Life. In Kruk, M. (Ed.), *Assessing the Effectiveness of Virtual Technologies in Foreign and Second Language Instruction* (pp. 61–85). IGI Global. https://doi.org/10.4018/978-1-5225-7286-2.ch003

Akella, N. R. (2022). Unravelling the Web of Qualitative Dissertation Writing!: A Student Reflects. In Zimmerman, A. (Ed.), *Methodological Innovations in Research and Academic Writing* (pp. 260–282). IGI Global. https://doi.org/10.4018/978-1-7998-8283-1.ch014

Alegre de la Rosa, O. M., & Angulo, L. M. (2017). Social Inclusion and Intercultural Values in a School of Education. In Mukerji, S., & Tripathi, P. (Eds.), *Handbook of Research on Administration, Policy, and Leadership in Higher Education* (pp. 518–531). Hershey, PA: IGI Global. DOI: 10.4018/978-1-5225-0672-0.ch020

Alexander, C. (2019). Using Gamification Strategies to Cultivate and Measure Professional Educator Dispositions. *International Journal of Game-Based Learning*, 9(1), 15–29. https://doi.org/10.4018/IJGBL.2019010102

Alkhatib, G., & Bayouq, S. T. (2021). A TAM-Based Model of Technological Factors Affecting Use of E-Tourism. *International Journal of Tourism and Hospitality Management in the Digital Age*, 5(2), 50–67. https://doi.org/10.4018/IJTHMDA.20210701.oa1

Altinay Ozdemir, M. (2021). Virtual Reality (VR) and Augmented Reality (AR) Technologies for Accessibility and Marketing in the Tourism Industry. In C. Eusébio, L. Teixeira, & M. Carneiro (Eds.), *ICT Tools and Applications for Accessible Tourism* (pp. 277-301). IGI Global. https://doi.org/10.4018/978-1-7998-6428-8.ch013

Anantharaman, R. N., Rajeswari, K. S., Angusamy, A., & Kuppusamy, J. (2017). Role of Self-Efficacy and Collective Efficacy as Moderators of Occupational Stress Among Software Development Professionals. *International Journal of Human Capital and Information Technology Professionals*, 8(2), 45–58. DOI: 10.4018/IJHCITP.2017040103

Anderson, K. M. (2017). Preparing Teachers in the Age of Equity and Inclusion. In I. Management Association (Ed.), *Medical Education and Ethics: Concepts, Methodologies, Tools, and Applications* (pp. 1532-1554). Hershey, PA: IGI Global. DOI: 10.4018/978-1-5225-0978-3.ch069

Aninze, F., El-Gohary, H., & Hussain, J. (2018). The Role of Microfinance to Empower Women: The Case of Developing Countries. *International Journal of Customer Relationship Marketing and Management*, 9(1), 54–78. DOI: 10.4018/IJCRMM.2018010104

Antosova, G., Sabogal-Salamanca, M., & Krizova, E. (2021). Human Capital in Tourism: A Practical Model of Endogenous and Exogenous Territorial Tourism Planning in Bahía Solano, Colombia. In Costa, V., Moura, A., & Mira, M. (Eds.), *Handbook of Research on Human Capital and People Management in the Tourism Industry* (pp. 282–302). IGI Global. https://doi.org/10.4018/978-1-7998-4318-4.ch014

Arsenijević, O. M., Orčić, D., & Kastratović, E. (2017). Development of an Optimization Tool for Intangibles in SMEs: A Case Study from Serbia with a Pilot Research in the Prestige by Milka Company. In Vemić, M. (Ed.), *Optimal Management Strategies in Small and Medium Enterprises* (pp. 320–347). Hershey, PA: IGI Global. DOI: 10.4018/978-1-5225-1949-2.ch015

Aryanto, V. D., Wismantoro, Y., & Widyatmoko, K. (2018). Implementing Eco-Innovation by Utilizing the Internet to Enhance Firm's Marketing Performance: Study of Green Batik Small and Medium Enterprises in Indonesia. *International Journal of E-Business Research*, 14(1), 21–36. DOI: 10.4018/IJEBR.2018010102

Asero, V., & Billi, S. (2022). New Perspective of Networking in the DMO Model. In Valeri, M. (Ed.), *New Governance and Management in Touristic Destinations* (pp. 105–118). IGI Global. https://doi.org/10.4018/978-1-6684-3889-3.ch007

Atiku, S. O., & Fields, Z. (2017). Multicultural Orientations for 21st Century Global Leadership. In Baporikar, N. (Ed.), *Management Education for Global Leadership* (pp. 28–51). Hershey, PA: IGI Global. DOI: 10.4018/978-1-5225-1013-0.ch002

Atiku, S. O., & Fields, Z. (2018). Organisational Learning Dimensions and Talent Retention Strategies for the Service Industries. In Baporikar, N. (Ed.), *Global Practices in Knowledge Management for Societal and Organizational Development* (pp. 358–381). Hershey, PA: IGI Global. DOI: 10.4018/978-1-5225-3009-1.ch017

Atsa'am, D. D., & Kuset Bodur, E. (2021). Pattern Mining on How Organizational Tenure Affects the Psychological Capital of Employees Within the Hospitality and Tourism Industry: Linking Employees' Organizational Tenure With PsyCap. *International Journal of Tourism and Hospitality Management in the Digital Age*, 5(2), 17–28. https://doi.org/10.4018/IJTHMDA.2021070102

Ávila, L., & Teixeira, L. (2018). The Main Concepts Behind the Dematerialization of Business Processes. In M. Khosrow-Pour, D.B.A. (Ed.), *Encyclopedia of Information Science and Technology, Fourth Edition* (pp. 888-898). Hershey, PA: IGI Global. https://doi.org/DOI: 10.4018/978-1-5225-2255-3.ch076

Awdziej, M. (2017). Case Study as a Teaching Method in Marketing. In Latusek, D. (Ed.), *Case Studies as a Teaching Tool in Management Education* (pp. 244–263). Hershey, PA: IGI Global. DOI: 10.4018/978-1-5225-0770-3.ch013

Ayorekire, J., Mugizi, F., Obua, J., & Ampaire, G. (2022). Community-Based Tourism and Local People's Perceptions Towards Conservation: The Case of Queen Elizabeth Conservation Area, Uganda. In Mensah, I., & Afenyo-Agbe, E. (Eds.), *Prospects and Challenges of Community-Based Tourism and Changing Demographics* (pp. 56–82). IGI Global. https://doi.org/10.4018/978-1-7998-7335-8.ch003

Bakos, J. (2019). Sociolinguistic Factors Influencing English Language Learning. In Erdogan, N., & Wei, M. (Eds.), *Applied Linguistics for Teachers of Culturally and Linguistically Diverse Learners* (pp. 403–424). IGI Global. https://doi.org/10.4018/978-1-5225-8467-4.ch017

Baleiro, R. (2022). Tourist Literature and the Architecture of Travel in Olga Tokarczuk and Patti Smith. In R. Baleiro & R. Pereira (Eds.), *Global Perspectives on Literary Tourism and Film-Induced Tourism* (pp. 202-216). IGI Global. https://doi.org/10.4018/978-1-7998-8262-6.ch011

Banas, J. R., & York, C. S. (2017). Pre-Service Teachers' Motivation to Use Technology and the Impact of Authentic Learning Exercises. In Tomei, L. (Ed.), *Exploring the New Era of Technology-Infused Education* (pp. 121–140). Hershey, PA: IGI Global. DOI: 10.4018/978-1-5225-1709-2.ch008

Barat, S. (2021). Looking at the Future of Medical Tourism in Asia. *International Journal of Tourism and Hospitality Management in the Digital Age*, 5(1), 19–33. https://doi.org/10.4018/IJTHMDA.2021010102

Barbosa, C. A., Magalhães, M., & Nunes, M. R. (2021). Travel Instagramability: A Way of Choosing a Destination? In M. Dinis, L. Bonixe, S. Lamy, & Z. Breda (Eds.), *Impact of New Media in Tourism* (pp. 173-190). IGI Global. https://doi.org/10.4018/978-1-7998-7095-1.ch011

Bari, M. W., & Khan, Q. (2021). Pakistan as a Destination of Religious Tourism. In E. Alaverdov & M. Bari (Eds.), *Global Development of Religious Tourism* (pp. 1-10). IGI Global. https://doi.org/10.4018/978-1-7998-5792-1.ch001

Bartens, Y., Chunpir, H. I., Schulte, F., & Voß, S. (2017). Business/IT Alignment in Two-Sided Markets: A COBIT 5 Analysis for Media Streaming Business Models. In De Haes, S., & Van Grembergen, W. (Eds.), *Strategic IT Governance and Alignment in Business Settings* (pp. 82–111). Hershey, PA: IGI Global. DOI: 10.4018/978-1-5225-0861-8.ch004

Barton, T. P. (2021). Empowering Educator Allyship by Exploring Racial Trauma and the Disengagement of Black Students. In Reneau, C., & Villarreal, M. (Eds.), *Handbook of Research on Leading Higher Education Transformation With Social Justice, Equity, and Inclusion* (pp. 186–197). IGI Global. https://doi.org/10.4018/978-1-7998-7152-1.ch013

Bashayreh, A. M. (2018). Organizational Culture and Organizational Performance. In Lee, W., & Sabetzadeh, F. (Eds.), *Contemporary Knowledge and Systems Science* (pp. 50–69). Hershey, PA: IGI Global. DOI: 10.4018/978-1-5225-5655-8.ch003

Bechthold, L., Lude, M., & Prügl, R. (2021). Crisis Favors the Prepared Firm: How Organizational Ambidexterity Relates to Perceptions of Organizational Resilience. In Zehrer, A., Glowka, G., Schwaiger, K., & Ranacher-Lackner, V. (Eds.), *Resiliency Models and Addressing Future Risks for Family Firms in the Tourism Industry* (pp. 178–205). IGI Global. https://doi.org/10.4018/978-1-7998-7352-5.ch008

Bedford, D. A. (2018). Sustainable Knowledge Management Strategies: Aligning Business Capabilities and Knowledge Management Goals. In Baporikar, N. (Ed.), *Global Practices in Knowledge Management for Societal and Organizational Development* (pp. 46–73). Hershey, PA: IGI Global. DOI: 10.4018/978-1-5225-3009-1.ch003

Bekjanov, D., & Matyusupov, B. (2021). Influence of Innovative Processes in the Competitiveness of Tourist Destination. In Soares, J. (Ed.), *Innovation and Entrepreneurial Opportunities in Community Tourism* (pp. 243–263). IGI Global. https://doi.org/10.4018/978-1-7998-4855-4.ch014

Benhima, M. (2021). Moroccan English Department Student Attitudes Towards the Use of Distance Education During COVID-19: Moulay Ismail University as a Case Study. *International Journal of Information and Communication Technology Education*, 17(3), 105–122. https://doi.org/10.4018/IJICTE.20210701.oa7

Beycioglu, K., & Wildy, H. (2017). Principal Preparation: The Case of Novice Principals in Turkey. In I. Management Association (Ed.), *Educational Leadership and Administration: Concepts, Methodologies, Tools, and Applications* (pp. 1152-1169). Hershey, PA: IGI Global. https://doi.org/DOI: 10.4018/978-1-5225-1624-8.ch054

Bharwani, S., & Musunuri, D. (2018). Reflection as a Process From Theory to Practice. In M. Khosrow-Pour, D.B.A. (Ed.), *Encyclopedia of Information Science and Technology, Fourth Edition* (pp. 1529-1539). Hershey, PA: IGI Global. DOI: 10.4018/978-1-5225-2255-3.ch132

Bharwani, S., & Musunuri, D. (2018). Reflection as a Process From Theory to Practice. In M. Khosrow-Pour, D.B.A. (Ed.), *Encyclopedia of Information Science and Technology, Fourth Edition* (pp. 1529-1539). Hershey, PA: IGI Global. DOI: 10.4018/978-1-5225-2255-3.ch132

Bhatt, G. D., Wang, Z., & Rodger, J. A. (2017). Information Systems Capabilities and Their Effects on Competitive Advantages: A Study of Chinese Companies. *Information Resources Management Journal*, 30(3), 41–57. DOI: 10.4018/IRMJ.2017070103

Bhushan, A., Garza, K. B., Perumal, O., Das, S. K., Feola, D. J., Farrell, D., & Birnbaum, A. (2022). Lessons Learned From the COVID-19 Pandemic and the Implications for Pharmaceutical Graduate Education and Research. In Ford, C., & Garza, K. (Eds.), *Handbook of Research on Updating and Innovating Health Professions Education: Post-Pandemic Perspectives* (pp. 324–345). IGI Global. https://doi.org/10.4018/978-1-7998-7623-6.ch014

Bhushan, M., & Yadav, A. (2017). Concept of Cloud Computing in ESB. In Bhadoria, R., Chaudhari, N., Tomar, G., & Singh, S. (Eds.), *Exploring Enterprise Service Bus in the Service-Oriented Architecture Paradigm* (pp. 116–127). Hershey, PA: IGI Global. DOI: 10.4018/978-1-5225-2157-0.ch008

Bhushan, S. (2017). System Dynamics Base-Model of Humanitarian Supply Chain (HSCM) in Disaster Prone Eco-Communities of India: A Discussion on Simulation and Scenario Results. *International Journal of System Dynamics Applications*, 6(3), 20–37. DOI: 10.4018/IJSDA.2017070102

Binder, D., & Miller, J. W. (2021). A Generations' Perspective on Employer Branding in Tourism. In Costa, V., Moura, A., & Mira, M. (Eds.), *Handbook of Research on Human Capital and People Management in the Tourism Industry* (pp. 152–174). IGI Global. https://doi.org/10.4018/978-1-7998-4318-4.ch008

Bintz, W., Ciecierski, L. M., & Royan, E. (2021). Using Picture Books With Instructional Strategies to Address New Challenges and Teach Literacy Skills in a Digital World. In Haas, L., & Tussey, J. (Eds.), *Connecting Disciplinary Literacy and Digital Storytelling in K-12 Education* (pp. 38–58). IGI Global. https://doi.org/10.4018/978-1-7998-5770-9.ch003

Birch Freeman, A. A., Mensah, I., & Antwi, K. B. (2022). Smiling vs. Frowning Faces: Community Participation for Sustainable Tourism in Ghanaian Communities. In Mensah, I., & Afenyo-Agbe, E. (Eds.), *Prospects and Challenges of Community-Based Tourism and Changing Demographics* (pp. 83–106). IGI Global. https://doi.org/10.4018/978-1-7998-7335-8.ch004

Biswas, A., & De, A. K. (2017). On Development of a Fuzzy Stochastic Programming Model with Its Application to Business Management. In Trivedi, S., Dey, S., Kumar, A., & Panda, T. (Eds.), *Handbook of Research on Advanced Data Mining Techniques and Applications for Business Intelligence* (pp. 353–378). Hershey, PA: IGI Global. DOI: 10.4018/978-1-5225-2031-3.ch021

Bohjanen, S. L., Cameron-Standerford, A., & Meidl, T. D. (2018). Capacity Building Pedagogy for Diverse Learners. In Keengwe, J. (Ed.), *Handbook of Research on Pedagogical Models for Next-Generation Teaching and Learning* (pp. 195–212). Hershey, PA: IGI Global. DOI: 10.4018/978-1-5225-3873-8.ch011

Boragnio, A., & Faracce Macia, C. (2021). "Taking Care of Yourself at Home": Use of E-Commerce About Food and Care During the COVID-19 Pandemic in the City of Buenos Aires. In Korstanje, M. (Ed.), *Socio-Economic Effects and Recovery Efforts for the Rental Industry: Post-COVID-19 Strategies* (pp. 45–71). IGI Global. https://doi.org/10.4018/978-1-7998-7287-0.ch003

Borges, V. D. (2021). Happiness: The Basis for Public Policy in Tourism. In Perinotto, A., Mayer, V., & Soares, J. (Eds.), *Rebuilding and Restructuring the Tourism Industry: Infusion of Happiness and Quality of Life* (pp. 1–25). IGI Global. https://doi.org/10.4018/978-1-7998-7239-9.ch001

Brewer, J. C. (2018). Measuring Text Readability Using Reading Level. In M. Khosrow-Pour, D.B.A. (Ed.), *Encyclopedia of Information Science and Technology, Fourth Edition* (pp. 1499-1507). Hershey, PA: IGI Global. DOI: 10.4018/978-1-5225-2255-3.ch129

Brookbanks, B. C. (2022). Student Perspectives on Business Education in the USA: Current Attitudes and Necessary Changes in an Age of Disruption. In Zhuplev, A., & Koepp, R. (Eds.), *Global Trends, Dynamics, and Imperatives for Strategic Development in Business Education in an Age of Disruption* (pp. 214–231). IGI Global. DOI: 10.4018/978-1-7998-7548-2.ch011

Brown, L. V., Dari, T., & Spencer, N. (2019). Addressing the Impact of Trauma in High Poverty Elementary Schools: An Ecological Model for School Counseling. In Daniels, K., & Billingsley, K. (Eds.), *Creating Caring and Supportive Educational Environments for Meaningful Learning* (pp. 135–153). IGI Global. https://doi.org/10.4018/978-1-5225-5748-7.ch008

Brown, S. L. (2017). A Case Study of Strategic Leadership and Research in Practice: Principal Preparation Programs that Work – An Educational Administration Perspective of Best Practices for Master's Degree Programs for Principal Preparation. In Wang, V. (Ed.), *Encyclopedia of Strategic Leadership and Management* (pp. 1226–1244). Hershey, PA: IGI Global. DOI: 10.4018/978-1-5225-1049-9.ch086

Brzozowski, M., & Ferster, I. (2017). Educational Management Leadership: High School Principal's Management Style and Parental Involvement in School Management in Israel. In Potocan, V., Ünğan, M., & Nedelko, Z. (Eds.), *Handbook of Research on Managerial Solutions in Non-Profit Organizations* (pp. 55–74). Hershey, PA: IGI Global. DOI: 10.4018/978-1-5225-0731-4.ch003

Bücker, J., & Ernste, K. (2018). Use of Brand Heroes in Strategic Reputation Management: The Case of Bacardi, Adidas, and Daimler. In Erdemir, A. (Ed.), *Reputation Management Techniques in Public Relations* (pp. 126–150). Hershey, PA: IGI Global. DOI: 10.4018/978-1-5225-3619-2.ch007

Buluk Eşitti, B. (2021). COVID-19 and Alternative Tourism: New Destinations and New Tourism Products. In Demir, M., Dalgıç, A., & Ergen, F. (Eds.), *Handbook of Research on the Impacts and Implications of COVID-19 on the Tourism Industry* (pp. 786–805). IGI Global. https://doi.org/10.4018/978-1-7998-8231-2.ch038

Bureš, V. (2018). Industry 4.0 From the Systems Engineering Perspective: Alternative Holistic Framework Development. In Brunet-Thornton, R., & Martinez, F. (Eds.), *Analyzing the Impacts of Industry 4.0 in Modern Business Environments* (pp. 199–223). Hershey, PA: IGI Global. DOI: 10.4018/978-1-5225-3468-6.ch011

Buzady, Z. (2017). Resolving the Magic Cube of Effective Case Teaching: Benchmarking Case Teaching Practices in Emerging Markets – Insights from the Central European University Business School, Hungary. In Latusek, D. (Ed.), *Case Studies as a Teaching Tool in Management Education* (pp. 79–103). Hershey, PA: IGI Global. DOI: 10.4018/978-1-5225-0770-3.ch005

Cahapay, M. B. (2020). Delphi Technique in the Development of Emerging Contents in High School Science Curriculum. *International Journal of Curriculum Development and Learning Measurement*, 1(2), 1–9. https://doi.org/10.4018/IJCDLM.2020070101

Camacho, L. F., & Leon Guerrero, A. E. (2022). Indigenous Student Experience in Higher Education: Implementation of Culturally Sensitive Support. In Pangelinan, P., & McVey, T. (Eds.), *Learning and Reconciliation Through Indigenous Education in Oceania* (pp. 254–266). IGI Global. https://doi.org/10.4018/978-1-7998-7736-3.ch016

Camillo, A. (2021). *Legal Matters, Risk Management, and Risk Prevention: From Forming a Business to Legal Representation*. IGI Global. DOI: 10.4018/978-1-7998-4342-9.ch004

Cannaday, J. (2017). The Masking Effect: Hidden Gifts and Disabilities of 2e Students. In Dickenson, P., Keough, P., & Courduff, J. (Eds.), *Preparing Pre-Service Teachers for the Inclusive Classroom* (pp. 220–231). Hershey, PA: IGI Global. DOI: 10.4018/978-1-5225-1753-5.ch011

Căpusneanu, S., & Topor, D. I. (2018). Business Ethics and Cost Management in SMEs: Theories of Business Ethics and Cost Management Ethos. In Oncioiu, I. (Ed.), *Ethics and Decision-Making for Sustainable Business Practices* (pp. 109–127). Hershey, PA: IGI Global. DOI: 10.4018/978-1-5225-3773-1.ch007

Cederquist, S., Fishman, B., & Teasley, S. D. (2022). What's Missing From the College Transcript?: How Employers Make Sense of Student Skills. In Huang, Y. (Ed.), *Handbook of Research on Credential Innovations for Inclusive Pathways to Professions* (pp. 234–253). IGI Global. https://doi.org/10.4018/978-1-7998-3820-3.ch012

Chan, R. L., Mo, P. L., & Moon, K. K. (2018). Strategic and Tactical Measures in Managing Enterprise Risks: A Study of the Textile and Apparel Industry. In Strang, K., Korstanje, M., & Vajjhala, N. (Eds.), *Research, Practices, and Innovations in Global Risk and Contingency Management* (pp. 1–19). Hershey, PA: IGI Global. DOI: 10.4018/978-1-5225-4754-9.ch001

Charlier, S. D., Burke-Smalley, L. A., & Fisher, S. L. (2018). Undergraduate Programs in the U.S: A Contextual and Content-Based Analysis. In Mendy, J. (Ed.), *Teaching Human Resources and Organizational Behavior at the College Level* (pp. 26–57). Hershey, PA: IGI Global. DOI: 10.4018/978-1-5225-2820-3.ch002

Chumillas, J., Güell, M., & Quer, P. (2022). The Use of ICT in Tourist and Educational Literary Routes: The Role of the Guide. In Ramos, C., Quinteiro, S., & Gonçalves, A. (Eds.), *ICT as Innovator Between Tourism and Culture* (pp. 15–29). IGI Global. https://doi.org/10.4018/978-1-7998-8165-0.ch002

Cockrell, P., & Gibson, T. (2019). The Untold Stories of Black and Brown Student Experiences in Historically White Fraternities and Sororities. In Hoffman-Miller, P., James, M., & Hermond, D. (Eds.), *African American Suburbanization and the Consequential Loss of Identity* (pp. 153–171). IGI Global. https://doi.org/10.4018/978-1-5225-7835-2.ch009

Cohen, M. (2022). Leveraging Content Creation to Boost Student Engagement. In Driscoll, T.III, (Ed.), *Designing Effective Distance and Blended Learning Environments in K-12* (pp. 223–239). IGI Global. https://doi.org/10.4018/978-1-7998-6829-3.ch013

Contreras, E. C., & Contreras, I. I. (2018). Development of Communication Skills through Auditory Training Software in Special Education. In M. Khosrow-Pour, D.B.A. (Ed.), *Encyclopedia of Information Science and Technology, Fourth Edition* (pp. 2431-2441). Hershey, PA: IGI Global. DOI: 10.4018/978-1-5225-2255-3.ch212

Cooke, L., Schugar, J., Schugar, H., Penny, C., & Bruning, H. (2020). Can Everyone Code?: Preparing Teachers to Teach Computer Languages as a Literacy. In Mitchell, J., & Vaughn, E. (Eds.), *Participatory Literacy Practices for P-12 Classrooms in the Digital Age* (pp. 163–183). IGI Global. https://doi.org/10.4018/978-1-7998-0000-2.ch009

Cooley, D., & Whitten, E. (2017). Special Education Leadership and the Implementation of Response to Intervention. In Topor, F. (Ed.), *Handbook of Research on Individualism and Identity in the Globalized Digital Age* (pp. 265–286). Hershey, PA: IGI Global. DOI: 10.4018/978-1-5225-0522-8.ch012

Cosner, S., Tozer, S., & Zavitkovsky, P. (2017). Enacting a Cycle of Inquiry Capstone Research Project in Doctoral-Level Leadership Preparation. In I. Management Association (Ed.), *Educational Leadership and Administration: Concepts, Methodologies, Tools, and Applications* (pp. 1460-1481). Hershey, PA: IGI Global. DOI: 10.4018/978-1-5225-1624-8.ch067

Crawford, C. M. (2018). Instructional Real World Community Engagement. In M. Khosrow-Pour, D.B.A. (Ed.), *Encyclopedia of Information Science and Technology, Fourth Edition* (pp. 1474-1486). Hershey, PA: IGI Global. DOI: 10.4018/978-1-5225-2255-3.ch127

Crosby-Cooper, T., & Pacis, D. (2017). Implementing Effective Student Support Teams. In Dickenson, P., Keough, P., & Courduff, J. (Eds.), *Preparing Pre-Service Teachers for the Inclusive Classroom* (pp. 248–262). Hershey, PA: IGI Global. DOI: 10.4018/978-1-5225-1753-5.ch013

Curran, C. M., & Hawbaker, B. W. (2017). Cultivating Communities of Inclusive Practice: Professional Development for Educators – Research and Practice. In Curran, C., & Petersen, A. (Eds.), *Handbook of Research on Classroom Diversity and Inclusive Education Practice* (pp. 120–153). Hershey, PA: IGI Global. DOI: 10.4018/978-1-5225-2520-2.ch006

Dahlberg, T., Kivijärvi, H., & Saarinen, T. (2017). IT Investment Consistency and Other Factors Influencing the Success of IT Performance. In De Haes, S., & Van Grembergen, W. (Eds.), *Strategic IT Governance and Alignment in Business Settings* (pp. 176–208). Hershey, PA: IGI Global. DOI: 10.4018/978-1-5225-0861-8.ch007

Damnjanović, A. M. (2017). Knowledge Management Optimization through IT and E-Business Utilization: A Qualitative Study on Serbian SMEs. In Vemić, M. (Ed.), *Optimal Management Strategies in Small and Medium Enterprises* (pp. 249–267). Hershey, PA: IGI Global. DOI: 10.4018/978-1-5225-1949-2.ch012

Daneshpour, H. (2017). Integrating Sustainable Development into Project Portfolio Management through Application of Open Innovation. In Vemić, M. (Ed.), *Optimal Management Strategies in Small and Medium Enterprises* (pp. 370–387). Hershey, PA: IGI Global. DOI: 10.4018/978-1-5225-1949-2.ch017

Daniel, A. D., & Reis de Castro, V. (2018). Entrepreneurship Education: How to Measure the Impact on Nascent Entrepreneurs. In Carrizo Moreira, A., Guilherme Leitão Dantas, J., & Manuel Valente, F. (Eds.), *Nascent Entrepreneurship and Successful New Venture Creation* (pp. 85–110). Hershey, PA: IGI Global. DOI: 10.4018/978-1-5225-2936-1.ch004

Dass, S., & Dabbagh, N. (2018). Faculty Adoption of 3D Avatar-Based Virtual World Learning Environments: An Exploratory Case Study. In I. Management Association (Ed.), *Technology Adoption and Social Issues: Concepts, Methodologies, Tools, and Applications* (pp. 1000-1033). Hershey, PA: IGI Global. https://doi.org/ DOI: 10.4018/978-1-5225-5201-7.ch045

David, R., Swami, B. N., & Tangirala, S. (2018). Ethics Impact on Knowledge Management in Organizational Development: A Case Study. In Baporikar, N. (Ed.), *Global Practices in Knowledge Management for Societal and Organizational Development* (pp. 19–45). Hershey, PA: IGI Global. DOI: 10.4018/978-1-5225-3009-1.ch002

Davison, A. M., & Scholl, K. G. (2017). Inclusive Recreation as Part of the IEP Process. In Curran, C., & Petersen, A. (Eds.), *Handbook of Research on Classroom Diversity and Inclusive Education Practice* (pp. 311–330). Hershey, PA: IGI Global. DOI: 10.4018/978-1-5225-2520-2.ch013

De Uña-Álvarez, E., & Villarino-Pérez, M. (2022). Fostering Ecocultural Resources, Identity, and Tourism in Inland Territories (Galicia, NW Spain). In G. Fernandes (Ed.), *Challenges and New Opportunities for Tourism in Inland Territories: Ecocultural Resources and Sustainable Initiatives* (pp. 1-16). IGI Global. https://doi.org/10.4018/978-1-7998-7339-6.ch001

DeCoito, I. (2018). Addressing Digital Competencies, Curriculum Development, and Instructional Design in Science Teacher Education. In M. Khosrow-Pour, D.B.A. (Ed.), *Encyclopedia of Information Science and Technology, Fourth Edition* (pp. 1420-1431). Hershey, PA: IGI Global. https://doi.org/DOI: 10.4018/978-1-5225-2255-3.ch122

DeCoito, I., & Richardson, T. (2017). Beyond Angry Birds™: Using Web-Based Tools to Engage Learners and Promote Inquiry in STEM Learning. In Levin, I., & Tsybulsky, D. (Eds.), *Digital Tools and Solutions for Inquiry-Based STEM Learning* (pp. 166–196). Hershey, PA: IGI Global. DOI: 10.4018/978-1-5225-2525-7.ch007

Delias, P., & Lakiotaki, K. (2018). Discovering Process Horizontal Boundaries to Facilitate Process Comprehension. *International Journal of Operations Research and Information Systems*, 9(2), 1–31. DOI: 10.4018/IJORIS.2018040101

Delmas, P. M. (2017). Research-Based Leadership for Next-Generation Leaders. In Styron, R.Jr, & Styron, J. (Eds.), *Comprehensive Problem-Solving and Skill Development for Next-Generation Leaders* (pp. 1–39). Hershey, PA: IGI Global. DOI: 10.4018/978-1-5225-1968-3.ch001

Demiray, U., & Ekren, G. (2018). Administrative-Related Evaluation for Distance Education Institutions in Turkey. In Buyuk, K., Kocdar, S., & Bozkurt, A. (Eds.), *Administrative Leadership in Open and Distance Learning Programs* (pp. 263–288). Hershey, PA: IGI Global. DOI: 10.4018/978-1-5225-2645-2.ch011

Denholm, J., & Lee-Davies, L. (2018). Success Factors for Games in Business and Project Management. In *Enhancing Education and Training Initiatives Through Serious Games* (pp. 34–68). Hershey, PA: IGI Global. DOI: 10.4018/978-1-5225-3689-5.ch002

Deshpande, M. (2017). Best Practices in Management Institutions for Global Leadership: Policy Aspects. In Baporikar, N. (Ed.), *Management Education for Global Leadership* (pp. 1–27). Hershey, PA: IGI Global. DOI: 10.4018/978-1-5225-1013-0.ch001

Deshpande, M. (2018). Policy Perspectives for SMEs Knowledge Management. In Baporikar, N. (Ed.), *Knowledge Integration Strategies for Entrepreneurship and Sustainability* (pp. 23–46). Hershey, PA: IGI Global. DOI: 10.4018/978-1-5225-5115-7.ch002

Dezdar, S. (2017). ERP Implementation Projects in Asian Countries: A Comparative Study on Iran and China. *International Journal of Information Technology Project Management*, 8(3), 52–68. DOI: 10.4018/IJITPM.2017070104

Dickenson, P. (2017). What do we Know and Where Can We Grow?: Teachers Preparation for the Inclusive Classroom. In Dickenson, P., Keough, P., & Courduff, J. (Eds.), *Preparing Pre-Service Teachers for the Inclusive Classroom* (pp. 1–22). Hershey, PA: IGI Global. DOI: 10.4018/978-1-5225-1753-5.ch001

Ding, Q., & Zhu, H. (2021). Flipping the Classroom in STEM Education. In Keengwe, J. (Ed.), *Handbook of Research on Innovations in Non-Traditional Educational Practices* (pp. 155–173). IGI Global. https://doi.org/10.4018/978-1-7998-4360-3.ch008

Dixon, T., & Christison, M. (2021). Teaching English Grammar in a Hybrid Academic ESL Course: A Mixed Methods Study. In Kelch, K., Byun, P., Safavi, S., & Cervantes, S. (Eds.), *CALL Theory Applications for Online TESOL Education* (pp. 229–251). IGI Global. https://doi.org/10.4018/978-1-7998-6609-1.ch010

Domingos, D., Respício, A., & Martinho, R. (2017). Reliability of IoT-Aware BPMN Healthcare Processes. In Reis, C., & Maximiano, M. (Eds.), *Internet of Things and Advanced Application in Healthcare* (pp. 214–248). Hershey, PA: IGI Global. DOI: 10.4018/978-1-5225-1820-4.ch008

Donne, V., & Hansen, M. (2017). Teachers' Use of Assistive Technologies in Education. In Tomei, L. (Ed.), *Exploring the New Era of Technology-Infused Education* (pp. 86–101). Hershey, PA: IGI Global. DOI: 10.4018/978-1-5225-1709-2.ch006

Donne, V., & Hansen, M. A. (2018). Business and Technology Educators: Practices for Inclusion. In I. Management Association (Ed.), *Business Education and Ethics: Concepts, Methodologies, Tools, and Applications* (pp. 471-484). Hershey, PA: IGI Global. https://doi.org/DOI: 10.4018/978-1-5225-3153-1.ch026

Dos Santos, L. M. (2022). Completing Student-Teaching Internships Online: Instructional Changes During the COVID-19 Pandemic. In Alaali, M. (Ed.), *Assessing University Governance and Policies in Relation to the COVID-19 Pandemic* (pp. 106–127). IGI Global. https://doi.org/10.4018/978-1-7998-8279-4.ch007

Dosumu, O., Hussain, J., & El-Gohary, H. (2017). An Exploratory Study of the Impact of Government Policies on the Development of Small and Medium Enterprises in Developing Countries: The Case of Nigeria. *International Journal of Customer Relationship Marketing and Management*, 8(4), 51–62. DOI: 10.4018/IJCRMM.2017100104

Dreon, O., Shettel, J., & Bower, K. M. (2017). Preparing Next Generation Elementary Teachers for the Tools of Tomorrow. In Grassetti, M., & Brookby, S. (Eds.), *Advancing Next-Generation Teacher Education through Digital Tools and Applications* (pp. 143–159). Hershey, PA: IGI Global. DOI: 10.4018/978-1-5225-0965-3.ch008

Durak, H. Y., & Güyer, T. (2018). Design and Development of an Instructional Program for Teaching Programming Processes to Gifted Students Using Scratch. In Cannaday, J. (Ed.), *Curriculum Development for Gifted Education Programs* (pp. 61–99). Hershey, PA: IGI Global. DOI: 10.4018/978-1-5225-3041-1.ch004

Durst, S., Bruns, G., & Edvardsson, I. R. (2017). Retaining Knowledge in Smaller Building and Construction Firms. *International Journal of Knowledge and Systems Science*, 8(3), 1–12. DOI: 10.4018/IJKSS.2017070101

Edvardsson, I. R., & Durst, S. (2017). Outsourcing, Knowledge, and Learning: A Critical Review. *International Journal of Knowledge-Based Organizations*, 7(2), 13–26. DOI: 10.4018/IJKBO.2017040102

Edwards, J. S. (2018). Integrating Knowledge Management and Business Processes. In M. Khosrow-Pour, D.B.A. (Ed.), *Encyclopedia of Information Science and Technology, Fourth Edition* (pp. 5046-5055). Hershey, PA: IGI Global. DOI: 10.4018/978-1-5225-2255-3.ch437

Egorkina, E., Ivanov, M., & Valyavskiy, A. Y. (2018). Students' Research Competence Formation of the Quality of Open and Distance Learning. In Mkrttchian, V., & Belyanina, L. (Eds.), *Handbook of Research on Students' Research Competence in Modern Educational Contexts* (pp. 364–384). Hershey, PA: IGI Global. DOI: 10.4018/978-1-5225-3485-3.ch019

Eichelberger, S., & Peters, M. (2021). Family Firm Management in Turbulent Times: Opportunities for Responsible Tourism. In Zehrer, A., Glowka, G., Schwaiger, K., & Ranacher-Lackner, V. (Eds.), *Resiliency Models and Addressing Future Risks for Family Firms in the Tourism Industry* (pp. 103–124). IGI Global. https://doi.org/10.4018/978-1-7998-7352-5.ch005

Eide, D., Hjalager, A., & Hansen, M. (2022). Innovative Certifications in Adventure Tourism: Attributes and Diffusion. In R. Augusto Costa, F. Brandão, Z. Breda, & C. Costa (Eds.), *Planning and Managing the Experience Economy in Tourism* (pp. 161-175). IGI Global. https://doi.org/10.4018/978-1-7998-8775-1.ch009

Ejiogu, A. O. (2018). Economics of Farm Management. In *Agricultural Finance and Opportunities for Investment and Expansion* (pp. 56–72). Hershey, PA: IGI Global. DOI: 10.4018/978-1-5225-3059-6.ch003

Ekanem, I., & Abiade, G. E. (2018). Factors Influencing the Use of E-Commerce by Small Enterprises in Nigeria. *International Journal of ICT Research in Africa and the Middle East*, 7(1), 37–53. DOI: 10.4018/IJICTRAME.2018010103

Ekanem, I., & Alrossais, L. A. (2017). Succession Challenges Facing Family Businesses in Saudi Arabia. In Zgheib, P. (Ed.), *Entrepreneurship and Business Innovation in the Middle East* (pp. 122–146). Hershey, PA: IGI Global. DOI: 10.4018/978-1-5225-2066-5.ch007

Ekren, G., Karataş, S., & Demiray, U. (2017). Understanding of Leadership in Distance Education Management. In I. Management Association (Ed.), *Educational Leadership and Administration: Concepts, Methodologies, Tools, and Applications* (pp. 34-50). Hershey, PA: IGI Global. https://doi.org/DOI: 10.4018/978-1-5225-1624-8.ch003

El Faquih, L., & Fredj, M. (2017). Ontology-Based Framework for Quality in Configurable Process Models. *Journal of Electronic Commerce in Organizations*, 15(2), 48–60. DOI: 10.4018/JECO.2017040104

Elmore, W. M., Young, J. K., Harris, S., & Mason, D. (2017). The Relationship between Individual Student Attributes and Online Course Completion. In Shelton, K., & Pedersen, K. (Eds.), *Handbook of Research on Building, Growing, and Sustaining Quality E-Learning Programs* (pp. 151–173). Hershey, PA: IGI Global. DOI: 10.4018/978-1-5225-0877-9.ch008

Ercegovac, I. R., Alfirević, N., & Koludrović, M. (2017). School Principals' Communication and Co-Operation Assessment: The Croatian Experience. In I. Management Association (Ed.), *Educational Leadership and Administration: Concepts, Methodologies, Tools, and Applications* (pp. 1568-1589). Hershey, PA: IGI Global. https://doi.org/DOI: 10.4018/978-1-5225-1624-8.ch072

Everhart, D., & Seymour, D. M. (2017). Challenges and Opportunities in the Currency of Higher Education. In Rasmussen, K., Northrup, P., & Colson, R. (Eds.), *Handbook of Research on Competency-Based Education in University Settings* (pp. 41–65). Hershey, PA: IGI Global. DOI: 10.4018/978-1-5225-0932-5.ch003

Faisal, M. N., & Talib, F. (2017). Building Ambidextrous Supply Chains in SMEs: How to Tackle the Barriers? *International Journal of Information Systems and Supply Chain Management*, 10(4), 80–100. DOI: 10.4018/IJISSCM.2017100105

Farmer, L. S. (2017). Managing Portable Technologies for Special Education. In Wang, V. (Ed.), *Encyclopedia of Strategic Leadership and Management* (pp. 977–987). Hershey, PA: IGI Global. DOI: 10.4018/978-1-5225-1049-9.ch068

Farmer, L. S. (2018). Optimizing OERs for Optimal ICT Literacy in Higher Education. In Keengwe, J. (Ed.), *Handbook of Research on Mobile Technology, Constructivism, and Meaningful Learning* (pp. 366–390). Hershey, PA: IGI Global. DOI: 10.4018/978-1-5225-3949-0.ch020

Ferguson, B. T. (2019). Supporting Affective Development of Children With Disabilities Through Moral Dilemmas. In Ikuta, S. (Ed.), *Handmade Teaching Materials for Students With Disabilities* (pp. 253–275). IGI Global. DOI: 10.4018/978-1-5225-6240-5.ch011

Fernandes, T. M., Gomes, J., & Romão, M. (2017). Investments in E-Government: A Benefit Management Case Study. *International Journal of Electronic Government Research*, 13(3), 1–17. DOI: 10.4018/IJEGR.2017070101

Figueira, L. M., Honrado, G. R., & Dionísio, M. S. (2021). Human Capital Management in the Tourism Industry in Portugal. In Costa, V., Moura, A., & Mira, M. (Eds.), *Handbook of Research on Human Capital and People Management in the Tourism Industry* (pp. 1–19). IGI Global. DOI: 10.4018/978-1-7998-4318-4.ch001

Fındık, L. Y. (2017). Self-Assessment of Principals Based on Leadership in Complexity. In I. Management Association (Ed.), *Educational Leadership and Administration: Concepts, Methodologies, Tools, and Applications* (pp. 978-991). Hershey, PA: IGI Global. https://doi.org/DOI: 10.4018/978-1-5225-1624-8.ch047

Flor, A. G., & Gonzalez-Flor, B. (2018). Dysfunctional Digital Demeanors: Tales From (and Policy Implications of) eLearning's Dark Side. In I. Management Association (Ed.), The Dark Web: Breakthroughs in Research and Practice (pp. 37-50). Hershey, PA: IGI Global. https://doi.org/DOI: 10.4018/978-1-5225-3163-0.ch003

Floyd, K. K., & Shambaugh, N. (2017). Instructional Design for Simulations in Special Education Virtual Learning Spaces. In Kidd, T., & Morris, L.Jr., (Eds.), *Handbook of Research on Instructional Systems and Educational Technology* (pp. 202–215). Hershey, PA: IGI Global. DOI: 10.4018/978-1-5225-2399-4.ch018

Freeland, S. F. (2020). Community Schools: Improving Academic Achievement Through Meaningful Engagement. In Kronick, R. (Ed.), *Emerging Perspectives on Community Schools and the Engaged University* (pp. 132–144). IGI Global. https://doi.org/10.4018/978-1-7998-0280-8.ch008

Gao, S. S., Oreal, S., & Zhang, J. (2018). Contemporary Financial Risk Management Perceptions and Practices of Small-Sized Chinese Businesses. In I. Management Association (Ed.), *Global Business Expansion: Concepts, Methodologies, Tools, and Applications* (pp. 917-931). Hershey, PA: IGI Global. DOI: 10.4018/978-1-5225-5481-3.ch041

Garg, R., & Berning, S. C. (2017). Indigenous Chinese Management Philosophies: Key Concepts and Relevance for Modern Chinese Firms. In Christiansen, B., & Koc, G. (Eds.), *Transcontinental Strategies for Industrial Development and Economic Growth* (pp. 43–57). Hershey, PA: IGI Global. DOI: 10.4018/978-1-5225-2160-0.ch003

Gencer, Y. G. (2017). Supply Chain Management in Retailing Business. In Akkucuk, U. (Ed.), *Ethics and Sustainability in Global Supply Chain Management* (pp. 197–210). Hershey, PA: IGI Global. DOI: 10.4018/978-1-5225-2036-8.ch011

Gera, R., Arora, S., & Malik, S. (2021). Emotional Labor in the Tourism Industry: Strategies, Antecedents, and Outcomes. In Costa, V., Moura, A., & Mira, M. (Eds.), *Handbook of Research on Human Capital and People Management in the Tourism Industry* (pp. 73–91). IGI Global. https://doi.org/10.4018/978-1-7998-4318-4.ch004

Ghanbarzadeh, R., & Ghapanchi, A. H. (2019). Applied Areas of Three Dimensional Virtual Worlds in Learning and Teaching: A Review of Higher Education. In I. Management Association (Ed.), *Virtual Reality in Education: Breakthroughs in Research and Practice* (pp. 172-192). IGI Global. https://doi.org/10.4018/978-1-5225-8179-6.ch008

Giacosa, E. (2018). The Increasing of the Regional Development Thanks to the Luxury Business Innovation. In Carvalho, L. (Ed.), *Handbook of Research on Entrepreneurial Ecosystems and Social Dynamics in a Globalized World* (pp. 260–273). Hershey, PA: IGI Global. DOI: 10.4018/978-1-5225-3525-6.ch011

Giovannini, J. M. (2017). Technology Integration in Preservice Teacher Education Programs: Research-based Recommendations. In Grassetti, M., & Brookby, S. (Eds.), *Advancing Next-Generation Teacher Education through Digital Tools and Applications* (pp. 82–102). Hershey, PA: IGI Global. DOI: 10.4018/978-1-5225-0965-3.ch005

Glowka, G., Tusch, M., & Zehrer, A. (2021). The Risk Perception of Family Business Owner-Manager in the Tourism Industry: A Qualitative Comparison of the Intra-Firm Senior and Junior Generation. In Zehrer, A., Glowka, G., Schwaiger, K., & Ranacher-Lackner, V. (Eds.), *Resiliency Models and Addressing Future Risks for Family Firms in the Tourism Industry* (pp. 126–153). IGI Global. https://doi.org/10.4018/978-1-7998-7352-5.ch006

Glykas, M., & George, J. (2017). Quality and Process Management Systems in the UAE Maritime Industry. *International Journal of Productivity Management and Assessment Technologies*, 5(1), 20–39. DOI: 10.4018/IJPMAT.2017010102

Glykas, M., Valiris, G., Kokkinaki, A., & Koutsoukou, Z. (2018). Banking Business Process Management Implementation. *International Journal of Productivity Management and Assessment Technologies*, 6(1), 50–69. DOI: 10.4018/IJPMAT.2018010104

Gomes, J., & Romão, M. (2017). The Balanced Scorecard: Keeping Updated and Aligned with Today's Business Trends. *International Journal of Productivity Management and Assessment Technologies*, 5(2), 1–15. DOI: 10.4018/IJPMAT.2017070101

Gomes, J., & Romão, M. (2017). Aligning Information Systems and Technology with Benefit Management and Balanced Scorecard. In De Haes, S., & Van Grembergen, W. (Eds.), *Strategic IT Governance and Alignment in Business Settings* (pp. 112–131). Hershey, PA: IGI Global. DOI: 10.4018/978-1-5225-0861-8.ch005

Good, S., & Clarke, V. B. (2017). An Integral Analysis of One Urban School System's Efforts to Support Student-Centered Teaching. In Keengwe, J., & Onchwari, G. (Eds.), *Handbook of Research on Learner-Centered Pedagogy in Teacher Education and Professional Development* (pp. 45–68). Hershey, PA: IGI Global. DOI: 10.4018/978-1-5225-0892-2.ch003

Goyal, A. (2021). Communicating and Building Destination Brands With New Media. In M. Dinis, L. Bonixe, S. Lamy, & Z. Breda (Eds.), *Impact of New Media in Tourism* (pp. 1-20). IGI Global. https://doi.org/10.4018/978-1-7998-7095-1.ch001

Grefen, P., & Turetken, O. (2017). Advanced Business Process Management in Networked E-Business Scenarios. *International Journal of E-Business Research*, 13(4), 70–104. DOI: 10.4018/IJEBR.2017100105

Guasca, M., Van Broeck, A. M., & Vanneste, D. (2021). Tourism and the Social Reintegration of Colombian Ex-Combatants. In J. da Silva, Z. Breda, & F. Carbone (Eds.), *Role and Impact of Tourism in Peacebuilding and Conflict Transformation* (pp. 66-86). IGI Global. https://doi.org/10.4018/978-1-7998-5053-3.ch005

Guetzoian, E. (2022). Gamification Strategies for Higher Education Student Worker Training. In Lane, C. (Ed.), *Handbook of Research on Acquiring 21st Century Literacy Skills Through Game-Based Learning* (pp. 164–179). IGI Global. https://doi.org/10.4018/978-1-7998-7271-9.ch009

Haider, A., & Saetang, S. (2017). Strategic IT Alignment in Service Sector. In Rozenes, S., & Cohen, Y. (Eds.), *Handbook of Research on Strategic Alliances and Value Co-Creation in the Service Industry* (pp. 231–258). Hershey, PA: IGI Global. DOI: 10.4018/978-1-5225-2084-9.ch012

Hajilari, A. B., Ghadaksaz, M., & Fasghandis, G. S. (2017). Assessing Organizational Readiness for Implementing ERP System Using Fuzzy Expert System Approach. *International Journal of Enterprise Information Systems*, 13(1), 67–85. DOI: 10.4018/IJEIS.2017010105

Haldorai, A., Ramu, A., & Murugan, S. (2018). Social Aware Cognitive Radio Networks: Effectiveness of Social Networks as a Strategic Tool for Organizational Business Management. In Bansal, H., Shrivastava, G., Nguyen, G., & Stanciu, L. (Eds.), *Social Network Analytics for Contemporary Business Organizations* (pp. 188–202). Hershey, PA: IGI Global. DOI: 10.4018/978-1-5225-5097-6.ch010

Hall, O. P.Jr. (2017). Social Media Driven Management Education. *International Journal of Knowledge-Based Organizations*, 7(2), 43–59. DOI: 10.4018/IJKBO.2017040104

Hamidi, F., Owuor, P. M., Hynie, M., Baljko, M., & McGrath, S. (2017). Potentials of Digital Assistive Technology and Special Education in Kenya. In Ayo, C., & Mbarika, V. (Eds.), *Sustainable ICT Adoption and Integration for Socio-Economic Development* (pp. 125–151). Hershey, PA: IGI Global. DOI: 10.4018/978-1-5225-2565-3.ch006

Hamim, T., Benabbou, F., & Sael, N. (2022). Student Profile Modeling Using Boosting Algorithms. *International Journal of Web-Based Learning and Teaching Technologies*, 17(5), 1–13. https://doi.org/10.4018/IJWLTT.20220901.oa4

Hanifah, H., Halim, H. A., Ahmad, N. H., & Vafaei-Zadeh, A. (2017). Innovation Culture as a Mediator Between Specific Human Capital and Innovation Performance Among Bumiputera SMEs in Malaysia. In Ahmad, N., Ramayah, T., Halim, H., & Rahman, S. (Eds.), *Handbook of Research on Small and Medium Enterprises in Developing Countries* (pp. 261–279). Hershey, PA: IGI Global. DOI: 10.4018/978-1-5225-2165-5.ch012

Hartlieb, S., & Silvius, G. (2017). Handling Uncertainty in Project Management and Business Development: Similarities and Differences. In Raydugin, Y. (Ed.), *Handbook of Research on Leveraging Risk and Uncertainties for Effective Project Management* (pp. 337–362). Hershey, PA: IGI Global. DOI: 10.4018/978-1-5225-1790-0.ch016

Hass, K. B. (2017). Living on the Edge: Managing Project Complexity. In Raydugin, Y. (Ed.), *Handbook of Research on Leveraging Risk and Uncertainties for Effective Project Management* (pp. 177–201). Hershey, PA: IGI Global. DOI: 10.4018/978-1-5225-1790-0.ch009

Hawking, P., & Carmine Sellitto, C. (2017). Developing an Effective Strategy for Organizational Business Intelligence. In Tavana, M. (Ed.), *Enterprise Information Systems and the Digitalization of Business Functions* (pp. 222–237). Hershey, PA: IGI Global. DOI: 10.4018/978-1-5225-2382-6.ch010

Hawking, P., & Sellitto, C. (2017). A Fast-Moving Consumer Goods Company and Business Intelligence Strategy Development. *International Journal of Enterprise Information Systems*, 13(2), 22–33. DOI: 10.4018/IJEIS.2017040102

Hawking, P., & Sellitto, C. (2017). Business Intelligence Strategy: Two Case Studies. *International Journal of Business Intelligence Research*, 8(2), 17–30. DOI: 10.4018/IJBIR.2017070102

Hee, W. J., Jalleh, G., Lai, H., & Lin, C. (2017). E-Commerce and IT Projects: Evaluation and Management Issues in Australian and Taiwanese Hospitals. *International Journal of Public Health Management and Ethics*, 2(1), 69–90. DOI: 10.4018/IJPHME.2017010104

Henderson, L. K. (2017). Meltdown at Fukushima: Global Catastrophic Events, Visual Literacy, and Art Education. In Shin, R. (Ed.), *Convergence of Contemporary Art, Visual Culture, and Global Civic Engagement* (pp. 80–99). Hershey, PA: IGI Global. DOI: 10.4018/978-1-5225-1665-1.ch005

Hernandez, A. A. (2018). Exploring the Factors to Green IT Adoption of SMEs in the Philippines. *Journal of Cases on Information Technology*, 20(2), 49–66. DOI: 10.4018/JCIT.2018040104

Hollman, A., Bickford, S., & Hollman, T. (2017). Cyber InSecurity: A Post-Mortem Attempt to Assess Cyber Problems from IT and Business Management Perspectives. *Journal of Cases on Information Technology*, 19(3), 42–70. DOI: 10.4018/JCIT.2017070104

Hudgins, T., & Holland, J. L. (2018). Digital Badges: Tracking Knowledge Acquisition Within an Innovation Framework. In I. Management Association (Ed.), *Wearable Technologies: Concepts, Methodologies, Tools, and Applications* (pp. 1118-1132). Hershey, PA: IGI Global. https://doi.org/DOI: 10.4018/978-1-5225-5484-4.ch051

Hwang, R., Lin, H., Sun, J. C., & Wu, J. (2019). Improving Learning Achievement in Science Education for Elementary School Students via Blended Learning. *International Journal of Online Pedagogy and Course Design*, 9(2), 44–62. https://doi.org/10.4018/IJOPCD.2019040104

Ibrahim, F., & Zainin, N. M. (2021). Exploring the Technological Impacts: The Case of Museums in Brunei Darussalam. *International Journal of Tourism and Hospitality Management in the Digital Age*, 5(1), 1–18. https://doi.org/10.4018/IJTHMDA.2021010101

Igbinakhase, I. (2017). Responsible and Sustainable Management Practices in Developing and Developed Business Environments. In Fields, Z. (Ed.), *Collective Creativity for Responsible and Sustainable Business Practice* (pp. 180–207). Hershey, PA: IGI Global. DOI: 10.4018/978-1-5225-1823-5.ch010

Iwata, J. J., & Hoskins, R. G. (2017). Managing Indigenous Knowledge in Tanzania: A Business Perspective. In Jain, P., & Mnjama, N. (Eds.), *Managing Knowledge Resources and Records in Modern Organizations* (pp. 198–214). Hershey, PA: IGI Global. DOI: 10.4018/978-1-5225-1965-2.ch012

Jain, P. (2017). Ethical and Legal Issues in Knowledge Management Life-Cycle in Business. In Jain, P., & Mnjama, N. (Eds.), *Managing Knowledge Resources and Records in Modern Organizations* (pp. 82–101). Hershey, PA: IGI Global. DOI: 10.4018/978-1-5225-1965-2.ch006

James, S., & Hauli, E. (2017). Holistic Management Education at Tanzanian Rural Development Planning Institute. In Baporikar, N. (Ed.), *Management Education for Global Leadership* (pp. 112–136). Hershey, PA: IGI Global. DOI: 10.4018/978-1-5225-1013-0.ch006

Jančec, L., & Vodopivec, J. L. (2019). The Implicit Pedagogy and the Hidden Curriculum in Postmodern Education. In Vodopivec, J., Jančec, L., & Štemberger, T. (Eds.), *Implicit Pedagogy for Optimized Learning in Contemporary Education* (pp. 41–59). IGI Global. https://doi.org/10.4018/978-1-5225-5799-9.ch003

Janošková, M., Csikósová, A., & Čulková, K. (2018). Measurement of Company Performance as Part of Its Strategic Management. In Leon, R. (Ed.), *Managerial Strategies for Business Sustainability During Turbulent Times* (pp. 309–335). Hershey, PA: IGI Global. DOI: 10.4018/978-1-5225-2716-9.ch017

Janus, M., & Siddiqua, A. (2018). Challenges for Children With Special Health Needs at the Time of Transition to School. In I. Management Association (Ed.), *Autism Spectrum Disorders: Breakthroughs in Research and Practice* (pp. 339-371). Hershey, PA: IGI Global. DOI: 10.4018/978-1-5225-3827-1.ch018

Jean-Vasile, A., & Alecu, A. (2017). Theoretical and Practical Approaches in Understanding the Influences of Cost-Productivity-Profit Trinomial in Contemporary Enterprises. In Jean Vasile, A., & Nicolò, D. (Eds.), *Sustainable Entrepreneurship and Investments in the Green Economy* (pp. 28–62). Hershey, PA: IGI Global. DOI: 10.4018/978-1-5225-2075-7.ch002

Jesus, R. A. (2018). Screencasts and Learning Styles. In M. Khosrow-Pour, D.B.A. (Ed.), *Encyclopedia of Information Science and Technology, Fourth Edition* (pp. 1548-1558). Hershey, PA: IGI Global. DOI: 10.4018/978-1-5225-2255-3.ch134

John, G., Francis, N., & Santhakumar, A. B. (2022). Student Engagement: Past, Present, and Future. In Ramlall, S., Cross, T., & Love, M. (Eds.), *Handbook of Research on Future of Work and Education: Implications for Curriculum Delivery and Work Design* (pp. 329–341). IGI Global. https://doi.org/10.4018/978-1-7998-8275-6.ch020

Joia, L. A., & Correia, J. C. (2018). CIO Competencies From the IT Professional Perspective: Insights From Brazil. *Journal of Global Information Management*, 26(2), 74–103. DOI: 10.4018/JGIM.2018040104

Juma, A., & Mzera, N. (2017). Knowledge Management and Records Management and Competitive Advantage in Business. In Jain, P., & Mnjama, N. (Eds.), *Managing Knowledge Resources and Records in Modern Organizations* (pp. 15–28). Hershey, PA: IGI Global. DOI: 10.4018/978-1-5225-1965-2.ch002

K., I., & A, V. (2018). Monitoring and Auditing in the Cloud. In K. Munir (Ed.), *Cloud Computing Technologies for Green Enterprises* (pp. 318-350). Hershey, PA: IGI Global. https://doi.org/DOI: 10.4018/978-1-5225-3038-1.ch013

Kabra, G., Ghosh, V., & Ramesh, A. (2018). Enterprise Integrated Business Process Management and Business Intelligence Framework for Business Process Sustainability. In Paul, A., Bhattacharyya, D., & Anand, S. (Eds.), *Green Initiatives for Business Sustainability and Value Creation* (pp. 228–238). Hershey, PA: IGI Global. DOI: 10.4018/978-1-5225-2662-9.ch010

Kaoud, M. (2017). Investigation of Customer Knowledge Management: A Case Study Research. *International Journal of Service Science, Management, Engineering, and Technology*, 8(2), 12–22. DOI: 10.4018/IJSSMET.2017040102

Karpinski, A. C., D'Agostino, J. V., Williams, A. K., Highland, S. A., & Mellott, J. A. (2018). The Relationship Between Online Formative Assessment and State Test Scores Using Multilevel Modeling. In M. Khosrow-Pour, D.B.A. (Ed.), *Encyclopedia of Information Science and Technology, Fourth Edition* (pp. 5183-5192). Hershey, PA: IGI Global. DOI: 10.4018/978-1-5225-2255-3.ch450

Kats, Y. (2017). Educational Leadership and Integrated Support for Students with Autism Spectrum Disorders. In I. Management Association (Ed.), *Educational Leadership and Administration: Concepts, Methodologies, Tools, and Applications* (pp. 101-114). Hershey, PA: IGI Global. https://doi.org/DOI: 10.4018/978-1-5225-1624-8.ch007

Katuu, S. (2018). A Comparative Assessment of Enterprise Content Management Maturity Models. In Gwangwava, N., & Mutingi, M. (Eds.), *E-Manufacturing and E-Service Strategies in Contemporary Organizations* (pp. 93–118). Hershey, PA: IGI Global. DOI: 10.4018/978-1-5225-3628-4.ch005

Kaya, G., & Altun, A. (2018). Educational Ontology Development. In M. Khosrow-Pour, D.B.A. (Ed.), *Encyclopedia of Information Science and Technology, Fourth Edition* (pp. 1441-1450). Hershey, PA: IGI Global. DOI: 10.4018/978-1-5225-2255-3.ch124

Keough, P. D., & Pacis, D. (2017). Best Practices Implementing Special Education Curriculum and Common Core State Standards using UDL. In Dickenson, P., Keough, P., & Courduff, J. (Eds.), *Preparing Pre-Service Teachers for the Inclusive Classroom* (pp. 107–123). Hershey, PA: IGI Global. DOI: 10.4018/978-1-5225-1753-5.ch006

Khan, M. Y., & Abir, T. (2022). The Role of Social Media Marketing in the Tourism and Hospitality Industry: A Conceptual Study on Bangladesh. In Ramos, C., Quinteiro, S., & Gonçalves, A. (Eds.), *ICT as Innovator Between Tourism and Culture* (pp. 213–229). IGI Global. https://doi.org/10.4018/978-1-7998-8165-0.ch013

Kilburn, M., Henckell, M., & Starrett, D. (2018). Factors Contributing to the Effectiveness of Online Students and Instructors. In M. Khosrow-Pour, D.B.A. (Ed.), *Encyclopedia of Information Science and Technology, Fourth Edition* (pp. 1451-1462). Hershey, PA: IGI Global. DOI: 10.4018/978-1-5225-2255-3.ch125

Kinnunen, S., Ylä-Kujala, A., Marttonen-Arola, S., Kärri, T., & Baglee, D. (2018). Internet of Things in Asset Management: Insights from Industrial Professionals and Academia. *International Journal of Service Science, Management, Engineering, and Technology*, 9(2), 104–119. DOI: 10.4018/IJSSMET.2018040105

Klein, A. Z., Sabino de Freitas, A., Machado, L., Freitas, J. C.Jr, Graziola, P. G.Jr, & Schlemmer, E. (2017). Virtual Worlds Applications for Management Education. In Tomei, L. (Ed.), *Exploring the New Era of Technology-Infused Education* (pp. 279–299). Hershey, PA: IGI Global. DOI: 10.4018/978-1-5225-1709-2.ch017

Koban Koç, D. (2021). Gender and Language: A Sociolinguistic Analysis of Second Language Writing. In Hancı-Azizoglu, E., & Kavaklı, N. (Eds.), *Futuristic and Linguistic Perspectives on Teaching Writing to Second Language Students* (pp. 161–177). IGI Global. https://doi.org/10.4018/978-1-7998-6508-7.ch010

Konecny, L. T. (2017). Hybrid, Online, and Flipped Classrooms in Health Science: Enhanced Learning Environments. In I. Management Association (Ed.), *Flipped Instruction: Breakthroughs in Research and Practice* (pp. 355-370). Hershey, PA: IGI Global. https://doi.org/DOI: 10.4018/978-1-5225-1803-7.ch020

Kővári, E., Saleh, M., & Steinbachné Hajmásy, G. (2022). The Impact of Corporate Digital Responsibility (CDR) on Internal Stakeholders' Satisfaction in Hungarian Upscale Hotels. In Valeri, M. (Ed.), *New Governance and Management in Touristic Destinations* (pp. 35–51). IGI Global. https://doi.org/10.4018/978-1-6684-3889-3.ch003

Kożuch, B., & Jabłoński, A. (2017). Adopting the Concept of Business Models in Public Management. In Lewandowski, M., & Kożuch, B. (Eds.), *Public Sector Entrepreneurship and the Integration of Innovative Business Models* (pp. 10–46). Hershey, PA: IGI Global. DOI: 10.4018/978-1-5225-2215-7.ch002

Kumar, J., Adhikary, A., & Jha, A. (2017). Small Active Investors' Perceptions and Preferences Towards Tax Saving Mutual Fund Schemes in Eastern India: An Empirical Note. *International Journal of Asian Business and Information Management*, 8(2), 35–45. DOI: 10.4018/IJABIM.2017040103

Kupietz, K. D. (2021). Gaming and Simulation in Public Education: Teaching Others to Help Themselves and Their Neighbors. In Drumhiller, N., Wilkin, T., & Srba, K. (Eds.), *Simulation and Game-Based Learning in Emergency and Disaster Management* (pp. 41–62). IGI Global. https://doi.org/10.4018/978-1-7998-4087-9.ch003

Kwee, C. T. (2022). Assessing the International Student Enrolment Strategies in Australian Universities: A Case Study During the COVID-19 Pandemic. In Alaali, M. (Ed.), *Assessing University Governance and Policies in Relation to the COVID-19 Pandemic* (pp. 162–188). IGI Global. https://doi.org/10.4018/978-1-7998-8279-4.ch010

Latusi, S., & Fissore, M. (2021). Pilgrimage Routes to Happiness: Comparing the Camino de Santiago and Via Francigena. In Perinotto, A., Mayer, V., & Soares, J. (Eds.), *Rebuilding and Restructuring the Tourism Industry: Infusion of Happiness and Quality of Life* (pp. 157–182). IGI Global. https://doi.org/10.4018/978-1-7998-7239-9.ch008

Lauricella, S., & McArthur, F. A. (2022). Taking a Student-Centred Approach to Alternative Digital Credentials: Multiple Pathways Toward the Acquisition of Microcredentials. In Piedra, D. (Ed.), *Innovations in the Design and Application of Alternative Digital Credentials* (pp. 57–69). IGI Global. https://doi.org/10.4018/978-1-7998-7697-7.ch003

Lavassani, K. M., & Movahedi, B. (2017). Applications Driven Information Systems: Beyond Networks toward Business Ecosystems. *International Journal of Innovation in the Digital Economy*, 8(1), 61–75. DOI: 10.4018/IJIDE.2017010104

Lazzareschi, V. H., & Brito, M. S. (2017). Strategic Information Management: Proposal of Business Project Model. In Jamil, G., Soares, A., & Pessoa, C. (Eds.), *Handbook of Research on Information Management for Effective Logistics and Supply Chains* (pp. 59–88). Hershey, PA: IGI Global. DOI: 10.4018/978-1-5225-0973-8.ch004

Lechuga Sancho, M. P., & Martín Navarro, A. (2022). Evolution of the Literature on Social Responsibility in the Tourism Sector: A Systematic Literature Review. In Fernandes, G. (Ed.), *Challenges and New Opportunities for Tourism in Inland Territories: Ecocultural Resources and Sustainable Initiatives* (pp. 169–186). IGI Global. https://doi.org/10.4018/978-1-7998-7339-6.ch010

Lederer, M., Kurz, M., & Lazarov, P. (2017). Usage and Suitability of Methods for Strategic Business Process Initiatives: A Multi Case Study Research. *International Journal of Productivity Management and Assessment Technologies*, 5(1), 40–51. DOI: 10.4018/IJPMAT.2017010103

Lee, I. (2017). A Social Enterprise Business Model and a Case Study of Pacific Community Ventures (PCV). In Potocan, V., Ünğan, M., & Nedelko, Z. (Eds.), *Handbook of Research on Managerial Solutions in Non-Profit Organizations* (pp. 182–204). Hershey, PA: IGI Global. DOI: 10.4018/978-1-5225-0731-4.ch009

Leon, L. A., Seal, K. C., Przasnyski, Z. H., & Wiedenman, I. (2017). Skills and Competencies Required for Jobs in Business Analytics: A Content Analysis of Job Advertisements Using Text Mining. *International Journal of Business Intelligence Research*, 8(1), 1–25. DOI: 10.4018/IJBIR.2017010101

Levy, C. L., & Elias, N. I. (2017). SOHO Users' Perceptions of Reliability and Continuity of Cloud-Based Services. In Moore, M. (Ed.), *Cybersecurity Breaches and Issues Surrounding Online Threat Protection* (pp. 248–287). Hershey, PA: IGI Global. DOI: 10.4018/978-1-5225-1941-6.ch011

Levy, M. (2018). Change Management Serving Knowledge Management and Organizational Development: Reflections and Review. In Baporikar, N. (Ed.), *Global Practices in Knowledge Management for Societal and Organizational Development* (pp. 256–270). Hershey, PA: IGI Global. DOI: 10.4018/978-1-5225-3009-1.ch012

Lewandowski, M. (2017). Public Organizations and Business Model Innovation: The Role of Public Service Design. In Lewandowski, M., & Kożuch, B. (Eds.), *Public Sector Entrepreneurship and the Integration of Innovative Business Models* (pp. 47–72). Hershey, PA: IGI Global. DOI: 10.4018/978-1-5225-2215-7.ch003

Lhannaoui, H., Kabbaj, M. I., & Bakkoury, Z. (2017). A Survey of Risk-Aware Business Process Modelling. *International Journal of Risk and Contingency Management*, 6(3), 14–26. DOI: 10.4018/IJRCM.2017070102

Li, J., Sun, W., Jiang, W., Yang, H., & Zhang, L. (2017). How the Nature of Exogenous Shocks and Crises Impact Company Performance?: The Effects of Industry Characteristics. *International Journal of Risk and Contingency Management*, 6(4), 40–55. DOI: 10.4018/IJRCM.2017100103

Llamas, M. F. (2019). Intercultural Awareness in Teaching English for Early Childhood: A Film-Based Approach. In Domínguez Romero, E., Bobkina, J., & Stefanova, S. (Eds.), *Teaching Literature and Language Through Multimodal Texts* (pp. 54–68). IGI Global. https://doi.org/10.4018/978-1-5225-5796-8.ch004

Lokhtina, I., & Kkese, E. T. (2022). Reflecting and Adapting to an Academic Workplace Before and After the Lockdown in Greek-Speaking Cyprus: Opportunities and Challenges. In Zhuplev, A., & Koepp, R. (Eds.), *Global Trends, Dynamics, and Imperatives for Strategic Development in Business Education in an Age of Disruption* (pp. 126–148). IGI Global. https://doi.org/10.4018/978-1-7998-7548-2.ch007

Lopez-Fernandez, M., Perez-Perez, M., Serrano-Bedia, A., & Cobo-Gonzalez, A. (2021). Small and Medium Tourism Enterprise Survival in Times of Crisis: "El Capricho de Gaudí. In Toubes, D., & Araújo-Vila, N. (Eds.), *Risk, Crisis, and Disaster Management in Small and Medium-Sized Tourism Enterprises* (pp. 103–129). IGI Global. DOI: 10.4018/978-1-7998-6996-2.ch005

Lovell, K. L. (2017). Development and Evaluation of Neuroscience Computer-Based Modules for Medical Students: Instructional Design Principles and Effectiveness. In Stefaniak, J. (Ed.), *Advancing Medical Education Through Strategic Instructional Design* (pp. 262–276). Hershey, PA: IGI Global. DOI: 10.4018/978-1-5225-2098-6.ch013

Mahajan, A., Maidullah, S., & Hossain, M. R. (2022). Experience Toward Smart Tour Guide Apps in Travelling: An Analysis of Users' Reviews on Audio Odigos and Trip My Way. In R. Augusto Costa, F. Brandão, Z. Breda, & C. Costa (Eds.), *Planning and Managing the Experience Economy in Tourism* (pp. 255-273). IGI Global. https://doi.org/10.4018/978-1-7998-8775-1.ch014

Maher, D. (2019). The Use of Course Management Systems in Pre-Service Teacher Education. In Keengwe, J. (Ed.), *Handbook of Research on Blended Learning Pedagogies and Professional Development in Higher Education* (pp. 196–213). IGI Global. https://doi.org/10.4018/978-1-5225-5557-5.ch011

Makewa, L. N. (2019). Teacher Technology Competence Base. In Makewa, L., Ngussa, B., & Kuboja, J. (Eds.), *Technology-Supported Teaching and Research Methods for Educators* (pp. 247–267). IGI Global. https://doi.org/10.4018/978-1-5225-5915-3.ch014

Malega, P. (2017). Small and Medium Enterprises in the Slovak Republic: Status and Competitiveness of SMEs in the Global Markets and Possibilities of Optimization. In Vemić, M. (Ed.), *Optimal Management Strategies in Small and Medium Enterprises* (pp. 102–124). Hershey, PA: IGI Global. DOI: 10.4018/978-1-5225-1949-2.ch006

Malewska, K. M. (2017). Intuition in Decision-Making on the Example of a Non-Profit Organization. In Potocan, V., Ünğan, M., & Nedelko, Z. (Eds.), *Handbook of Research on Managerial Solutions in Non-Profit Organizations* (pp. 378–399). Hershey, PA: IGI Global. DOI: 10.4018/978-1-5225-0731-4.ch018

Mallett, C. A. (2022). School Resource (Police) Officers in Schools: Impact on Campus Safety, Student Discipline, and Learning. In Crews, G. (Ed.), *Impact of School Shootings on Classroom Culture, Curriculum, and Learning* (pp. 53–70). IGI Global. https://doi.org/10.4018/978-1-7998-5200-1.ch004

Marinho, J. E., Freitas, I. R., Leão, I. B., Pacheco, L. O., Gonçalves, M. P., Castro, M. J., Silva, P. D., & Moreira, R. J. (2022). Project-Based Learning Application in Higher Education: Student Experiences and Perspectives. In Alves, A., & van Hattum-Janssen, N. (Eds.), *Training Engineering Students for Modern Technological Advancement* (pp. 146–164). IGI Global. https://doi.org/10.4018/978-1-7998-8816-1.ch007

Maroofi, F. (2017). Entrepreneurial Orientation and Organizational Learning Ability Analysis for Innovation and Firm Performance. In Baporikar, N. (Ed.), *Innovation and Shifting Perspectives in Management Education* (pp. 144–165). Hershey, PA: IGI Global. DOI: 10.4018/978-1-5225-1019-2.ch007

Marques, M., Moleiro, D., Brito, T. M., & Marques, T. (2021). Customer Relationship Management as an Important Relationship Marketing Tool: The Case of the Hospitality Industry in Estoril Coast. In M. Dinis, L. Bonixe, S. Lamy, & Z. Breda (Eds.), *Impact of New Media in Tourism* (pp. 39-56). IGI Global. https://doi.org/ DOI: 10.4018/978-1-7998-7095-1.ch003

Martins, P. V., & Zacarias, M. (2017). A Web-based Tool for Business Process Improvement. *International Journal of Web Portals*, 9(2), 68–84. DOI: 10.4018/ IJWP.2017070104

Matthies, B., & Coners, A. (2017). Exploring the Conceptual Nature of e-Business Projects. *Journal of Electronic Commerce in Organizations*, 15(3), 33–63. DOI: 10.4018/JECO.2017070103

Mayer, V. F., Fraga, C. C., & Silva, L. C. (2021). Contributions of Neurosciences to Studies of Well-Being in Tourism. In Perinotto, A., Mayer, V., & Soares, J. (Eds.), *Rebuilding and Restructuring the Tourism Industry: Infusion of Happiness and Quality of Life* (pp. 108–128). IGI Global. https://doi.org/10.4018/978-1-7998-7239-9.ch006

McCleskey, J. A., & Melton, R. M. (2022). Rolling With the Flow: Online Faculty and Student Presence in a Post-COVID-19 World. In Ramlall, S., Cross, T., & Love, M. (Eds.), *Handbook of Research on Future of Work and Education: Implications for Curriculum Delivery and Work Design* (pp. 307–328). IGI Global. https://doi.org/10.4018/978-1-7998-8275-6.ch019

McCormack, V. F., Stauffer, M., Fishley, K., Hohenbrink, J., Mascazine, J. R., & Zigler, T. (2018). Designing a Dual Licensure Path for Middle Childhood and Special Education Teacher Candidates. In Polly, D., Putman, M., Petty, T., & Good, A. (Eds.), *Innovative Practices in Teacher Preparation and Graduate-Level Teacher Education Programs* (pp. 21–36). Hershey, PA: IGI Global. DOI: 10.4018/978-1-5225-3068-8.ch002

McDaniel, R. (2017). Strategic Leadership in Instructional Design: Applying the Principles of Instructional Design through the Lens of Strategic Leadership to Distance Education. In Wang, V. (Ed.), *Encyclopedia of Strategic Leadership and Management* (pp. 1570–1584). Hershey, PA: IGI Global. DOI: 10.4018/978-1-5225-1049-9.ch109

McKee, J. (2018). Architecture as a Tool to Solve Business Planning Problems. In M. Khosrow-Pour, D.B.A. (Ed.), *Encyclopedia of Information Science and Technology, Fourth Edition* (pp. 573-586). Hershey, PA: IGI Global. DOI: 10.4018/978-1-5225-2255-3.ch050

McKinney, R. E., Halli-Tierney, A. D., Gold, A. E., Allen, R. S., & Carroll, D. G. (2022). Interprofessional Education: Using Standardized Cases in Face-to-Face and Remote Learning Settings. In Ford, C., & Garza, K. (Eds.), *Handbook of Research on Updating and Innovating Health Professions Education: Post-Pandemic Perspectives* (pp. 24–42). IGI Global. https://doi.org/10.4018/978-1-7998-7623-6.ch002

McMurray, A. J., Cross, J., & Caponecchia, C. (2018). The Risk Management Profession in Australia: Business Continuity Plan Practices. In Bajgoric, N. (Ed.), *Always-On Enterprise Information Systems for Modern Organizations* (pp. 112–129). Hershey, PA: IGI Global. DOI: 10.4018/978-1-5225-3704-5.ch006

Meddah, I. H., & Belkadi, K. (2018). Mining Patterns Using Business Process Management. In Hamou, R. (Ed.), *Handbook of Research on Biomimicry in Information Retrieval and Knowledge Management* (pp. 78–89). Hershey, PA: IGI Global. DOI: 10.4018/978-1-5225-3004-6.ch005

Meintjes, H. H. (2021). Learner Views of a Facebook Page as a Supportive Digital Pedagogical Tool at a Public South African School in a Grade 12 Business Studies Class. *International Journal of Smart Education and Urban Society*, 12(2), 32–45. https://doi.org/10.4018/IJSEUS.2021040104

Melero-García, F. (2022). Training Bilingual Interpreters in Healthcare Settings: Student Perceptions of Online Learning. In LeLoup, J., & Swanson, P. (Eds.), *Handbook of Research on Effective Online Language Teaching in a Disruptive Environment* (pp. 288–310). IGI Global. https://doi.org/10.4018/978-1-7998-7720-2.ch015

Meletiadou, E. (2022). The Use of Peer Assessment as an Inclusive Learning Strategy in Higher Education Institutions: Enhancing Student Writing Skills and Motivation. In Meletiadou, E. (Ed.), *Handbook of Research on Policies and Practices for Assessing Inclusive Teaching and Learning* (pp. 1–26). IGI Global. https://doi.org/10.4018/978-1-7998-8579-5.ch001

Melian, A. G., & Camprubí, R. (2021). The Accessibility of Museum Websites: The Case of Barcelona. In Eusébio, C., Teixeira, L., & Carneiro, M. (Eds.), *ICT Tools and Applications for Accessible Tourism* (pp. 234–255). IGI Global. https://doi.org/10.4018/978-1-7998-6428-8.ch011

Memon, R. N., Ahmad, R., & Salim, S. S. (2018). Critical Issues in Requirements Engineering Education. In I. Management Association (Ed.), *Computer Systems and Software Engineering: Concepts, Methodologies, Tools, and Applications* (pp. 1953-1976). Hershey, PA: IGI Global. DOI: 10.4018/978-1-5225-3923-0.ch081

Mendenhall, R. (2017). Western Governors University: CBE Innovator and National Model. In Rasmussen, K., Northrup, P., & Colson, R. (Eds.), *Handbook of Research on Competency-Based Education in University Settings* (pp. 379–400). Hershey, PA: IGI Global. DOI: 10.4018/978-1-5225-0932-5.ch019

Mendes, L. (2017). TQM and Knowledge Management: An Integrated Approach Towards Tacit Knowledge Management. In Jaziri-Bouagina, D., & Jamil, G. (Eds.), *Handbook of Research on Tacit Knowledge Management for Organizational Success* (pp. 236–263). Hershey, PA: IGI Global. DOI: 10.4018/978-1-5225-2394-9.ch009

Menezes, V. D., & Cavagnaro, E. (2021). Communicating Sustainable Initiatives in the Hotel Industry: The Case of the Hotel Jakarta Amsterdam. In F. Brandão, Z. Breda, R. Costa, & C. Costa (Eds.), *Handbook of Research on the Role of Tourism in Achieving Sustainable Development Goals* (pp. 224-234). IGI Global. https://doi .org/10.4018/978-1-7998-5691-7.ch013

Menezes, V. D., & Cavagnaro, E. (2021). Communicating Sustainable Initiatives in the Hotel Industry: The Case of the Hotel Jakarta Amsterdam. In F. Brandão, Z. Breda, R. Costa, & C. Costa (Eds.), *Handbook of Research on the Role of Tourism in Achieving Sustainable Development Goals* (pp. 224-234). IGI Global. https://doi .org/10.4018/978-1-7998-5691-7.ch013

Mense, E. G., Griggs, D. M., & Shanks, J. N. (2018). School Leaders in a Time of Accountability and Data Use: Preparing Our Future School Leaders in Leadership Preparation Programs. In Mense, E., & Crain-Dorough, M. (Eds.), *Data Leadership for K-12 Schools in a Time of Accountability* (pp. 235–259). Hershey, PA: IGI Global. DOI: 10.4018/978-1-5225-3188-3.ch012

Mense, E. G., Griggs, D. M., & Shanks, J. N. (2018). School Leaders in a Time of Accountability and Data Use: Preparing Our Future School Leaders in Leadership Preparation Programs. In Mense, E., & Crain-Dorough, M. (Eds.), *Data Leadership for K-12 Schools in a Time of Accountability* (pp. 235–259). Hershey, PA: IGI Global. DOI: 10.4018/978-1-5225-3188-3.ch012

Mestry, R., & Naicker, S. R. (2017). Exploring Distributive Leadership in South African Public Primary Schools in the Soweto Region. In I. Management Association (Ed.), *Educational Leadership and Administration: Concepts, Methodologies, Tools, and Applications* (pp. 1041-1064). Hershey, PA: IGI Global. DOI: 10.4018/978-1-5225-1624-8.ch050

Mitas, O., Bastiaansen, M., & Boode, W. (2022). If You're Happy, I'm Happy: Emotion Contagion at a Tourist Information Center. In R. Augusto Costa, F. Brandão, Z. Breda, & C. Costa (Eds.), *Planning and Managing the Experience Economy in Tourism* (pp. 122-140). IGI Global. https://doi.org/10.4018/978-1-7998-8775-1.ch007

Mnjama, N. M. (2017). Preservation of Recorded Information in Public and Private Sector Organizations. In Jain, P., & Mnjama, N. (Eds.), *Managing Knowledge Resources and Records in Modern Organizations* (pp. 149–167). Hershey, PA: IGI Global. DOI: 10.4018/978-1-5225-1965-2.ch009

Mokoqama, M., & Fields, Z. (2017). Principles of Responsible Management Education (PRME): Call for Responsible Management Education. In Fields, Z. (Ed.), *Collective Creativity for Responsible and Sustainable Business Practice* (pp. 229–241). Hershey, PA: IGI Global. DOI: 10.4018/978-1-5225-1823-5.ch012

Monaghan, C. H., & Boboc, M. (2017). (Re) Defining Leadership in Higher Education in the U.S. In Wang, V. (Ed.), *Encyclopedia of Strategic Leadership and Management* (pp. 567–579). Hershey, PA: IGI Global. DOI: 10.4018/978-1-5225-1049-9.ch040

Monteiro, A., Lopes, S., & Carbone, F. (2021). Academic Mobility: Bridging Tourism and Peace Education. In J. da Silva, Z. Breda, & F. Carbone (Eds.), *Role and Impact of Tourism in Peacebuilding and Conflict Transformation* (pp. 275-301). IGI Global. https://doi.org/10.4018/978-1-7998-5053-3.ch016

Morall, M. B. (2021). Reimagining Mobile Phones: Multiple Literacies and Digital Media Compositions. In C. Moran (Eds.), *Affordances and Constraints of Mobile Phone Use in English Language Arts Classrooms* (pp. 41-53). IGI Global. https://doi.org/10.4018/978-1-7998-5805-8.ch003

Mthethwa, V. (2022). Student Governance and the Academic Minefield During COVID-19 Lockdown in South Africa. In Alaali, M. (Ed.), *Assessing University Governance and Policies in Relation to the COVID-19 Pandemic* (pp. 255–276). IGI Global. https://doi.org/10.4018/978-1-7998-8279-4.ch015

Muniapan, B. (2017). Philosophy and Management: The Relevance of Vedanta in Management. In Ordóñez de Pablos, P. (Ed.), *Managerial Strategies and Solutions for Business Success in Asia* (pp. 124–139). Hershey, PA: IGI Global. DOI: 10.4018/978-1-5225-1886-0.ch007

Murad, S. E., & Dowaji, S. (2017). Using Value-Based Approach for Managing Cloud-Based Services. In Turuk, A., Sahoo, B., & Addya, S. (Eds.), *Resource Management and Efficiency in Cloud Computing Environments* (pp. 33–60). Hershey, PA: IGI Global. DOI: 10.4018/978-1-5225-1721-4.ch002

Mutahar, A. M., Daud, N. M., Thurasamy, R., Isaac, O., & Abdulsalam, R. (2018). The Mediating of Perceived Usefulness and Perceived Ease of Use: The Case of Mobile Banking in Yemen. *International Journal of Technology Diffusion*, 9(2), 21–40. DOI: 10.4018/IJTD.2018040102

Muthee, J. M., & Murungi, C. G. (2018). Relationship Among Intelligence, Achievement Motivation, Type of School, and Academic Performance of Kenyan Urban Primary School Pupils. In M. Khosrow-Pour, D.B.A. (Ed.), *Encyclopedia of Information Science and Technology, Fourth Edition* (pp. 1540-1547). Hershey, PA: IGI Global. https://doi.org/DOI: 10.4018/978-1-5225-2255-3.ch133

Naidoo, V. (2017). E-Learning and Management Education at African Universities. In Baporikar, N. (Ed.), *Management Education for Global Leadership* (pp. 181–201). Hershey, PA: IGI Global. DOI: 10.4018/978-1-5225-1013-0.ch009

Naidoo, V., & Igbinakhase, I. (2018). Opportunities and Challenges of Knowledge Retention in SMEs. In Baporikar, N. (Ed.), *Knowledge Integration Strategies for Entrepreneurship and Sustainability* (pp. 70–94). Hershey, PA: IGI Global. DOI: 10.4018/978-1-5225-5115-7.ch004

Naranjo, J. (2018). Meeting the Need for Inclusive Educators Online: Teacher Education in Inclusive Special Education and Dual-Certification. In Polly, D., Putman, M., Petty, T., & Good, A. (Eds.), *Innovative Practices in Teacher Preparation and Graduate-Level Teacher Education Programs* (pp. 106–122). Hershey, PA: IGI Global. DOI: 10.4018/978-1-5225-3068-8.ch007

Naumov, N., & Costandachi, G. (2021). Creativity and Entrepreneurship: Gastronomic Tourism in Mexico. In Soares, J. (Ed.), *Innovation and Entrepreneurial Opportunities in Community Tourism* (pp. 90–108). IGI Global. https://doi.org/10.4018/978-1-7998-4855-4.ch006

Nayak, S., & Prabhu, N. (2017). Paradigm Shift in Management Education: Need for a Cross Functional Perspective. In Baporikar, N. (Ed.), *Management Education for Global Leadership* (pp. 241–255). Hershey, PA: IGI Global. DOI: 10.4018/978-1-5225-1013-0.ch012

Nedelko, Z., & Potocan, V. (2017). Management Solutions in Non-Profit Organizations: Case of Slovenia. In Potocan, V., Üngan, M., & Nedelko, Z. (Eds.), *Handbook of Research on Managerial Solutions in Non-Profit Organizations* (pp. 1–22). Hershey, PA: IGI Global. DOI: 10.4018/978-1-5225-0731-4.ch001

Nedelko, Z., & Potocan, V. (2017). Priority of Management Tools Utilization among Managers: International Comparison. In Wang, V. (Ed.), *Encyclopedia of Strategic Leadership and Management* (pp. 1083–1094). Hershey, PA: IGI Global. DOI: 10.4018/978-1-5225-1049-9.ch075

Nedelko, Z., Raudeliūnienė, J., & Črešnar, R. (2018). Knowledge Dynamics in Supply Chain Management. In Baporikar, N. (Ed.), *Knowledge Integration Strategies for Entrepreneurship and Sustainability* (pp. 150–166). Hershey, PA: IGI Global. DOI: 10.4018/978-1-5225-5115-7.ch008

Nguyen, H. T., & Hipsher, S. A. (2018). Innovation and Creativity Used by Private Sector Firms in a Resources-Constrained Environment. In Hipsher, S. (Ed.), *Examining the Private Sector's Role in Wealth Creation and Poverty Reduction* (pp. 219–238). Hershey, PA: IGI Global. DOI: 10.4018/978-1-5225-3117-3.ch010

Nkabinde, Z. P. (2017). Multiculturalism in Special Education: Perspectives of Minority Children in Urban Schools. In Keengwe, J. (Ed.), *Handbook of Research on Promoting Cross-Cultural Competence and Social Justice in Teacher Education* (pp. 382–397). Hershey, PA: IGI Global. DOI: 10.4018/978-1-5225-0897-7.ch020

Nkabinde, Z. P. (2018). Online Instruction: Is the Quality the Same as Face-to-Face Instruction? In Keengwe, J. (Ed.), *Handbook of Research on Digital Content, Mobile Learning, and Technology Integration Models in Teacher Education* (pp. 300–314). Hershey, PA: IGI Global. DOI: 10.4018/978-1-5225-2953-8.ch016

Nugroho, A., & Albusaidi, S. S. (2022). Internationalization of Higher Education: The Methodological Critiques on the Research Related to Study Overseas and International Experience. In Magd, H., & Kunjumuhammed, S. (Eds.), *Global Perspectives on Quality Assurance and Accreditation in Higher Education Institutions* (pp. 75–89). IGI Global. https://doi.org/10.4018/978-1-7998-8085-1.ch005

Nulty, Z., & West, S. G. (2022). Student Engagement and Supporting Students With Accommodations. In Bull, P., & Patterson, G. (Eds.), *Redefining Teacher Education and Teacher Preparation Programs in the Post-COVID-19 Era* (pp. 99–116). IGI Global. https://doi.org/10.4018/978-1-7998-8298-5.ch006

O'Connor, J. R.Jr, & Jackson, K. N. (2017). The Use of iPad® Devices and "Apps" for ASD Students in Special Education and Speech Therapy. In Kats, Y. (Ed.), *Supporting the Education of Children with Autism Spectrum Disorders* (pp. 267–283). Hershey, PA: IGI Global. DOI: 10.4018/978-1-5225-0816-8.ch014

Obicci, P. A. (2017). Risk Sharing in a Partnership. In *Risk Management Strategies in Public-Private Partnerships* (pp. 115–152). Hershey, PA: IGI Global. DOI: 10.4018/978-1-5225-2503-5.ch004

Obidallah, W. J., & Raahemi, B. (2017). Managing Changes in Service Oriented Virtual Organizations: A Structural and Procedural Framework to Facilitate the Process of Change. *Journal of Electronic Commerce in Organizations*, 15(1), 59–83. DOI: 10.4018/JECO.2017010104

Ojo, O. (2017). Impact of Innovation on the Entrepreneurial Success in Selected Business Enterprises in South-West Nigeria. *International Journal of Innovation in the Digital Economy*, 8(2), 29–38. DOI: 10.4018/IJIDE.2017040103

Okdinawati, L., Simatupang, T. M., & Sunitiyoso, Y. (2017). Multi-Agent Reinforcement Learning for Value Co-Creation of Collaborative Transportation Management (CTM). *International Journal of Information Systems and Supply Chain Management*, 10(3), 84–95. DOI: 10.4018/IJISSCM.2017070105

Okolie, U. C., & Yasin, A. M. (2017). TVET in Developing Nations and Human Development. In Okolie, U., & Yasin, A. (Eds.), *Technical Education and Vocational Training in Developing Nations* (pp. 1–25). Hershey, PA: IGI Global. DOI: 10.4018/978-1-5225-1811-2.ch001

Olivera, V. A., & Carrillo, I. M. (2021). Organizational Culture: A Key Element for the Development of Mexican Micro and Small Tourist Companies. In Soares, J. (Ed.), *Innovation and Entrepreneurial Opportunities in Community Tourism* (pp. 227–242). IGI Global. DOI: 10.4018/978-1-7998-4855-4.ch013

Ossorio, M. (2022). Corporate Museum Experiences in Enogastronomic Tourism. In R. Augusto Costa, F. Brandão, Z. Breda, & C. Costa (Eds.), *Planning and Managing the Experience Economy in Tourism* (pp. 107-121). IGI Global. https://doi .org/DOI: 10.4018/978-1-7998-8775-1.ch006

Ossorio, M. (2022). Enogastronomic Tourism in Times of Pandemic. In Fernandes, G. (Ed.), *Challenges and New Opportunities for Tourism in Inland Territories: Ecocultural Resources and Sustainable Initiatives* (pp. 241–255). IGI Global. https://doi.org/10.4018/978-1-7998-7339-6.ch014

Özekici, Y. K. (2022). ICT as an Acculturative Agent and Its Role in the Tourism Context: Introduction, Acculturation Theory, Progress of the Acculturation Theory in Extant Literature. In Ramos, C., Quinteiro, S., & Gonçalves, A. (Eds.), *ICT as Innovator Between Tourism and Culture* (pp. 42–66). IGI Global. https://doi.org/10.4018/978-1-7998-8165-0.ch004

Pack, A., & Barrett, A. (2021). A Review of Virtual Reality and English for Academic Purposes: Understanding Where to Start. *International Journal of Computer-Assisted Language Learning and Teaching*, 11(1), 72–80. https://doi.org/10.4018/IJCALLT.2021010105

Pal, K. (2018). Building High Quality Big Data-Based Applications in Supply Chains. In Kumar, A., & Saurav, S. (Eds.), *Supply Chain Management Strategies and Risk Assessment in Retail Environments* (pp. 1–24). Hershey, PA: IGI Global. DOI: 10.4018/978-1-5225-3056-5.ch001

Palos-Sanchez, P. R., & Correia, M. B. (2018). Perspectives of the Adoption of Cloud Computing in the Tourism Sector. In Rodrigues, J., Ramos, C., Cardoso, P., & Henriques, C. (Eds.), *Handbook of Research on Technological Developments for Cultural Heritage and eTourism Applications* (pp. 377–400). Hershey, PA: IGI Global. DOI: 10.4018/978-1-5225-2927-9.ch018

Papadopoulou, G. (2021). Promoting Gender Equality and Women Empowerment in the Tourism Sector. In F. Brandão, Z. Breda, R. Costa, & C. Costa (Eds.), *Handbook of Research on the Role of Tourism in Achieving Sustainable Development Goals* (pp. 152-174). IGI Global. https://doi.org/DOI: 10.4018/978-1-7998-5691-7.ch009

Papp-Váry, Á. F., & Tóth, T. Z. (2022). Analysis of Budapest as a Film Tourism Destination. In R. Baleiro & R. Pereira (Eds.), *Global Perspectives on Literary Tourism and Film-Induced Tourism* (pp. 257-279). IGI Global. https://doi.org/10.4018/978-1-7998-8262-6.ch014

Pashollari, E. (2019). Building Sustainability Through Environmental Education: Education for Sustainable Development. In L. Wilson, & C. Stevenson (Eds.), *Building Sustainability Through Environmental Education* (pp. 72-88). IGI Global. https://doi.org/10.4018/978-1-5225-7727-0.ch004

Patiño, B. E. (2017). New Generation Management by Convergence and Individual Identity: A Systemic and Human-Oriented Approach. In Baporikar, N. (Ed.), *Innovation and Shifting Perspectives in Management Education* (pp. 119–143). Hershey, PA: IGI Global. DOI: 10.4018/978-1-5225-1019-2.ch006

Patro, C. S. (2021). Digital Tourism: Influence of E-Marketing Technology. In M. Dinis, L. Bonixe, S. Lamy, & Z. Breda (Eds.), *Impact of New Media in Tourism* (pp. 234-254). IGI Global. https://doi.org/10.4018/978-1-7998-7095-1.ch014

Paulson, E. N. (2017). Adapting and Advocating for an Online EdD Program in Changing Times and "Sacred" Cultures. In I. Management Association (Ed.), *Educational Leadership and Administration: Concepts, Methodologies, Tools, and Applications* (pp. 1849-1876). Hershey, PA: IGI Global. https://doi.org/DOI: 10.4018/978-1-5225-1624-8.ch085

Pawliczek, A., & Rössler, M. (2017). Knowledge of Management Tools and Systems in SMEs: Knowledge Transfer in Management. In Bencsik, A. (Ed.), *Knowledge Management Initiatives and Strategies in Small and Medium Enterprises* (pp. 180–203). Hershey, PA: IGI Global. DOI: 10.4018/978-1-5225-1642-2.ch009

Pejic-Bach, M., Omazic, M. A., Aleksic, A., & Zoroja, J. (2018). Knowledge-Based Decision Making: A Multi-Case Analysis. In Leon, R. (Ed.), *Managerial Strategies for Business Sustainability During Turbulent Times* (pp. 160–184). Hershey, PA: IGI Global. DOI: 10.4018/978-1-5225-2716-9.ch009

Perano, M., Hysa, X., & Calabrese, M. (2018). Strategic Planning, Cultural Context, and Business Continuity Management: Business Cases in the City of Shkoder. In Presenza, A., & Sheehan, L. (Eds.), *Geopolitics and Strategic Management in the Global Economy* (pp. 57–77). Hershey, PA: IGI Global. DOI: 10.4018/978-1-5225-2673-5.ch004

Pereira, R., Mira da Silva, M., & Lapão, L. V. (2017). IT Governance Maturity Patterns in Portuguese Healthcare. In De Haes, S., & Van Grembergen, W. (Eds.), *Strategic IT Governance and Alignment in Business Settings* (pp. 24–52). Hershey, PA: IGI Global. DOI: 10.4018/978-1-5225-0861-8.ch002

Pérez-Uribe, R. I., Torres, D. A., Jurado, S. P., & Prada, D. M. (2018). Cloud Tools for the Development of Project Management in SMEs. In Perez-Uribe, R., Salcedo-Perez, C., & Ocampo-Guzman, D. (Eds.), *Handbook of Research on Intrapreneurship and Organizational Sustainability in SMEs* (pp. 95–120). Hershey, PA: IGI Global. DOI: 10.4018/978-1-5225-3543-0.ch005

Petersen, A. J., Elser, C. F., Al Nassir, M. N., Stakey, J., & Everson, K. (2017). The Year of Teaching Inclusively: Building an Elementary Classroom for All Students. In Curran, C., & Petersen, A. (Eds.), *Handbook of Research on Classroom Diversity and Inclusive Education Practice* (pp. 332–348). Hershey, PA: IGI Global. DOI: 10.4018/978-1-5225-2520-2.ch014

Petrisor, I., & Cozmiuc, D. (2017). Global Supply Chain Management Organization at Siemens in the Advent of Industry 4.0. In Saglietto, L., & Cezanne, C. (Eds.), *Global Intermediation and Logistics Service Providers* (pp. 123–142). Hershey, PA: IGI Global. DOI: 10.4018/978-1-5225-2133-4.ch007

Pfannenstiel, K. H., & Sanders, J. (2017). Characteristics and Instructional Strategies for Students With Mathematical Difficulties: In the Inclusive Classroom. In Curran, C., & Petersen, A. (Eds.), *Handbook of Research on Classroom Diversity and Inclusive Education Practice* (pp. 250–281). Hershey, PA: IGI Global. DOI: 10.4018/978-1-5225-2520-2.ch011

Phan, A. N. (2022). Quality Assurance of Higher Education From the Glonacal Agency Heuristic: An Example From Vietnam. In Magd, H., & Kunjumuhammed, S. (Eds.), *Global Perspectives on Quality Assurance and Accreditation in Higher Education Institutions* (pp. 136–155). IGI Global. https://doi.org/10.4018/978-1-7998-8085-1.ch008

Pierce, J. M., Velliaris, D. M., & Edwards, J. (2017). A Living Case Study: A Journey Not a Destination. In Silton, N. (Ed.), *Exploring the Benefits of Creativity in Education, Media, and the Arts* (pp. 158–178). Hershey, PA: IGI Global. DOI: 10.4018/978-1-5225-0504-4.ch008

Pipia, S., & Pipia, S. (2021). Challenges of Religious Tourism in the Conflict Region: An Example of Jerusalem. In E. Alaverdov & M. Bari (Eds.), *Global Development of Religious Tourism* (pp. 135-148). IGI Global. https://doi.org/10.4018/978-1-7998-5792-1.ch009

Poulaki, P., Kritikos, A., Vasilakis, N., & Valeri, M. (2022). The Contribution of Female Creativity to the Development of Gastronomic Tourism in Greece: The Case of the Island of Naxos in the South Aegean Region. In Valeri, M. (Ed.), *New Governance and Management in Touristic Destinations* (pp. 246–258). IGI Global. https://doi.org/10.4018/978-1-6684-3889-3.ch015

Preast, J. L., Bowman, N., & Rose, C. A. (2017). Creating Inclusive Classroom Communities Through Social and Emotional Learning to Reduce Social Marginalization Among Students. In Curran, C., & Petersen, A. (Eds.), *Handbook of Research on Classroom Diversity and Inclusive Education Practice* (pp. 183–200). Hershey, PA: IGI Global. DOI: 10.4018/978-1-5225-2520-2.ch008

Radosavljevic, M., & Andjelkovic, A. (2017). Multi-Criteria Decision Making Approach for Choosing Business Process for the Improvement: Upgrading of the Six Sigma Methodology. In Stanković, J., Delias, P., Marinković, S., & Rochhia, S. (Eds.), *Tools and Techniques for Economic Decision Analysis* (pp. 225–247). Hershey, PA: IGI Global. DOI: 10.4018/978-1-5225-0959-2.ch011

Radovic, V. M. (2017). Corporate Sustainability and Responsibility and Disaster Risk Reduction: A Serbian Overview. In Camilleri, M. (Ed.), *CSR 2.0 and the New Era of Corporate Citizenship* (pp. 147–164). Hershey, PA: IGI Global. DOI: 10.4018/978-1-5225-1842-6.ch008

Raghunath, K. M., Devi, S. L., & Patro, C. S. (2018). Impact of Risk Assessment Models on Risk Factors: A Holistic Outlook. In Strang, K., Korstanje, M., & Vajjhala, N. (Eds.), *Research, Practices, and Innovations in Global Risk and Contingency Management* (pp. 134–153). Hershey, PA: IGI Global. DOI: 10.4018/978-1-5225-4754-9.ch008

Raman, A., & Goyal, D. P. (2017). Extending IMPLEMENT Framework for Enterprise Information Systems Implementation to Information System Innovation. In Tavana, M. (Ed.), *Enterprise Information Systems and the Digitalization of Business Functions* (pp. 137–177). Hershey, PA: IGI Global. DOI: 10.4018/978-1-5225-2382-6.ch007

Randolph, K. M., & Brady, M. P. (2018). Evolution of Covert Coaching as an Evidence-Based Practice in Professional Development and Preparation of Teachers. In Bryan, V., Musgrove, A., & Powers, J. (Eds.), *Handbook of Research on Human Development in the Digital Age* (pp. 281–299). Hershey, PA: IGI Global. DOI: 10.4018/978-1-5225-2838-8.ch013

Rao, Y., & Zhang, Y. (2017). The Construction and Development of Academic Library Digital Special Subject Databases. In Ruan, L., Zhu, Q., & Ye, Y. (Eds.), *Academic Library Development and Administration in China* (pp. 163–183). Hershey, PA: IGI Global. DOI: 10.4018/978-1-5225-0550-1.ch010

Ravasan, A. Z., Mohammadi, M. M., & Hamidi, H. (2018). An Investigation Into the Critical Success Factors of Implementing Information Technology Service Management Frameworks. In Jakobs, K. (Ed.), *Corporate and Global Standardization Initiatives in Contemporary Society* (pp. 200–218). Hershey, PA: IGI Global. DOI: 10.4018/978-1-5225-5320-5.ch009

Rell, A. B., Puig, R. A., Roll, F., Valles, V., Espinoza, M., & Duque, A. L. (2017). Addressing Cultural Diversity and Global Competence: The Dual Language Framework. In Leavitt, L., Wisdom, S., & Leavitt, K. (Eds.), *Cultural Awareness and Competency Development in Higher Education* (pp. 111–131). Hershey, PA: IGI Global. DOI: 10.4018/978-1-5225-2145-7.ch007

Rezaie, S., Mirabedini, S. J., & Abtahi, A. (2018). Designing a Model for Implementation of Business Intelligence in the Banking Industry. *International Journal of Enterprise Information Systems*, 14(1), 77–103. DOI: 10.4018/IJEIS.2018010105

Richards, M., & Guzman, I. R. (2020). Academic Assessment of Critical Thinking in Distance Education Information Technology Programs. In I. Management Association (Ed.), *Learning and Performance Assessment: Concepts, Methodologies, Tools, and Applications* (pp. 1-19). IGI Global. https://doi.org/10.4018/978-1-7998-0420-8.ch001

Richards, V., Matthews, N., Williams, O. J., & Khan, Z. (2021). The Challenges of Accessible Tourism Information Systems for Tourists With Vision Impairment: Sensory Communications Beyond the Screen. In Eusébio, C., Teixeira, L., & Carneiro, M. (Eds.), *ICT Tools and Applications for Accessible Tourism* (pp. 26–54). IGI Global. https://doi.org/10.4018/978-1-7998-6428-8.ch002

Riel, J., Lawless, K. A., & Brown, S. W. (2017). Defining and Designing Responsive Online Professional Development (ROPD): A Framework to Support Curriculum Implementation. In Kidd, T., & Morris, L.Jr., (Eds.), *Handbook of Research on Instructional Systems and Educational Technology* (pp. 104–115). Hershey, PA: IGI Global. DOI: 10.4018/978-1-5225-2399-4.ch010

Roberts, C. (2017). Advancing Women Leaders in Academe: Creating a Culture of Inclusion. In Mukerji, S., & Tripathi, P. (Eds.), *Handbook of Research on Administration, Policy, and Leadership in Higher Education* (pp. 256–273). Hershey, PA: IGI Global. DOI: 10.4018/978-1-5225-0672-0.ch012

Rodgers, W. J., Kennedy, M. J., Alves, K. D., & Romig, J. E. (2017). A Multimedia Tool for Teacher Education and Professional Development. In Martin, C., & Polly, D. (Eds.), *Handbook of Research on Teacher Education and Professional Development* (pp. 285–296). Hershey, PA: IGI Global. DOI: 10.4018/978-1-5225-1067-3.ch015

Rodrigues de Souza Neto, V., & Marques, O. (2021). Rural Tourism Fostering Welfare Through Sustainable Development: A Conceptual Approach. In Perinotto, A., Mayer, V., & Soares, J. (Eds.), *Rebuilding and Restructuring the Tourism Industry: Infusion of Happiness and Quality of Life* (pp. 38–57). IGI Global. https://doi.org/10.4018/978-1-7998-7239-9.ch003

Romano, L., Grimaldi, R., & Colasuonno, F. S. (2017). Demand Management as a Success Factor in Project Portfolio Management. In Romano, L. (Ed.), *Project Portfolio Management Strategies for Effective Organizational Operations* (pp. 202–219). Hershey, PA: IGI Global. DOI: 10.4018/978-1-5225-2151-8.ch008

Romanowski, M. H. (2017). Qatar's Educational Reform: Critical Issues Facing Principals. In I. Management Association (Ed.), *Educational Leadership and Administration: Concepts, Methodologies, Tools, and Applications* (pp. 1758-1773). Hershey, PA: IGI Global. https://doi.org/DOI: 10.4018/978-1-5225-1624-8.ch080

Rubio-Escuderos, L., & García-Andreu, H. (2021). Competitiveness Factors of Accessible Tourism E-Travel Agencies. In Eusébio, C., Teixeira, L., & Carneiro, M. (Eds.), *ICT Tools and Applications for Accessible Tourism* (pp. 196–217). IGI Global. https://doi.org/10.4018/978-1-7998-6428-8.ch009

Rucci, A. C., Porto, N., Darcy, S., & Becka, L. (2021). Smart and Accessible Cities?: Not Always – The Case for Accessible Tourism Initiatives in Buenos Aries and Sydney. In Eusébio, C., Teixeira, L., & Carneiro, M. (Eds.), *ICT Tools and Applications for Accessible Tourism* (pp. 115–145). IGI Global. https://doi.org/10.4018/978-1-7998-6428-8.ch006

Ruffin, T. R., Hawkins, D. P., & Lee, D. I. (2018). Increasing Student Engagement and Participation Through Course Methodology. In M. Khosrow-Pour, D.B.A. (Ed.), *Encyclopedia of Information Science and Technology, Fourth Edition* (pp. 1463-1473). Hershey, PA: IGI Global. DOI: 10.4018/978-1-5225-2255-3.ch126

Ruhi, U. (2018). Towards an Interdisciplinary Socio-Technical Definition of Virtual Communities. In M. Khosrow-Pour, D.B.A. (Ed.), *Encyclopedia of Information Science and Technology, Fourth Edition* (pp. 4278-4295). Hershey, PA: IGI Global. DOI: 10.4018/978-1-5225-2255-3.ch371

Ryan, L., Catena, M., Ros, P., & Stephens, S. (2021). Designing Entrepreneurial Ecosystems to Support Resource Management in the Tourism Industry. In Costa, V., Moura, A., & Mira, M. (Eds.), *Handbook of Research on Human Capital and People Management in the Tourism Industry* (pp. 265–281). IGI Global. https://doi.org/10.4018/978-1-7998-4318-4.ch013

Sabina, L. L., Curry, K. A., Harris, E. L., Krumm, B. L., & Vencill, V. (2017). Assessing the Performance of a Cohort-Based Model Using Domestic and International Practices. In I. Management Association (Ed.), *Educational Leadership and Administration: Concepts, Methodologies, Tools, and Applications*(pp. 913-929). Hershey, PA: IGI Global. https://doi.org/DOI: 10.4018/978-1-5225-1624-8.ch044

Sabuncu, I. (2021). Understanding Tourist Perceptions and Expectations During Pandemic Through Social Media Big Data. In Demir, M., Dalgıç, A., & Ergen, F. (Eds.), *Handbook of Research on the Impacts and Implications of COVID-19 on the Tourism Industry* (pp. 330–350). IGI Global. https://doi.org/10.4018/978-1-7998-8231-2.ch016

Safari, M. R., & Jiang, Q. (2018). The Theory and Practice of IT Governance Maturity and Strategies Alignment: Evidence From Banking Industry. *Journal of Global Information Management*, 26(2), 127–146. DOI: 10.4018/JGIM.2018040106

Sahoo, J., Pati, B., & Mohanty, B. (2017). Knowledge Management as an Academic Discipline: An Assessment. In Gunjal, B. (Ed.), *Managing Knowledge and Scholarly Assets in Academic Libraries* (pp. 99–126). Hershey, PA: IGI Global. DOI: 10.4018/978-1-5225-1741-2.ch005

Saini, D. (2017). Relevance of Teaching Values and Ethics in Management Education. In Baporikar, N. (Ed.), *Management Education for Global Leadership* (pp. 90–111). Hershey, PA: IGI Global. DOI: 10.4018/978-1-5225-1013-0.ch005

Sambhanthan, A. (2017). Assessing and Benchmarking Sustainability in Organisations: An Integrated Conceptual Model. *International Journal of Systems and Service-Oriented Engineering*, 7(4), 22–43. DOI: 10.4018/IJSSOE.2017100102

Sambhanthan, A., & Potdar, V. (2017). A Study of the Parameters Impacting Sustainability in Information Technology Organizations. *International Journal of Knowledge-Based Organizations*, 7(3), 27–39. DOI: 10.4018/IJKBO.2017070103

Samkian, A., Pascarella, J., & Slayton, J. (2022). Towards an Anti-Racist, Culturally Responsive, and LGBTQ+ Inclusive Education: Developing Critically-Conscious Educational Leaders. In Cain-Sanschagrin, E., Filback, R., & Crawford, J. (Eds.), *Cases on Academic Program Redesign for Greater Racial and Social Justice* (pp. 150–175). IGI Global. https://doi.org/10.4018/978-1-7998-8463-7.ch007

Sánchez-Fernández, M. D., & Manríquez, M. R. (2018). The Entrepreneurial Spirit Based on Social Values: The Digital Generation. In Isaias, P., & Carvalho, L. (Eds.), *User Innovation and the Entrepreneurship Phenomenon in the Digital Economy* (pp. 173–193). Hershey, PA: IGI Global. DOI: 10.4018/978-1-5225-2826-5.ch009

Sanchez-Ruiz, L., & Blanco, B. (2017). Process Management for SMEs: Barriers, Enablers, and Benefits. In Vemić, M. (Ed.), *Optimal Management Strategies in Small and Medium Enterprises* (pp. 293–319). Hershey, PA: IGI Global. DOI: 10.4018/978-1-5225-1949-2.ch014

Santamaría, A. P., Webber, M., & Santamaría, L. J. (2017). Effective School Leadership for Māori Achievement: Building Capacity through Indigenous, National, and International Cross-Cultural Collaboration. In I. Management Association (Ed.), *Educational Leadership and Administration: Concepts, Methodologies, Tools, and Applications* (pp. 1547-1567). Hershey, PA: IGI Global. https://doi.org/DOI: 10.4018/978-1-5225-1624-8.ch071

Santamaría, L. J. (2017). Culturally Responsive Educational Leadership in Cross-Cultural International Contexts. In I. Management Association (Ed.), *Educational Leadership and Administration: Concepts, Methodologies, Tools, and Applications* (pp. 1380-1400). Hershey, PA: IGI Global. https://doi.org/DOI: 10.4018/978-1-5225-1624-8.ch064

Sanz, L. F., Gómez-Pérez, J., & Castillo-Martinez, A. (2018). Analysis of the European ICT Competence Frameworks. In Ahuja, V., & Rathore, S. (Eds.), *Multidisciplinary Perspectives on Human Capital and Information Technology Professionals* (pp. 225–245). Hershey, PA: IGI Global. DOI: 10.4018/978-1-5225-5297-0.ch012

Sarvepalli, A., & Godin, J. (2017). Business Process Management in the Classroom. *Journal of Cases on Information Technology*, 19(2), 17–28. DOI: 10.4018/JCIT.2017040102

Saxena, G. G., & Saxena, A. (2021). Host Community Role in Medical Tourism Development. In Singh, M., & Kumaran, S. (Eds.), *Growth of the Medical Tourism Industry and Its Impact on Society: Emerging Research and Opportunities* (pp. 105–127). IGI Global. https://doi.org/10.4018/978-1-7998-3427-4.ch006

Saygili, E. E., Ozturkoglu, Y., & Kocakulah, M. C. (2017). End Users' Perceptions of Critical Success Factors in ERP Applications. *International Journal of Enterprise Information Systems*, 13(4), 58–75. DOI: 10.4018/IJEIS.2017100104

Saygili, E. E., & Saygili, A. T. (2017). Contemporary Issues in Enterprise Information Systems: A Critical Review of CSFs in ERP Implementations. In Tavana, M. (Ed.), *Enterprise Information Systems and the Digitalization of Business Functions* (pp. 120–136). Hershey, PA: IGI Global. DOI: 10.4018/978-1-5225-2382-6.ch006

Schwaiger, K. M., & Zehrer, A. (2021). The COVID-19 Pandemic and Organizational Resilience in Hospitality Family Firms: A Qualitative Approach. In Zehrer, A., Glowka, G., Schwaiger, K., & Ranacher-Lackner, V. (Eds.), *Resiliency Models and Addressing Future Risks for Family Firms in the Tourism Industry* (pp. 32–49). IGI Global. https://doi.org/10.4018/978-1-7998-7352-5.ch002

Scott, N., & Campos, A. C. (2022). Cognitive Science of Tourism Experiences. In R. Augusto Costa, F. Brandão, Z. Breda, & C. Costa (Eds.), *Planning and Managing the Experience Economy in Tourism* (pp. 1-21). IGI Global. https://doi.org/DOI: 10.4018/978-1-7998-8775-1.ch001

Segredo, M. R., Cistone, P. J., & Reio, T. G. (2017). Relationships Between Emotional Intelligence, Leadership Style, and School Culture. *International Journal of Adult Vocational Education and Technology*, 8(3), 25–43. DOI: 10.4018/IJAVET.2017070103

Seidenstricker, S., & Antonino, A. (2018). Business Model Innovation-Oriented Technology Management for Emergent Technologies. In M. Khosrow-Pour, D.B.A. (Ed.), *Encyclopedia of Information Science and Technology, Fourth Edition* (pp. 4560-4569). Hershey, PA: IGI Global. DOI: 10.4018/978-1-5225-2255-3.ch396

Selvi, M. S. (2021). Changes in Tourism Sales and Marketing Post COVID-19. In Demir, M., Dalgıç, A., & Ergen, F. (Eds.), *Handbook of Research on the Impacts and Implications of COVID-19 on the Tourism Industry* (pp. 437–460). IGI Global. DOI: 10.4018/978-1-7998-8231-2.ch021

Senaratne, S., & Gunarathne, A. D. (2017). Excellence Perspective for Management Education from a Global Accountants' Hub in Asia. In Baporikar, N. (Ed.), *Management Education for Global Leadership* (pp. 158–180). Hershey, PA: IGI Global. DOI: 10.4018/978-1-5225-1013-0.ch008

Sensuse, D. I., & Cahyaningsih, E. (2018). Knowledge Management Models: A Summative Review. *International Journal of Information Systems in the Service Sector*, 10(1), 71–100. DOI: 10.4018/IJISSS.2018010105

Seth, M., Goyal, D., & Kiran, R. (2017). Diminution of Impediments in Implementation of Supply Chain Management Information System for Enhancing its Effectiveness in Indian Automobile Industry. *Journal of Global Information Management*, 25(3), 1–20. DOI: 10.4018/JGIM.2017070101

Seyal, A. H., & Rahman, M. N. (2017). Investigating Impact of Inter-Organizational Factors in Measuring ERP Systems Success: Bruneian Perspectives. In Tavana, M. (Ed.), *Enterprise Information Systems and the Digitalization of Business Functions* (pp. 178–204). Hershey, PA: IGI Global. DOI: 10.4018/978-1-5225-2382-6.ch008

Shalev, N. (2017). Empathy and Leadership From the Organizational Perspective. In Nedelko, Z., & Brzozowski, M. (Eds.), *Exploring the Influence of Personal Values and Cultures in the Workplace* (pp. 348–363). Hershey, PA: IGI Global. DOI: 10.4018/978-1-5225-2480-9.ch018

Shaqrah, A. A. (2018). Analyzing Business Intelligence Systems Based on 7s Model of McKinsey. *International Journal of Business Intelligence Research*, 9(1), 53–63. DOI: 10.4018/IJBIR.2018010104

Sharma, A. J. (2017). Enhancing Sustainability through Experiential Learning in Management Education. In Baporikar, N. (Ed.), *Management Education for Global Leadership* (pp. 256–274). Hershey, PA: IGI Global. DOI: 10.4018/978-1-5225-1013-0.ch013

Shetty, K. P. (2017). Responsible Global Leadership: Ethical Challenges in Management Education. In Baporikar, N. (Ed.), *Innovation and Shifting Perspectives in Management Education* (pp. 194–223). Hershey, PA: IGI Global. DOI: 10.4018/978-1-5225-1019-2.ch009

Siamak, M., Fathi, S., & Isfandyari-Moghaddam, A. (2018). Assessment and Measurement of Education Programs of Information Literacy. In Bhardwaj, R. (Ed.), *Digitizing the Modern Library and the Transition From Print to Electronic* (pp. 164–192). Hershey, PA: IGI Global. DOI: 10.4018/978-1-5225-2119-8.ch007

Sinthupundaja, J., & Kohda, Y. (2017). Effects of Corporate Social Responsibility and Creating Shared Value on Sustainability. *International Journal of Sustainable Entrepreneurship and Corporate Social Responsibility*, 2(1), 27–38. DOI: 10.4018/IJSECSR.2017010103

Siu, K. W., & García, G. J. (2017). Disruptive Technologies and Education: Is There Any Disruption After All? In I. Management Association (Ed.), *Educational Leadership and Administration: Concepts, Methodologies, Tools, and Applications* (pp. 757-778). Hershey, PA: IGI Global. https://doi.org/DOI: 10.4018/978-1-5225-1624-8.ch037

Škarica, I., & Hrgović, A. V. (2018). Implementation of Total Quality Management Principles in Public Health Institutes in the Republic of Croatia. *International Journal of Productivity Management and Assessment Technologies*, 6(1), 1–16. DOI: 10.4018/IJPMAT.2018010101

Skokic, V. (2021). How Small Hotel Owners Practice Resilience: Longitudinal Study Among Small Family Hotels in Croatia. In Zehrer, A., Glowka, G., Schwaiger, K., & Ranacher-Lackner, V. (Eds.), *Resiliency Models and Addressing Future Risks for Family Firms in the Tourism Industry* (pp. 50–73). IGI Global. DOI: 10.4018/978-1-7998-7352-5.ch003

Slagter van Tryon, P. J. (2017). The Nurse Educator's Role in Designing Instruction and Instructional Strategies for Academic and Clinical Settings. In Stefaniak, J. (Ed.), *Advancing Medical Education Through Strategic Instructional Design* (pp. 133–149). Hershey, PA: IGI Global. DOI: 10.4018/978-1-5225-2098-6.ch006

Slattery, C. A. (2018). Literacy Intervention and the Differentiated Plan of Instruction. In *Developing Effective Literacy Intervention Strategies: Emerging Research and Opportunities* (pp. 41–62). Hershey, PA: IGI Global. DOI: 10.4018/978-1-5225-5007-5.ch003

Smith, A. R. (2017). Ensuring Quality: The Faculty Role in Online Higher Education. In Shelton, K., & Pedersen, K. (Eds.), *Handbook of Research on Building, Growing, and Sustaining Quality E-Learning Programs* (pp. 210–231). Hershey, PA: IGI Global. DOI: 10.4018/978-1-5225-0877-9.ch011

Smuts, H., Kotzé, P., Van der Merwe, A., & Loock, M. (2017). Framework for Managing Shared Knowledge in an Information Systems Outsourcing Context. *International Journal of Knowledge Management*, 13(4), 1–30. DOI: 10.4018/IJKM.2017100101

Souders, T. M. (2017). Understanding Your Learner: Conducting a Learner Analysis. In Stefaniak, J. (Ed.), *Advancing Medical Education Through Strategic Instructional Design* (pp. 1–29). Hershey, PA: IGI Global. DOI: 10.4018/978-1-5225-2098-6.ch001

Sousa, M. J., Cruz, R., Dias, I., & Caracol, C. (2017). Information Management Systems in the Supply Chain. In Jamil, G., Soares, A., & Pessoa, C. (Eds.), *Handbook of Research on Information Management for Effective Logistics and Supply Chains* (pp. 469–485). Hershey, PA: IGI Global. DOI: 10.4018/978-1-5225-0973-8.ch025

Spremic, M., Turulja, L., & Bajgoric, N. (2018). Two Approaches in Assessing Business Continuity Management Attitudes in the Organizational Context. In Bajgoric, N. (Ed.), *Always-On Enterprise Information Systems for Modern Organizations* (pp. 159–183). Hershey, PA: IGI Global. DOI: 10.4018/978-1-5225-3704-5.ch008

Spring, K. J., Graham, C. R., & Ikahihifo, T. B. (2018). Learner Engagement in Blended Learning. In M. Khosrow-Pour, D.B.A. (Ed.), *Encyclopedia of Information Science and Technology, Fourth Edition* (pp. 1487-1498). Hershey, PA: IGI Global. DOI: 10.4018/978-1-5225-2255-3.ch128

Steenkamp, A. L. (2018). Some Insights in Computer Science and Information Technology. In *Examining the Changing Role of Supervision in Doctoral Research Projects: Emerging Research and Opportunities* (pp. 113–133). Hershey, PA: IGI Global. DOI: 10.4018/978-1-5225-2610-0.ch005

Stipanović, C., Rudan, E., & Zubović, V. (2022). Reaching the New Tourist Through Creativity: Sustainable Development Challenges in Croatian Coastal Towns. In Valeri, M. (Ed.), *New Governance and Management in Touristic Destinations* (pp. 231–245). IGI Global. https://doi.org/10.4018/978-1-6684-3889-3.ch014

Storey, V. A., Anthony, A. K., & Wahid, P. (2017). Gender-Based Leadership Barriers: Advancement of Female Faculty to Leadership Positions in Higher Education. In Wang, V. (Ed.), *Encyclopedia of Strategic Leadership and Management* (pp. 244–258). Hershey, PA: IGI Global. DOI: 10.4018/978-1-5225-1049-9.ch018

Stottlemyer, D. (2018). Develop a Teaching Model Plan for a Differentiated Learning Approach. In *Differentiated Instructional Design for Multicultural Environments: Emerging Research and Opportunities* (pp. 106–130). Hershey, PA: IGI Global. DOI: 10.4018/978-1-5225-5106-5.ch005

Stottlemyer, D. (2018). Developing a Multicultural Environment. In *Differentiated Instructional Design for Multicultural Environments: Emerging Research and Opportunities* (pp. 1–27). Hershey, PA: IGI Global. DOI: 10.4018/978-1-5225-5106-5.ch001

Swagerty, T. (2022). Digital Access to Culturally Relevant Curricula: The Impact on the Native and Indigenous Student. In Reeves, E., & McIntyre, C. (Eds.), *Multidisciplinary Perspectives on Diversity and Equity in a Virtual World* (pp. 99–113). IGI Global. https://doi.org/10.4018/978-1-7998-8028-8.ch006

Swami, B. N., Gobona, T., & Tsimako, J. J. (2017). Academic Leadership: A Case Study of the University of Botswana. In Baporikar, N. (Ed.), *Innovation and Shifting Perspectives in Management Education* (pp. 1–32). Hershey, PA: IGI Global. DOI: 10.4018/978-1-5225-1019-2.ch001

Swanson, K. W., & Collins, G. (2018). Designing Engaging Instruction for the Adult Learners. In M. Khosrow-Pour, D.B.A. (Ed.), *Encyclopedia of Information Science and Technology, Fourth Edition* (pp. 1432-1440). Hershey, PA: IGI Global. DOI: 10.4018/978-1-5225-2255-3.ch123

Swartz, B. A., Lynch, J. M., & Lynch, S. D. (2018). Embedding Elementary Teacher Education Coursework in Local Classrooms: Examples in Mathematics and Special Education. In Polly, D., Putman, M., Petty, T., & Good, A. (Eds.), *Innovative Practices in Teacher Preparation and Graduate-Level Teacher Education Programs* (pp. 262–292). Hershey, PA: IGI Global. DOI: 10.4018/978-1-5225-3068-8.ch015

Tabach, A., & Croteau, A. (2017). Configurations of Information Technology Governance Practices and Business Unit Performance. *International Journal of IT/Business Alignment and Governance*, 8(2), 1–27. DOI: 10.4018/IJITBAG.2017070101

Talaue, G. M., & Iqbal, T. (2017). Assessment of e-Business Mode of Selected Private Universities in the Philippines and Pakistan. *International Journal of Online Marketing*, 7(4), 63–77. DOI: 10.4018/IJOM.2017100105

Taliadorou, N., & Pashiardis, P. (2017). Emotional Intelligence and Political Skill Really Matter in Educational Leadership. In I. Management Association (Ed.), *Educational Leadership and Administration: Concepts, Methodologies, Tools, and Applications* (pp. 1274-1303). Hershey, PA: IGI Global. https://doi.org/DOI: 10.4018/978-1-5225-1624-8.ch060

Tam, G. C. (2017). Project Manager Sustainability Competence. In *Managerial Strategies and Green Solutions for Project Sustainability* (pp. 178–207). Hershey, PA: IGI Global. DOI: 10.4018/978-1-5225-2371-0.ch008

Tambo, T. (2018). Fashion Retail Innovation: About Context, Antecedents, and Outcome in Technological Change Projects. In I. Management Association (Ed.), *Fashion and Textiles: Breakthroughs in Research and Practice* (pp. 233-260). Hershey, PA: IGI Global. https://doi.org/DOI: 10.4018/978-1-5225-3432-7.ch010

Tandoh, K. A., & Ebe-Arthur, J. E. (2018). Effective Educational Leadership in the Digital Age: An Examination of Professional Qualities and Best Practices. In Keengwe, J. (Ed.), *Handbook of Research on Digital Content, Mobile Learning, and Technology Integration Models in Teacher Education* (pp. 244–265). Hershey, PA: IGI Global. DOI: 10.4018/978-1-5225-2953-8.ch013

Tantau, A. D., & Frăţilă, L. C. (2018). Information and Management System for Renewable Energy Business. In *Entrepreneurship and Business Development in the Renewable Energy Sector* (pp. 200–244). Hershey, PA: IGI Global. DOI: 10.4018/978-1-5225-3625-3.ch006

Teixeira, N., Pardal, P. N., & Rafael, B. G. (2018). Internationalization, Financial Performance, and Organizational Challenges: A Success Case in Portugal. In Carvalho, L. (Ed.), *Handbook of Research on Entrepreneurial Ecosystems and Social Dynamics in a Globalized World* (pp. 379–423). Hershey, PA: IGI Global. DOI: 10.4018/978-1-5225-3525-6.ch017

Teixeira, P., Teixeira, L., Eusébio, C., Silva, S., & Teixeira, A. (2021). The Impact of ICTs on Accessible Tourism: Evidence Based on a Systematic Literature Review. In Eusébio, C., Teixeira, L., & Carneiro, M. (Eds.), *ICT Tools and Applications for Accessible Tourism* (pp. 1–25). IGI Global. DOI: 10.4018/978-1-7998-6428-8.ch001

Tobin, M. T. (2018). Multimodal Literacy. In M. Khosrow-Pour, D.B.A. (Ed.), *Encyclopedia of Information Science and Technology, Fourth Edition* (pp. 1508-1516). Hershey, PA: IGI Global. DOI: 10.4018/978-1-5225-2255-3.ch130

Torres, K. M., Arrastia-Chisholm, M. C., & Tackett, S. (2019). A Phenomenological Study of Pre-Service Teachers' Perceptions of Completing ESOL Field Placements. *International Journal of Teacher Education and Professional Development*, 2(2), 85–101. https://doi.org/10.4018/IJTEPD.2019070106

Torres, M. C., Salamanca, Y. N., Cely, J. P., & Aguilar, J. L. (2020). All We Need is a Boost! Using Multimodal Tools and the Translanguaging Strategy: Strengthening Speaking in the EFL Classroom. *International Journal of Computer-Assisted Language Learning and Teaching*, 10(3), 28–47. DOI: 10.4018/IJCALLT.2020070103

Torres, M. L., & Ramos, V. J. (2018). Music Therapy: A Pedagogical Alternative for ASD and ID Students in Regular Classrooms. In Epler, P. (Ed.), *Instructional Strategies in General Education and Putting the Individuals With Disabilities Act (IDEA) Into Practice* (pp. 222–244). Hershey, PA: IGI Global. DOI: 10.4018/978-1-5225-3111-1.ch008

Toulassi, B. (2017). Educational Administration and Leadership in Francophone Africa: 5 Dynamics to Change Education. In Mukerji, S., & Tripathi, P. (Eds.), *Handbook of Research on Administration, Policy, and Leadership in Higher Education* (pp. 20–45). Hershey, PA: IGI Global. DOI: 10.4018/978-1-5225-0672-0.ch002

Trad, A., & Kalpić, D. (2018). The Business Transformation Framework, Agile Project and Change Management. In M. Khosrow-Pour, D.B.A. (Ed.), *Encyclopedia of Information Science and Technology, Fourth Edition* (pp. 620-635). Hershey, PA: IGI Global. https://doi.org/DOI: 10.4018/978-1-5225-2255-3.ch054

Trad, A., & Kalpić, D. (2018). The Business Transformation and Enterprise Architecture Framework: The Financial Engineering E-Risk Management and E-Law Integration. In Sergi, B., Fidanoski, F., Ziolo, M., & Naumovski, V. (Eds.), *Regaining Global Stability After the Financial Crisis* (pp. 46–65). Hershey, PA: IGI Global. DOI: 10.4018/978-1-5225-4026-7.ch003

Trengereid, V. (2022). Conditions of Network Engagement: The Quest for a Common Good. In R. Augusto Costa, F. Brandão, Z. Breda, & C. Costa (Eds.), *Planning and Managing the Experience Economy in Tourism* (pp. 69-84). IGI Global. https://doi.org/10.4018/978-1-7998-8775-1.ch004

Turulja, L., & Bajgoric, N. (2018). Business Continuity and Information Systems: A Systematic Literature Review. In Bajgoric, N. (Ed.), *Always-On Enterprise Information Systems for Modern Organizations* (pp. 60–87). Hershey, PA: IGI Global. DOI: 10.4018/978-1-5225-3704-5.ch004

Umair, S., & Sharif, M. M. (2018). Predicting Students Grades Using Artificial Neural Networks and Support Vector Machine. In M. Khosrow-Pour, D.B.A. (Ed.), *Encyclopedia of Information Science and Technology, Fourth Edition* (pp. 5169-5182). Hershey, PA: IGI Global. DOI: 10.4018/978-1-5225-2255-3.ch449

Vargas-Hernández, J. G. (2017). Professional Integrity in Business Management Education. In Baporikar, N. (Ed.), *Management Education for Global Leadership* (pp. 70–89). Hershey, PA: IGI Global. DOI: 10.4018/978-1-5225-1013-0.ch004

Varnacı Uzun, F. (2021). The Destination Preferences of Foreign Tourists During the COVID-19 Pandemic and Attitudes Towards: Marmaris, Turkey. In Demir, M., Dalgıç, A., & Ergen, F. (Eds.), *Handbook of Research on the Impacts and Implications of COVID-19 on the Tourism Industry* (pp. 285–306). IGI Global. https://doi.org/10.4018/978-1-7998-8231-2.ch014

Vasista, T. G., & AlAbdullatif, A. M. (2017). Role of Electronic Customer Relationship Management in Demand Chain Management: A Predictive Analytic Approach. *International Journal of Information Systems and Supply Chain Management*, 10(1), 53–67. DOI: 10.4018/IJISSCM.2017010104

Vettraino, L., Castello, V., Guspini, M., & Guglielman, E. (2018). Self-Awareness and Motivation Contrasting ESL and NEET Using the SAVE System. In M. Khosrow-Pour, D.B.A. (Ed.), *Encyclopedia of Information Science and Technology, Fourth Edition* (pp. 1559-1568). Hershey, PA: IGI Global. DOI: 10.4018/978-1-5225-2255-3.ch135

Vieru, D., & Bourdeau, S. (2017). Survival in the Digital Era: A Digital Competence-Based Multi-Case Study in the Canadian SME Clothing Industry. *International Journal of Social and Organizational Dynamics in IT*, 6(1), 17–34. DOI: 10.4018/IJSODIT.2017010102

Vijayan, G., & Kamarulzaman, N. H. (2017). An Introduction to Sustainable Supply Chain Management and Business Implications. In Khan, M., Hussain, M., & Ajmal, M. (Eds.), *Green Supply Chain Management for Sustainable Business Practice* (pp. 27–50). Hershey, PA: IGI Global. DOI: 10.4018/978-1-5225-0635-5.ch002

Vlachvei, A., & Notta, O. (2017). Firm Competitiveness: Theories, Evidence, and Measurement. In Vlachvei, A., Notta, O., Karantininis, K., & Tsounis, N. (Eds.), *Factors Affecting Firm Competitiveness and Performance in the Modern Business World* (pp. 1–42). Hershey, PA: IGI Global. DOI: 10.4018/978-1-5225-0843-4.ch001

Wang, C., Schofield, M., Li, X., & Ou, X. (2017). Do Chinese Students in Public and Private Higher Education Institutes Perform at Different Level in One of the Leadership Skills: Critical Thinking?: An Exploratory Comparison. In Wang, V. (Ed.), *Encyclopedia of Strategic Leadership and Management* (pp. 160–181). Hershey, PA: IGI Global. DOI: 10.4018/978-1-5225-1049-9.ch013

Wang, J. (2017). Multi-Agent based Production Management Decision System Modelling for the Textile Enterprise. *Journal of Global Information Management*, 25(4), 1–15. DOI: 10.4018/JGIM.2017100101

Wiedemann, A., & Gewald, H. (2017). Examining Cross-Domain Alignment: The Correlation of Business Strategy, IT Management, and IT Business Value. *International Journal of IT/Business Alignment and Governance*, 8(1), 17–31. DOI: 10.4018/IJITBAG.2017010102

Wiemelt, J. (2017). Critical Bilingual Leadership for Emergent Bilingual Students. In I. Management Association (Ed.), *Educational Leadership and Administration: Concepts, Methodologies, Tools, and Applications* (pp. 1606-1631). Hershey, PA: IGI Global. DOI: 10.4018/978-1-5225-1624-8.ch074

Wolf, F., Seyfarth, F. C., & Pflaum, E. (2018). Scalable Capacity-Building for Geographically Dispersed Learners: Designing the MOOC "Sustainable Energy in Small Island Developing States (SIDS)". In Pandey, U., & Indrakanti, V. (Eds.), *Open and Distance Learning Initiatives for Sustainable Development* (pp. 58–83). Hershey, PA: IGI Global. DOI: 10.4018/978-1-5225-2621-6.ch003

Wolf, R., & Thiel, M. (2018). Advancing Global Business Ethics in China: Reducing Poverty Through Human and Social Welfare. In Hipsher, S. (Ed.), *Examining the Private Sector's Role in Wealth Creation and Poverty Reduction* (pp. 67–84). Hershey, PA: IGI Global. DOI: 10.4018/978-1-5225-3117-3.ch004

Woodley, X. M., Mucundanyi, G., & Lockard, M. (2017). Designing Counter-Narratives: Constructing Culturally Responsive Curriculum Online. *International Journal of Online Pedagogy and Course Design*, 7(1), 43–56. DOI: 10.4018/IJOPCD.2017010104

Yablonsky, S. (2018). Innovation Platforms: Data and Analytics Platforms. In *Multi-Sided Platforms (MSPs) and Sharing Strategies in the Digital Economy: Emerging Research and Opportunities* (pp. 72–95). Hershey, PA: IGI Global. DOI: 10.4018/978-1-5225-5457-8.ch003

Yaşar, B. (2021). The Impact of COVID-19 on Volatility of Tourism Stocks: Evidence From BIST Tourism Index. In Demir, M., Dalgıç, A., & Ergen, F. (Eds.), *Handbook of Research on the Impacts and Implications of COVID-19 on the Tourism Industry* (pp. 23–44). IGI Global. https://doi.org/10.4018/978-1-7998-8231-2.ch002

Yell, M. L., & Christle, C. A. (2017). The Foundation of Inclusion in Federal Legislation and Litigation. In Curran, C., & Petersen, A. (Eds.), *Handbook of Research on Classroom Diversity and Inclusive Education Practice* (pp. 27–52). Hershey, PA: IGI Global. DOI: 10.4018/978-1-5225-2520-2.ch002

Yusoff, A., Ahmad, N. H., & Halim, H. A. (2017). Agropreneurship among Gen Y in Malaysia: The Role of Academic Institutions. In Ahmad, N., Ramayah, T., Halim, H., & Rahman, S. (Eds.), *Handbook of Research on Small and Medium Enterprises in Developing Countries* (pp. 23–47). Hershey, PA: IGI Global. DOI: 10.4018/978-1-5225-2165-5.ch002

Zacher, D., & Pechlaner, H. (2021). Resilience as an Opportunity Approach: Challenges and Perspectives for Private Sector Participation on a Community Level. In Zehrer, A., Glowka, G., Schwaiger, K., & Ranacher-Lackner, V. (Eds.), *Resiliency Models and Addressing Future Risks for Family Firms in the Tourism Industry* (pp. 75–102). IGI Global. https://doi.org/10.4018/978-1-7998-7352-5.ch004

Zanin, F., Comuzzi, E., & Costantini, A. (2018). The Effect of Business Strategy and Stock Market Listing on the Use of Risk Assessment Tools. In *Management Control Systems in Complex Settings: Emerging Research and Opportunities* (pp. 145–168). Hershey, PA: IGI Global. DOI: 10.4018/978-1-5225-3987-2.ch007

Zgheib, P. W. (2017). Corporate Innovation and Intrapreneurship in the Middle East. In Zgheib, P. (Ed.), *Entrepreneurship and Business Innovation in the Middle East* (pp. 37–56). Hershey, PA: IGI Global. DOI: 10.4018/978-1-5225-2066-5.ch003

Zinner, L. (2019). Fostering Academic Citizenship With a Shared Leadership Approach. In Zhu, C., & Zayim-Kurtay, M. (Eds.), *University Governance and Academic Leadership in the EU and China* (pp. 99–117). IGI Global. https://doi.org/10.4018/978-1-5225-7441-5.ch007

About the Contributors

Dale T. Mathews is an Associate Professor of international business and economics at the Rio Piedras campus of the University of Puerto Rico. He earned his Ph.D. in Development Studies at the Institute of Development Studies, Sussex University, England, and his MA in Economics at the University of Puerto Rico. To date he has published numerous articles in peer-review journals, books and daily newspapers on topics related to Caribbean and Central American commerce. His latest work is titled "Competing in the US Market: Central American Garment Assemblers", published in Social and Economic Studies (2020): 155-175. He has a forthcoming article on a similar topic to be published in "Ciencia & Sociedad" at the Instituto Tecnológico de Santo Domingo in the Dominican Republic.

Bryan Christiansen is the Chief Executive Officer at Soluvex, LLC, which is a global technology consulting firm in the USA. A former adjunct professor at Southern New Hampshire University, Christiansen earned his MBA at Capella University and his BS in Marketing degree at the University of the State of New York. To date he has published 45 Reference books on various topics of which over 60 percent are Scopus- and/or Web of Science-indexed. Christiansen is a Book Series Editor-in-Chief of "Advances in Psychology, Mental Health, and Behavioral Studies" and "Advances in Digital Crime, Forensics, and Cyber Terrorism". His works have been cited in articles, books, doctoral dissertations, and master's theses in Chinese, Czech, English, French, Greek, Russian, Spanish, and Turkish.

* * *

Clifton Armstrong holds a Master's Degree in Music Theory from Florida State University, a Master's Degree in English Education from the Mayaguez campus of the University of Puerto Rico, and a Doctorate in Linguistics from the Rio Piedras campus of the University of Puerto Rico. He has published work on creole languages, given presentations in Holland, Germany, and St. Lucia on creoles. He has given presentations on Second Langauge Acquisition, performed piano recitals, published a writing textbook titled "Excursions into the Art of Writing," and self-published a series of music books titled "Inventions: Piano Music for Learners." He has participated in over ten humanitarian trips to the Dominican Republic and oversaw a donation of computers to a needy public school in St. Lucia.

Segundo Castro-Gonzáles, currently works in the Management Department and in the Graduate School of the College of Business Administration at the University of Puerto Rico, Rio Piedras Campus. Previously, he served at the IEN Business School of Ana G. Méndez University - Carolina Campus (UAGM-CA) and as Prometheus Researcher of the National Secretariat of Science and Technology of Ecuador (CONCYTEC), he was assigned to the College of Business Administration and Accounting Sciences of the Technical University of Machala - Ecuador. Professor Castro-Gonzales has published in academic journals such as: Global Business Journal (Hawaii-USA), OIKOS (Chile), European Research on Management and Business Economics (Spain), Strategies Journal (Colombia), Journal of Distribution Science (South Korea), among others. Dr Castro-Gonzáles has presented his research in several International conferences, such as: CLADEA (Peru, Chile and Costa Rica), Academy of International Business (Miami, Tampa-Consumel and San Antonio-TX), Quest (San Juan-Puerto Rico), Coidine, among others.

Kathleen A. Corrales is an assistant professor, researcher, and the Academic Coordinator of the Instituto de Idiomas, Universidad del Norte. Her research interests include the intersection of language teaching and learning, CLIL and EMI, internationalization, the development of international and intercultural competences, and global business communication and has published in these areas.

Kurt Desender is an assistant professor (with tenure) in the Department of Business Administration at the University Carlos III. His research interests lie in the areas of corporate governance, corporate social responsibility, strategic management, and financial accounting. He is an editorial board member of Journal of International Business Studies and Corporate Governance: An International Review. His research has been published in the Academy of Management Annals, the Strategic Management Journal, and the Journal of International Business Studies, among others.

Jahir Lombana is an academic with a demonstrated history of working in administration of higher education industry (e.g.: accreditations, assurance of learning, curriculum development). Strong business development professional skilled in Academic Research, Intercultural Communication, E-Learning, Strategic

Planning, and Lecturing. Teaching and research topics of interest: competitiveness, strategy, competencies and international trade.

Mónica López-Puertas Lamy is an assistant professor (with tenure) in the Department of Business Administration at the University Carlos III. Her research interests focus on determinants and consequences of accounting, corporate governance, and corporate finance decisions on firms' access to credit, and bank risk on the implications. Her research has been published in the Strategic Management Journal, Journal of International Business Studies, and Journal of Business Finance and Accounting, among others.

Lorena Palacios-Chacón is a Full Time Assistant Professor of the International Business and Logistics Department at Tecnologico de Monterrey, Business School, Guadalajara Campus in Mexico. Dr. Palacios-Chacon earned her Ph.D. in management from the University of Puerto Rico, and her two bachelors in economics and finance and international trade from the Sergio Arboleda University. One of her main interests is the writing of teaching cases, she has participated in a number of conferences, having won multiple best case awards, and she coauthored the case FIFA 2010: Choosing the best coach in the world that was published in HBP through the CALDEA-BALAS case consortium. She is the current President of the Latin American Case Association (ALAC). Dr. Palacios-Chacon has written books and articles in the areas of internationalization of the firm, financial deepening in Colombia, the processes of offshore and outsourcing of companies, and international economic integration between countries.

Lourdes Rey-Paba is the Director of the Instituto de Idiomas, Universidad Del Norte. Her research interests include language teacher development, language learning, English mediated instruction, curriculum design and evaluation and Intercultural competence development.

Surjit Singha is an academician with a broad spectrum of interests, including UN Sustainable Development Goals, Organizational Climate, Workforce Diversity, Organizational Culture, HRM, Marketing, Finance, IB, Global Business, Business, AI, Women Studies, and Cultural Studies. Currently a faculty member at Kristu Jayanti College, Dr. Surjit also serves as an Editor, reviewer, and author for prominent global publications and journals, including being on the Editorial review board of Information Resources Management Journal and a contributor to IGI Global. With over 15 years of experience in Administration, Teaching, and Research, Dr. Surjit is dedicated to imparting knowledge and guiding students in their research pursuits. As a research mentor, Dr. Surjit has nurtured young minds and fostered academic growth. Dr. Surjit has an impressive track record of over 100 publications, including articles, book chapters, and textbooks, holds two US Copyrights, and has successfully completed and published two fully funded minor research projects from Kristu Jayanti College.

Duane Windsor (PhD, Harvard University) is the Lynette S. Autrey Professor of Management in Rice University's Jones Graduate School of Business. He specializes in corporate social responsibility, stakeholder theory, and anti-corruption reform.

Index

O

P

Q

R

S

T

U

V

www.ingramcontent.com/pod-product-compliance
Lightning Source LLC
LaVergne TN
LVHW061547290926
849162LV00004B/937